Studies of the Oxford Institute of European and Comparative Law

Editor
Professor Birke Häcker

Board of Advisory Editors
Professor Mark Freedland, FBA
Professor Stephen Weatherill
Professor Stefan Enchelmaier

Recent titles in this Series

Volume 20: The EU Charter of Fundamental Rights as a Binding Instrument: Five Years Old and Growing
Edited by Sybe de Vries, Ulf Bernitz and Stephen Weatherill

Volume 21: The Images of the Consumer in EU Law: Legislation, Free Movement and Competition Law
Edited by Dorota Leczykiewicz and Stephen Weatherill

Volume 22: Passing Wealth on Death: Will-Substitutes in Comparative Perspective
Edited by Alexandra Braun and Anne Röthel

Volume 23: General Principles of Law: European and Comparative Perspectives
Edited by Stefan Vogenauer and Stephen Weatherill

Volume 24: The Future of Contract Law in Latin America: The Principles of Latin American Contract Law
Edited by Rodrigo Momberg and Stefan Vogenauer

Volume 25: The Code Napoléon Rewritten: French Contract Law after the 2016 Reforms
Edited by John Cartwright and Simon Whittaker

Volume 26: Discretion in EU Public Procurement Law
Edited by Sanja Bogojevic, Xavier Groussot and Jörgen Hettne

Volume 27: New Economic Constitutionalism in Europe
George Gerapetritis

Volume 28: French Civil Liability in Comparative Perspective
Edited by Jean-Sébastien Borghetti and Simon Whittaker

Volume 29: Better Regulation in EU Contract Law: The Fitness Check and the New Deal for Consumers
Edited by Esther van Schagen and Stephen Weatherill

Volume 30: Property and Contract: Comparative Reflections on English Law and Spanish Law
Edited by John Cartwright and Ángel M López y López

PROPERTY AND CONTRACT

This book explores a range of comparative issues in, and in the relationship between, property law and contract law in English and Spanish law. It also draws on other jurisdictions. The purpose is to give readers access to discussions of these areas of private law that are not easily accessible elsewhere. It goes further, however, than simply setting out similarities and differences: it provides an insightful analysis of key points of interest in the comparison of the legal systems discussed.

Volume 30: Studies of the Oxford Institute of European and Comparative Law

Property and Contract

Comparative Reflections on English Law and Spanish Law

Edited by
John Cartwright
and
Ángel M López y López

•HART•
OXFORD • LONDON • NEW YORK • NEW DELHI • SYDNEY

HART PUBLISHING

Bloomsbury Publishing Plc

Kemp House, Chawley Park, Cumnor Hill, Oxford, OX2 9PH, UK

1385 Broadway, New York, NY 10018, USA

29 Earlsfort Terrace, Dublin 2, Ireland

First published in Great Britain 2021

A catalogue record for this book is available from the British Library.

Library of Congress Cataloging-in-Publication data

Names: Comparative Law Workshop : Property and Contracts (2018) : (Universidad de Sevilla) | Cartwright, John, 1957- editor. | López y López, Ángel M, editor. | Universidad de Sevilla. Centro de Derecho Comparado, sponsoring body. | University of Oxford. Institute of European and Comparative Law, sponsoring body.

Title: Property and contract law : comparative reflections on English law and Spanish law / edited by John Cartwright and Ángel M López y López.

Description: Oxford ; New York : Hart, 2021. | Series: Studies of the Oxford Institute of European and comparative law ; volume 30 | "This volume in the Studies of the Oxford Institute of European and Comparative Law is the result of a research workshop held at the University of Seville in 2018 to coincide with the 500th anniversary of the Law Faculty of Seville. The workshop was organised by the Centro de Derecho Comparado of the Law Faculty of the University of Seville and the Institute of European and Comparative Law of the Law Faculty of the University of Oxford."—ECIP Preface. | Includes bibliographical references and index.

Identifiers: LCCN 2021031535 (print) | LCCN 2021031536 (ebook) | ISBN 9781509929337 (hardback) | ISBN 9781509954483 (paperback) | ISBN 9781509929351 (ePDF) | ISBN 9781509929344 (Epub)

Subjects: LCSH: Real property—England—Congresses. | Real property—Spain—Congresses.

Classification: LCC KJC1315.A6 C66 2018 (print) | LCC KJC1315.A6 (ebook) | DDC 346.4204/3—dc23

LC record available at https://lccn.loc.gov/2021031535

LC ebook record available at https://lccn.loc.gov/2021031536

ISBN: HB: 978-1-50992-933-7
ePDF: 978-1-50992-935-1
ePub: 978-1-50992-934-4

Typeset by Compuscript Ltd, Shannon

PREFACE

This volume in the Studies of the Oxford Institute of European and Comparative Law is the result of a research workshop held at the University of Seville in 2018 to coincide with the 500th anniversary of the Law Faculty of Seville. The workshop was organised by the Centro de Derecho Comparado of the Law Faculty of the University of Seville and the Institute of European and Comparative Law of the Law Faculty of the University of Oxford.

The workshop explored a range of comparative issues in, and in the relationship between, property law and contract law in English law, Spanish law and other jurisdictions. The workshop was conducted in both English and Spanish, and contributors presented papers in one or other language. The purpose of this volume is to present papers from the workshop in a form that will be accessible to an English-speaking audience, and thereby to give readers access to discussions and comparisons of these areas of private law that are not easily accessible elsewhere. Papers that were originally written in Spanish have been translated either by (or on behalf of) their authors, or by the editors of this volume.

We should like to thank the Law Faculty at the University of Seville for the warm and enthusiastic welcome and hospitality extended to the participants at the workshop, and for its financial support for the workshop, as well as to the Institute of European and Comparative Law for its financial support for the participants from Oxford. Above all, we thank those who participated in the workshop, especially those who presented papers and have re-worked them for publication in this volume.

John Cartwright
Ángel M López y López
Oxford and Seville
April 2021

CONTENTS

Preface v
List of Contributors xiii
List of Abbreviations xv
Note on Translations Used in this Volume xxi

1. *Introduction* *1*
John Cartwright and Ángel M López y López

I. General Scope and Purpose of the Book 1
II. Institutions and Terminology of the Spanish Law of Property 11

2. *Contract and the Transfer of Ownership in Spanish and Latin American Law: An Overview* *19*
Ángel M López y López

I. Limited Scope of the Discussion 19
II. The Roman-Canon Law Tradition 20
III. The Break from the Traditional Mechanism of Transfer Made by the French Civil Code 21
IV. The System of '*Titulus et Modus*' for the Transfer of Ownership in Spain, in Austria and widely in Latin America 22
V. Features of the Modern Spanish System 24
A. The Need for a *iusta causa traditionis*, and the Problem of Fiduciary Transfers 24
B. *Traditio* as a Mechanism of Publicity 26
VI. *Traditio* of Movables and the Rule 'Possession is Equivalent to Title' 27
VII. *Traditio* of Immovables and Registration in the Public Register 29

3. *The Dual Role of the* Escritura Pública *in the Sale of Immovable Property* 33
Manuel Espejo Lerdo de Tejada

I. Introduction 33
II. Delivery as an Obligation of the Vendor and Delivery as *Traditio* 34
III. Some Special Features of the Transfer of Ownership by *Escritura Pública* 42
A. Defects in the Instrument of Sale or in the Vendor's Title 42
B. Sale with Reservation of Ownership 47

C. Sale of a Future Thing.....51
D. *Traditio* by a Person Who is Not in Possession of the Thing Sold.....55

4. A Non Domino *Acquisitions and Protection of Third-Party Purchasers of Immovable Property in the Spanish Legal System*.....*61*
Juan Pablo Murga Fernández

I. Introduction.....61
A. The Notion of *A Non Domino* Acquisition.....62
B. The Spanish Land Registration System.....64
II. The Principle and Requirements of Conclusive Title through Registration.....66
A. Existence of a Third Party.....67
B. Acquisition of a Property Right Over Immovable Property.....68
C. The Purchaser's Good Faith.....69
i. The 'Configuration' of Good Faith.....71
ii. The Timing of Good Faith under Article 34.....75
D. Acquisition for Value.....78
E. The Transferor's Registered Ownership and Power of Disposition.....79
F. Title Registration.....81
G. Validity of the Title of a Protected Third Party.....84
III. The Fundamental Effect of Conclusive Title: Curing the Transferor's Lack of Power of Disposition and Establishing a True *A Non Domino* Acquisition.....86

5. *Contract and Conveyance: The Further Repercussions of Different Transfer Systems*.....*89*
Birke Häcker

I. Introduction, or: On the Importance of Understanding Rules in Context.....89
II. Outline of the Different Property Transfer Regimes.....92
A. Two or Three Basic Questions.....92
B. France: A Pure Causal Consensual System.....93
C. Germany: A Fully-Fledged Principle of Abstraction.....95
D. Austria: An Example of Separation without Abstraction.....97
E. England: A Muddle?.....98
III. The Passing of Risk.....101
IV. The Nature of the Buyer's Claim against the Seller.....106
V. Security Mechanisms and Protection against Insolvency.....109
A. The Buyer's Position.....109
B. The Seller's Position.....111
VI. The Effects of Rescission of Contract.....114

VII. The Size and Structure of the Law of Unjust(ified) Enrichment 118
VIII. The Rules on Bona Fide Purchase 124
A. The First Connection: Bona Fide Purchase Rules and Derivative Acquisition....................124
B. The Second Connection: Protecting Third Parties in Conveyance Chains 129
IX. Conclusion 135

6. *The Creation and Transfer of Property Rights by Contract in English Law* *137*
John Cartwright

I. Introduction. Contract and Property: Independence and Interdependence....................137
II. Contracts to Transfer Rights in Land: The Creation of Property Rights in Equity....................138
A. The Distinction between Legal and Equitable Rights in Land: Historical Context 140
B. The Creation of Equitable Interests by Contract: The Doctrine of *Walsh v Lonsdale*....................141
C. The Strength Against Third Parties of the Purchaser's Equitable Interest Arising under a Contract of Sale of Land....................143
D. The Basis of the Purchaser's Equitable Interest in the Remedy of Specific Performance 145
E. The Operation of the Principle Outside the Context of Land 147
III. Passing the (Legal) Property in Movables by Contract....................148
IV. Conclusions....................151

7. *The Transfer of Ownership of Goods in the Draft Common Frame of Reference*....................*153*
Francisco Oliva Blázquez

I. Introduction....................153
II. The Proposal for Harmonising the Transfer of Ownership of Goods: The Work of the Study Group on a European Civil Code....................155
III. The Basic Structure of Article VIII-2:101 DCFR 158
IV. Autonomy of Will and Transfer of Ownership 159
V. The Principle of Delivery and the Greater Protection of the Interests of All the Parties Involved (Creditors)....................160
VI. Abstract Transfer versus Causal Transfer....................164
VII. Conclusion 165

8. *The Assignment of Contract: Some Comparative Reflections on French and English Law* *167*
Agnès Kwiatkowski

I. Introduction. The Assignment of Contract: An Intriguing Recognition 167
A. General Definition of Assignment 168
B. A Specific Context in French law: The Reform of Contract Law 169
C. A Bit of History 170
D. The Idea of Transfer 171
II. Opposing Visions of the Mechanism of Assignment 173
A. Technically Different 173
i. A Problematic Construction in French Law 173
ii. A Comparison with English Law 176
B. Conceptually Different 178
i. The Contract as Object of the Assignment 178
ii. The Transfer 179
III. A Mechanism Revealing the Proprietary Character of the Contract 180
A. The Nature of Contractual Rights 180
i. Contract and Property: A Difficult Line to Draw in the Context of Assignment 180
ii. A Chose in Action as the Central Element in English Law 181
iii. Contractual Rights as Property 183
B. The Contract as an Asset 185
i. The Contract Behaves Like Property 185
ii. Recognising a Real Assignment of 'the Contract' 186
IV. Conclusion 187

9. *Mistakes in Wills* *189*
Simon Douglas

I. Introduction 189
II. Mistakes 190
III. Remedies 191
A. Knowledge and Approval 191
B. Construction 196
i. The Traditional Approach to Construction 196
ii. Parol Evidence 197
iii. Modern Approach to Construction 198
C. Rectification 201
i. Construction versus Rectification 202
ii. Meaning Errors 203
iii. Parol Terms 204
IV. Conclusion 206

10. *Private Property and Forced Expropriation: Current Challenges in Spanish Law* *207*
Encarnación Montoya Martín

I. Introduction 207
II. Private Property in the Spanish Constitution of 1978 207
A. The Nature of the Fundamental Right to Property 209
B. Constitutional Guarantees of Property 210
i. Formal Guarantee: Reservation to Legislation 210
ii. Material Guarantee: The Essential Content 211
III. Forced Expropriation 212
A. The Concept 213
B. Constitutional Guarantees of Forced Expropriation 215
i. The Ground of Public Utility or Social Interest is the Legitimate Burden of Forced Expropriation 216
ii. Providing Proper Compensation: Compensation as a Patrimonial Guarantee 217
iii. Procedural Guarantee or the Right to an Effective Defence Against Expropriation 218
IV. Weak Points or Aspects Most in Need of Reform in the LEF 219
A. Forced Expropriation and the Autonomic Model 220
B. Administrations with Expropriation Powers 221
C. The Need to Strengthen Effective Protection of the Expropriated Party in the Expropriation Procedures 221
i. The Declaration of the Ground of Public Utility or Social Interest 221
ii. Reinforce the Procedure for Declaring the Need for Occupation and Reduce the Generalisation of Implicit Declarations 222
iii. The Generalisation of Emergency Expropriations 223
iv. The Problem of Valuations 223
V. The United Kingdom before the European Court of Human Rights on the Basis of Expropriation 224

Index *229*

LIST OF CONTRIBUTORS

John Cartwright is Emeritus Professor of the Law of Contract at the University of Oxford, and Research Fellow of the Institute of European and Comparative Law. He was formerly Director of the Institute.

Simon Douglas is Associate Professor of Law at the University of Oxford, and Law Fellow at Jesus College.

Manuel Espejo Lerdo de Tejada is Professor of Civil Law at the University of Seville.

Birke Häcker is Professor of Comparative Law at the University of Oxford and Fellow of Brasenose College; and Director of the Institute of European and Comparative Law.

Agnès Kwiatkowski is *Docteure en droit* of the University of Lille, and was formerly *Maison Française d'Oxford* Visiting Scholar at the Institute of European and Comparative Law, Oxford.

Ángel M López y López is Emeritus Professor of Civil Law at the University of Seville.

Encarnación Montoya Martín is Professor of Administrative Law at the University of Seville.

Juan Pablo Murga Fernández is Associate Professor of Civil Law at the University of Seville and Visiting Research Fellow of the Institute of European and Comparative Law, Oxford.

Francisco Oliva Blázquez is Professor of Civil Law at the University Pablo de Olavide, Seville.

LIST OF ABBREVIATIONS

AAMN	Anales de la Academia Matritense del Notariado
ABGB	Allgemeines bürgerliches Gesetzbuch (General Civil Code of Austria) (1811)
AC	Law Reports, Appeal Cases (Third Series) (1891–)
ADC	Anuario de Derecho Civil
ADHGB	Allgemeines Deutsches Handelsgesetzbuch (General German Commercial Code) (1861)
All ER	All England Law Reports
ALR	Allgemeines Landrecht für die Preußischen Staaten (Prussian General State Law) (1794)
App Cas	Law Reports, Appeal Cases (Second Series) (1875–1890)
Art(s)/art(s)	article(s)
BCC	British Company Cases
BGB	Bürgerliches Gesetzbuch (German Civil Code) (1896)
Burr	Burrow's King's Bench Reports
CA	Court of Appeal
Can J Law & Juris	Canadian Journal of Law & Jurisprudence
Cass civ (1), (3)	First or third civil chamber of the Cour de cassation (French Supreme Court)
Cass com	Commercial chamber of the Cour de cassation (French Supreme Court)
Cass req	Chambre de requêtes ('chamber of petitions') of the Cour de cassation (French Supreme Court)
CC	Código Civil español (Spanish Civil Code) (1889)
Cc	Code civil français (French Civil Code) (1804; with later amendments). References are to the latest version except where otherwise made clear.
CCJC	Cuadernos Civitas de Jurisprudencia Civil

CCom	Código de Comercio (Spanish Commercial Code) (1885)
CE	Constitución Española (Spanish Constitution) (1978)
Cf/cf	compare
Ch	Law Reports, Chancery Division (1890–)
Ch D	Law Reports, Chancery Division of the High Court of Justice (Second Series) (1875–1890)
Ch or ChD	Chancery Division
Ch Rep	Reports in Chancery
Ch/ch	Chapter
chron	chroniques
CISG	UN Convention on Contracts for the International Sale of Goods (1980) (Vienna Sales Convention)
Cl & Fin	Clark & Finnelly's House of Lords Cases (1831–1846)
CLC	Commercial Law Cases
CLJ	Cambridge Law Journal
CLP	Current Legal Problems
Cmnd	Command (identifier for published parliamentary papers)
Conv	Conveyancer and Property Lawyer
Ct	Court
D	Recueil Dalloz
DCFR	Draft Common Frame of Reference (2009)
Dig	Digest of Justinian
DLR	Dominion Law Reports (Canada)
DP	Dalloz, Recueil périodique et critique de jurisprudence, de législation et de doctrine (1825–1940)
Drew	Drewry's Reports (1852–1859)
ECHR	European Convention for the Protection of Human Rights and Fundamental Freedoms
ECLI	European Case Law Identifier
ECtHR	European Court of Human Rights
ed(s)	editor(s)

edn	edition
eg	for example
EHRR	European Human Rights Reports
El & Bl	Ellis & Blackburn's Queen's Bench Reports (1852–1858)
EPLJ	European Property Law Journal
ER	English Reports
esp	especially
EWCA Civ	Decision of the Court of Appeal (Civil Division)
EWHC	Decision of the High Court
ExCh	Court of Exchequer Chamber
f(f)	and following
FJ	Fundamento jurídico (numbered section of decision of the Spanish Constitutional Court giving its legal reasoning)
G	Institutes of Gaius
GG	Grundgesetz für die Bundesrepublik Deutschland (Basic Law for the Federal Republic of Germany) (1949)
HCA	Decision of the High Court of Australia
HL	House of Lords
HL(Sc)	House of Lords (Scottish Appeal)
HRA	Human Rights Act
ie	that is / in other words
Inst	Institutes of Justinian
IR	Irish Reports
J	Mr (or Mrs) Justice (Justice of the High Court in England and Wales)
JCP G	Juris-classeur périodique, La semaine juridique, édition générale
JORF	Journal officiel de la République française (Official Journal of the French Republic)
JSC	Justice of the Supreme Court
JUR	Repertorio de Jurisprudencia Aranzadi
KB	Law Reports, King's Bench Division (1901–1952)

KBD	King's Bench Division
Law Com	Law Commission
LCA	Land Charges Act
LEF	Ley de 16 de diciembre de 1954 sobre expropiación forzosa (Boletín Oficial del Estado, núm. 351, de 17/12/1954) (Forced Expropriation Law)
LH	Ley Hipotecaria (Spanish Mortgage Act) (1944, revised version in force from 1946)
LJ	Lord (or Lady) Justice (Justice of the Court of Appeal in England and Wales)
LP(MP)A	Law of Property (Miscellaneous Provisions) Act
LPA	Law of Property Act
LQR	Law Quarterly Review
LR CP	Law Reports, Common Pleas (First Series) (1865–1875)
LR P & D	Law Reports, Probate & Divorce Cases
LR PD	Law Reports, Probate Division (First Series) (1865–1875)
LR QB	Law Reports, Queen's Bench (First Series) (1865–1875)
LRA	Land Registration Act
LT	Law Times Reports
Madd	Maddock's Chancery Reports (1815–1821)
MLR	Modern Law Review
MR	Master of the Rolls
n	note
No(s), no(s)	Number(s)
NSWCA	New South Wales Court of Appeal
NSWLR	New South Wales Law Reports
OED	Oxford English Dictionary
OGH	Oberster Gerichtshof (Austrian Supreme Court)
OJ	Official Journal of the European Communities/Union
OR	Schweizerisches Obligationenrecht (Swiss Law of Obligations)
P	Law Reports, Probate Division (1891–1971)
P & CR	Property, Planning and Compensation Reports

para	paragraph
PC	Judicial Committee of the Privy Council
PD	Law Reports, Probate Division of the High Court of Justice (Second Series) (1875–1890)
PDA	Probate, Divorce and Admiralty Division
PECL	Principles of European Contract Law (2000–2003)
Ph	Phillips (Reports 1841–1849)
QB	Court of Queen's Bench; Law Reports, Queen's Bench Division (1891–1901, 1952–)
QBD	Queen's Bench Division
r	rule
RAP	Revista de Administración Pública
RCDI	Revista Crítica de Derecho Inmobiliario
RDC	Revue des contrats
RDGRN	Resolución de la Dirección General de los Registros y del Notariado (decisions of the Spanish Directorate-General of Registries and Notaries)
RDI	Revue de droit immobilier
RDP	Revista Aranzadi de Derecho Patrimonial
REF	Decreto de 26 de abril de 1957 por el que se aprueba el Reglamento de la Ley de Expropiación Forzosa (Boletín Oficial del Estado, núm. 160, de 20/06/1957) (Decree Approving the Regulation of the Forced Expropriation Law)
RH	Reglamento Hipotecario, Decreto de 14 de febrero de 1947 (Boletín Oficial del Estado, núm. 106, de 16/04/1947) (Spanish Mortgage Regulation)
RJ	Repertorio de Jurisprudencia Aranzadi
RJDA	Revue de Jurisprudence de Droit des affaires
RLR	Restitution Law Review
RTD civ	Revue trimestrielle de droit civil
RUE	Revista de Urbanismo y Edificación
s(s)	section(s)
SC	Supreme Court

SCC	Decision of the Supreme Court of Canada
Sched	Schedule
SGA	Sale of Goods Act
SGECC	Study Group on a European Civil Code
SI	Statutory Instrument
STC	Simon's Tax Cases
STC	Sentencia del Tribunal Constitucional (decision of the Spanish Constitutional Court)
STS	Sentencia del Tribunal Supremo (decision of the Spanish Supreme Court)
Sw & Tr	Swabey & Tristram's Probate & Divorce Reports (1858–1865)
SZ	Entscheidungen des Österreichischen Obersten Gerichtshofes in Zivil- und Justizverwaltungssachen (decisions of the OGH in private law and administration of justice)
TC	Tribunal Constitucional Español (Spanish Constitutional Court)
TE	Teilentwurf (draft)
TLI	Trust Law International
TLR	Times Law Reports
trans	translated (by)
Tul LR	Tulane Law Review
UKHL	Decision of the House of Lords
UKSC	Decision of the UK Supreme Court
VC	Vice Chancellor
Vol(s)/vol(s)	Volume(s)
WLR	Weekly Law Reports
WTLR	Wills and Trusts Law Reports
ZEuP	Zeitschrift für Europäisches Privatrecht
ZGB	Schweizerisches Zivilgesetzbuch (Swiss Civil Code) (1907)
ZPO	Zivilprozessordnung (German Code of Civil Procedure)
ZRG (RA)	Zeitschrift der Savigny-Stiftung für Rechtsgeschichte (Romanistische Abteilung)

NOTE ON TRANSLATIONS USED IN THIS VOLUME

Translations of the text of the Spanish Civil Code (*Código Civil*: CC) are based on the translation dated 2016 published by the Spanish Ministry of Justice (but with some amendments by the authors and editors of this volume): see www.mjusticia.gob.es/es/AreaTematica/DocumentacionPublicaciones/Documents/Spanish%20Civil%20Code.pdf.

Translations of the Spanish Constitution (*Constitución Española*: CE) of 1978 are based on the translation published by the Spanish Ministry of Justice (but with some amendments by the authors and editors of this volume): see www.congreso.es/constitucion/ficheros/c78/cons_ingl.pdf.

Translations of the provisions of the French Civil Code (*Code civil*: Cc) which were reformed in 2016 (and further revised in 2018) are taken from the translation by J Cartwright, S Whittaker and B Fauvarque-Cosson commissioned by the *Direction des affaires civiles et du sceau, Ministère de la Justice, République française*, printed in J Cartwright, B Fauvarque-Cosson and S Whittaker, *La Réécriture du code civil: le droit français des contrats après la réforme de 2016* (Paris, Société de législation comparée, 2018) Annexe 1, and also available at www.textes.justice.gouv.fr/dossiers-thematiques-10083/loi-du-170215-sur-la-simplification-du-droit-12766/traduction-de-lordonnance-du-10-fevrier-2016-en-langue-anglaise-28998.html.

Except where otherwise indicated, translations of Latin materials from the Digest of Justinian are based on the translation by A Watson, *The Digest of Justinian* (Philadelphia, University of Pennsylvania Press, revised 1998) (with some amendments by the authors and editors of this volume).

Translations of other foreign language materials are by the authors and/or editors of this volume.

1

Introduction

JOHN CARTWRIGHT AND ÁNGEL M LÓPEZ Y LÓPEZ*

I. General Scope and Purpose of the Book

The following chapters of this book are based on presentations made at a workshop held at the University of Seville which explored a range of comparative issues in, and the relationship between, property law and contract law in English law, Spanish law and other jurisdictions. The purpose of the book is to make accessible to an English-speaking audience the discussions and comparisons of these areas of private law that are not easily accessible elsewhere.

Chapters 2 to 7 explore various different aspects of the rules for the creation and transfer of property, within particular systems or comparatively across systems.

We begin with a general introduction by Ángel López y López (Chapter 2) to the relationship between contract and the transfer of ownership in Spanish law and Latin American law. This chapter sets the scene for the approach to the transfer of ownership in modern Spanish law, discussed in more detail in Chapters 3 and 4, and the comparative discussion of approaches in other civil law systems in Chapters 5 and 7. López y López illustrates the significance of the historical background to our topic within civil law systems,[1] noting the development from Roman law through to the modern law, and he highlights a number of points which will be key not only for an understanding of the modern Spanish law but also for its comparison with other systems: the system of '*titulus et modus*', which requires both a *legal ground* (*titulus*) for the transfer of ownership and an effective *method* (*modus*) of transfer, and takes us to consider the notion of *causa* (the 'cause' for the effective transfer of property, and therefore – at the heart of our topic in this book – the relationship between the (valid) contract and the (valid) transfer

* The drafting of this chapter, which constitutes the Editors' joint introduction to the book, was undertaken by John Cartwright.

[1] For further discussion of importance of historical context, see Häcker, below, Ch 5 sections II.C, D and E, III, V.B and VIII.B (discussing the historical background to modern civil law systems and the common law in the context of different aspects of their property law); Cartwright, below, Ch 6, esp section II.A (historical background of the different approaches of the common law and equity to the creation and protection of both property rights and rights arising under contracts for the transfer of property).

of property); differences between movable and immovable property; the role of publicity in the transfer of property (including different concepts and effects of registration systems); and the significance of possession as a source of ownership – and in particular the rule that 'possession is equivalent to title' (*posesión vale título*).

Chapters 3 and 4 both focus on aspects of the transfer of ownership of immovable property within Spanish law.

Manuel Espejo Lerdo de Tejada (Chapter 3) takes the classic case of sale of immovable property and explains the use of a special formal written instrument (*escritura pública*) as the equivalent of delivery – the *modus* within the Spanish system of *titulus et modus* in the transfer of ownership of immovables. He focuses on a number of problematic cases in which there can be difficulties in determining whether (and, if so, when) the *escritura pública* has the effect of transferring ownership without further physical delivery: where the seller has no title at the time of executing the *escritura pública* but later acquires it; where there is delivery of possession but subject to a reservation of ownership (for example, subject to a condition as to the payment of the price) but the condition for the transfer of ownership is later satisfied; the sale of a thing which does not yet exist or has not yet been defined, but later comes into existence or is defined; and the sale by a person who is not in fact in possession of the property at the time of executing the *escritura pública* (and therefore the 'fictitious' delivery which is deemed to be effected by the execution of the *escritura pública* could not have taken place).

In Chapter 4, the principal focus of Juan Pablo Murga Fernández's contribution is the acquisition of ownership of immovable property from a non-owner – *a non domino*. The focus on ownership of immovable property takes him to the Spanish land registry system, and the notion under Land Registry law of conclusive title to land in favour of a purchaser in good faith once it is registered, including difficulties which arise in the interpretation of the requirement of good faith, and whether registration of the instrument of transfer has the effect of curing or overriding defects in the contract which forms the ground (the *causa* – the *titulus*) of the transfer. This chapter gives a general introduction to the Spanish land registry system; later in this Introduction we draw attention to some of the features of the Spanish system which Murga Fernández lays out, and how they compare with the English system of land registration.[2]

In Chapter 5, Birke Häcker moves our focus from Spanish law to other legal systems – mainly English, French and German law, but also Austrian law (which bears striking similarities to the Spanish property law, as López y López indicated earlier in Chapter 2) and Swiss law; and her primary focus is the transfer not of land, but of movables, especially in the context of contracts for the sale of goods. She presents a broad comparative discussion of different property transfer systems, drawing out key distinctions between 'unitary' systems (where the contractual consent also brings about the transfer of property) and those which

[2] Below, section II.

adopt a principle of 'separation' (where the contract and the transfer are separate legal transactions); and between those which see the validity of the transfer as depending on the validity of the contract ('causal' systems) and those where there is no such interdependence of validity ('abstract' systems). Within this taxonomy, we see at the two extremes the French system (unitary, causal, consensual)[3] and the German (wholly abstract).[4] For the purposes of our comparison with Spanish law, however, it is important to note Häcker's categorisation of the Austrian system, which lies between the two extremes of France and Germany: Austria has separation without abstraction, because – as also Spanish law – it adopts the system of *titulus et modus*, requiring the transfer (*traditio*) separate from the contract, but making the validity of the transfer depend on the validity of the underlying contract.[5] Another system which does not belong fully to either extreme is English law which, largely because of its history, has a mix of approaches:[6] the common law generally adopts an abstract system, certainly for interests in land, and also probably for movables – except for the transfer pursuant to a contract for the sale of goods, which appears to be causal and consensual, although Häcker raises a question about whether even in this case the contract may be separate from the transfer, rather than unitary. She also notes that the picture is complicated by the (proprietary) effect given to the contract in equity, a topic which is then left for more detailed discussion by Cartwright (Chapter 6).

Häcker's explanation of the different transfer systems is important for us to understand the different choices available to legal systems in devising their property transfer systems, although for the purpose of her own chapter it is designed only to set the context: her main focus is to consider in detail the implications of the choice of transfer system on other parts of the legal order and the interaction between property law and these parts.[7] What repercussions (if any) does the choice of transfer system have on the legal system's rules for, or general approach to, the passing of risk? Or on the nature of the buyer's claim (including the availability of remedies) against seller? Or on security mechanisms and the protection of each party against the insolvency of the other? Or on the effects of rescission (retroactive avoidance) of the contract on the transfer of property? Or on the size and structure of the law of unjust(ified) enrichment within the system? Or on the operation of the system's rules on bona fide purchase?

In Chapter 6, John Cartwright takes up in more detail some particular aspects of English law which were raised by Häcker in the previous chapter: he discusses the way in which property rights can be created or transferred *by contract*; and (in that context) the way in which the rules of contract law – and in particular, the (equitable) remedy of specific performance of the contract – have a direct or indirect

[3] A 'pure causal consensual system': see below, Ch 5 section II.B.
[4] A 'fully-fledged principle of abstraction': see below, Ch 5 section II.C.
[5] A 'causal tradition system': see below, Ch 5 section II.D.
[6] A 'muddle': see below, Ch 5 section II.E.
[7] See below, Ch 5 sections III to VIII.

bearing on the nature and strength of the property rights thereby created or transferred. This picks up the direct link between contract and property, in particular through the operation of equity, peculiar to English law and other systems in the common law world which follow the English tradition in their property law. The main focus of the chapter is the contract for the sale or creation of an interest in land, where the traditional approach of equity is to say that, as long as the contract would be enforced specifically by a court of equity, then equity treats the contract as already transferring or creating the right which the contract has promised. Two aspects of this are worthy of note, especially by lawyers from the civil law tradition. First, this involves the creation of an (equitable) property right in the hands of the transferee concurrently with the (legal) property right that has not (yet) been transferred or disposed of. Second, the existence and validity of the (equitable) property right depends not just on the validity of the contract, but on whether the court would grant the remedy of specific performance of it; and its enforceability depends on matters that other systems would readily recognise: rules of bona fide purchase, and the system of registration in the Land Register. More is said below by way of comparison of the Spanish and English systems of registration of property rights in land.[8]

As a secondary element of his discussion, Cartwright also considers the way in which (legal) property in movables can be passed by contract. Although – as Häcker has already shown in Chapter 5 – the English contract of sale of goods may not de iure pass the property (as in, say, the causal consensual system of French law), in many cases the property will pass when the contract is made, based on the parties' consent. But the strength of that transferred title to property is not what a civil lawyer might expect it to be. In the case of movables, it is rare that the holder of a contractual right to property can obtain it, either by enforcing the contract, or by enforcing his title that has been passed by or under the contract. There is therefore a sharply different strength of title passed by contract, depending on whether the property is land or movables. But at the heart of this difference we find the different views taken of the remedy of specific performance of the contract in these different cases (ie, specific performance protects interests in land more strongly than interests in movables).

In Chapter 7, Francisco Oliva Blázquez takes us back to the context which Birke Häcker discussed in Chapter 5: the contract for the sale of goods, and comparison of different systems' approaches to the moment at which the transfer of ownership takes effect. This time, however, the focus is not the national systems, but on whether a universal and common solution can be found, using the provision of the Draft Common Frame of Reference (DCFR, article VIII–2:101) as a model for discussion and analysis, and drawing on the studies published by Lurger and Faber, chairing the 'Acquisition and Loss of Ownership in Movables' working

[8] Below, section II.

group within the 'Common Principles of European Contract Law' project.[9] Given that – as we have seen in Häcker's review of just a few European systems – there is no common (even functionally equivalent) solution across national systems in the EU, Oliva Blázquez asks which solution should be preferred. He notes that the DCFR solution allows the parties to determine the moment of transfer of ownership; failing that, it adopts a rule of *modus* – delivery (or equivalent), rather than mere consent. But it requires also *titulus* – thereby following the causal principle for the underlying agreement, rather than abstraction. So the solution is similar to Austria or Spain, not to Germany or France. Oliva Blázquez argues that there are good reasons for preferring this solution, based on a fair balance of treatment of the parties' creditors, as well as of the parties themselves.

In the final three chapters of the book, we have discussions of specific topics in contract or property law which raise issues that should be of interest to comparative lawyers.

Agnès Kwiatkowski (Chapter 8) has French law as her focus. She highlights – and criticises – the recognition in the reforms made to the French Civil Code in 2016/2018 of the concept of 'assignment of the contract', which now appears in the Code in addition to the (separate) institutions of assignment of the benefit of rights, assignment of the burden of rights and novation. Kwiatkowski's criticism is directed not at the idea that a contract (as a unit, containing both benefits and burdens of the obligations it creates) can be assigned, but at the form in which the French Code has defined it: assignment of the 'status of party', rather than of the contract itself. This discussion highlights a significant idea for the purposes of this book, showing a link between contract and property: that assignment of a contract – even of the benefit, but certainly of its burden or of the ('whole') contract – involves a shift from the inter partes, personal nature of contract, to treating the contract as an object of property, or, as Kwiatkowski puts it, 'why should we not see the contract itself as a transferable asset? An asset represents rights that have an economic value. This perceptible property aspect could turn some contracts into assets'.[10] This involves, in effect, breaking down the boundaries between the static patrimonial right (the contract) and the dynamic patrimonial right (property).[11]

This chapter is comparative, but between French law and English law. As Kwiatkowski makes clear,[12] the language of 'assignment of the contract' is alien to English law. However, the idea of the same contract being transferred (its burdens, as well as its benefits) is not unknown in certain particular contexts: leases are perhaps the best example, although the lease is already seen as a hybrid figure, belonging to both contract and property; but there are also other cases such as the

[9] B Lurger and W Faber, *Principles of European Law: Acquisition and Loss of Ownership of Goods (PEL Acq Own)* (Munich, Sellier, 2011); see also the six volumes of national reports in W Faber and B Lurger (eds), *National Reports on the Transfer of Movables in Europe* (München, Sellier, 2008–2011).

[10] See below, Ch 8 section III.B.i.

[11] Cf Oliva Blázquez, below, Ch 7 section I.

[12] See below, Ch 8 section II.A.ii.

transfer of employment contracts. The same concerns apply in all legal systems (protection of both parties in the continuing relationship of landlord and tenant on the sale of the reversion by the landlord or on the assignment of the lease by the tenant; protection of the employee on change of undertaking by the employer), so there is here a very useful point of comparison about the techniques by which different systems achieve the transfer. Given that common law systems generally adopt a piecemeal approach, by contrast with the more general principles of the civil law,[13] it is perhaps less surprising that a codified system such as France should elevate to a general principle the concept of transfer of the contract (or of transfer of the contractual relationship, or of the 'status' of parties to the contract). Indeed, as Kwiatkowski notes towards the end of her chapter, the idea of an 'assignment of contract' is not unknown in other systems in the Continental civil law tradition – even in Spain, where it does not figure in the Civil Code, but has been developed by case-law to respond to commercial needs.[14] The precise concept or mechanism at play, however, may vary, together with the extent to which (and the theory according to which) systems depart from the notion of contractual obligation as being purely personal, with effect inter partes and not erga omnes, a notion which is the starting point not only for the common law but also for civilian systems following the Roman law tradition.[15]

In Chapter 9, Simon Douglas takes us to a special area of the law that sits between property and obligations and is concerned with testamentary dispositions over property. He discusses the three principal methods by which mistakes

[13] J Cartwright, *Contract Law: An Introduction to the English Law of Contract for the Civil Lawyer*, 3rd edn (Oxford, Hart Publishing, 2016) ch 2, esp 16–17.

[14] See, eg, STS 532/2014, 13 October where the Spanish Supreme Court referred to a number of its earlier decisions dating back to the 1960s, which together demonstrated that there can be an assignment of contract (*la cesión de contrato*) as long as it is a bilateral contract in which some or all of the duties on both sides remain to be performed, and the other party to the contract has given his consent prior to, at the same time as or after the transaction of assignment (the consent of all three parties therefore being involved). The assignment of the contract involves the transfer of the contractual relationship in its entirety, with a continuation of the same rights and obligations but with the substitution of one of the parties of the contract. The institution of assignment of contract is included within (eg) the Italian Civil Code, arts 1406–10 (*la cessione del contratto*) and the Dutch Civil Code, art 6:159 (*contractsoverneming*); and in PECL art 12:201 ('transfer of contract'), DCFR art III.-5:302 ('transfer of contractual position'). There are other useful references in the Comments and Notes to those provisions of PECL and the DCFR: see O Lando, E Clive, A Prüm and R Zimmermann, *Principles of European Contract Law Part III* (The Hague, Kluwer Law International, 2003) 134–37; C von Bar and E Clive (eds), *Principles, Definitions and Model Rules of European Private Law: Draft Common Frame of Reference* (DCFR) (Munich, Sellier, 2009) vol 2, 1102–07.

[15] In Roman law, even the assignment of the benefit of contractual obligations was developed only with difficulty, evading the non-assignability of the (personal) obligation by the use of mandate to allow the 'assignee' (mandatary) to sue on the creditor's behalf, but without a duty to account to the creditor for the proceeds: B Nicholas, *An Introduction to Roman Law* (Oxford, Clarendon Press, 1962) 200–01; WW Buckland, *A Textbook of Roman Law from Augustus to Justinian*, 3rd edn, revised P Stein (Cambridge, Cambridge University Press, 1963) 520–21. Assignment of burdens, or of the whole contract, was not conceivable: in order to achieve (functionally) such transactions a new contract was required – a novation (*novatio*): Nicholas 199–200; Buckland 568–71. As Kwiatkowski makes clear, the requirement of novation for this purpose is still the approach taken by English law.

affecting a will (testament) can be cured in English law: the doctrine of 'knowledge and approval', construction and rectification. The first of these is a particular doctrine developed in the context of the English process of registration of a will (so-called probate): words of which the testator had no knowledge are not entered into probate, and they are effectively deleted from the will. Construction (interpretation) and rectification (re-writing the will) are doctrines that are used generally in relation to written legal instruments, including contracts – and Douglas discusses the development of the rules of construction in relation to wills, in parallel to development of the modern rules of construction of contracts, which have abandoned literalism and adopted a more contextual interpretation. A broadening of the rules of construction as a means of correcting errors in written instruments has the effect of narrowing the circumstances in which a court needs to take the more obviously intrusive step of rectifying the instrument, to order a change in its (literal) wording. However, Douglas argues that rectification is still needed, to address particular kinds of mistake where the rules of construction cannot help.

This chapter discusses the use of similar doctrines (in particular, construction and rectification) in relation to written contracts and one particular form of disposition of property (the will – the testament), within English law. It therefore considers the core legal issue covered by this book – the interrelationship between contract and property – but it does not aim to be comparative with other systems, such as Spain. However, the argument in the chapter will invite readers from other jurisdictions to consider similar issues in their own systems. We can all see the same questions. Setting aside any mandatory rules which legal systems may impose on freedom of testation,[16] we would all say that voluntary dispositions of property on death are based on the will of the testator; but we would also generally say that a contract (bilateral or unilateral) is also based on the will, or intention, of the parties concerned. However, this immediately raises questions for the comparative lawyer: how our different systems identify a party's 'will' or 'intention', whether in subjective or objective terms; and whether the processes of construction of wills (and other dispositions of property) and of contracts have a

[16] Spain does not have a unitary succession law: extensive provisions setting out general rules are contained in Book III, Title III of the Spanish Civil Code, but these constitute default rules which may be displaced by specific local legislation enacted by the Autonomous Communities. However, one feature of the Spanish system is forced heirship, under which a reserved share of the estate (*la legítima*) cannot be disposed of by will but is reserved to certain 'forced heirs' (*herederos forzosos*): art 806 CC. See generally S Cámara Lapuente, 'Testamentary Formalities in Spain' in KGC Reid, MJ de Waal and R Zimmermann (eds), *Comparative Succession Law: Volume I: Testamentary Formalities* (Oxford, Oxford University Press, 2011) ch 4. This limitation on freedom of testation is also known in other civil law systems, such as France (*'la réserve héréditaire'*: art 912 Cc). Although in principle there is no such limitation on the freedom of testation in English law, the Inheritance (Provision for Family and Dependants) Act 1975 empowers the court to order financial provision out of an estate in favour of certain persons for whom the testator's will, or the law of intestate succession, does not make reasonable financial provision. The functional difference between systems may therefore not be as wide as first appears: M J De Waal, 'Comparative Succession Law' in M Reimann and R Zimmermann, *The Oxford Handbook of Comparative Law*, 2nd edn (Oxford, Oxford University Press, 2019) 1058, 1073–75.

common set of rules or whether, for example, the special context of a testamentary disposition means that its construction follows different rules or at least an adaptation of the rules generally applied in the interpretation of written instruments.[17] We cannot go into the matter here in detail to explain the Spanish position, by comparison with the position of English law as it is given by Douglas in his chapter. But we should mention that there are special provisions in the Spanish Civil Code for how a will is to be construed, apparently giving priority to the (objective) language of the will, although it yields to contrary evidence of the testator's intention[18] and in practice where the meaning of a disposition is challenged there needs to be an investigation into the true intention of the testator.[19] Extrinsic evidence can be used to establish the testator's intention as to the language he used,[20] and the contextual evidence of the aim sought to be achieved by the testator by his will.[21] The question of whether the general rules for the construction of contracts should also apply to the construction of wills has also arisen in Spain. The basic rule for contracts appears at first sight to be similar to the rule for testamentary dispositions: the literal meaning of a contract has priority if the terms are clear, but this yields to contrary evidence of the subjective intention of the parties.[22] However, the practice of construction of contracts goes beyond the enquiry into the parties' subjective intentions, and the Spanish Supreme Court has made clear that there is a difference of principle between the construction of wills and the construction of contracts:

> The interpretation of contracts, and in general that of inter vivos legal transactions, is guided not only by the will, but also by the so-called self-responsibility of the party making the declaration, and the reliance of the party to whom the declaration

[17] We set aside here the question of the circumstances in which there can be a valid *oral* will; and whether the rules for the interpretation of transactions (contract or property) effected orally may differ from those effected by writing.

[18] The general provision is in art 675.1 CC: 'Every testamentary disposition shall be construed according to the literal meaning of its words, unless it is appears clearly that the testator's intention was otherwise. In case of doubt, what appears to conform closest to the testator's intention, according to the wording of the will, shall be observed' ('Toda disposición testamentaria deberá entenderse en el sentido literal de sus palabras, a no ser que aparezca claramente que fue otra la voluntad del testador. En caso de duda se observará lo que aparezca más conforme a la intención del testador, según el tenor del mismo testamento'). There are also a number of other provisions giving particular rules of interpretation, such as how to identify the intended beneficiaries of the will, and how to interpret the testator's intention as to the nature/extent of the benefit to be taken by beneficiaries, but these are generally default rules of interpretation, overridden where a contrary intention of the testator is clearly evidenced.

[19] See, eg, STS 160/2011, 18 March; STS 691/2010, 2 November.

[20] See, eg, STS 1208/2007, 20 November (letter from testator to indicate that he included the contents of a safe deposit box within 'deposits' referred to in his will).

[21] See, eg, STS 624/2012, 30 October.

[22] Art 1281 CC: 'If the terms of a contract are clear and do not leave any doubt as to the intention of the contracting parties, the literal meaning of its clauses shall stand. If the words seem contrary to the evident intention of the contracting parties, the latter shall prevail over the former' ('Si los términos de un contrato son claros y no dejan duda sobre la intención de los contratantes, se estará al sentido literal de sus cláusulas. Si las palabras parecieren contrarias a la intención evidente de los contratantes, prevalecerá ésta sobre aquéllas'). There are also a number of more particular rules of interpretation in arts 1282–89, some of which are relevant particularly to bilateral transactions.

> is addressed, both of which derive from the objective principle of good faith. But the interpretation of a testament must be guided solely by a subjective test based on the testator's declarations of his last will. Case-law has recognised as a general rule in our law that the real will is preferred over the declared will, with the clarification that, in case of possible divergence between them, it is for those who allege this disparity to prove it, since the law takes as its starting-point that the declared will coincides with the real will.[23]

In the final chapter in the book (Chapter 10), Encarnación Montoya Martín takes us to a different area, within public law. She explains the legal controls on forced expropriation of private property in Spain in a way which will cast light on this significant issue of Spanish law for the non-Spanish reader. There are some special contextual aspects of this topic for Spain: in particular, the constitutionalisation of individual rights (including property) in the Spanish Constitution in 1978, enforced by the Spanish Constitutional Court, although the designation of rights which qualify as (constitutionally protected) property rights are in the hands of the national legislator – directly, or by (delegated) legislative decrees – since the right to property is not itself one of the 'fundamental rights and public liberties' which are subjected to special legislative procedures by reason of the Constitution. This is significant, as Montoya Martín says,[24] since it is the (ordinary) legislator's definition of the property right, and the limitations on it, designed to fulfil a social function, that will determine whether on the facts of a case there is an interference with the right which goes so far as to give rise to the right to compensation for forced expropriation under the Constitution. But, given that the Constitutional Court controls the right to property, there is a balance to be struck between the constitutional right to property, and the powers of the ordinary legislator which must respect the essential content of the right. The chapter explains the historical background to the Spanish legislation on forced appropriation, from its nineteenth century origins to the Forced Expropriation Law (*la Ley de Expropiación Forzosa*) of 1954 which is still in force, and which includes within permitted expropriation (subject always to compensation and, under the Constitution, to procedural guarantees) not only deprivation for reasons of public utility, but also of 'social interest' – which raises a tension with the concept of the 'social function' of the right which the (ordinary) legislator can define and therefore put outside the scope of constitutional protection as long as the essential content of the right is not infringed. The chapter includes discussion of areas which are in need of reform within Spanish law, as well as (by way of coda) a discussion of two cases in which Acts of the United Kingdom Parliament,[25] which had the effect of depriving owners of their property, were challenged (unsuccessfully) before the European Court of Human Rights.

[23] STS 947/2003, 9 October.

[24] See below, Ch 10 section III.A.

[25] *James v United Kingdom* (1986) 8 EHRR 123 (Leasehold Reform Act 1967: immovable property); *Lithgow v United Kingdom* (1986) 8 EHRR 329 (Aircraft and Shipbuilding Industries Act 1977: nationalisation of companies and shares in the aircraft and shipbuilding sector).

We do not have a full comparative discussion within this book on the approach to the constitutionalisation of property rights in English law – which would take us rather outside the general scope of the book, given that it would need to cover the means by which rights under the European Convention on Human Rights are protected within English law, including the (limited) scope of the implementation of the Convention by the Human Rights Act 1998[26] and the limited powers of the domestic courts under the 1998 Act,[27] as well as the approach taken in the UK courts to the application of the Convention. However, the two UK cases which Montoya Martín discusses point readers towards the direction that such a discussion might take, including the fact that the national authorities have a wide margin of appreciation on the balancing of interests involved in implementing social policies.[28] Further reading must be sought elsewhere.[29]

[26] Under HRA 1998, the domestic courts now have jurisdiction in relation to the alleged breach of an individual's ECHR rights by public authorities, although the Act does not expressly create rights enforceable directly between private individuals which would override the contractual rights and obligations that they have entered into: *McDonald v McDonald* [2016] UKSC 28, [2017] AC 273, confirmed by the ECtHR in *FJM v UK* (2019) 68 EHRR SE5. However, the Act gives private individuals directly enforceable rights against public authorities, for example, public sector tenants against their landlords.

[27] The courts cannot disapply legislation which they find to be incompatible with the ECHR, nor require the legislature to enact amending legislation to comply with the ECHR: HRA 1998, s 4(6). They must, however, read and give effect to primary and subordinate legislation in a way which is compliant with the Convention rights '[s]o far as it is possible to do so': s 3(1), and if that proves impossible, they can make a declaration that a provision of primary or subordinate legislation is incompatible with a Convention right: s 4. The domestic courts must take into account relevant jurisprudence of the European Court of Human Rights: s 2; and they normally follow the Strasbourg jurisprudence unless there is very good reason not to do so: see *Ofulue v Bossert* [2008] EWCA Civ 7, [2009] Ch 1 at [32].

[28] See, eg, *Regina (Mott) v Environment Agency* [2018] UKSC 10, [2018] 1 WLR 1022 (Environment Agency breached leaseholder's right to peaceful enjoyment of his possessions under art 1 of the first Protocol (A1P1) to the ECHR by rendering his commercial rights uneconomic when it imposed without compensation conditions on his right to fish for salmon. See, however, at [37] (Lord Carnwath JSC): 'I would emphasise that this was an exceptional case on the facts, because of the severity and the disproportion (as compared to others) of the impact on Mr Mott. As the Strasbourg cases show, the national authorities have a wide margin of discretion in the imposition of necessary environmental controls, and A1P1 gives no general expectation of compensation for adverse effects. Furthermore, where (unlike this case) the authorities have given proper consideration to the issues of fair balance, the courts should give weight to their assessment').

[29] See, eg, S Bridge, E Cooke and M Dixon (eds), *Megarry & Wade, The Law of Real Property*, 9th edn (London, Sweet & Maxwell, 2019) [1-021]–[1-031], esp the discussion of deprivation of possessions (art 1 of the first Protocol) at [1-027]–[1-028]; S Gardner and E MacKenzie, *An Introduction to Land Law*, 4th edn (Oxford, Hart Publishing, 2015) ch 2; R Smith, *Property Law*, 10th edn (Harlow, Pearson, 2020) ch 3. For the law of compulsory purchase (broadly, the exercise of a statutory power to compel landowners to sell their land, at a proper price, for the purpose of development projects carried out in the public interest), see M Barnes, *The Law of Compulsory Purchase and Compensation* (Oxford, Hart Publishing 2014) (the HRA 1998 is discussed at [1.13]); R Honey, R Fookes and J Pereira (eds), *The Law of Compulsory Purchase*, 3rd edn (Haywards Heath, Bloomsbury Professional, 2018) (the human rights dimension is discussed at ch A4). And for a recent example of the courts' consideration of the relationship between art 8 ECHR (right to respect for private life and home) and the tort of private nuisance (which protects against unreasonable interference with property interests in land), see *Fearn v Tate Gallery Board of Trustees* [2020] EWCA Civ 104, [2020] Ch 621 at [86]–[95] (CA, rejecting the argument that the common law tort of nuisance should be extended in light of art 8 to overlooking of property; an appeal to SC is pending).

In 2018, the UK Government asked the Law Commission to review the process for enfranchisement of long residential leaseholds (those granted for more than 21 years) – ie, the tenant's right to

II. Institutions and Terminology of the Spanish Law of Property

It may be helpful for us to explain at the outset some of the institutions and terminology of Spanish property law, since they may not be well known to the English reader. This is not, of course, a comprehensive introduction to the subject; we limit ourselves to those matters which will be referred to in later chapters of this book.

Many of the institutions of Spanish property law – and, indeed, much of its technical language – follow from its Roman heritage. There is a core distinction between movable and immovable property;[30] and between ownership (*la propiedad*)[31] and possession (*la posesión*),[32] which receive different forms of protection: the owner has a form of *vindicatio* – the right to claim recovery of the thing against whoever holds it;[33] the person who has possession (without ownership) has only an action to protect against a dispossession, or to reverse a dispossession that has taken place, without settling the question of ownership.[34] The different ways of

buy the freehold, or to have an extension of the lease: the tenant's right to buy the freehold was the subject of the claim in *James v United Kingdom*, above, n 25). The Commission's terms of reference included 'to consider the case to improve [the tenant's] access to enfranchisement' and 'to examine the options to reduce the premium (price) payable by existing and future leaseholders to enfranchise, whilst ensuring sufficient compensation is paid to landlords to reflect their legitimate property interests'. The Law Commission published its *Report on options to reduce the price payable* on enfranchisement by the tenant (Law Com No 387) in January 2020, and in July 2020 its Report *Leasehold home ownership: buying your freehold or extending your lease* (Law Com No 392) which recommends (inter alia) widening the scope of the tenant's powers to enfranchise a long leasehold. The Commission explicitly considered the human rights law implications of its recommendations, particularly in relation to the proposals to reduce the compensation payable by the tenant to the landlord in the event of enfranchisement, and sought the independent Opinion of a specialist human rights barrister on the compliance with human rights law of the options they set out: see Law Com No 387, paras 1.41–1.55. The Commission published the Opinion alongside its own Report. In January 2021 the Government announced its intention to bring forward residential leasehold legislation. See generally www.lawcom.gov.uk/project/leasehold-enfranchisement/.

[30] Art 333 CC: 'All objects which are or may be subject to appropriation are deemed either movable or immovable goods' ('Todas las cosas que son o pueden ser objeto de apropiación se consideran como bienes muebles o inmuebles'). Immovables are defined in art 334 CC; movables are defined and further categorised in arts 335–36.

[31] Art 348.1 CC: 'Ownership is the right to enjoy and dispose of an object, without other limitations than those set out in legislation' ('La propiedad es el derecho de gozar y disponer de una cosa, sin más limitaciones que las establecidas en las leyes').

[32] Arts 430ff CC.

[33] Art 348.2 CC: 'The owner shall have an action against the holder and the possessor of the thing to claim it' ('El propietario tiene acción contra el tenedor y el poseedor de la cosa para reivindicarla'). This is commonly referred to as *la acción reivindicatoria*.

[34] Art 446 CC: 'Every possessor is entitled to be respected in his possession; and, if he were to be disturbed in it, he shall be protected or such possession shall be restored to him by the means set out in the laws of procedure' ('Todo poseedor tiene derecho a ser respetado en su posesión; y, si fuere inquietado en ella, deberá ser amparado o restituido en dicha posesión por los medios que las leyes de procedimiento establecen'). The summary claim for protection of possession is provided by *Ley 1/2000, de 7 de enero, de Enjuiciamiento Civil*, art 250.1.4º. This action is commonly referred to as *la acción interdictal*, and art 1651 of the former law of civil procedure (of 1881) referred to the 'interdict to retain or recover' ('*el interdicto de retener o recobrar*'), although the 2000 Law has abandoned the use of this term.

acquiring ownership are set out in the Civil Code:[35] the two which mainly concern us are *traditio* (*tradición*) and prescription (*prescripción*).

Traditio is delivery of the thing, although special cases have been devised by which an owner can be deemed to have delivered the thing (and therefore to have transferred his ownership) without physical delivery, or at least at a time which differs from the actual delivery.[36] Particularly important for our purpose is the special rule of the Civil Code that the execution of an *escritura pública* – a public instrument authenticated by a Spanish notary – to give effect to a contract for the sale is 'equivalent to delivery of the thing constituting the subject-matter of the contract unless it should result or it should clearly be deduced otherwise from the escritura pública'.[37] The use of the *escritura pública* as the means of transfer of ownership of land, and various difficulties which arise from the operation of the *escritura pública* and from the interpretation of the Code, are discussed in detail by Espejo Lerdo de Tejada in Chapter 3.

Possession for a specified period of time can be a source of a new right of ownership through 'acquisitive prescription' (*la prescripción adquisitiva*), commonly referred to also as *usucapio* (*la usucapión*). Ownership is acquired either by 'ordinary' prescription for a relatively short period fixed by law, as long as strict conditions are satisfied, including that the possession of the thing was acquired in good faith and pursuant to a 'just title' – a good legal ground by which (but for some defect, such as the seller's lack of title) ownership might have been acquired;[38] or by possession for a longer period without the requirements of good faith and 'just title'.[39]

[35] Art 609 CC:

> 'Ownership is acquired by occupation.
>
> Ownership and other rights over property are acquired and transmitted by law, by gift, by testate and intestate succession and, as a result of certain contracts, by *traditio*.
>
> They may also be acquired by prescription'.
>
> ('La propiedad se adquiere por la ocupación.
>
> La propiedad y los demás derechos sobre los bienes se adquieren y transmiten por la ley, por donación, por sucesión testada e intestada, y por consecuencia de ciertos contratos mediante la tradición.
>
> Pueden también adquirirse por medio de la prescripción'.)

[36] eg, by symbolic delivery of the means of control of the thing (such as its keys) or by agreeing to a borrower keeping goods of which he already has possession: art 1463 CC. See also López y López, below, Ch 2 section V.B.

[37] Art 1462 CC ('… el otorgamiento de ésta equivaldrá a la entrega de la cosa objeto del contrato, si de la misma escritura no resultare o se dedujere claramente lo contrario').

[38] Art 1940 CC: 'Para la prescripción ordinaria del dominio y demás derechos reales se necesita poseer las cosas con buena fe y justo título por el tiempo determinado en la ley' ('Ordinary prescription of ownership and other rights in rem shall require bona fide possession of the thing and pursuant and a just title for the period provided in the law'). Further details of these requirements are set out in arts 1941ff. The period is three years' continuous possession in good faith for movables, and 10 years' for immovables (against a person who is present) or 20 years' (against a person who is absent): arts 1955.1, 1957 CC.

[39] Art 1955.2 CC (movables: six years), art 1959 CC (immovables: 30 years).

All these concepts and institutions are familiar from classical and post-classical Roman law,[40] and are known also in other modern civilian systems in many of which,[41] as in Spanish law, even the terminology often closely matches the Latin terms of the old Roman law.[42] This does not, of course, mean that the modern systems have interpreted and adopted the institutions of the Roman law of property in all respects, or in the same way. One later (non-Roman) development, which is generally shared in some form amongst systems of the modern civil law tradition, is the protection of a person who takes possession of property in good faith from a non-owner. Spanish law has the rule that 'possession of movable property, acquired in good faith, is equivalent to title'[43] although its operation is not identical to that in other systems[44] and, indeed, there is some debate amongst authors about the technical effect of this provision within Spanish law.[45]

An example of a key rule within Spanish law which differs from many other civil law systems is the relationship between the contract for the transfer of property, and the transfer of property itself. This is a topic which is at the heart of this book, and is discussed by a number of our contributors.[46] Roman law kept the

[40] See Nicholas (n 15) 105 (movable/immovable), 100 (*vindicatio*), 107–09 (possession and its protection by the interdicts), 117–20 (*traditio*, including its special forms devised over time in Roman law), 122–23, 128 (*usucapio* and acquisitive prescription); Buckland (n 15) 186 (movable/immovable), 187, 675 (ownership and its protection by the *vindicatio*), 196, 734–35 (possession and interdicts to retain or recover possession); 226–29 (*traditio*); 241–52 (*usucapio* and acquisitive prescription).

[41] Notably, in the so-called Romanistic (or Latin) systems: see López y López, below, Ch 2 section III; K Zweigert and H Kötz, *An Introduction to Comparative Law*, 3rd edn (trans T Weir, Oxford, Oxford University Press, 1998) ch 5. We do not seek here to engage in the debate about how (if at all) to categorise 'legal families' generally for the purposes of comparative law.

[42] Cf Häcker, below, Ch 5 section IV, discussing the owner's claim (*action en revendication*) in French law. For an outline (in English) of French property law, see J Bell, S Boyron and S Whittaker, *Principles of French Law*, 2nd edn (Oxford, Oxford University Press, 2008) ch 9, although some details, and some references within the French Civil Code, have now changed, notably following a reform of the law of prescription by *Loi no 2008-561 du 17 juin 2008 portant réforme de la prescription en matière civile*. This reform had the effect of changing the numbering (from art 2279 to art 2276) of the classic article which provides that 'In the case of movable property, possession is equivalent to title' ('En fait de meubles, la possession vaut titre'). See also E Cashin Ritaine, 'National Report on the Transfer of Movables in France' in W Faber and B Lurger (eds), *National Reports on the Transfer of Movables in Europe* (n 9) vol 4 (Munich, Sellier, 2011).

[43] Art 464.1 CC ('La posesión de los bienes muebles, adquirida de buena fe, equivale al título. …'). cf in French law art 2276 Cc (above, n 42).

[44] Systems differ, for example, as to whether and when they require the acquirer not only to take possession in good faith but also to be a *purchaser for value* in order to trigger the acquisition of ownership from a non-owner. Under a separate legislative text (art 34 LH) Spanish law requires acquisition from the non-owner to be for value in order to give the protection of the conclusive effect of registration of title to immovable property (see Murga Fernández, below, Ch 4 section II.D), but purchase for value is not required under art 464.1 CC for movable property. See also the general comparative discussion of this issue in relation to movables by Häcker, below, Ch 5 section VIII.A.

[45] In particular, whether the effect of the acquisition of possession in good faith is to give immediate ownership, or only to form a good 'title' (*titulus*) for the acquisition of ownership in due course by *usucapio*: see López y López, below, Ch 2 section VI; Murga Fernández, below, Ch 4 section I.A. Cf Häcker, below, Ch 5 section VIII.A (discussing English, French and German law); Oliva Blázquez, below, Ch 7 section VI (DCFR).

[46] For a general discussion see Häcker, below, Ch 5 section II; and for further explanation, discussion and defence of the Spanish system of *titulus et modus* see López y López, below, Ch 2 sections IV and V.A; Murga Fernández, below, Ch 4 section I; Oliva Blázquez, below, Ch 7 section VII.

contract of sale (with obligational effect) separate from the transfer of ownership (with proprietary effect)[47] but modern systems have varied or departed from this approach in different ways. The Spanish approach is the system of '*titulus et modus*' (*título y modo*): the transfer requires both a *legal ground* (*titulus*) for the transfer of ownership and an effective *method* (*modus*) of transfer, keeping the transfer (by *traditio* – delivery, or its equivalent[48]) separate from the preceding contract, but also linking the validity of the transfer to the validity of the contract,[49] thus making it a causal system, but with separation and not abstraction.[50]

Another important feature of the Spanish system, in relation to immovable property, is its Land Registry system. Most modern legal systems have developed systems of registration of property rights in relation to land – the ownership of the land itself, as well as other rights for which the holders of those rights need protection not just against the owner but also against third parties, such as later purchasers or mortgagees. The nature and strength of the protection which registration gives to the owner of the land and to other right-holders varies from one system to another: for example, in the case of the landowner, some systems make registration constitutive of the right of ownership; others regard ownership as acquired by means which are independent of registration but allow the owner, or the person who has some other right against the land, to register the right in order to make it enforceable against third parties.[51] An account of the Spanish land registration system is given by Murga Fernández in Chapter 4, and this does not need to be repeated in detail here. As Murga Fernández shows, there are a number of debatable issues in the operation of the land registration system and the circumstances in which (and the extent to which) it protects third parties, but key features are the scrutiny of instruments of title (and other documents), before they can be entered on the register, by a Registrar – a lawyer who has a special qualification in Spain;[52] the principle that once registered, title to the property is conclusive within Land Registry law (although, it should be noted, it is not necessarily immune from challenge under the civil law, for example where the instrument of acquisition is a nullity);[53]

[47] See Nicholas (n 15) 103–04, 178–79.

[48] The *titulus et modus* system is therefore sometimes referred to as 'title and delivery'.

[49] This again picks up one aspect of the old Roman system, that an effective *traditio* required a *iustus titulus*, or a *iusta causa*: see Nicholas (n 15) 117–18; Buckland (n 15) 228–29. The modern Spanish rule does not, however, simply adopt the Roman position: see López y López, below, Ch 2 section II.

[50] See the classification by Häcker, below, Ch 5 section II.

[51] See generally López y López, below, Ch 2 section VII. For sources (in English) on the registration systems in Germany, Austria, England and France, see S van Erp and B Akkermans (eds), *Cases, Materials and Text on Property Law* (Oxford, Hart Publishing, 2012) ch 8 section II.

[52] 'Registrars of Ownership, Mercantile and Movable Goods' (*Registradores de la Propiedad, Mercantiles y de Bienes Muebles*) are qualified lawyers appointed after a competitive examination to a public office: see www.mjusticia.gob.es/eu/ciudadanos/empleo-publico/acceso-convocatorias-perfiles/cuerpo-registradores. The website of the Registrars is at www.registradores.org, with links to the Property Register and information about its operation at www.registradores.org/el-colegio/registro-de-la-propiedad.

[53] The scope of this exception to the principle of conclusive title by registration raises some controversial points of interpretation: see Murga Fernández, below, Ch 4 section II.G.

and the protection of third parties acquiring property for value in good faith on the basis of what appears in the register. This *fe pública registral* (public faith in the Register) is said to be a cornerstone of the Spanish land registration system.[54]

There are some echoes here of the English system of land registration, and what the Land Registry claims for it. Perhaps it is not surprising that HM Land Registry also asserts the importance of public faith in the register:[55]

> Land is our nation's greatest asset. Clarity and security of land ownership is essential to a functioning property market. A healthy market is essential to a successful economy and society. Land is used to support all dimensions of life – agricultural, business, social and personal. Its financial value may fluctuate, but its vital role in life remains the same.
>
> We provide that necessary clarity and security in property ownership and interests. We do this by maintaining a land register of more than 25 million land and property titles in England and Wales estimated to be worth more than £7 trillion. The records are state guaranteed. This supports secured lending on £1–1.5 trillion of property. We enable property transactions to be registered accurately, efficiently and safely. This provides trust and confidence in the property market and thereby in the economy generally.

There are, however, differences of principle and practice in the two systems. We cannot give a full account of the system of land registration in England, in order to make a comprehensive comparison with the account of the Spanish system given by Murga Fernández,[56] but two points are worth highlighting.

First, the English equivalent of the Spanish principle of conclusive title by registration. Under the current English legislation,[57] the general rule is that entry into the land register of a person as proprietor of the legal estate[58] is (a) *necessary* to make him the full holder at law of the estate;[59] and (b) *conclusive* of his title: 'If … the legal estate would not otherwise be vested in him, it shall be deemed to be vested in him as a result of the registration.'[60] In principle, registration cures a defect in the title, and is constitutive of the title. There can, however, be a challenge

[54] See Murga Fernández, below, Ch 4 section I.B. Since January 2020, following a restructuring and renaming of ministerial departments, oversight of the Registry is now entrusted (under the Ministry of Justice) to *La Dirección General de Seguridad Jurídica y Fe Pública* (the Directorate-General of Legal Security and Public Faith), formerly *La Dirección General de los Registros y del Notariado* (the Directorate-General of Registries and Notaries): *Real Decreto 139/2020, de 28 de enero, por el que se establece la estructura orgánica básica de los departamentos ministeriales.*

[55] *HM Land Registry Annual Report and Accounts 2019/20*, p 4 ('Our Primary Role').

[56] For discussion of the English land registry system, see *Megarry & Wade* (n 29) ch 6; and for the fullest treatment, see TBF Ruoff and RB Roper, *The Law and Practice of Registered Conveyancing*, new looseleaf edn (London, Sweet & Maxwell, 2003).

[57] LRA 2002. Not all land in England is yet registered (see Cartwright, below, Ch 6 n 33) but we are not here concerned with the rules which apply in the case of unregistered land.

[58] The 'legal estate in fee simple absolute in possession' approximates to the civil law notion of ownership: see Cartwright, below, Ch 6 n 3.

[59] LRA 2002, s 27: the transfer, which must be by deed (see LPA 1925, s 52), 'does not operate at law until the relevant registration requirements are met'. For discussion of *equitable* title to property, see Cartwright, below, Ch 6 section II.

[60] LRA 2002, s 58.

to the registered title if there is a ground for obtaining rectification of the register by the court or by the registrar. Rectification is an alteration to the register in order to correct a mistake (a notion that is rather widely interpreted) which prejudicially affects the title of a registered proprietor, although it will not be ordered against a registered proprietor in possession unless he consents, or has by fraud or lack of proper care caused or substantially contributed to the mistake, or it would for any other reason be unjust for the alteration not to be made.[61] The approach here is different from that adopted in Spain, although any system that has as its basic rule that the register is conclusive must decide in what circumstances to allow a claim based on a defect in a transaction which is incorrectly recorded or reflected in the register. English law adopts a general rule of abstraction in the transfer of title to land: the deed of conveyance, once registered, effects the transfer independently of the validity of the preceding contract.[62] However, the purity of this principle has to give way in exceptional cases. It should be added that an important aspect of the English principle of conclusive registration is that it is 'guaranteed by the State': there is a statutory right to compensation (an 'indemnity') for loss suffered by reason of rectification of the register or mistakes in the register, which is not limited to mistakes made by the Land Registry but includes (for example) mistakes resulting from frauds perpetrated by third parties.[63]

The second point of comparison is the extent to which a person who acquires the land might be affected by proprietary rights which have been created in favour of third parties but do not appear on the register. This is a question of the reliability of the register not in the sense of the accuracy of the entries which appear in it, but in the sense of its completeness: can the acquirer assume that all third-party proprietary rights are entered on the register, or at least that he will not be bound by any that do not appear? A situation in which this issue can arise is the double sale of property, where the first-in-time sale has not yet been registered when the second purchaser registers his acquisition. This is a core case discussed in relation to the sale of land in Spanish law by Murga Fernández, where he shows that the person who relies on the accuracy and completeness of the register can do so only if (inter alia) he is *in good faith* and acquires the property *for value* from the existing registered owner.[64] There are again echoes here for the English reader although, as Cartwright explains in his chapter, considering also the case of double sale in English land law,[65] the discussion of 'good faith' and absence of 'notice' as the basis of protection of the (second) purchaser of land has now been superseded within the English system of land registration by an inquiry into whether

[61] LRA 2002, Sched 4; *Megarry & Wade* (n 29) [6-131]–[6-139].

[62] See Häcker, below, Ch 5 section II.E.

[63] LRA 2002, Sched 8; *Megarry & Wade* (n 29) [6-140]–[6-145]. The most financially significant category of claims is for fraud and forgery. During 2019/2020 the Land Registry paid indemnities to cover losses (excluding costs) totalling £4.1m for 845 claims, including £1.9m for 12 fraud and forgery claims: *HM Land Registry Annual Report and Accounts 2019/20*, p 108.

[64] See Murga Fernández, below, Ch 4 section II.C (good faith), D (acquisition for value).

[65] See Cartwright, below, Ch 6 section II.C.

(a) the third-party right (such as the first-in-time purchase) has been entered on the register of the title so that the (second) purchaser will see it when he inspects the register to see the title that he is buying, or (b) whether the prior interest is an 'overriding interest' – such as the interest of a person in 'actual occupation' of the land in question, since a purchaser ought to make inquiries of anyone in occupation of the land he is buying.[66] This may be seen as, in effect, a modified statutory version of the old English principle of the 'bona fide purchaser without notice'[67] and therefore close in its underlying thinking to the approach adopted in Spain. Another common link is the requirement also in English law that the acquisition be for value: a donee is bound by the same rights affecting the property as his predecessor in title.[68]

When comparing legal systems, we must not assume that their rules will be identical. This book contains much evidence of differences in legal rules, not only between two systems of such different traditions as English law and Spanish law but also between systems of similar or at least much more closely related traditions.[69] Nor must we even assume that the (functional) effects of their different rules will be identical:[70] there may well be historical, social and other system-specific contextual justifications for their substantive differences.[71] However, we should not be surprised when, from time to time, we discover similarities in the rules, or at least in their functional effects, and in some of their underlying policies as reflected in those rules.

[66] LRA 2002, Sched 3 para 2. The interest does not override if the first purchaser (who has not registered his interest) did not disclose it if asked by the second purchaser, or if the first purchaser's occupation would not have been obvious on a reasonably careful inspection of the land (and as long as the second purchaser did not actually know of the interest).

[67] It has been said that 'the system [of land registration] is designed to free the purchaser from the hazards of notice – real or constructive – which, in the case of unregistered land, involved him in enquiries, often quite elaborate, failing which he might be bound by equities. … The only kind of notice recognised is by entry on the register': *Williams & Glyn's Bank Ltd v Boland* [1981] AC 487 (HL) 503–04 (Lord Wilberforce). However, the expectation that the purchaser will investigate the state of the register, together with the existence of the category of (unregistered but binding) overriding interests of a person in actual occupation except where, broadly speaking, he (and his interest) is not discoverable if the purchaser makes enquiries, brings us back a little closer towards a modified version of the principle of notice.

[68] LRA 2002, s 28. Protection is given only to the transferee of the registered title who acquires 'for valuable consideration': s 29(1).

[69] See, eg, differences between English law and civil law systems discussed by Häcker, below, Ch 5, and within the civil law systems discussed by López y López, below, Ch 2.

[70] cf Zweigert and Kötz (n 41) 40, who claim that 'a "*praesumptio similitudinis*", a presumption that the practical results are similar' can be a very useful 'working rule', at least in areas of private law which are 'relatively "unpolitical"' – that is, 'if we leave aside the topics which are heavily impressed by moral views or values, mainly to be found in family law and in the law of succession'.

[71] On the importance of seeing a whole system's legal rules in context, see Häcker, below, Ch 5 section I. On the significance of historical context, see above, n 1.

2

Contract and the Transfer of Ownership in Spanish and Latin American Law

An Overview

ÁNGEL M LÓPEZ Y LÓPEZ

I. Limited Scope of the Discussion

This chapter will give an overview of the relationship between contract and the transfer of ownership in Spanish law and Latin American law. The limited scope of this discussion should be made clear at the outset. We shall not deal with—

(a) acquisition of original title, such as by *ocupación* (occupation of ownerless property – *res nullius*);[1]
(b) acquisition by succession on death, which is subject to separate regulation;[2]
(c) gratuitous transfers,[3] since the typical donation is not a contract;[4] or

[1] Arts 610 to 617 CC. *Ocupación* is limited in Spanish law to movable things, since all immovables without a known owner belong to the State or to the Autonomous Communities.

It should be added that, in this context, *usucapión* (acquisition of ownership by possession for a defined period) is an instrument of closure: see arts 1940–1960 CC. *Usucapión* is traditionally (and incorrectly) classified as acquisitive prescription, by contrast with extinctive prescription (referred to by the Code as prescription (or limitation) of actions): arts 1961–1975 CC. Common effects follow from both: arts 1930–1939 CC (Book IV, Title XVIII, Prescription; Chapter I, General Provisions), although these include provisions that apply only to one or the other. In any event, they are intertwined in a rather complex way, the details of which do not concern us here: see ÁM López y López, *Fundamentos de Derecho Civil. Doctrinas generales y bases constitucionales* (Valencia, Tirant Lo Blanch, 2012) 233–47; and an overview by A Luna Serrano in *Comentario del Código Civil*, vol II (Madrid, *Ministerio de Justicia*, 1991) 2095, 2149 (arts 1940–1960); M Yzquierdo Tolsada in A Cañizares Laso and others (eds), *Código Civil comentado*, vol IV (Cizur Menor, Civitas/Thomson Reuters, 2011) 1564–617 (arts 1940–1960).

[2] Arts 657–1087 CC. It should be remembered that the inheritance contract – a private contractual agreement varying the application of the general law of succession relating to the testator's estate, entered into in advance of his death – is permitted only in limited circumstances in the common law (the general national law) of Spain: art 1271 CC.

[3] Arts 618–656 CC.

[4] This is the majority thesis, although it is debated. The case-law of the Supreme Court is similarly divided, and in a similar proportion. However, there seems to be a consensus that the typical donation

(d) transfer of limited rights over land (rather than the transfer of ownership itself). The transfer of limited rights has certain peculiarities which would complicate this overview without adding anything useful to the discussion.

II. The Roman-Canon Law Tradition

The Spanish system for the transfer of ownership – as, indeed, also the Austrian system, and the dominant system in most of Latin America – belongs fully to the Roman-Canon Law tradition as it has derived from Roman law through the intervening centuries up to the Spanish and Austrian codifications, and most of those in Latin America.

It is well known that *traditio* was a mode of transfer of ownership in classical Roman law, alongside the (possibly earlier) *mancipatio* and *in iure cessio*.[5] It consisted of a transfer of possession which, unlike those other two modes of acquisition, was neither formal nor abstract, but had to be based on a *iusta causa* (a 'good cause'), sometimes referred to as a *iustus titulus* (a 'good title').[6] This is not the place to explore in detail the Roman concept of *iusta causa*, but only to note that, in general terms, it meant a valid legal act antecedent to the transfer of possession, and whose purpose was precisely that of transferring the ownership. Preceded by that legal act, *traditio* is simply the factual transfer of possession from the transferor to the acquirer, who will then enjoy the very significant protection accorded to possession.[7]

It must be said immediately that the principle of *iusta causa*, as originally conceived, and following its evolution over the centuries to the modern era, is quite different from the general principle of lack of form for contractual obligations found in the Canon Law rule *solus consensus obligat* (an obligation is formed by consent alone). Indeed, this lack of form is reflected in the question whether

(that is, that regulated by the Code) does not need delivery (*traditio*) in order to effect the transfer of ownership, and therefore we do not need to explore this in depth here. For a brief account of these issues (but with extensive citation of decisions and the key literature), see M Anderson in A Cañizares Laso, S Cámara Laso and C Sánchez Hernández (eds), *Código Civil comentado*, vol II (Cizur Menor, Civitas/Thomson Reuters, 2011) 91–97 (art 618).

[5] *Mancipatio* was a formal transfer, in the presence of witnesses; *in iure cessio* was a procedure before the Praetor involving a fictitious assertion of the right to recovery as owner (*vindicatio*) by the intended transferee, in which the original owner (the transferor) acquiesced. For certain items of property (*res mancipi*) one of these forms was mandatory if ownership (rather than mere possession) was to be transferred. See B Nicholas, *An Introduction to Roman Law* (Oxford, Clarendon Press, 1962) 63–64, 116–17; WW Buckland, *A Textbook of Roman Law from Augustus to Justinian*, 3rd edn, revised P Stein (Cambridge, Cambridge University Press, 1963) 233–41.

[6] Dig 41.1.31 pr: 'Nunquam nuda traditio transfert dominium, sed ita, si venditio aut aliqua iusta causa praecesserit, propter quam traditio sequeretur' ('bare delivery of itself never transfers ownership, but only when there is a prior sale or other ground on account of which the delivery follows'). See also Nicholas (n 5) 117–18; Buckland (n 5) 246–47.

[7] For comprehensive treatment of the subject, see J Belda Mercado, *Presupuestos romanísticos de la transmisión de la propiedad y compraventa en la dogmática moderna* (Granada, Comares, 2001).

anything more than mere consent is required for the binding force of a contract; in continental law this has been the 'cause' of the obligation, and in the common law consideration. Put briefly, the challenge to the consensualist principle was one that required a cause as the basis of the obligation – *causa civilis obligandi* – rather than the need for a legal transaction antecedent to the transfer of property, which in the modern theories of the civil law we have come to call the 'cause of the patrimonial attribution'. As demonstrated by the rule *pacta sunt servanda*, which bears the undeniable imprint of Canon Law, but also of the *lex mercatoria*, it is presented as overcoming the requirement of uttering particular words to perfect the contract (as was the case of the old formulae of *sponsio* and *stipulatio*),[8] or as overcoming the requirement of a *vestimentum*, or a particular form, which came to support the establishment of the effectiveness of mere formless agreements – *pacta nuda* as opposed to *pacta vestita*.[9]

III. The Break from the Traditional Mechanism of Transfer Made by the French Civil Code

The French Civil Code of 1804 made a notable break from this system. Contrary to the common legal tradition (the *ius commune*), and doubtless under the influence of individualist-rationalist philosophy, it established the rule that the transfer of ownership is effected by the mere consent of the contracting parties, without the need for delivery of possession.

This is an especially interesting point for comparative law. The French Code is seen as the archetype of the 'Latin' systems – civil law systems in the Roman tradition. But its value in this respect is contradicted in one essential point – the system of transfer of property – since many codes of the first wave of Romanistic codification did not follow it: it was not followed by the Italian Civil Code of 1865, nor by the first Portuguese Civil Code of 1867, nor by the Spanish Code of 1889; nor was it followed by a large number of Latin American codifications.

Even so, it is worth reflecting briefly on the value of the French Code as archetype, given not only that has it not been followed in relation to the system of transfer by a large part of the Romanistic world, but also that its system of succession, substantially Germanic, has not been accepted either. Its primacy as a model is based on having given a constitutional basis to the ideology of codification, and on the adoption of the categories of obligations drawn from the *ius commune* – the bulk of which are based on Justinian's Institutional scheme, with greater or lesser local variants which are of no real significance – although not without some

[8] Nicholas (n 5) 193–96; Buckland (n 5) 434–37.

[9] ÁM López y López, 'El contrato', in *Derecho Civil Constitucional* (Seville, Universidad de Sevilla, 2015) 609–25.

noticeable influence from French customary law (*le droit coutumier*). We obviously do not want to displace the *Code civil des français* from its position as venerable ancestor, but, just as the science of comparative law has warned us that there can be profound differences within other legal systems or 'families', the same must be observed within the 'Latin family', even in relation to the legendary leading text.

IV. The System of '*Titulus et Modus*' for the Transfer of Ownership in Spain, in Austria and widely in Latin America

The system of '*titulus et modus*' requires both a *legal ground* (*titulus*) for the transfer of ownership and an effective *method* (*modus*) of transfer. This system was adopted in Austria[10] and very widely by the Latin American codifications,[11] having effect in the great majority of the Republics, after the emancipation from Spain and Portugal – in practically all the great countries, with the notable exception of Mexico. Indeed, the three countries whose codifications are linked to the names of the greatest Latin American jurists of the nineteenth century, Bello, Vélez Sarsfield and Teixeira da Freitas – that is, Chile, Argentina and Brazil – opted for the theory of *titulus et modus*. It is worth highlighting the fact that the first Peruvian Civil Code, of 1852, also chose this system of transfer, with the entire Code as a public demonstration – a sort of traditionalist revolt against French influence. This subject requires further historical study which has not yet been undertaken, but the political ideal that was represented for the young new nations by the French code was not enough to make them forget their own tradition, which was that of the colonial law. They saw no need to reject texts that had been exported by the

[10] ABGB § 380: 'It is impossible to obtain ownership without a title and a recognised mode of acquisition' ('Ohne Titel und ohne rechtliche Erwerbungsart kann kein Eigenthum erlangt werden'); §424: 'the legal ground of an intermediate acquisition may consist in a contract' ('Der Titel der mittelbaren Erwerbung liegt in einem Vertrage'); §425: 'a mere legal ground for acquisition does not give ownership. Ownership and all real rights may be acquired, except in the cases specified by law, only by delivery and acceptance that are legally valid' ('Der bloße Titel gibt noch kein Eigenthum. Das Eigenthum und alle dingliche Rechte überhaupt können, außer den in dem Gesetze bestimmten Fällen, nur durch die rechtliche Uebergabe und Uebernahme erworben werden'). See also Häcker, below, Ch 5 section II.D.

[11] See Civil Code of Argentina, arts 2601, 2602, 2603; Civil Code of Colombia, art 673; Civil Code of Chile, art 588; Civil Code of Cuba, art 178; Civil Code of Guatemala, art 1809; Civil Code of Honduras, art 697; Civil Code of Panama, art 123; Civil Code of Nicaragua, art 1278; Civil Code of Peru, art 947; Civil Code Puerto Rica, art 549; Civil Code of El Salvador, art 651; Civil Code of Uruguay, art 758; Civil Code of Venezuela, art 1487. These are the provisions that establish the principle, although their systematic positioning is not always the same, ranging from a separate and detailed treatment of *traditio*, to the formulation of the theory of *titulus et modus* within a general rule about the modes of acquisition of ownership, and going through regulation on the time of transfer of ownership in sales. In any case, the common Roman basis is immediately very evident.

The Bolivian Civil Code, the Costa Rican Civil Code, the Dominican Civil Code and the Mexican Civil Code adopt the consensual system.

former imperial motherland – *Las Partidas*,[12] a monument of common principles of law, and enormously prestigious, before even the discovery of America: Cardinal De Luca referred to them as *Pandectae castellanae*. It should not be forgotten that the great Latin American jurists of the period of emancipation had received their basic training in the texts of the Royal Law of Castilla. In addition, we can advance a hypothesis, although it is evidently not easy to demonstrate. It is this: the ruling class that led the emancipation was a very conservative patrician class, inheriting directly their interests from those that preceded them in the period when viceroys governed, although the relationship with the distant and turbulent motherland was irremediably broken, and with little possibility of rehabilitation, since the wretched Spain of the nineteenth century was not in a position to be a benchmark for its former colonies, as Britain was in relation to the United States. It is curious that the civilian political enthusiasm for things French, much less strong than commonly claimed, is limited to the field of private law, because from the constitutional point of view the particular model to be imitated is the North American constitution. In any case – and there are very significant statements about this by Andrés Bello – the Latin American civil codification was conceived as a consolidation of what already existed, and what already existed was without doubt Spanish. The evidence for this is becoming increasingly clear, and has not been highlighted as it should be, not even in the leading works of comparative law.[13] No doubt this is not unconnected with the deep depression of Spain during the nineteenth century and a good part of the twentieth century, and the limited development of the Latin American Republics. Finally, there is the point that it is not usually appreciated that, although the lateness of the Spanish codification suggests that it had no

[12] *Las Siete Partidas del sabio Rey don Alonso el nono*, glossed by Gregorio López (Salamanca, Andrea de Portonaris, 1555), published in facsimile edition by Boletín Oficial del Estado (2011) and available in digital form at www.boe.es/biblioteca_juridica. *Las Partidas* clearly include the system of *titulus et modus*: Third Part, Title XXVIII, Law 46, opening words: 'Apoderan unos omes á otros en sus cosas vendiendo gelas, o dando gelas en dote, o en otra manera, o cambiando las, o por otra alguna derecha razón. E por ende dezimos que por tal apoderamiento como este que faga un un ome á otro de su cosa, ó que lo faga otro alguno por su mandado, que passa el señorío dela cosa a aquel á quien apoderasse della'. A relatively free translation into modern Spanish (in which, obviously, the ancient language loses its sparkle and grace) would be 'Apoderan como dueños unos hombres a otros de sus cosas, vendiéndoselas, dándoselas en dote, o en otra manera, o permutándolas o por otro justo derecho. Y por ende, decimos que por tal apoderamiento como este que haga un hombre a otro, o lo haga otro por su mandato, que pasa la propiedad de la cosa a quien la ponga bajo su poder' ('Some owners entrust things to others, to be sold, to be given in dowry or on some other basis, or to be exchanged or for some other legal transaction. And therefore we say that by such entrusting by one to another, directly or by mandate, ownership of the thing passes to the one to whom it is entrusted').

[13] However, some time ago studies began to appear that highlighted emphatically this legal unity of the Hispanic world, from the emancipation to the modern day, by force of tradition and the individual choice of Latin American jurists, despite the unfortunate situation of the old motherland. Especially worth reading, for its rigor and the prestige of the author, is the study by B Bravo Lira, 'El Derecho Indiano despues de independencia en América española' in his book *Derecho común y Derecho propio en el Nuevo Mundo* (Santiago de Chile, Editorial Jurídica de Chile, 1989), a monumental contribution on the influence (and limits) of European legal systems, especially Spanish, in Latin America with (of course) special reference to Chile. It is still curious – and very reprehensible – that Spanish academics, with only a few exceptions, pay little attention to this subject.

influence on the formulation of the codes of the American Republics, given that they were of course earlier, this ignores the fact that the underlying source materials were identical. Before ending this discussion, we should note that in the draft Spanish Civil Code of 1851, so important for understanding the current Spanish Code, the consensualist principle of the French Code was adopted for the system of transfer, although in 1889 it returned to the traditional Roman formulation.

V. Features of the Modern Spanish System

The features of the current system of transfer correspond to the Romanistic scheme described above on two particular points: the need for *cause* for the effective transfer of patrimonial rights, and the requirements of publicity of property rights.

A. The Need for a *iusta causa traditionis*, and the Problem of Fiduciary Transfers

To take the first point: we again emphasise that the cause of the transfer, and the cause of the obligation (necessary for the binding force of the contract for the effective transfer of property), operate at quite different levels. Of course, for a contract which precedes a transfer of property to be a good cause of the transfer, in the sense discussed above, it is obvious that the contract must be binding, and this means that there must be an existing cause of the obligation. But the cause of the transfer must have different conditions, even though the starting point is that it is based on a valid and effective contract.

The first condition – outside the contract itself – is that the transferor has a power of disposition that enables the transfer to take effect. In the traditional Roman legal thinking, this corresponds to the requirement of a so-called power of disposition or, as it is sometimes put, legitimate title.[14] The second is that the antecedent legal transaction, regardless of the existence of the power of disposition, must be of the kind that is designed to effect the complete and irrevocable transfer of ownership. This requirement gives rise to some difficult cases. The first of these is *fiduciary* transfers, which in traditional Romanistic terminology are divided into the so-called *fiducia cum amico* and *fiducia cum creditore*.[15] Although it is debatable,

[14] Dig 50.17.54: 'Nemo plus iuris ad alium transferre potest, quam ipse haberet' ('No one can transfer greater rights to someone else than he possesses himself').

[15] *Fiducia* was an agreement attached to a transfer of ownership of property directing what should be done with it: it could be contracted either with one's creditor by way of security, on the basis that the property would be reconveyed when the debt was repaid (*fiducia cum creditore*), or with a friend for the safekeeping of the property (*fiducia cum amico*): G.2.60; Nicholas (n 5) 151; Buckland (n 5) 431–33, 473–74.

it seems that in the Spanish legal system, as it stands today after a long period of uncertainty, the creation of these fiduciary figures is structurally impossible,[16] since the *fiducia cum amico*, by interposing a person to hold the property, would be contrary to the principle that simulated (or sham) transactions are invalid; and the *fiducia cum creditore* would contravene the prohibition of the so-called *pacto comisorio*, which prevents in general terms the transfer of the property for the purposes of security, in particular where a sale is often used as a security with a (concealed) repurchase. Even if a sale-as-security could be formulated in such a way that answers the underlying reason for the prohibition of a *pacto comisorio* – which is simply to stop usury – it would be doubtful that it would not involve a transaction constituting a fraud on the procedures for the enforcement of a pledge and, above all, of a mortgage, procedures that are not available to private individuals as a general principle in the essential rules of civil procedure for the trial process, and even more so in the enforcement process.

The question of fiduciary transfers is a key issue of legislative policy, because all these difficulties would be avoided if the *trust* were to be adopted. If it is used appropriately, the division of ownership involved in a trust can – and in fact does – address in a practical and lawful way the aims of the *fiducia cum creditore* and the *fiducia cum amico*. It is well known that, within the Romanistic systems, we are moving towards the adoption of the trust, although by various different routes and in different degrees: this has already been done in the French Civil Code,[17] and a form of the trust is being incorporated into Italian law. Notwithstanding this movement of the Civil Law systems to accepting the concept of the trust,[18] it is difficult to leave aside all the questions arising from the very different structure of property law on the Roman model (which allowed neither degrees of ownership, nor a divided right of ownership)[19] by contrast with another system based on a feudal model, in which the flexibility of 'property' is almost infinite. As a side note – but it is a significant point – it must be said that divided ownership is not alien to the Spanish legal system, because it is the essential core of the institution

[16] The authoritative treatment of fiduciary transactions is found in F de Castro y Bravo, *El negocio jurídico* (Madrid, Instituto Nacional de Estudios Jurídicos, 1971) 379–443.

[17] Arts 2011–2030 Cc (*la fiducie*), introduced in 2007, with later modifications.

[18] For Spanish law, see a brilliant exposition of the difficulties of the trust, as well as its potential, in the essay by S Cámara Lapuente, 'Trusts y patrimonios fiduciarios: acerca de sus posibles aplicaciones en el derecho de la persona, familia y sucesiones y su eventual regulación' *Diario La Ley*, no 7675, 2011. All things considered, a general adoption of the institution of the trust is unthinkable. Proof of this is found in the regulation of *la fiducie* in the French Civil Code, after its recent introduction. Cámara had already highlighted this before the reform in an essay destined, in my opinion, to become a classic: 'Trust a la francesa. Las doce preguntas de siempre y un reto desesperado a partir de la proposición de ley de 8 de febrero de 2005 que instituye la "fiducie"' *Indret: Revista para el Análisis del Derecho*, no 2, 2005 (available only online).

[19] Dig 13.6.5.15: 'duorum quidem in solidum dominium vel possessionem esse non posse: nec quemquam partis corporis dominum esse, sed totius corporis pro indiviso pro parte dominium habere' ('it is impossible for two people each to own or possess the entirety of something, also … a man cannot be owner of a part of a unit but can be part-owner of the whole unit in an undivided share').

of *enfiteusis*[20] regulated by extension in the Civil Code[21] and the codes of Catalonia[22] and the Balearic Islands.[23] In the latter two, it is a common form of legal relationship between farmers and their landowners.

Another problem of some significance in drawing up a system of transfer of ownership is the possible use of types of contract that are not designed to transfer ownership. Although it is not the only case, the most relevant is the contract of mandate to sell or buy, in which the purpose of the mandate is simply to effect a transaction on behalf of another, but which would not be sufficient as a legal basis (*titulus*) for either the acquisition or the transfer of ownership. However, in our opinion, this problem is very artificial, once it is understood that there is no such thing as a non-representative mandate – not even when the mandated party acts in his own name and on behalf of another. That is our thesis,[24] although it is in the minority amongst legal scholars. There are, however, judicial decisions that appear to point in its favour.

B. *Traditio* as a Mechanism of Publicity

The second function of a system founded on *traditio* is to use the transfer of possession that is thereby involved as a mechanism for publicising the transfer of ownership. In fact, in the case of movable property, most people do not notice the publicity of possession; and in the case of immovables it can be ambiguous, since certain acts involving the exercise of authority in relation to property can be done equally by the owner or by one who has only a personal right. However, the publicity is shown very easily ('*possideo quia possideo*': I have possession because I possess) and, given the strong protection that possession deserves, even where the possessor is not the true owner, it creates a picture of effects which are practically identical to those that derive from the publicity of a right by its registration in a public Registry. This functional equivalence is seen very clearly in the regulation of a double sale contained in article 1473 CC:

> If the same thing were to have been sold to different purchasers, ownership shall be transferred to the person who first took possession of it in good faith, if it were a movable thing. If it were an immovable, ownership shall belong to the acquirer who first registered it with the Registry. In the absence of registration, ownership shall belong to the person who first takes possession of it in good faith; and, in the absence thereof, to the person who presents a deed with a prior date, provided that he has acted in good faith.[25]

[20] *Emphyteusis* was developed in Roman law as an agreement to grant land for a long period, or even for ever – as long as the agreed regular rent was paid: Nicholas (n 5) 148–49; Buckland (n 5) 275.

[21] Arts 1628–1657 CC.

[22] Arts 565-15 to 565-28 Civil Code of Catalonia.

[23] Arts 55–63 Civil Code of the Balearic Islands.

[24] ÁM López y López, 'La gestión típica derivada del mandato' *Revista de Derecho Privado*, Jul–Aug 1996, 553–65.

[25] Art 1473 CC: 'Si una misma cosa se hubiese vendido a diferentes compradores la propiedad se transferirá a la persona que primero haya tomado posesión de ella con buena fe si fuere mueble. Si fuere

In this case, the force of the *traditio* resides in generating a state of possession, although it seems clear that over time *traditio* has developed to become more and more removed from a material transfer of factual possession, starting from the time when the so-called 'dematerialisation' of *traditio* gained importance through mechanisms such as the *traditio chartae, traditio ficta, constitutum possessorium,*[26] and even in certain circumstances the mere agreement of the contracting parties: see articles 1462 and 1463 CC.[27]

VI. *Traditio* of Movables and the Rule 'Possession is Equivalent to Title'

When it comes to movable property, it is necessary to consider the relationship between *traditio* and the rule 'possession is equivalent to title' ('posesión vale título'), a rule that is reflected in one way or another in the Latin systems, although the rule itself is thought to be of Germanic origin, or, at least, non-Romanistic. When the transferor of the movable thing is the owner, clearly the rule does not come into play, since there is then a straightforward application of the system of *titulus et modus*. But where the transferor is not the true owner, the rule 'possession is equivalent to title' fulfils one of two functions: either it is a 'good basis of title' (*iustus titulus*) for *usucapio*, or it forms the basis of the acquisition of ownership.

inmueble, la propiedad pertenecerá al adquirente que antes la haya inscrito en el Registro. Cuando no haya inscripción, pertenecerá la propiedad a quien de buena fe sea primero en la posesión; y faltando ésta, a quien presente título de fecha más antigua, siempre que haya buena fe'.

[26] These extended forms of *traditio*, without physical delivery of the thing itself of which ownership is to be transferred, were developed in later Roman law: delivery of an immovable by handing over a written deed of transfer (*traditio chartae*), a symbolic handing over of another thing (eg keys to the property to be transferred) (*traditio ficta*), and an agreement by which the owner of property transfers legal possession to the transferee but retains physical control (detention) on behalf of the transferee (eg a sale and immediate lease back of land) (*constitutum possessorium*).

[27] Art 1462 CC: 'The thing sold shall be deemed to have been delivered when it is put in the power and possession of the purchaser. Where the sale has been made pursuant to a public deed (*escritura pública*), the execution of the document shall be equivalent to the delivery of the thing constituting the subject matter of the contract, unless it should result or it should clearly be deduced otherwise from the *escritura pública*' ('Se entenderá entregada la cosa vendida cuando se ponga en poder y posesión del comprador. Cuando se haga la venta mediante escritura pública, el otorgamiento de ésta equivaldrá a la entrega de la cosa objeto del contrato, si de la misma escritura no resultare o se dedujere claramente lo contrario').

Art 1463 CC: 'Outside the cases stated in the preceding article, delivery of movable property shall take place: by delivery of the keys of the place or location where they are stored or kept; and by mere agreement or conformity between the contracting parties, if the thing sold cannot be moved to the possession of the purchaser at the time of the sale, or if the latter already had it in his power for some other reason' ('Fuera de los casos que expresa el artículo precedente, la entrega de los bienes muebles se efectuará: por la entrega de las llaves del lugar o sitio donde se hallan almacenados o guardados, y por el solo acuerdo o conformidad de los contratantes, si la cosa vendida no puede trasladarse a poder del comprador en el instante de la venta, o si éste la tenía ya en su poder por algún otro motivo)'.

In determining which of these two approaches is taken by Spanish law, there is heated controversy about the interpretation of article 464 CC[28] and its related provisions – a controversy to which there is no clear answer as a matter of theory. In our opinion, the thesis (referred to as Romanist) that the 'title' is a title for *usucapio* is the one that is consonant with the historical inspiration of Spanish law. But there is no doubt that the demands of a modern economy, involving significant (indeed, essential) exchange of movables, would give more weight to the thesis (referred to as Germanic) that the 'title' is a ground of ownership, from that moment already having the effect of acquisition *a non domino* – from a non-owner; already a kind of bar to the claim for recovery by the owner.[29] If the latter thesis is accepted, however, possession would establish at a stroke the acquisition of property, with a total disregard for whether there is a power of disposal. This would be a significant exception to the principle of legitimacy of title,[30] which is considered key in a system of transfer of ownership.

This is certainly all consistent with the wording of article 464,[31] although on some points there are also significant uncertainties,[32] and we have no judicial decisions that can be considered definitive on the issue.[33] It should perhaps be added that the uncertainty about article 464 has remained unresolved because the structure of Spanish private law still separates civil law and commercial law, and in relation to commercial transactions (a focus for disputes relating to movables), article 85 CCom[34] establishes a genuine acquisition *a non domino* on the basis

[28] Art 464.1 CC: 'Possession of movable property, acquired in good faith, is equivalent to title. Notwithstanding the foregoing, any person who has lost movable property or has been deprived of it unlawfully may claim it from its possessor' ('La posesión de los bienes muebles, adquirida de buena fe, equivale al título. Sin embargo, el que hubiese perdido una cosa mueble o hubiese sido privado de ella ilegalmente podrá reivindicarla de quien la posea').

[29] 'Mobilia non habet sequelam', a possible transposition in the procedural sense of the rule 'Hand muß Hand wahren, Wo Du deinen Glauben gelassen hast, da mußt Du ihn wiedersuchen' ('Hand must warrant hand. Look for your faith where you have reposed it'). This is indicative of the protection of the purchaser's legitimate expectations vis-à-vis the true owner, which is characteristic of Germanic legal systems.

[30] Discussed above, text to n 14, with the saying 'nemo plus iuris ad alium transferre potest, quam ipse haberet'.

[31] It must be added that the acquisition must be onerous – for value. This is not expressed by the rule, but is always required. It follows from the fact that Romanistic systems in general give less protection to gratuitous acquisitions: 'Qui certat de damno vitando anteponendum est ei qui certat de lucro captando' ('One who seeks to avoid loss is to be preferred over one who seeks to make a profit'), a general extension of the principle found in Dig 50.17.41.1: 'In re obscura melius est favere repetitioni quam adventicio lucro' ('In an uncertain case, it is better to favour a claim for restitution than an adventitious gain').

[32] In particular, the meaning of 'unlawful deprivation' ('any person who … has been deprived of [movable property] unlawfully may claim it from its possessor'), which is a key point to be understood in deciding whether to accept the 'Romanist' or the 'Germanic' thesis.

[33] For an overview of the significant difficulties posed by art 464 CC, see JM Miquel Gonzalez in *Comentario del Código Civil, Ministerio de Justicia* (n 1) vol II, 1240–48; PP De Pablo Contreras in *Código civil comentado* (n 1) vol I, 1878–86.

[34] Art 85 CCom:

> 'The purchase of merchandise in stores or shops open to the public shall cause prescription, as of right, with regard to the purchased merchandise in favour of the purchaser, except for the rights, if

that there is an *instantaneous prescription*[35] which bars the true owner's action to recover the property where it is sold in establishments open to the public.

VII. *Traditio* of Immovables and Registration in the Public Register

The *traditio* of immovables, by the very nature of the property which is its subject matter, gives rise to a state of possession which is more public and visible than that of movable property. But this does not mean that the external signs of the fact of taking possession are not so unambiguous that it is entirely clear whether such taking of possession corresponds to ownership or to some other right – including a personal right (as opposed to a property right) such as a lease. For this reason, in many legal systems, a mechanism has been established that guarantees the existence of ownership as a right vested in a specific holder, by placing the instrument of transfer on a public register.

This public register is generally held by administrative authorities, rather than judicial authorities, but is always under judicial control. It is the basis of a declaration to the general public, with legally binding force, indicating who holds the legal title as owner, regardless of who is actually in possession.

That said, we must make some important clarifications. The first is that possession derived from *traditio*, as a mere fact, may be different from the outset, or may vary over time, and therefore does not necessarily match what appears from the entry in the register, since the latter is nothing more than a reproduction of a written entry, at a fixed moment in time, of the instrument of acquisition,

any, of the owner of the sold objects to lodge civil or criminal proceedings against one selling the merchandise wrongfully.

For the purposes of this prescription, the following shall be deemed to be stores or shops open to the public:

1. Those established by registered merchants.
2. Those established by non-registered merchants, provided that the stores or shops remain open to the public for a period of eight consecutive days or have been announced by means of signs, samples or titles directly on the actual premises or by flyers distributed to the public or advertising placed in local newspapers'.

('La compra de mercaderías en almacenes o tiendas abiertas al público causará prescripción de derecho a favor del comprador, respecto de las mercaderías adquiridas, quedando a salvo, en su caso, los derechos del propietario de los objetos vendidos para ejercitar las acciones civiles o criminales que puedan corresponderle contra el que los vendiere indebidamente.

Para los efectos de esta prescripción, se reputarán almacenes o tiendas abiertas al público:

1.° Los que establezcan los comerciantes inscritos.

2.° Los que establezcan los comerciantes no inscritos, siempre que los almacenes o tiendas permanezcan abiertas al público por espacio de ocho días consecutivos, o se hayan anunciado, por medio de rótulos, muestras o títulos, en el local mismo, o por avisos repartidos al público o insertos en los diarios de la localidad').

[35] This use of the concept of prescription shows that it is malleable, but also technically incorrect.

and of the hypothetical possession which might at some time correspond to it. This possible duality of possession-as-fact held by one person over an immovable, and the possession of another that theoretically should accompany the ownership declared in the register, may give rise to a number of difficult problems where there is conflict between the two, although the starting point is to prefer the possession derived from the registration of ownership over the possession that is held in fact. We cannot go into details here but, in outline, this preference is manifested in two ways: first, the availability of summary judicial proceedings to restore the factual possession to the registered owner; secondly, the institutional difficulty of effecting *usucapio contra tabulas* – prescription against the recorded title.[36]

The second clarification does not concern conflicts in relation to possession, but rather the most important function of the register: to settle conflicts of ownership. This function depends upon the registry system that is adopted. Although registry systems are very varied, they can be reduced to three types.[37]

(a) The first is the so-called Torrens system, also known as the Australian system. This is based on a very simple principle: immovable property circulates in the same way as credit contained in security documents, of which there are no more than two identical copies, one contained in a central registry and another in the hands of individuals, which must always agree; in both instruments, successive transfers of the estate must appear as an uninterrupted chain, similar to that of endorsements. We need give no further details of such instruments here.

(b) Another system would be what is known as the Latin type of register, or a transcription system, also called the Latin system, whose main examples are those in France and Italy. The transcription system only guarantees that, irrespective of the date of the instrument of acquisition of title, it cannot be set up ('opposed') against another title whose instrument is already transcribed in the register; but this does not mean that the real owner of an immovable cannot bring a successful claim for return of the property against a person whose title appears on the register. (This is why the Latin registry system is also known as one of 'mere opposability'.) The typical case of conflict solved by the transcription system is the double transfer, of which the double sale is the paradigm. In such a case, the buyer who registers his title can set it up against another who has not registered his own title, although the latter acquired his title first. However, it is not guaranteed against the true owner of the thing sold – at least, where the true owner is not the person who sold it to him.

[36] On the very complex framework of the relationship between *usucapio* and Land Register, there is a useful presentation of the economic approach in J Puig Brutau, *Fundamentos de Derecho Civil, III-I* (Barcelona, Bosch, 1971) 375–80.

[37] For a presentation of the three systems, exemplary for its simplicity and precision, see JL Lacruz Berdejo, *Derecho inmobiliario registral* (Barcelona, Bosch, 1984) 25–32.

(c) To achieve the effect that the registered owner is protected against the real owner, we must use a type of register that reflects the system of registration also referred to as the Germanic system. In this system, the person who acquires ownership based on the acquisition of a title that was already then entered on the register cannot be defeated by the claim of the true owner for return of the property, because his acquisition is based on what appears from the declaration to the general public. Needless to say, the true owner has claims against those who have caused his loss, or have profited from it: actions for payment of money (including, under this general heading, actions for unjustified enrichment), but never specific recovery of the thing that has been transferred, which remains definitively in the hands of the registered owner. It is important to make clear that the price of such strong protection is that the acquisition must be for value and – of particular relevance for our subject – the contract must be valid:[38] the only thing that registration cures is a lack of power of disposal on the part of the transferor. This system is the one that has been adopted in Spain since the mid-nineteenth century, which makes the Spanish real estate business one of the most secure, in legal terms, in the world – a judgement that must be extended to the Latin American world that has not followed the transcription system.

In registration systems, a particular problem that arises is the relationship between *traditio* and registration, although it must be added immediately that this problem does not arise in systems where the registration is constitutive of title – where the acquisition of ownership occurs by registration alone. This happens in the German registration system, and even more intensely in the Swiss system. But where the registration is not constitutive (such as in Spain) the process of acquisition is completed by *traditio*, which raises the question of what relationship *traditio* has

[38] Art 33 LH: 'Registration does not validate instruments or contracts that are a nullity according to legislative enactments' ('La inscripción no convalida los actos o contratos que sean nulos con arreglo a las leyes').

Art 34 LH: 'Where a third party in good faith acquires a right for value from a person who appears in the Land Register as having the power to transfer it, the right shall be upheld once entered in the Register, even if thereafter the right of the transferor is annulled or cancelled for reasons not recorded in the Register'.

Third parties are always presumed to act in good faith, unless it is proved that they were aware of the inaccuracy in the Register.

Parties acquiring property or rights gratuitously shall not enjoy greater protection by registration than that to which their predecessor or transferor was entitled'.

('El tercero que de buena fe adquiera a título oneroso algún derecho de persona que en el Registro aparezca con facultades para transmitirlo, será mantenido en su adquisición, una vez que haya inscrito su derecho, aunque después se anule o resuelva el del otorgante por virtud de causas que no consten en el mismo Registro.

La buena fe del tercero se presume siempre mientras no se pruebe que conocía la inexactitud del Registro.

Los adquirentes a título gratuito no gozarán de más protección registral que la que tuviere su causante o transferente'.)

with registration. Given the intensity of the effect of registration, some argue that registration acts as a substitute. This view is challenged by others who say that in practical terms the problem does not arise, because it is only public documents that can be entered into the register of ownership – practically always the notarial deed of transfer (*escritura pública*), and we know that the execution of this deed is equivalent to *traditio*. There is also a lively debate on this point, but we shall not enter into that.[39]

[39] For the *escritura pública* and its effect as *traditio* in the transfer of ownership of land, see generally Espejo Lerdo de Tejada, below, Ch 3; and for the Spanish system of land registration, see Murga Fernández, below, Ch 4.

3

The Dual Role of the *Escritura Pública* in the Sale of Immovable Property

MANUEL ESPEJO LERDO DE TEJADA*

I. Introduction

In Chapter 2 of this volume, Professor López y López describes the Spanish system for transferring property rights by means of the system of '*titulus et modus*', which in practice requires a valid *title* (*titulus* – legal ground) and *delivery* (*traditio*) as the effective method (*modus*) of transfer.[1] We shall therefore refer to it in this chapter as as a title-and-delivery system. This chapter focuses on one of the forms of delivery, *traditio* by means of *escritura pública*, which is recognised in article 1462.2 CC. Although article 1462 does not mention immovable property,[2] in practice *escrituras públicas* are used mainly in sales of immovables, because property transfers qualify for publicity in the Property Register only if they are documented in an *escritura pública*, a public instrument authenticated by a Spanish notary. For this reason, the cases mentioned in this chapter almost always refer to sales of immovables,

* This chapter was written under the research project *Sujetos e instrumentos del tráfico privado (VII): Mercado inmobiliario y crisis económica* (DER 2015-66043-P) and the project *Red de Excelencia Registro, mercado crediticio y crisis económica* (DER16-81966-RED), both funded by the Spanish Ministry of the Economy, Industry and Competitiveness; and as part of the work of University of Seville Research Group SEJ584 on *Sociedad, Mercado y Derecho*. Our most recent publications on the subject are: 'En qué casos la escritura pública no equivale a la entrega' in A Carrasco Perera (ed), *Tratado de la compraventa homenaje a Rodrigo Bercovitz*, vol II (Navarra, Aranzadi, 2013) 1203–14; 'La escritura pública de compraventa ¿Produce siempre la tradición?' in JP Murga Fernández and S Tomás Tomás (eds), *Il Diritto patrimoniale di fronte alla crisi economica in Italia e in Spagna* (Milan, Cedam, 2014) 77–96; *La tercería de dominio y la transmisión de inmuebles. La defensa de los derechos reales en la ejecución singular* (Pamplona, Aranzadi, 2015). This chapter draws heavily on our previous work but deals with some issues in greater depth and re-examines others, such as eviction. It gives a more detailed, up-to-date treatment of case-law and takes into account more recent scholarly writings.

[1] See art 609.2 CC: 'Ownership and other rights over property are acquired and transmitted …, as a result of certain contracts, by *traditio*' ('La propiedad y los demás derechos sobre los bienes se adquieren y transmiten … por consecuencia de ciertos contratos mediante la tradición'). For further discussion of the system of *titulus et modus*, see Cartwright and López y López, above, Ch 1 section II.

[2] This point was underlined at the time by F García Goyena, *Concordancias, motivos y comentarios del Código civil español*, reprint of the 1852 Madrid edition (Zaragoza, Universidad de Zaragoza, Cátedra de Derecho Civil, 1974) 738, in the commentary on art 1385 of the 1851 draft of the Civil Code.

although we shall also use some particularly significant judicial decisions dealing with the sale of movables in order to explain certain concepts, such as reservation of ownership, and the sale of property belonging to another.[3]

In the Spanish courts, disputes about the ownership of property very often turn on whether or not there was *traditio*, ie, whether a transfer of ownership has taken place. This question arises particularly frequently in cases involving third-party claims to ownership, where there is an *escritura pública* documenting a sale that predates an attachment of the property, but there is also much litigation claiming a vendor's failure to fulfil the duty to deliver possession. During times of economic crisis, these problems become even more pressing, and it is imperative to have clear principles for the resolution of disputes. This chapter looks at the main doubts raised by the fact that the Spanish system treats an *escritura pública* as equivalent to *traditio*, and especially possible exceptions to the *traditio* mechanism of transfer, and the relationship between *traditio* and the duty to deliver real, effective possession.

The cases discussed here may happen in any form of *traditio*, but they present some unique features when they occur in *traditio* by means of *escritura pública*. The cases are: (a) a defect in the instrument of sale or the vendor's title and, in the latter case, the treatment of a sale of property belonging to another; (b) sale with reservation of ownership; (c) sale of a future thing; and (d) *traditio* by a person who is not in possession of the thing sold. Before taking up these topics, we shall examine the dual nature of delivery: as an obligation of the vendor, and as *traditio*.

II. Delivery as an Obligation of the Vendor and Delivery as *Traditio*

The place to begin is the rule governing delivery (*traditio*) in the contract of sale. This is article 1462.2 CC, which provides:

> Where the sale has been made pursuant to an *escritura pública*, the execution of the document shall be equivalent to the delivery of the thing constituting the subject matter of the contract, *unless it should result or it should clearly be deduced otherwise from the* escritura pública.[4]

Legal scholars have underlined the different legal significance that can be attributed to the delivery of a thing under Spanish patrimonial law. First, delivery is a component of the act of performance, conduct that must be effected by the vendor to

[3] In those cases, we shall make it clear where the litigation involved movable property and therefore no *escritura pública* as a means of *traditio*.

[4] 'Cuando se haga la venta mediante escritura pública, el otorgamiento de ésta equivaldrá a la entrega de la cosa objeto del contrato, *si de la misma escritura no resultare o se dedujere claramente lo contrario*' (emphasis added).

satisfy the purchaser in aspects such as the use, enjoyment and disposition of the asset that is the subject matter of the contract.[5] Secondly, however, delivery is a necessary requirement for the transfer of property rights in the thing sold (cf articles 609 and 1095 CC). It is the 'mode of acquisition' (*modus*) necessary to acquire property under the Spanish system for transfer of ownership, the classic title and delivery ('*titulus et modus*').[6]

Naturally, in claims of ownership by third parties, it is important to determine when (or, indeed, whether) ownership has been transferred. But it is also important to determine whether the equivalence between the *escritura pública* and delivery can be decisive in disputes concerning only the obligational level, such as over performance and non-performance.[7]

[5] A Gordillo Cañas, 'La inscripción en el Registro de la Propiedad (su contenido causal, su carácter voluntario y su función publicadora de la realidad jurídico-inmobiliaria o generadora de su apariencia jurídica)' ADC 2001, 177–78. In this context, we can speak of delivery of possession: M Cuena Casas, *Función del poder de disposición en los sistemas de transmisión onerosa de los derechos reales* (Barcelona, JM Bosch, 1996) 253; I González Pacanowska, 'Comentario al art. 1462' in R Bercovitz Rodríguez-Cano (ed), *Comentarios al Código Civil*, VII (Valencia, Tirant lo Blanch, 2013) 10320ff.

[6] This is accepted by (inter alia) STS 11 October 2006 (RJ 2006\6693): delivery has 'a dual significance, because in obligational terms it constitutes an act owed or of discharge (arts 1156 and 1160 CC) and, in terms of property, it is the delivery that complements the title or contract (arts 609 and 1095 CC)'. Amongst scholars, see González Pacanowska (n 5) 10318–19; Gordillo Cañas (n 5) 177–78; C Jerez Delgado, *Tradición y Registro* (Madrid, Colegio de Registradores de la Propiedad, Mercantiles y Bienes Muebles de España, 2004) 97ff; JL Lacruz Berdejo, *Elementos de Derecho Civil*, III, 1 (Barcelona, JM Bosch, 1991) 231; AM Morales Moreno, *Posesión y usucapión* (Madrid, Colegio de Registradores de la Propiedad, Mercantiles y Bienes Muebles de España, 1972) 214–15, 229. For a different account, identifying a possible third function of delivery – to transfer possession as owner – see B Rodríguez-Rosado, 'La equivalencia de la escritura a la entrega y el valor de la tradición instrumental' in L Díez-Picazo (ed), *Estudios jurídicos en homenaje al profesor José María Miquel* vol II (Navarra, Cizur Menor, 2014) 2813ff. This view can be supported by a range of historical and systematic arguments which the author makes convincingly, as well as by incidental statements made in some Spanish Supreme Court judgments: STS 10 November 1994 (RJ 1994\8465), which holds that 'the efficacy … of *traditio* in any of its forms is weakened only when the person making delivery did not have possession of the thing as its owner (directly, or indirectly through possession by another in some capacity other than as owner)'; and 13 May 1995 (RJ 1995\4233): '[T]he equivalence between *traditio* and execution of an *escritura pública* pursuant to art 1462.2 does not operate when the vendor does not have possession of the thing as its owner, but that does not hinder equivalence where possession (either direct or as a matter of fact) is held by another person by virtue of a right granted by the vendor'. This thesis differs from the thesis put forward in this chapter, because it claims that the *escritura pública* is not an efficacious medium of transfer if the owner has illegitimately lost possession and can no longer protect himself by a summary action based on possession *(la acción interdictal)* but can only resort to action for recovery of the property as its owner (*la acción reivindicatoria*). We shall explain why this exclusion poses a sufficiently serious drawback to reject the underlying thesis.

[7] Consider eviction, for example. Does an *escritura pública*, without actual possession, provide sufficient grounds to constitute dispossession and therefore trigger the application of the rules governing the warranty against eviction? For legal writers, eviction presupposes a real, effective delivery. In the words of G García Cantero, *Comentarios al Código civil y compilaciones forales*, XIX, 2nd edn (Madrid, Edersa, 1991) 305, 'the "deprivation" suffered by the purchaser before actual delivery entitles him to other kinds of action – such as enforced performance of the contract with the seller, or compensation for his loss – but not the action based on the warranty against eviction'. This line is followed by FA Rodríguez Morata, *Venta de cosa ajena y evicción* (Barcelona, Bosch, 1990) 18–19, 178–79; similarly R Durán Rivacoba, *Evicción y saneamiento* (Cizur Menor (Navarra), Aranzadi, 2002) 121; J Ataz López,

Would delivery as the method of transfer be thought to have the same requirements as delivery as performance of the obligation? Or, to put it another way, does a failure in performance of the obligational duty of delivery mean that no transfer of the property has happened? And would the reverse be true? Can a property right be transferred if the purchaser has never obtained effective possession (and therefore the vendor failed to perform)? We think these are different questions. Performance involves satisfying the purchaser, and that means the purchaser must have possession of the thing for which he contracted; therefore, performance requires some form of delivery other than the purely fictitious delivery that an *escritura pública* can procure. But ownership could be transferred without the need for actual possession: if neither the purchaser nor the vendor is in possession; or if the vendor continues to hold the thing and there is no actual delivery.[8]

To summarise, the rule does not prevent an *escritura pública* from being used to effect the purchaser's acquisition of a property right in a thing, regardless of its possession. What is important in terms of the rule is that the purchaser may exercise his ownership of the asset *erga omnes* and therefore against whosoever possesses it.[9] Consequently, the equivalence between an *escritura pública* and

'Comentario al art. 1475' in Bercovitz Rodríguez-Cano (n 5) 10457. This proposed solution is not entirely convincing. If the purchaser sues the possessor of the thing to recover it (as he surely can, now that he is the owner) but the action fails, naturally the purchaser must apply the requirements of eviction against the vendor. We cannot go into the problem of the relationship between eviction and non-performance, with all its implications – for which see Durán Rivacoba, 49ff.

[8] Lacruz Berdejo (n 6) 231–32, 235. STS 25 November 2013 (RJ 2013\7826) explicitly addresses a case of this type. The purchaser brought an action to recover certain properties which he had bought in an *escritura pública*, but which had been possessed by the vendor since the time of the contract by the purchaser's grace and favour ('por mera tolerancia o concesión graciosa'). The court's argument is clear:

> despite the fictitious nature of instrumental *traditio* with respect to genuine *traditio*, whose core feature would have been physical or effective delivery of the house sold, the Spanish conveyancing system allows a legal equivalence to be established between the delivery of the thing and the execution of the *escritura pública* documenting the sale, as may be gathered from the second paragraph of article 1462 CC, so that execution of the *escritura pública* in itself entails investiture of possession for these purposes. No express will in that respect is necessary, because such a will is implicit in the purpose or consequence of the purchase as a prior or antecedent transaction. Accordingly, taking a literal interpretation of the article, this reason of legal equivalence can be weakened when the contrary is clearly inferred or deduced from the *escritura pública* itself. This point of interpretation leads necessarily to an investigation of the possibility that the effect in transferring ownership might have been contradicted by either facts recorded in the *escritura pública* itself or the declared will of the parties to defer the *traditio* stemming from delivery until some later time in the performance of the contract.

In the same sense in a similar case, STS 14 January 2009 (RJ 2010\2323) reads:

> We cannot agree that there was no delivery of the owner's title. If we accept that delivery occurs by virtue of the *escritura pública* documenting the sale, provided that the *escritura pública* contains no clear statement to the contrary, the interpretation of the *escritura pública* made by the judgment under appeal allows us to affirm that this latter circumstance is not present …. [T]he argument that the spouse who continues to use the home has title as possessor stemming from joint possession by both spouses [vendors] is irrelevant.

[9] RDGRN 8 September 2005 (RJ 2005\6938): 'the *escritura pública* may be equivalent to delivery for the purpose of effecting *traditio* of ownership, even when it does not result in a transfer of possession,

delivery under article 1462.2 CC plays its main role in regard to the transfer of ownership. It does not refer to the fulfilment of the delivery obligation, which requires a physical form.

The problems concerning the value of an *escritura pública* in transferring ownership have come up in Spanish legal writing and case-law mainly in the following situations: when the sale is coupled with a special condition reserving ownership for the vendor until the purchaser has paid the price in full; when the vendor named in the *escritura pública* does not possess the thing; when the asset to be delivered is partly or completely a future asset; and, lastly, when the asset does not belong to the vendor.[10] These, then, are the situations that deserve close attention.

In these instances, or at least in some of them, one might well ask whether the arrival of the anticipated future event will automatically trigger the transfer of ownership, this time truly as an effect of the *escritura pública*. On the other hand, will the instrument by that time have lost its power to effect the transfer virtually, requiring instead a form of delivery that will necessarily have to be real or effective? It seems to us that the *escritura pública* is generally sufficient and there is no need to wait for effective delivery of possession because, in these circumstances, the obstacle which initially prevented the *escritura pública* from having the effect of transferring ownership will have been overcome.[11]

The 1851 draft of the Spanish Civil Code established a system of consensual transfer of ownership but contained a rule identical to today's article 1462.2. García Goyena thought this exception to the general rule of equivalence between an *escritura pública* and delivery could be seen, for example, in cases where the public instrument calls for delivery at a scheduled time or place, or delivery in instalments.[12] In such cases it would be obvious that delivery as the vendor's obligation would not have taken place even if there was an *escritura pública*. If the vendor defaults, it will be of no assistance to have documented the contract in an *escritura pública*; the key point to resolve the dispute will be whether performance has been effected, in full or in part, correctly or incorrectly.[13]

such that, despite the transfer of ownership, the obligation of delivery may not be completely discharged'; see also the decisions of 30 March 2001 (RJ 2002\2194) and 25 January 2001 (RJ 2002\2142). Something similar appears in STS 31 January 2013 (RJ 2013\1838); for the court 'the physical occupation of the home' is not enough 'to undermine instrumental *traditio* … as represented by the *escritura pública*'.

[10] See M Peña Bernaldo de Quirós, *Derechos reales. Derecho hipotecario,* I (Madrid, Colegio de Registradores de la Propiedad, Mercantiles y de Bienes Muebles de España, 2001) 101–02 (reservation of ownership), 106–07, 109–10 (things not possessed by the vendor), 109 n 22 (sale of a future thing or a thing belonging to another).

[11] This is the view of C Rogel Vide, *La compraventa de cosa futura* (Bolonia, Real Colegio de Espana, 1975) 307, who says that, in the case of a sale of a future thing, *traditio* takes place automatically because 'the obstacles preventing … the application of 1462.2 have seemingly been removed', and González Pacanowska (n 5) 10348, who states that, in a reservation of ownership, once the obligation to pay the price is fulfilled, ownership is acquired immediately.

[12] García Goyena (n 2) 738. This is not the place to discuss how pointless a rule like this is in a system where property rights are transferred by consent.

[13] G Bercovitz Álvarez, *Tradición instrumental y posesión* (Pamplona, Aranzadi, 1999) 86; L Díez-Picazo, *Fundamentos del Derecho Civil Patrimonial*, IV (Pamplona, Civitas, 2010) 91–92;

Let us move on to the question of whether, under the system contained in the current Civil Code, an *escritura pública* has force as a means of transferring ownership in the examples just mentioned.

When an *escritura pública* provides for a thing to be delivered at a place other than where the instrument is itself executed, the duty of delivery cannot always be considered discharged. In most cases, if the purchaser is at the place where the *escritura pública* is being signed, he cannot be elsewhere taking possession. The deciding point will be the effective discharge of the duty of delivery.[14] The transfer of ownership does, however, happen as an effect of the *escritura pública*, because the very rule that establishes the *escritura pública* as equivalent to delivery can prove useful when delivery is difficult.

In cases where an *escritura pública* calls for delivery of the thing within a particular time, or in instalments, delivery (as the vendor's obligation) clearly does not take place at the time of execution of the *escritura pública*. In our opinion, the delay in handing over physical possession does not necessarily exclude the proprietary effect of the instrument, because the delay might easily be taken to refer to the obligational aspect of delivery.[15] In short, the transfer of ownership may be held to take place at the scheduled time (whether or not there has been actual delivery) as an effect of the *escritura pública*, and it is also feasible to maintain that what is being discharged by instalments is effective delivery, not the transfer of ownership (*traditio*). However, according to the provisions of article 1462.2 CC, the parties must be able to agree to exclude the proprietary effect of the *escritura pública*, by a provision which appears expressly in the *escritura pública* itself, or must be inferred from the instrument.[16]

In practice this issue is not so clear-cut. If the *escritura pública* expressly states that it is not effective to transfer ownership, there is no particular difficulty. But how can the exclusion of proprietary effect be inferred in the absence of express provision? The problem is exemplified by two Spanish Supreme Court judgments, in which the reasoning may provide some guidance for similar cases.[17]

González Pacanowska (n 5) 10319; Jerez Delgado (n 6) 233; A Hernández Gil, *La posesión* (Madrid, Civitas, 1980) 303; M Navarro Castro, *La tradición instrumental* (Barcelona, Bosch, 1996) 165ff; T Rubio Garrido, *Contrato de compraventa y transmisión de la propiedad* (Bolonia, Publicaciones del Real Colegio de España, 1993) 172–73.

[14] For example, let us imagine that the purchaser has an agent sign the *escritura pública* or deliver the physical item for him. Then it is perfectly plausible that the two acts could be simultaneous.

[15] M Albaladejo García, *Derecho Civil*, III, 1 (Barcelona, Bosch, 1977) 150ff; González Pacanowska (n 5) 10347–48. For L Díez-Picazo, *Fundamentos del Derecho Civil Patrimonial*, III (Madrid, Civitas, 1995) 630, the mere postponement of delivery does not in itself prevent the equivalence between *escritura pública* and delivery. Consequently, what must be recorded in the *escritura pública* is the clear intention to exclude the proprietary effect: Díez-Picazo, *Fundamentos del Derecho Civil Patrimonial*, IV (n 13) 92.

[16] Bercovitz Álvarez (n 13) 137ff; Díez-Picazo, *Fundamentos del Derecho Civil Patrimonial*, IV (n 13) 92; Peña Bernaldo de Quirós (n 10) 109.

[17] On the other hand, the reasoning of STS 5 November 2010 (RJ 2010\8025) is difficult to follow. It asserts that the literal wording of the *escritura pública* in the case showed that 'the efficacy of the sale, and therefore also its proprietary effect, depend on registration of the *escritura pública* …. [B]oth parties regarded registration of the contract to be equivalent of the *traditio* or delivery necessary

According to the judgment of 19 July 2011,

> under article 1462 of the Civil Code the fictitious delivery of the immovable thing by means of the execution of an *escritura pública* is conditional on it not being stated or clearly inferred otherwise from the *escritura pública*. In this case not only does the *escritura pública* set a maximum deadline of six months for the delivery of the (immovable) property by the vendor, free of charges and encumbrances, and as a whole; it also postpones the obligation to pay part of the agreed price until the time of effective delivery. Therefore, effective delivery cannot be held to have occurred automatically when the *escritura pública* was executed, and therefore the purchaser cannot be held to have acquired the ownership pursuant to article 609 of the Civil Code.[18]

We can certainly support the solution as formulated in this judgment. The transfer of ownership did not occur at the time of execution of the *escritura pública*. But perhaps the ownership should have been considered transferred as an effect of the *escritura pública* once the prescribed delivery deadline had passed. On this point, it is important to note that, according to the findings of fact, the purchaser was already in possession of the property before the sale and continued to possess it after the sale. It therefore seems clear that the 'effective delivery' to which the *escritura pública* referred was the delivery of ownership (*traditio*), not delivery of possession. The purchaser already had possession, albeit under a different title. Furthermore, the document said that delivery should coincide with payment of the deferred price, so there seemed to be a sort of implicit reservation of ownership, in the sense that the parties deliberately timed delivery to coincide with payment of the price. It can therefore be inferred that the ownership was not to be transferred when the payment deadline arrived, but when payment was made. One conclusion to be drawn from this case is that the vendor's reservation of ownership until full payment of the price does not have to be expressly stipulated. All that is necessary is to be able to deduce the clear wish that the ownership be transferred only when payment is complete. For example, the same thing could happen in cases where the *escritura pública* simply states that the vendor retains possession of the thing until the price has been paid in full.[19] Naturally, once payment is made, the *escritura pública* is the only mechanism of *traditio* necessary.

A second, very interesting case examining the practical relationship between the efficacy of an *escritura pública* as an instrument of *traditio*, the transfer of ownership and contractual non-performance, is found in the Supreme Court judgment of 15 July 2011.[20] The case concerned immovable property that was both *future property* (the *escritura pública* stated the number of square metres it was to have, but it could not be finally defined without urban planning approval) and

to transfer the undivided half'. We do not deny that this was the correct interpretation of the parties' wishes, but in our opinion the failure of the judgment to explain the particular contents of the clause that it was interpreting means that the criterion used in the judgment cannot be applied to other cases.

[18] STS 19 July 2011 (RJ 2011\5223).

[19] Similarly Rodríguez-Rosado (n 6) 2824, n 18.

[20] STS 15 July 2011 (RJ 2011\6118).

belonged to a third party (at least technically, though not actually; the property belonged to a property holding company entirely controlled by the vendor).

In this case, several properties were sold in an *escritura pública*: a property with a spring, the elements necessary for the commercial development of the spring and a portion of land whose size was fixed but whose location and identification depended on the administrative approval of an urban development project that was underway. The exact details of the land were to be established on one of two alternative bases: the land might be made up of two particular parcels defined in the as-yet unapproved draft development project; or, if a different project were ultimately approved, the purchaser would receive any two parcels defined in the final project whose location and area were similar to those of the parcels in the first alternative.

The vendor claimed that the purchaser was in default by failing to pay part of the price, and therefore sought termination of the contract of sale. The purchaser, however, claimed that the vendor had committed an earlier breach by failing to deliver the expected portion of land, even though the urban development project had been approved several years ago. The purchaser therefore claimed that the contract should not be terminated but enforced.

The Supreme Court found that the lower courts were correct in dismissing the vendor's claim, upholding the counterclaim and ordering the vendor to execute the necessary *escritura pública* to transfer the portion of land to the purchaser, at which time the vendor was to receive the payments still owed toward the purchase price.

According to the Supreme Court, the vendor's appeal contained the contradiction of both affirming that the portion of land had already been delivered and claiming that the land was pending delivery until the vendor and the purchaser reached a bilateral agreement 'specifying or identifying' the portion of land.

For the Supreme Court,

> The origin of the contradiction lies in the assumption that, through the execution of the *escritura pública*, the said portion of land was delivered pursuant to article 1462 CC. It is true that, according to article 1462, the execution of an *escritura pública* is equivalent to the delivery of the thing that is the subject matter of the contract, but it is also true that this equivalence is subject to the proviso 'unless it should result or it should clearly be deduced otherwise from the *escritura pública*.' And this is what happens in this case. Even though the *escritura pública* states that the purchaser took legal possession of the two properties, that is, [the property with the spring] and the 800 m^2 portion of land, in reality, as the *escritura pública* itself quite clearly shows, the latter property could not be *definitively specified* until the development project became final. *This necessarily left also pending the delivery*, either of parcels NUM008 and NUM009 according the map attached to the *escritura pública* if the project turned out as planned, or of the equivalent 800 m^2 parcel.[21]

[21] Emphasis added.

Therefore, the *escritura pública* contained only an implicit, not explicit, rejection of its own proprietary effect.

In reality, 'the completion of the effect of transferring the 800 m^2 depended upon the suspensive condition of definitive approval of the plan for partition, and its consequential project of parcel redivision'; but since the

> suspensive condition was not fulfilled, because the original parcels NUM008 and NUM009 did not become reality, from that point Pablo was obligated to undertake the alternative performance that was provided for, that is to say, delivery of the 800 m^2 piece of land as near as possible to the original parcels NUM008 and NUM009, which necessarily meant delivery of 400 m^2 land units that added up to that area.

Indeed, 'according to the expert testimony, the substitute parcels were easy to identify. They were current parcels NUM006 and NUM007'. In that light, one might indeed maintain that the *escritura pública* did have value as *traditio*.

The Supreme Court left this possibility open, because it was not called upon to settle that particular question explicitly; all it had to do was to decide whether the vendor had failed to perform the contract. On that point, the court said that, even if it were accepted that the *escritura pública* had transferred ownership of the two parcels to the purchaser, the vendor could not be considered to have performed the contract correctly, because the vendor behaved as if the parcels remained a part of his personal or corporate assets. Moreover, the vendor did not have the parcels registered in his own name, but kept them registered in the name of the company, which prevented the purchaser from registering them as his.

In other words, discharge of the contractual duty of delivery encompasses aspects that are more varied and wider than those required by *traditio*, such as actual delivery of possession or the removal by the vendor of obstacles to the registration of the *escritura pública*. In our opinion, therefore, the property must be determinable pursuant to the rules of the Land Registry relating to property identification. And in fact, in addition to what the Supreme Court says, article 21.1 of the Spanish Mortgage Act (*Ley Hipotecaria*, 'LH') declares,

> Documents concerning contracts or instruments that must be registered shall make express mention of, at least, all the particulars that must necessarily appear in the registration entry and are relevant to the personality of the grantors, the property and the registered rights.

That means a sufficent reference to the particulars that article 9 LH requires for registration. In short, the vendor has to cooperate in everything necessary to enable the purchaser to register the property in the Land Register. On the other hand, at least prima facie, it would be enough for the purposes of transferring ownership if the *escritura pública* contained an adequate identification of the property, even if it fell short of all the particulars necessary for registration. Obviously, however, the only property that the *escritura pública* in this case could possibly have specified accurately was the first property that was anticipated, and not the alternative property, since that resulted from the urban development procedure which was not yet complete when the document was executed. That was why there could be no *traditio* as an effect of the *escritura pública.*

Where the subject matter of the sale is relatively indeterminate at its origin, the general rule could be said to be that the *escritura pública* cannot be equivalent to *traditio* as long as the property remains unidentifiable. On the other hand, case-law is not clear whether, once the property has been identified, the *escritura pública* causes the transfer of ownership or whether an act of physical delivery is necessary. Our view is that there should be no difficulty with the document's serving as *traditio*, but the question is better settled in the *escritura pública* itself, if the parties wish to avoid the uncertainty generated by this indecisive case-law.

III. Some Special Features of the Transfer of Ownership by *Escritura Pública*

A. Defects in the Instrument of Sale or in the Vendor's Title

An *escritura pública* does not guarantee the transfer of ownership if there is a defect in the contract. The Spanish system of real property would prevent the transfer from being effective, because the *traditio* is causally linked to the underlying legal ground for the transfer (*titulus*). For this reason, a void or defective contract is an obstacle to the acquisition of property rights.[22]

Nor is the transfer possible where the vendor does not hold title, does not have the power of disposition and never acquires the power: in such cases the principle is *nemo dat quod non habet.* Nevertheless, a purchaser might acquire the asset through prescription (*usucapio*)[23] or through the protection that registration accords to purchasers of immovables. In these latter cases, even where there has been no *traditio*, there is no failure in performance of the contract, because the acquisition of the property right will have taken place through these other mechanisms.

The problem of selling property belonging to another requires closer attention. Clearly, since Spain does not use the consensual system of property transfer, the fact that a vendor undertakes to transfer something that does not belong to him at the time does not mean the contract is invalid,[24] unless there is also another defect

[22] González Pacanowska (n 5) 10323. This refers to the validity of the *titulus*: Navarro Castro (n 13) 144.

[23] González Pacanowska (n 5) 10349; Jerez Delgado (n 6) 187ff.

[24] JP Murga Fernández, 'La doble venta judicial y el artículo 34 de la Ley Hipotecaria: recepción de la doctrina uniforme sentada en 2007' RCDI, no 732, 2012, p 1977, agrees that this argument is in favour of the sale of another's property being necessarily valid under Spanish law. See also JP Murga Fernández, 'Venta de cosa ajena y publicidad registral. Comentario a la Sentencia del Tribunal Supremo de 20 de junio de 2010 (RJ 2010, 6561)' RDP, no 27, 2011, p 326: 'The sale of another's property is valid as a necessary consequence of the Spanish system for the transfer of immovable property'.

such as a defect in consent.[25] The sale only gives rise to an obligatory relationship in which the vendor must deliver the thing that is sold, but this is not a dispositive act that itself effects the acquisition of the property right by the purchaser. Acquisition is effected only through delivery or *traditio*, at which time the vendor must be the owner of the right in order to enable the purchaser to acquire it.[26]

There could be cases where the purchaser never acquires title to the property (neither as an effect of the contract followed by delivery, nor through *usucapio*, nor through acquisition through registration) but is given a guarantee by the vendor of quiet enjoyment, albeit not ownership. This would not be a case of contractual non-performance either, despite the lack of *traditio*;[27] or, at least, it is not

[25] In favour of the validity of a contract of sale of property belonging to another: STS 31 December 1981 (RJ 1981\5358); similarly, but alluding to the possibility of inefficacy due to fraud: 11 May 2004 (RJ 2004\2733), 11 October 2006 (RJ 2006\6693) and 13 May 2013 (RJ 2013\3699). Amongst academic writers: JM Miquel González in *Comentario del Código Civil* I (Madrid, Ministerio de Justicia, 1993) art 609, p 1547; M Fernández de Villavicencio, *Compraventa de cosa ajena* (Barcelona, JM Bosch, 1994); AM López López in *Comentario del Código Civil* II (Madrid, Ministerio de Justicia, 1993) art 1445, p 888; Rubio Garrido (n 13) 258ff; Murga Fernández, 'La doble venta' (n 24) 1976–82.

[26] STS 11 October 2006 (RJ 2006\6693). Murga Fernández, 'La doble venta' (n 24) 2035 recently stressed that the power of disposition has to be found in the delivery, not the title (the *modus*, not the *titulus*, of the '*titulus et modus*' system): 'Judicial sales of another's property are valid, because the power of disposition is not a requirement of the validity of the sale as the title (*titulus*) of the acquisition, but as necessary in the delivery (*modus*), together with the earlier title, for the definitive completion of the acquisition process'.

[27] See, eg, STS 11 May 2004 (RJ 2004\2733), where 'the defendant purchaser [in a claim for termination for non-payment] received express permission from the owner of the car (the subject matter of the sale) to use it. That itself is at least evidence of a tolerated, non-contentious situation'. Accordingly, in this claim for termination, it is the purchaser who is considered to be in default, because he stopped paying. The purchaser cannot claim that, since the vendor was not the owner of the car, he had a well-founded fear of his possession being disturbed after conclusion of the contract and therefore could legitimately suspend payment of the price under art 1502 CC, because the particulars set out above were known. For the court,

> [N]o law requires the vendor to be the owner of the thing that is sold; it is enough if the thing can be delivered, in fulfilment of the vendor's obligation, since the sale is a contract that creates obligations, including the vendor's obligation to deliver the thing to the purchaser in exchange for the price.
>
> Furthermore, it is clear that a sale of another's property could have been completed even if the purchaser's consent was vitiated through mistake or even fraud. It is also clear that the purchaser has the right to delivery of the thing with quiet enjoyment (arts 1461 and 1462 CC) or to have ownership transferred to him if the agreement so provides. In such cases, the law provides the purchaser with means of defending his interests, in the form of actions for the annulment for vitiated consent, for enforcement of the promised performance, for termination of the contract for non-performance, or for damages for breach of contract.
>
> But the defendant's answer to the claim was limited to asking for its dismissal, without seeking any of the consequences flowing from the contract. Instead, he accepted a situation that the judgment appealed against correctly describes as contradictory, defending the continued legal force of a contractual relationship in which the thing does not belong to the vendor, and in which the purchaser, who possesses the thing (as shown in the proceedings), has paid less than half the agreed price.
>
> For this reason, the defect claimed as the basis of the appeal must be held to be non-existent. None of the consequences covered by Spanish law on sales of another's property are contradicted by the decision appealed against, which merely terminates the contractual relationship at the vendor's request because the court considers failure to pay the price sufficient cause for termination.

necessarily non-performance. Again, we can see the difference between delivery as fulfilment of an obligation and delivery as *traditio*.

The question arises, however, whether an *escritura pública* is sufficient to produce an automatic transfer of a property right once the vendor (after the date of the *escritura pública*) acquires title to the asset.[28] It has been authoritatively stated that in that case the *escritura pública* would preclude itself from having the effect of transferring the property, and that the only right stemming from it would be a personal right to have the other party fulfil in due course the obligation to deliver.[29] Therefore, in the event of a negative answer to this question, the vendor ought to be required to perform an act that does provide *traditio* (usually physical delivery) to avoid the drawbacks and expenses of having another *escritura pública* executed. To the best of our knowledge, there is no case on this point, but our opinion is that, although physical delivery is undoubtedly an obligation of the vendor and remains so until it has been fulfilled, the transfer of ownership is not linked to physical delivery. Since article 1462.2 CC establishes the *escritura pública* as equivalent to delivery, we could suppose that the purchaser's acquisition of the thing happens automatically when the vendor obtains ownership of the thing. The reason that seems decisive in in favour of this view is that if the initial efficacy of the *escritura pública* as a means of transfer of ownership was impeded merely by the transferor's lack of ownership, once that obstacle is removed, the problem is removed and the *escritura pública* would have its normal effect. A different solution would have to be found in the case of a sale under an *escritura pública* that expressly states that the document has no effect in relation to the transfer of ownership; in that case, the process would indeed have to be completed through some other form of *traditio*.

In connection with these problems of delivery as fulfilment of an obligation and as *traditio*, and also in connection with the application of the rules governing the warranty against eviction, it might be interesting to look at the problems that can be caused by the incorrect identification of boundaries in the sale of land. The Spanish Supreme Court's judgment of 31 January 2018[30] outlines a general approach to the issue. In that case, many years after the completion of a sale, the purchaser began to have problems with his possession of the property. He claimed that a third party was building on part of it. The purchaser took action against the third party to recover the land as its owner, but failed because he could not prove that his ownership included the piece of land on which the defendant was building.

Once the court had given its final decision, the purchaser sued the vendor, claiming termination of the sale for non-performance, or, in the alternative, that the sale be declared a completely nullity for lack of subject matter. The purchaser claimed that the things sold to him, as described in the instruments of transfer,

[28] Very similar to art 1478.2 of the Italian Civil Code: 'Il compratore diventa proprietario nel momento in cui il venditore acquista la proprietà dal titolare di essa' ('The buyer becomes the owner when the seller buys the property from the owner of it').

[29] Peña Bernaldo de Quirós (n 10) 109, n 22.

[30] STS 31 January 2018 (RJ 2018\313).

either did not exist (because their boundaries were not as described), or were impossible, or had been found to be located within the property of third parties. In the court's words, the problem with the sale agreement was that 'the description in the Register of the properties covered by the agreement did not correspond to the topographical reality to which the consent of all parties was given'. We might reasonably think that this error in description meant that this was a case of the sale of property belonging to another, and in fact the solutions suggested by the claimant correspond relatively well with the solutions that have been explained as applying in such a situation. However, this must be qualified. In a sale of another's property (in this case, property partly belonging to another), as has been said above and in the Supreme Court judgment, the complete nullity the claimant sought (which the claimant asserted was not subject to any prescription) was less feasible than a defect in contractual consent, error or fraud – in which case the plaintiff would have had to take action within four years of the conclusion of the contract, under article 1301 CC. And in the case at hand, the four-year period had long elapsed, so the right of action had been extinguished.

Furthermore, we should note that if the action for annulment was not brought in time, it was because there was *traditio* in this case, because the sale was executed in an *escritura pública*. And there was also performance, as shown by the purchaser's having engaged in effective acts of possession of the property that had been maintained for several years, although – and this is important – the Supreme Court did not go so far as to say that possession extended to the part of the land that the purchaser claimed had been encroached upon. Therefore, there was not only *traditio*, but also performance of the obligation to deliver, and the contract could not be terminated for non-performance.[31]

But we could consider whether this is a case of eviction. We think it probable that it was, at least if the purchaser could prove that his possession extended to the portion of land that he claimed had been invaded.[32] Under the Spanish Civil Code,

[31] According to the Supreme Court:

> [I]t is correct to deem that delivery has taken place, not only instrumentally through the execution of the *escrituras públicas* (art 1462.2 CC), but also because, as reasoned by the judgment under appeal, there were acts of possession on the part of the purchaser (arts 1462.1 and 438 CC). Because the properties were indeed delivered, we agree with the lower court in concluding that there was no breach of the sale agreements … [T]he appellant is mixing up different legal issues. He confuses the inexistence of the subject matter at the time when the contract was entered into, and non-performance of the contract with the subsequent occurrence of events (the appellant speaks of 'events after completion' and 'supervening non-performance') consisting in the fact that, years after the formation of the contracts, he lost the actions he brought against the person occupying part of his property because the instruments he used to prove his title could not prevail against the third party's titles. But it does not follow that the sales entered into earlier had no subject matter, or that the defendants did not deliver the properties which were the subject of the contracts as they identified them on the land, irrespective of whether the descriptions entered in the Register were inaccurate.

[32] But it is not certain that it is a case of eviction where the case raises the problem of identification of the property. It is possible that all that happened was that the purchaser was trying to take advantage of a defect in the description of his property in the Register and take over a piece of land that was actually the subject matter of the sale, land that did not belong to him and that he never possessed.

the vendor is obligated not only to deliver the thing he is selling, but also to provide a warranty over it (article 1461). That is to say, he must guarantee 'lawful and peaceful possession of the thing sold' (article 1474), and this duty is triggered 'when the purchaser is deprived of all or a part of the thing purchased by a final judgment by virtue of a right predating the purchase' (article 1475). These rules can refer to cases such as the one described above. In fact, the vendor himself thought the action the purchaser had taken against him was an action for warranty of title for dispossession. But the purchaser did not meet a requirement set by article 1481 CC for such liability to arise: the purchaser should have notified the vendor of his intention to sue the third-party possessor in defence of the purchased property. By failing to do so, the purchaser deprived the vendor of the opportunity to join in the action and provide evidence that the property was correctly identified.

It is interesting to notice that this case of eviction differs somewhat from what the Civil Code regards as normal. In the Code, the purchaser loses possession as a result of a final judgment when a third party has sued the purchaser, whilst in the case we have discussed, first the purchaser loses possession, then his loss is confirmed by a final judgment in a proceeding brought by the purchaser as plaintiff to defend the property from an intruding third party. Cases like this are referred to as 'reverse' or 'inverse' eviction.[33]

There have been times when the Supreme Court has allowed the purchaser to claim in the same proceedings against the possessor (to recover possession) and, in the alternative, against the vendor (for the eviction). The Supreme Court's argument in its judgment of 10 December 1996 is convincing:

> [A]s the defendant possessor has filed counterclaims and won, obviously we must examine the secondary action, ie, the eviction complaint, which is filed against the vendors. Having rejected their claim for recovery of the property as owner, we may now declare that the purchasers have been deprived of all rights stemming from their purchase, that they were so deprived by a judgment that is already final, and that it would be mere formalism – contrary to what is reasonable and to procedural economy – to force them to resort to a new set of proceedings, especially when the vendors' right of defence has been scrupulously respected.[34]

Another Supreme Court judgment,[35] however, applied rather a different approach and said that, in cases of reverse eviction, the purchaser

> must be required to instruct the vendor, before filing his claim, to state his defence or provide him with means of defence, which in effect replaces notice of the claim in a case

[33] FA Rodríguez Morata, 'La evicción inversa en la compraventa' in A Carrasco Perera (ed), *Tratado de la compraventa. Homenaje al profesor Rodrigo Bercovitz*, vol II (Navarra, Cizur Menor, 2013) 1353ff; Durán Rivacoba (n 7) 301ff; J Ataz López, 'Comentario a los arts. 1481–1482' in Bercovitz Rodríguez-Cano (n 5) 10501ff; C Martínez de Aguirre y Aldaz, 'Compraventa y permuta' in *Curso de Derecho civil (II). Derecho de obligaciones* (Madrid, Majadahonda, 2014) 535. The hypothesis is also referred to by García Cantero (n 7) 303–04.

[34] STS 10 December 1996 (RJ 1996\9191).

[35] STS 7 June 1995 (RJ 1995\4630).

where the purchaser is the defendant. What is unusual is for the purchaser to exercise a joinder of actions, as he has done here, ie, action for recovery of the property as owner and (in case it should be necessary) an action for eviction.[36]

Be that as it may, the fact is that this kind of claim could have been used in the case decided by the judgment of 31 January 2018 if the purchaser had been more careful.

B. Sale with Reservation of Ownership

In a sale contract containing a reservation of ownership clause, the vendor does not usually fail to fulfil the duty of delivery. In fact, reservation of ownership clauses are normally used to act as a form of guarantee in contracts in which the vendor fulfils the duty of delivery before the purchaser has paid the price. On the other hand, many doubts do arise about the *traditio* and the transfer of ownership.

Some think that reservation of ownership is the very paradigm of the case where an *escritura pública* has no effect as *traditio*.[37] To them, reservation of ownership is a suspensive condition that freezes the effect of the instrument;[38] the vendor continues to own the property until the entire price has been paid, and then the property right is automatically transferred.[39]

That solution has received well-deserved criticism from two directions. First, it has been said that the purchaser's legal position under a reservation of ownership clause hardly resembles the position of a mere creditor; the purchaser is usually the owner as well as the possessor of the asset, with the right of use and enjoyment, which he exercises as owner, and he also assumes the risk that the thing may become damaged in the meantime. It has been reasoned accordingly that a reservation of ownership cannot be a suspensive condition but is instead a 'resolutory' (defeasible) condition, and consequently 'the purchaser acquires a defeasible ownership'.[40]

[36] On both judgments, see L Muñoz Sabaté, '¿Puede el comprador reivindicar contra el despojo y acumular eventualmente contra el vendedor pretensionando la restitución del precio? Análisis de dos sentencias contradictorias del Tribunal Supremo', *Diario La Ley*, 'Doctrina' section, 1998, Ref D-24, vol 1 (quoted from the *laleydigital* version).

[37] G García Cantero in *Comentario del Código Civil*, II (Madrid, Ministerio de Justicia, 1993) art 1462, p 912.

[38] On this interpretation, and on the subject of reservation of ownership in general, see the bibliography in M Espejo Lerdo de Tejada, *La reserva de dominio inmobiliaria en el concurso* (Cizur Menor, Civitas, 2006) and the following commentaries: 'La eficacia de la reserva de dominio inmobiliaria: Comentario a la Sentencia del Tribunal Supremo de 16 de marzo de 2007 (RJ 2007, 1857)' RDP, no 20, 2008, pp 321–33; 'La reserva de dominio mobiliaria en el concurso del comprador. Comentario a la Sentencia núm. 592/2007 de 19 diciembre del Juzgado de lo Mercantil núm. 1 de Bilbao (AC 2007\2068)' RDP, no 23, 2009, pp 331–41. See also the articles by JM Miquel González 'La reserva de dominio' in S de Dios and others (eds), *Historia de la propiedad: crédito y garantía* (Salamanca, Servicio de Estudios del Colegio de Registradores, 2007) 523–600, and 'La reserva de dominio' in E Bosch Capdevila (ed), *Nuevas perspectivas del derecho contractual* (Barcelona, Bosch, 2012) 139–224.

[39] González Pacanowska (n 5) 10348.

[40] Díez-Picazo (n 15) 785–86.

Secondly, it has been said that, functionally, a reservation of ownership is a form of security, and for this purpose the vendor need not keep ownership, because a simple limited property right serves just as well. The conclusion then is that a reservation of ownership is a simple pledge (without transfer of possession, since the thing remains in the purchaser's possession) or mortgage (if the property of which ownership is reserved is real property).[41] Thus, the vendor has a guarantee that his money will be repaid, and the purchaser has ownership.

Neither critique is fully convincing, yet both serve to alter the scope of the meaning of the more widely held thesis (ie, that reservation of ownership is a suspensive condition that freezes the effects of the *escritura pública*) and to criticise some of its results. In this regard, we agree that greater importance should be given to the *cause*, inasmuch as the cause affects the value of *traditio*.

But we still believe that the explanation of reservation of ownership as a suspensive condition, correctly applied, is the explanation that best reflects the will of the parties. The more problematic issues that this doctrine has to face concern the legal attribution of proprietary rights in the case of immovable property that is sold and delivered (whether physically or instrumentally) but is subjected to a reservation of ownership clause until the price is paid in full. In this situation, third parties – be they creditors of the purchaser or of the vendor who have an attachment placed on the property, or sub-purchasers of the property by an act of the purchaser or of the vendor – should not be overprotected, because reservation of ownership should not play a decisive role in such matters. If the alternative interpretation in such cases were to decide which of the parties to the sale is the owner and which is the mere creditor (assuming a simplistic adherence to the meaning and effects of a condition that affects the transfer of ownership), we are doomed to reach unfair solutions that unnecessarily sacrifice some of the conflicting interests.

In our view, what is needed is a clear understanding of how a reservation of ownership clause works as a condition. Certain things must be established. First, the vendor retains ownership as security until the purchaser finishes paying the purchase price. Second, the purchaser acquires a right of ownership in the property from the time of *traditio*, pending its definitive consolidation at full payment. Third, these two rights are compatible with one another, because they are organised and defined reciprocally with respect to the condition that limits them both. Fourth, each party (purchaser and vendor) remains able to dispose freely of his property right, because in each case it is an unstable right. Therefore, as regards the freedom of disposition of each of the parties to the contract, the principle of *nemo dat quod non habet* will always be in issue. Each party can dispose of the right he holds, and only that right, no more.

[41] R Bercovitz, *La cláusula de reserva de dominio. Estudio sobre su naturaleza jurídica en la compraventa a plazos de bienes muebles* (Madrid, Moneda y Crédito, 1971) 17 and throughout. In later work Bercovitz said he still supported the same idea, with the additional nuance of accepting 'the immediate transfer of ownership (at the time of delivery) to the purchaser, subject to a resolutory condition (defeasance) if the deferred price is not paid': R Bercovitz, 'Comentario a la STS 19 de mayo de 1989' in CCJC, 20, 1989, 580. This looks more like a correction than a nuance.

It seems to us, then, that reservation of ownership does not alter the mechanism for the transfer of real property rights through the extension of a purely credit-based relationship between purchaser and vendor after the *escritura pública* is made (or after real delivery).[42] Rather, a reservation of ownership establishes an event that places a condition on the property right – a condition, therefore, affecting not only the obligatory relationship, but also the proprietary effects triggered by delivery, and enabling a property right in the thing to be ascribed to each party. That is to say, both the vendor's situation and the purchaser's situation are secured through a legal attribution of property rights.

The decision of 18 May 1933 of the Spanish Directorate-General of Registries and Notaries[43] said that a reservation of ownership clause 'changes … the essence of the [sale] contract by switching the object of the transfer from the right of ownership, which remains in the vendor's power, to other property rights limiting the right of ownership'. We do not think that this is entirely correct, if it means that the purchaser acquires a *limited property right*, because that sounds like the acquisition of traditional property rights; but it does seem to us that a reservation of ownership *limits the property right*, because through the condition it establishes, it enables two proprietary titles (titles of ownership) to the same right, the vendor's title and the purchaser's title, to coexist simultaneously and compatibly, trimmed neatly to fit together into a whole. This response addresses scholars' reasonable concern for balance between the legal spheres of the two parties to the contract, especially when third parties (purchasers or creditors through the purchaser or vendor) appear.

So-called reservation of ownership agreements are one of those acts that are significant enough in relation to property for the Land Registry to put on public record (see article 23 LH). The purchaser's right is not obligational; it is a full property right, once *traditio* has taken place; but it is subject to a real security until the price is paid in full. Unlike limited real security rights, the real security in this case is an ownership right, and consists in making the ownership acquired by the purchaser and retained by the vendor contingent upon an uncertain event, ie, full payment of the price. The purchaser's ownership and the vendor's ownership are contingent on the same event, but in a diverging sense.[44]

[42] Peña Bernaldo de Quirós (n 10) 101: '[E]ven if the parties have declared in their instrument that there is a sale and that possession will be delivered, but that they want to establish a reservation of ownership (to secure payment) instead of the *legal effect* of the transfer, with *traditio* there will be a transfer of a certain legal attribution of property rights pertaining to the thing if that is the *legal effect* that the law says corresponds to the practical causal purpose (as happens in so-called "sales with reservation of ownership")'.

[43] RDGRN 18 May 1933 (RJ 1933\197).

[44] See RM Roca Sastre and L Roca-Sastre Muncunill, *Derecho Hipotecario*, III (Barcelona, Bosch, 1995) 375–76. The ideas about reservation of ownership given in the text, which we have been expressing for some years, were quoted verbatim in STS 24 July 2012 (RJ 2012\9334) in a case of a sale of movables. They have also been used in other court decisions concerning immovables, such as the judgments of the Appellate Court of Las Palmas of 22 February 2017 (JUR 2017\81739) and 6 September 2016 (JUR 2016\234203). Finally, they were espoused in RDGRN 28 November 2017 (RJ 2017\5680),

This view is consistent with the possibility of registering in the Land Register the acquisition of a property right in real estate subject to a condition precedent, thus enabling it to encompass 'all the *restrictions* that more or less intensely affect the right to be entered … all the clauses *limiting* the ownership or property right that is transferred'.[45] And this solution with respect to registration is in turn consistent with the acceptance by the Spanish system of property rights of the criterion of *numerus apertus*, rather than a fixed number of rights decided by law.

The explanation above would settle cases such as attachments placed on property by the creditors of the vendor or purchaser. Only the unstable property right retained or acquired by the debtor could be attached. In this sense, the position (now outdated) of the Supreme Court in its judgment of 11 July 1983[46] may be criticised. The judgment prevented the purchaser from successfully exercising a third-party claim to ownership in the event of attachment of the asset by the vendor's creditors. The current position, represented by Supreme Court judgments in 1989, 1993, 1996 and 2007,[47] clearly aims to change direction by accepting the purchaser's claim in such circumstances. It would still be wise to specify that, until the purchaser pays the price, the attachment should be lifted only partially, so that it is limited to the real security right which the vendor still retains. On the other hand, if the purchase is cancelled because of the purchaser's default, the purchaser will no longer have legal standing to claim ownership, and the creditors can succeed in their enforcement.

When the attachment is enforced by the purchaser's creditors, the vendor, too, may assert a third-party claim to ownership, driven by the need to preserve the real security that ensures that he will collect his purchase price in full.[48] In our opinion, the correct decision would be to lift the attachment partially, that is, to acknowledge the existence of a security right (a right of ownership) in the asset, but not to lift the attachment completely; that would make no sense, because in fact the purchaser has bought a property right in the thing, even though he is still waiting for that right to be perfected. Naturally, the attachment could be lifted completely if the purchase is cancelled for non-payment of the price. Lastly, if the reservation of ownership is extinguished because the purchaser has paid the

which nevertheless upholds debatable solutions about the indisposability of the subject matter of the sale and the problems of penalty clauses that may accompany reservations of ownership, which it would be out of place to discuss here. For the problem of penalty clauses, readers are warmly recommended to consult the monograph by E Ramos Chaparro, *La cláusula penal del pacto resolutorio (Aspectos sustantivos y registrales)* (Seville, Universidad de Sevilla, 1999).

[45] P Gómez de la Serna, *La Ley Hipotecaria, comentada y concordada con la legislación anterior española y extranjera*, I (Madrid, Imprenta de la Revista de Legislación, 1862) 512–13, 256–57 and 465–66.

[46] STS 11 July 1983 (RJ 1983\4208).

[47] STS 19 May 1989 (RJ 1989\3778); STS 16 July 1993 (RJ 1993\6450); STS 3 July 1996 (RJ 1996\5555); STS 16 March 2007 (RJ 2007\1857, not directly related to the case).

[48] This was recognised in cases of reservation of ownership of movable property in STS 7 October 1995 (RJ 1995\7025), STS 12 July 1996 (RJ 1996\5886) and STS 20 June 2000 (RJ 2000\5294). We see no good reason why the same solution should not be applied to sales of immovables with reservation of ownership.

entire price, obviously the vendor cannot assert a successful third-party claim to ownership, because his right no longer exists.

Finally, the effect of full payment of the price, as we have already said, is automatic acquisition of definitive ownership[49] and lapse of the vendor's retained security right.

C. Sale of a Future Thing

We return now to another kind of sale agreement where problems may arise concerning the two dimensions of delivery: as fulfilment of an obligation, and as *traditio*. However, we shall only examine delivery as *traditio*, because the purely obligational aspects are especially complex. Let us just say here that, since the subject matter of the contract is a future thing, certain pre-delivery duties are incumbent upon one of the parties, and those duties consist in carrying out the activities necessary to make the thing come into existence.

In practice, future things that the vendor is in the process of bringing into existence are often sold in an *escritura pública*. The problem is seen most of all in cases of buildings bought off plan or under construction. An *escritura pública* cannot make up for the present non-existence of the subject matter of the contract,[50] and for that reason it is said that one of the instances where an *escritura pública* has no effect as *traditio* is where a future thing is concerned;[51] but that does not solve all the problems presented by this topic.[52] As we have already said, we believe that, once the element preventing the *escritura pública* from being effective as traditio has been overcome, that should mean the transfer is accomplished, without any need for another *traditio*, although there is no support for our solution in case-law.

One variation with some very particular features of its own is the case of a contract under which the vendor delivers land in exchange for part of the building the purchaser will eventually raise there.[53] The owner of the plot, who is not himself qualified to do the building work, engages a professional builder, and the deal is that in the end both parties obtain flats or business premises that can be

[49] González Pacanowska (n 5) 10348; MP Sánchez González and I Mondéjar Peña in M Pasquau Liaño (ed) *Jurisprudencia Civil comentada*, III (Granada, Comares, 2009) CC art 1461, p 2978.

[50] González Pacanowska (n 5) 10343.

[51] Peña Bernaldo de Quirós (n 10) 109 n 22.

[52] ibid; the author, who refers to STS 9 October 1997 (quoted below in the text), himself acknowledges that it is 'debtable whether the thing, in the case at issue, is a future thing'.

[53] On the subject of this section generally, see our monograph *La permuta de suelo por edificación futura. Entrega y transmisión de la propiedad en el sistema del Código Civil* (Seville, Universidad de Sevilla, 2011) and the articles 'La inscripción en el Registro de la Propiedad de la cesión de suelo a cambio de edificación futura: comentario a la RDGRN de 7 de mayo de 2009 (RJ 2009, 3004)', RDP, no 24, 2010, pp 323–29; 'Prehorizontalidad y transmisión del derecho de vuelo a cambio de edificación futura', RDP, no 26, 2011, pp 373–78; '¿Es conforme al ordenamiento el art. 13 RH sobre cesión de suelo por obra futura?' in ML Atienza Navarro and others (eds), *Pensamientos jurídicos y palabras dedicados a Rafael Ballarín* (Valencia, Universitat de València, 2009) 337ff. These works give a more detailed exposition with bibliographical references.

used independently. Obviously, a contract like this is hard to categorise. Although it could constitute a sale, if that is the parties' will, it could also be classified as an exchange (article 1446 CC), or a contract of works, or of partnership, and so on. At all events, it contains distinctive elements of all these various contract types, resulting in a sort of hybrid. We are not going to dwell on it but will just deal with delivery in terms of the two facets discussed in this chapter.

The most common explanation amongst scholars of how this contract works is that, in the beginning, the assignor transfers ownership of the entire plot. Thus, the *escritura pública* acts as *traditio.* Next, after the building has been completed, the assignee retransfers the appropriate property to the assignor in another delivery (for example, in a new *escritura pública*).[54] In this view, in exchange for giving up ownership of the plot now, the assignor just receives a credit, which in future may lead to the acquisition of a property right. But until that time comes, his position is highly insecure. In fact, there are plenty of cases in which arrangements like these lead to unsatisfactory solutions for the assignor. When, for example, the builder's creditors place an attachment on the building, the assignor no longer owns the plot, and he does not yet own any part of the building. A third-party claim to ownership on his part would inevitably be doomed to failure.

The arguments used in case-law have a direct impact on the problem of conveyancing. The Supreme Court's judgment of 15 June 1992 said,[55] '[T]he contract in question … gives rise only to obligational effects between the parties. For it to have effects in transferring ownership of the works (or the part of the works) whose completion is inexcusable requires delivery once the works are completed'. The Supreme Court judgment of 9 October 1997 reads similarly:

> When the contract is completed, the owner of the lot has it at his disposition as owner, and the execution of the *escritura pública* is equivalent to *traditio* or delivery, an effect that does not occur in connection with the performance to be provided by the other party, as it is the delivery of a future thing that has yet to be built on the lot. Thus, the execution of the document does not imply the *traditio ficta* under article 1462, paragraph 2, whereas the alleged transferor lacks possession as owner of the thing in either direct or indirect possession, since the thing does not exist, although it is possible. Hence, a necessary requirement for acquiring ownership through *traditio*, where

[54] An excellent example of this view is STS 6 July 2009 (RJ 2009\4453), which stated that 'there was initially no "traditio" of [the buildings that should have been constructed], because the *escritura pública* of 27 February 1996 established an agreement for future delivery and the need to execute the *escritura pública* documenting allocation in order for the transfer to take place'. Literally, the *escritura pública* stated that the party 'undertook to deliver … the six homes … to Leonardo and his wife Gregoria and to Conrado and his wife Ofelia within the maximum period of thirty months … by which time the works must have been declared completed and the occupancy certificate must have been secured. Said delivery shall be formalised in the proper *escritura pública* of allocation, with the undertaking to deliver the undivided shares of ownership free of all encumbrances'. Could not this delivery and *escritura pública* be held to affect things from the perspective of obligations, or at most the acquisition of the specific homes, but not from the perspective of the creation *ab initio* of an arrangement for joint ownership of the land?

[55] STS 15 June 1992 (RJ 1992\5134).

there is title, is the existence of the thing and possession of the thing in the capacity of owner, which the obligated party must deliver when the thing is made corporeal through construction.[56]

It is obvious, at least to us, that, because the consequences are so highly debatable, it is advisable to attempt a theoretical reconstruction of the concept from its foundations, to eliminate the imbalances to which this first, more common, thesis leads. In our opinion, this would require a re-evaluation of the meaning of the two deliveries involved in this type of contract: delivery of the land to the builder, and delivery by the builder of the finished result of his construction.

There is one interpretation amongst scholars that points in the direction of this re-balancing. It holds that the future flats are transferred to the assignor now, even though they are as-yet unbuilt, and that this is so by virtue of the *escritura pública* formalising the assignment of the plot, which acts as instrumental *traditio*. This thesis gained strong support in the Spanish Directorate-General of Registries and Notaries' decision of 16 May 1996:

> The *escritura pública* may be equivalent to delivery for the purposes of deeming the transfer of ownership to have been performed, even when it does not also cause a transfer of possession, such that despite the transfer of ownership the obligation of delivery might not be completely fulfilled.[57]

This view was continued in the Directorate-General's decision of 5 January 1999.[58]

The explanation seems unnecessary and contrived, because it means accepting that property rights in future things exist, and that seems to contradict the very concept of the property right. Consequently, this approach to the problem does not have many followers nowadays.

There is a way to achieve the same practical result of balance between the contractual positions. One need only rethink the meaning of the delivery involved in the contract so that the *escritura pública* produces a title shared between assignor and assignee instead of a transfer of exclusive ownership of the plot. The economics of this conceptualisation would obviously require the effective delivery

[56] STS 9 October 1997 (RJ 1997\7065). This criterion is repeated in STS 18 February 2005 (RJ 2005\1681), STS 26 April 2007 (RJ 2007\2393) and STS 14 June 2007 (RJ 2007\3515): 'The "delivery" requirement cannot be eliminated in these cases. The delivery necessary for the acquisition of ownership can be embodied only at the time of effective construction and delivery of possession of the home in question to the parties to the exchange, even in cases such as this, where the exchange agreement is made in an *escritura pública*'. On the other hand, STS 14 November 1997 (RJ 1997\8123) reached a different finding and admitted a third-party claim to ownership.

[57] RDGRN 16 May 1996 (RJ 1996\3950).

[58] RDGRN 5 January 1999 (RJ 1999\41). However, RDGRN 23 September 1999 (RJ 1999\6475) did not uphold the value of the *escritura pública* as *traditio*. In the wake of the Supreme Court's judgment of 31 January 2001 (3rd Chamber), the Directorate-General of Registries and Notaries' doctrine now distinguishes between assignments of land for future building on the basis of whether the character of the counterperformance is purely obligational, or real; see RDGRN 13 July 2005 (RJ 2005\5654) and 7 May 2009 (RJ 2009\3004). Therefore, if the contract places the plot under a joint property regime, the joint property undoubtedly qualifies for registration; but if the contract only envisages a right to part of what is built in future, no real and present right can exist.

of the land to the builder in order to enable him to construct the building. But that delivery, which also functions as *traditio* of the plot, would not transfer full ownership of it, because the plot is envisaged in the contract as an element belonging to both parties, and a full transfer to the assignee would be completely useless for the purpose of the contract, even if the transfer were only provisional.[59] In our opinion, then, *traditio* of the plot is sufficient by itself to allow it to be placed in a joint property regime.

How would the future buildings be acquired? Obviously there is no present acquisition of future assets. Acquisition will happen when the buildings come into existence. If we accept that the land is jointly owned, what is built on the land will be jointly owned too, via accession. But if the original contract has already clearly defined the distribution of the future building between the parties, then the arrangement will also work as an advance division of the eventual joint property. All that would remain would be to deliver physical possession of his part to the assignor of the land. No *traditio* would be required, because strictly speaking there is no transfer of assets, only the determination of the assets included in the share of each of the joint owners. If the assets corresponding to each of the parties are not specifically defined in the contract, this will have to be done later in another property division agreement, although normally the original contract lays down the rules of the division (and the task of determining the properties may even be left to one of the parties). At all events, this division of the joint property does not require any *traditio* as a prerequisite to the existence of each party's exclusive property rights in the assets allocated to him.

Indeed, this is the approach that best takes into account the cause of the contract, which explains its proprietary effect. Furthermore, it is an explanation that adapts quite well to the provisions of the Mortgage Act. Ownership of the land could be registered as ordinary joint ownership of property. But there is another possibility, too: the property could be registered directly as horizontal property (a legal situation known in Spain as *prehorizontalidad*, in which the wish to establish a horizontal property regime is fully formed, but the regime itself has yet to be established). Article 8.4 LH allows buildings under construction to be registered in a horizontal property regime. If construction on plan is regarded as having already begun, it is perfectly possible to register the legal position of both parties to the contract. In this case the law even considers it possible to register the resulting properties separately (article 8.5 LH).

This theoretical explanation can work in other cases, too, though they are rather few in number and almost purely academic, eg, an *escritura pública* transferring future real estate elements that will be produced by works that are still only on plan or under construction and are the exclusive property of the developer or builder. Admittedly, the usual course in such cases is sale in a private document,

[59] A Carrasco Perera, E Cordero Lobato and C González Carrasco, *Derecho de la construcción y la vivienda*, 7th edn (Pamplona, Aranzadi, 2012) 297–98.

leaving the *escritura pública* for when the works have finished.[60] In such cases the transfer of ownership of a share of land as proposed here would require another form of *traditio.* But if there is an *escritura pública, traditio* would happen as one of its effects, even if the obligation to deliver the flat is scheduled for later.[61] In other words, despite the need for delivery, we do not think the purchaser's position would be merely obligational.[62] Since ownership of the future flat involves current ownership of a fraction of the land on which the building is to be raised, we cannot not rule out the efficacy of the *escritura pública* as *traditio* with regard to the ownership share.[63] This solution would also be supported by the fact that legislation itself already says that situations of *prehorizontalidad* can qualify for registration, as we have explained.[64]

D. *Traditio* by a Person Who is Not in Possession of the Thing Sold

This is rather a controversial problem that Spanish scholars examine frequently and through a wide variety of lenses.[65] It would be impossible to list all the authors and their arguments here – details can be found in the publications cited in this chapter – but we should at least say which we feel is the right path to a solution.

[60] See also Rogel Vide (n 11) 288–89.

[61] Rogel Vide (n 11) 287.

[62] cf (to the contrary) Rogel Vide (n 11) 287.

[63] Rogel Vide (n 11) 289 himself acknowledges the possibility of immediately selling an undivided share of the plot and leaving the acquisition of the future flat to be conducted according to the conventional regulations governing the effects of accession. But in our view this should be the normal effect of a transaction of this kind. The interesting judgment STS 12 November 2007 (RJ 2007\8107) reaches its decision under a rule that may seem different from ours, although in reality, instead of the sale's having being made in an *escritura pública*, a contract was 'made between a government agency (Patronato de Casas para Funcionarios de la presidencia del Gobierno)' and the purchaser. The court ruled,

> [E]ven if it [the contract] were considered a public document, it could not have the effect of transferring ownership of the home in question, because in that case the formal award of said home to the purchaser would not have been necessary … nor would the later execution of an *escritura pública*. The delivery of the thing sold entails the effective transfer of possession to the purchaser, which … complements title with delivery, and the purchaser thus acquires the right of ownership, notwithstanding the fact that, as an exception, the law allows a so-called fictitious *traditio* when the parties so agree and the sale is made in an *escritura pública* (art 1462.2 CC), which "shall be equivalent to the delivery of the thing constituting the subject matter of the contract, unless it should result or it should clearly be deduced otherwise from the *escritura pública*." Thus, in no case could the delivery be understood to have been made fictitiously through the signing of the aforesaid document of 1979, not only because we have no record of the building's having been built by that date, but above all because the parties themselves evidenced it when the purchaser signed a document stating for the record that delivery occurred [at a later date].

[64] González Pacanowska (n 5) 10345–46.

[65] This is the main topic of the monograph by Bercovitz Álvarez (n 13); González Pacanowska (n 5) 10340ff. For an excellent exposition of scholarly views, see Gordillo Cañas (n 5) 164ff, with whom we agree; Jerez Delgado (n 6) 224ff; Navarro Castro (n 13) 171ff; Rodríguez-Rosado (n 6) 2813ff.

The starting point of the problem is that instrumental *traditio* is still just a symbolic form of delivery, and it could conceivably be rendered null if it is established that actual delivery is impossible. That is to say, if the transferor does not have indirect or direct possession, then the principle of *nemo dat quod non habet* comes into play, and the transfer of the property right becomes impossible due to defective delivery. A symbolic or fictitious form of *traditio* would have the same value as the reality it can represent, but if the represented reality proves on the facts to be impossible, then the symbolic *traditio* has no value and the transfer will not have taken place.[66] Are these ideas correct? We think not; we shall give our arguments briefly in the following pages.

The problem, in practical terms and in scholarly discussion, is almost always restricted to immovables, for the reason we already know: *escrituras públicas* are used in sales of immovables to facilitate their registration. There are those who say *traditio* is replaced by registration in cases of registration of ownership, whilst other authors consider that conclusive title through registration can make up for an absence of *traditio* in the case of a direct purchaser in good faith. We shall not go into this issue.

It is true that, in practice, the problem is eventually decided most of the time under the rules for double sales or the rules of publicity through the register, as we can see in the case-law cited below.[67] Anyway, we need not examine the criteria stemming from these rules to believe that one can confidently affirm that instrumental *traditio* under article 1462.2 CC in itself serves as delivery or *traditio*, and it is not an obstacle that the party making the *traditio* (the *tradens*) does not even possess the thing indirectly.[68] There would actually be two possibilities. One is that

[66] A similar conclusion can be drawn from the opinion of an early writer, QM Scaevola, *Código civil concordado y comentado extensamente*, XXIII (Madrid, Instituto Editorial Reus, 1906) 456–57: 'The last words of article 1462 reveal that the form of delivery that we explained is effective simply as a legal presumption. Even where there is an *escritura pública*, the reality of the facts may overcome the strength of the presumption'. And some lines later Scaevola thinks it possible that ownership may not belong to the purchaser. For Rodríguez-Rosado (n 6) 2831, '[T]he case of the dispossessed vendor [would still be] the only event where execution of an *escritura pública* could never make up for non-delivery of possession'; although Rodríguez-Rosado does consider it possible for the vendor to transfer his power to file proceedings within one year to recover possession (*la acción interdictal*) (pp 2817 and 2825). In short, in Rodríguez-Rosado's opinion, the only impossibility is for the vendor to transfer simply his right to take action to recover the thing as its owner (*la acción reivindicatoria*). It seems to us that case-law makes it clear that it is possible to transfer the right to bring the *acción reivindicatoria*. It would be pointless to prevent it, so this thesis refuses to integrate that case-law into the system. In short, in our opinion, the correct scholarly view is that given by Albaladejo García (n 15) 152ff: 'no matter how much proof there is that there was no real *traditio*, the execution of the *escritura pública* has in itself the value of an instrumental *traditio*'.

[67] We shall not dwell on this: it is covered in more detail by Murga Fernández, below, Ch 4.

[68] In this we agree with Lacruz Berdejo (n 6) 232, for the fundamental reason that this solution facilitates transfer of ownership without any detriment to the *escritura pública*'s functions of reflection, proof and publicity. See also Albaladejo García (n 15) 161; Cuena Casas (n 5) 266ff; Gordillo Cañas (n 5) 175ff. Naturally, it can be firmly asserted that 'possession by a lessee does not contradict the indirect possession of the property by its owner' when the owner transfers the property, as stated by STS 28 June 1961 (ECLI:ES:TS:1961:192) and STS 13 May 1995 (RJ 1995\4233).

the *tradens* has some form of possession; then, the instrumental *traditio* would constitute a transfer of legal possession without physical delivery (*un constituto posesorio*). If, on the other hand, the *tradens* has no form of possession at all, it is a case of *traditio ficta*, which means possession has not been effectively delivered, but *traditio ficta* is still good enough to transfer ownership.[69] We would not even need the legal subtlety of arguing (actually begging the question) that in such cases what is transferred is not the thing, but the proprietary right in it and consequently the standing to bring the action to recover it as owner (*la acción reivindicatoria*); then, delivery would not be legally necessary, because the case would fall under article 1526 CC, which apparently does not require any form of *traditio*.[70] And we say 'apparently' because article 609 CC establishes the title-and-delivery ('*títulus et modus*') system for 'ownership and other rights over property', and we think that, even if we imagine that we can distinguish between a sale and this alleged contract of transfer of ownership, nothing allows us to think that we could do away with the distinction between the assignor's obligation and the actual transfer of the right to the assignee. This last step must involve *traditio*, which would be possible if it happened through the execution of an *escritura pública*. Although article 1526.2 CC requires registration in order for an assignment to have effects vis-à-vis third parties, this requirement does not actually deny that the time of transfer is the time when the *escritura pública* is made.[71]

In order to confirm that instrumental *traditio* performed by an owner who is not in possession does enable ownership to be transferred, we need only consider article 36 LH. This refers to acquisitive prescription (*usucapión*) of property registered to another person, which can be completed in the year following registration of the challenged acquisition. The case covered by article 36 means that the transferor is an owner who is not in possession, and the purchaser has not received possession.[72] The legal consequence of this provision is clear: the purchaser is the owner against whom the prescription runs and is the person who must interrupt it. That is to say, the law assumes that the *escritura pública* does transfer the property right, even if it is not itself a form of delivery and is not necessarily accompanied by delivery.[73]

Some cases say that the *escritura pública* just gives rise to a presumption of *traditio* or delivery that can be rebutted if no *traditio* or delivery ever actually took place.[74] This doctrine should be understood to mean that the *escritura pública*

[69] Albaladejo García (n 15) 152. For these special forms of *traditio*, see López y López, above, Ch 2, section V.B.

[70] According to E Gimenez Roig, *Tráfico jurídico, compraventa, escritura e inscripción. Venta como cosa propia, de finca que otro posee en concepto de dueño* (Madrid, Centro de Estudios Registrales, 1998) 174, what exists in this case is 'a *transfer of ownership without the need for* traditio, by virtue of a legislative provision', ie, art 1526 CC.

[71] Gordillo Cañas (n 5) 179–80.

[72] Peña Bernaldo de Quirós (n 10) 110 n 25.

[73] Gordillo Cañas (n 5) 172–73.

[74] For example, the STS 10 December 1991 (RJ 1991\8928) states incidentally that 'a *traditio ficta* does not absolutely signify the actual *traditio* of the subject matter of the sale. It may happen that a

cannot confer possession if the vendor has no possession to confer, regardless of whether an owner who is not in possession can use an *escritura pública* to transfer ownership.[75] Naturally, in a case where the vendor is not the owner, this case-law need not even be taken into consideration, because the failure to transfer the property right is due simply to the vendor's lack of ownership, not a lack of *traditio*.[76] There is case-law, however, that clearly states that the instrumental *traditio* represented by an *escritura pública* takes place even if the vendor (who in the process

third party possesses the thing, attributing proprietary title to him such as to lead to the possibility of having to accept evidence to the contrary to combat the possible discordance between the legalistic instrumental *traditio* and the existing physical and legal reality'. This idea is not objectionable when understood correctly, ie, the purchaser can achieve actual delivery through an action to recover it, and the possessor's title can also be settled in the same proceedings. The existence of *traditio ficta* does not tip the scales toward any solution to these problems of title. The exact facts the court was dealing with are confusing (we do not know who had possession or if the person taking third-party action to claim ownership also held an *escritura pública* documenting his acquisition). What is clear is that a third-party claim to ownership was filed at the wrong time (when the judicial sale had already been concluded in an *escritura pública* and registered), so the solution to the case was grounded on a single reason:

> [A] trial on a third-party claim to ownership, which is of an incidental nature stemming from the execution process with which it is related, notwithstanding the fact that the rules for ordinary proceedings are being followed, is not the appropriate procedural framework for clarifying the nullity of the *escritura pública* documenting the judicial sale, as the appellants wish to do, disregarding the parties to the *escritura pública* and especially the purchaser, as the third-party purchaser of the property at issue. In this sense, the doctrine of this Chamber is consistent, firm and sustained and proclaims that, when the third-party claim is for ownership, the interested persons retain their right to take action however and against whoever is appropriate.

Also, in STS 10 December 1996 (RJ 1996\9191), the purchasers had never even possessed the property in dispute, nor had they delivered it to subsequent purchasers. As a result, *traditio* was lacking, since 'instrumental *traditio* as accepted by article 1462 is a *juris tantum* presumption that does not necessarily imply transfer of possession'. But the issue is not whether *traditio* was lacking: it is whether *traditio* can produce its effects in a case of double first registration where it is proved that the person who actually possessed the property had the better title. Nevertheless, the idea that delivery in the meaning of article 1462.2 is simply physical does not seem correct; that idea may be seen in some of the cases mentioned by JM Manresa y Navarro, *Comentarios al Código Civil español*, X-I (Madrid, Reus, 1969) 216–17: 'However, as far as its efficacy is concerned, this form of *traditio* is subject to the terms of the *escritura pública*, because if it results from it, or is deduced from it, that the parties did not intend to confirm delivery, no *traditio* can be understood to have happened. Such would be the case, for example, where a fixed date is set when the purchaser must take possession of the thing … or where the vendor reserves the right to use and enjoy the property until unharvested crops are gathered'. For similar Supreme Court judgments, see Rodríguez-Rosado (n 6) 2814 n 1, and 2828–29.

[75] Albaladejo García (n 15) 161; González Pacanowska (n 5) 10342; Peña Bernaldo de Quirós (n 10) 110. The analysis of case-law can be seen in Navarro Castro (n 13) 185ff. This is exactly what happened in the case in STS 8 May 1982 (RJ 1982\2559), which explicitly rejects the appellant's idea that the vendors 'could not transfer possession of the properties to the predecessors in title from the plaintiffs who claim them, despite the *traditio ficta* of the *escritura pública* … because they did not have possession of the properties'; the defendants did. Actually, as the Supreme Court's judgment says, '*traditio* is not always to be understood as a material and physical transfer of the thing being transferred by means of a contract, and not even a transfer or delivery entirely clear of all defects, if we want the obligatory relationship to be effective as well, precisely because what the law wants is for the thing to be placed sufficiently at the disposal of the lender or purchaser so that he can validly demand performance and accession to effective possession'.

[76] eg STS 1 July 1995 (RJ 1995\5421).

successfully demonstrates his ownership on that basis) lacks physical or de facto possession of the property (and if the possessor cannot actually prove that he himself has ownership).[77] And similarly we also agree with the Supreme Court judgment of 8 July 1983,[78] which states that the presumption established by article 36 can be rebutted not by proving that the thing was not effectively delivered, but by demonstrating that the effect of the *escritura pública* as *traditio* is excluded by the deed expressly or by clear implication.[79]

This distinction is important on the contractual level. If there is no real delivery, the purchaser can bring an action against the vendor to enforce the contract or for damages. Naturally, the purchaser may also recover the thing from a third party and thus acquire possession of it. If, after bringing this claim for the thing, the purchaser fails to have his possession recognised, the question is whether he can bring an action against the vendor for an indemnity based on the warranty against eviction. As we have already said, the general view of scholars is that eviction involves depriving the purchaser of a thing that has already been really and effectively received, so it could not be used in this case. Actually, the solution is

[77] See STS 31 March 1964 (ECLI:ES:TS:1964:4386); STS 8 May 1982 (RJ 1982\2559); STS 7 February 1985 (RJ 1985\538); STS 29 May 1997 (RJ 1997\4327); STS 22 December 2000 (RJ 2000\10136); STS 4 April 2002 (RJ 2002\3285); STS 23 November 2012 (RJ 2013\183).

In STS 29 May 1997 the Court said: 'The appellant argues that, because the vendor did not have possession of the property when he executed the *escritura pública* transferring it to the plaintiff, he could not transfer ownership of the property. This argument poses no obstacle to it [the declaration of property of the plaintiff], whereas modern scholarship and the most recent cases accept the view … that instrumental *traditio* takes place even if the vendor does not have physical or de facto possession of the property he is selling, because it is understood in such cases that the effect of transferring ownership can be undermined only by what results from, or is clearly deduced from, the *escritura pública* itself, in accordance with article 1462.2 CC.'

STS 22 December 2000 stated that the fact 'that the owner subject to attachment did not deliver the keys to the building does not allow us to affirm, as is claimed in the pleadings, that the successful bidders for the property and later the purchasers of it, the plaintiffs/respondents, did not acquire ownership of the property upon gaining both title and instrumental *traditio*, because no such thing is recorded in or can be deduced from the *escritura pública* documenting the sale. The retention of physical possession by the original possessor does not nullify the effect of the *escritura pública* as *traditio*.' Actually, the case here was really suggesting that the possessor of the property might be its true owner, since he acquired it at an auction, as did the plaintiff. Therefore, it is not true to say, as the Supreme Court does, that vis-à-vis the possessor 'the purchasers were empowered to demand performance of the delivery obligation stemming from the contract or to claim possession in their capacity as precarious possessors.' None of that was actually possible. The plaintiff's pleas show that the plaintiff was taking action to recover the property as owner, as was in fact proper for him to do.

STS 4 April 2002 also relates to acquisition at auction. For more on the special features of the conveyancing system for auctioned property, see the considerations we put forward in *La tercería de dominio y la transmisión de inmuebles. La defensa de los derechos reales en la ejecución singular* (Pamplona, Aranzadi, 2015) 216ff. A significant contribution to this subject is also made in JP Murga Fernández, *Profili civilistici della vendita giudiziale di beni immobili in Italia e in Spagna* (doctoral thesis, University of Bologna, 2014, available at: http://amsdottorato.unibo.it/6272/1/TESI_PROFILI_CIVILISTICI_DELLA_VENDITA_GIUDIZIALE._Marzo_2014._Juan_Pablo_Murga_Fern%C3%A1ndez.pdf) and *Subasta judicial y transmisión de la propiedad* (Cizur Menor, Aranzadi, 2015).

[78] STS 8 July 1983 (RJ 1983\4122).

[79] See also STS 22 March 1952 (RJ 1952\506) and STS 28 June 1961 (RJ 1961\3017).

not entirely satisfactory: the two cases resemble each other so closely that they call for similar solutions; and the requirements set for the warranty against eviction should be required also in claims against the vendor. Nevertheless, in practice what can happen in these cases is that the action to recover (as owner) the thing from the person in possession of it and the claim for an indemnity against the vendor end up being dealt with in the same proceedings, which means the requirements for eviction must be respected.

4

A Non Domino Acquisitions and Protection of Third-Party Purchasers of Immovable Property in the Spanish Legal System

JUAN PABLO MURGA FERNÁNDEZ*

I. Introduction

This book presents a comparative study of certain aspects of Spanish and English contract law and property law. One of the central themes is the system each country uses to transfer ownership and other property rights. This is a promising field for an exercise in comparison, because it encompasses several essential characteristics of the two legal systems, and it paints a good picture of the unique features that set Spain apart from the rest of Europe.[1] Contractual transfers of immovable property in Spain are governed by the system of '*titulus et modus*': title and delivery,[2] regulated by article 609.2 CC. Following, essentially, the Roman approach, the title-and-delivery system is, from the point of view of legal technique, undoubtedly much superior to French-style consensus-based systems, and its advantages are most evident when the system has to deal with transfers by a *non dominus*, ie, a party who lacks the power of disposition. Purely consensus-based systems (where contracts are not only a source of obligations, but also a source of property rights) confuse the obligational aspect of the transaction with the transfer of ownership, and so sale contracts in such systems require the vendor to have the power of disposition. Hence, any sale of third-party property by a person without the power

* This chapter was written under the research project *Sujetos e instrumentos del tráfico privado (VII): Mercado inmobiliario y crisis económica* (DER 2015-66043-P) and the project *Red de Excelencia Registro, mercado crediticio y crisis económica* (DER16-81966-RED), both funded by the Spanish Ministry of the Economy, Industry and Competitiveness.

[1] See AM López y López, above, Ch 2.

[2] See Espejo Lerdo de Tejada, above, Ch 3 section I, esp n 1. For further discussion of the system of *titulus et modus*, see Cartwright and López y López, above, Ch 1 section II.

of disposition – the quintessential case of *a non domino* transfer – is a nullity. Yet certain classic notions which date back to Roman law, such as the vendor's warranty against eviction and the requirement of a 'good title' (*iustus titulus*) for so-called 'ordinary' *usucapio* (where greater legal requirements need to be met, but a shorter time period is required), are actually underpinned by the necessary validity, from the contractual perspective, of *a non domino* acquisitions.[3] What else could explain how a contract that is a nullity (ie, by its very nature has no legal effect) because the transferring party has no power of disposition, can nevertheless have effects with respect to these classic notions? The issue has created headaches for French scholars, and it explains why the Italian Civil Code in 1942 qualified the country's consensus-based system by the inclusion of sales that have only obligational effects, for cases such as sales of future things and sales of property belonging to another.[4] Such problems do not arise in the Spanish system, where sales of property belonging to another are fully valid from the contractual and obligational perspective, because the power of disposition is conceived as an essential requirement not of title (*titulus*, the legal ground for the transfer – the contract), but of delivery (the *modus* of transfer). The system thus clearly separates the obligational phase from the proprietary phase.

A. The Notion of *A Non Domino* Acquisition

In order to understand fully a system of property transfer, one must look at how the law responds to *a non domino* transfers and acquisitions, a broad concept that, strictly speaking, covers distinct factual situations that are irregular:

(a) A wholly *a non domino* transfer. The transferor transfers a right that does not belong to him. Either he never owned the right, or he has already transferred the right to someone else. This transferor is called a *non dominus* or an *ex dominus*.
(b) A transfer by an owner whose title (without the knowledge of the purchaser) is defective (ie, subject to annulment or cancellation). Let us suppose the transferor (B) is the true owner (*verus dominus*), but B has agreed to a

[3] M Cuena Casas, *La función del poder de disposición en los sistemas de transmisión onerosa de los derechos reales* (Barcelona, JM Bosch, 1996) 89 correctly says, 'the peculiarity of the consensual conveyancing system lies in the fact that it has made the contract not only a source of obligations, but also an autonomous generator of property rights, without the need for any subsequent element. Contractual consent is sufficient for the transfer of property to be held to have occurred. This blurs the boundary between rights arising from obligations and property rights, between personal actions and actions available *erga omnes*'.

[4] See the so-called *vendita obbligatoria* in arts 1472 (sale of a future thing: 'Nella vendita che ha per oggetto una cosa futura, l'acquisto della proprietà si verifica non appena la cosa viene ad esistenza' '[in the sale of a future thing, the acquisition of ownership occurs as soon as the thing comes into existence']) and 1478 (sale of another's property: 'Il compratore diventa proprietario nel momento in cui il venditore acquista la proprietà dal titolare di essa' ['The buyer becomes owner at the moment when the seller acquires ownership in it']). This is also emphasised by Cuena Casas (n 3) 130–31.

condition in the contract by which another person (A) transferred it to B, that will retroactively discharge the contract if B fails to pay A the intended price after transferring title to a third party (C).[5]

In all these cases there is a series of clearly conflicting interests. There are the interests of the true owner, or the holder of title in whatever circumstance renders the right defective. There are the rights of C, the third-party purchaser, particularly if he is unaware that the transfer is irregular. In cases of *a non domino* transfers in the genuine, full sense ((a), in the situations given above), the traditional Roman rule of *nemo dat quod non habet* is followed, and a property right can be validly transferred only by a person who has the power to do so, ie, by a person who has legal standing to perform an act of disposition. Following this logic, only the holder of the right is protected; he cannot be deprived of his right unless he gives his consent in a transaction which is appropriate to transfer it (sale, barter, gift, etc). This static certainty of rights translates into manifest uncertainty for the dynamics of legal transactions: because no one can transfer greater property rights than belong to him, a purchaser can be secure in his purchase only if the right has been transferred to him by a person who has legal standing to enter into the transaction. This calls for *probatio diabolica* – the devil's proof. Proof must be shown of title ownership throughout the entire series of previous conveyances, however many there may be in the chain, at least as far back as necessary to acquire title by *usucapio*.[6] In these circumstances, a system that focuses solely on the security of rights would make an adequate circulation of wealth impossible: buyers would be afraid to lose the price paid because they could never be certain of undisturbed ownership.

Protection for the holders of individual rights therefore needs to be harmonised with protection for transactions. This can be done only by admitting exceptions to the rule of *nemo dat quod non habet* in certain cases where this favours a third-party purchaser.[7] Transactions receive such protection through what Spanish legal scholars term 'forms of publicity and legal appearance' (*formas de publicidad y apariencia*), which enable third parties to discover who legally owns the rights they would like to purchase, whether those rights are encumbered and, if so, how. Generally speaking, most legal systems have two main forms of publicity and legal appearance for property rights: possession and registration. In the case of possession, however, the legal standing that publicity lends is limited, for two reasons. First, there are property rights that are not subject to possession. Second, the publicity provided by possession is very limited, as it applies only to

[5] M Espejo Lerdo de Tejada, 'Principios esenciales del sistema inmobiliario registral español' *La Ley Argentina* 2017 no 229, 2.

[6] FJ Sánchez Calero and B Sánchez-Calero Arribas, *Manual de Derecho Inmobiliario Registral*, 5th edn (Valencia, Tirant Lo Blanch, 2017) 21.

[7] JL Lacruz Berdejo, *Lecciones de Derecho Inmobiliario Registral*, 2nd edn (Cizur-Menor, Aranzadi, 1957, reprinted 2011) 1: 'This book outlines the structure and operation of an organisation established by Spanish lawmakers to reconcile the security of rights acquired with regard to a person's immovable assets, ie, the security of individual rights and the security of legal acts, which is called security of transactions'.

the circle of persons who have the opportunity to learn of the situation. For this reason, the function of possession as a tool for publicity is essentially restricted to derivative acquisitions of movable property. In such cases special importance is given to article 464.1 CC, a controversial provision that establishes the rule that possession of movable property acquired in good faith is equivalent to title. The controversy the article inspires revolves around issues such as what is meant by 'title'. On this point, scholars are divided basically into two very different lines of thought:[8] the so-called Romanistic view, which identifies 'title' with the 'good title' ('*iustus titulus*') required for ordinary *usucapio* under article 1940 CC; and the Germanic position, which holds title to be equivalent to 'title as ownership' instead of 'title for *usucapio*'.[9] Thus, Germanic thought upholds the existence of a true *a non domino* acquisition, and in Spain this is also established without doubt in commercial matters by article 85 CCom for the purchase of merchandise in stores or shops open to the public.[10]

B. The Spanish Land Registration System

In immovable property, the area with which we are mainly concerned in this chapter, the instrument created by law to provide publicity and legal appearance is the Land Register. The land registration system is fundamentally regulated not by the Civil Code, but by the Mortgage Act ('LH'), which is still in force in a form dating from 1946.[11] This is for reasons that are largely historical. The Civil Code took a long time to pass due to, amongst other things, opposition from some regions of the country that had their own bodies of civil law. Legislators argued over whether a single Civil Code ought to be applied throughout Spain or the differences in private law between certain territories ought to continue to exist. Since the regional peculiarities of private law mostly concerned family economic regimes and succession on death, in 1861 the national legislators finally managed to pull together a Mortgage Act, which provided a single body of regulations for land registration throughout Spain. The legislators later felt it unnecessary to incorporate into the Civil Code of 1889 more than a few very general rules on land registration and a general reference to the special legislation.[12]

[8] There is an intermediate third way supported by a minority (including Vallet de Goytisolo and Díez-Picazo y Ponce de León) termed the 'theory of recovery of movable property' (*teoría de la reivindicación mobiliaria*). For an explanation of the theory, see P Grimalt Servera, 'Comentario al artículo 464' in R Bercovitz Rodríguez-Cano (ed), *Comentarios al Código Civil*, Vol III (Valencia, Tirant Lo Blanch, 2013) 3784–87.

[9] On scholars' varying positions on article 464 of the Civil Code and their respective arguments, see JM Miquel González, *La posesión de bienes muebles: estudio del artículo 464.1 del Código civil* (Madrid, Montecorvo 1979) 261–86; and more recently Grimalt Servera (n 8) 3768–87.

[10] See López y López, above, Ch 2 section VI n 34.

[11] The Mortgage Act of 1944 was revised into a new definitive text by *Decreto de 8 de febrero de 1946 por el que se aprueba la nueva redacción oficial de la Ley Hipotecaria*. The 1946 version has itself been revised from time to time.

[12] Espejo Lerdo de Tejada (n 5) 1.

Registration may be considered superior to possession. In Spain, the land registry system has certain unique features that, as with the general system for the transfer of ownership, are unlike those of any other European country. The Spanish registration system lies between the French system and the German system. It not only provides the typically Latin negative or preclusive effect of 'inopposibility' (under the principle that anything not registered has no force against third parties),[13] but it also adopts the automatic legal presumption that information published in the Land Register is accurate when all legal conditions[14] are met. The leading condition is good faith; good faith is the capital element of the guiding principle of the Spanish registration system, ie, that conclusive title stems from registration. The system not only gives registered situations legal priority over unregistered situations, but it also positively and unassailably guarantees any right that has been registered by a third party in good faith who meets the other requirements for earning conclusive title. For this reason, the Spanish registration system may be said to be more like the German registration system, though it does have an essential difference: the Spanish system aims to influence the substantive system as little as possible. How? First, the Spanish system continues to respect the system of contract based on consent rather than form; the system of transfer by title and delivery; and the consequential causalism in the transfer of property rights. Second, the registration system does not introduce constitutive registration.[15]

The greater resemblance to the Germanic system (subject to the not-inconsiderable caveats and nuances mentioned above) is explained by, amongst other things, the following characteristic features of the Spanish registration system:

(a) *Verification of instruments of title and other documents.* All documents must pass a legality check administered by a Registrar before registration. On submission, documents are subjected to a brief examination, check or scrutiny to ensure that only good, valid instruments of title are registered. The Registrar who conducts this pre-registration examination is an official who meets the special professional qualifications required for work of this importance.[16]

[13] See López y López, above, Ch 2 section VII.

[14] See art 34 LH, below, section II.

[15] Espejo Lerdo de Tejada (n 5) 1. The preamble to the 1861 Mortgage Act reads, 'The nations of Europe are divided as to how to settle the great questions to which this very interesting part of civil legislation gives rise. Two systems standing head to head dispute the field: the one introduced by the French Civil Code and imitated by many other peoples, and the other which, born in Prussia, has come to attract so many adherents to its capital rules and to dominate in so many countries'. Faced with this choice, the legislators drafting the Act began with the legal status of Spanish legislation: 'Our current mortgage legislation espouses a hybrid system: far from following what may be called the Germanic system, whose bases are absolute publicity and the rigorous speciality of mortgages, it admits a combination of this system with that of hidden and general mortgages'; and they advocated amending this traditional system: 'Yet the commission, which as a general rule inclines in all things towards the historical, towards the traditional … is obliged to take on the role of innovator, to plead that our mortgage system be seated upon fresh foundations, and that therefore all mortgage-related laws be amended'. The sense of novelty is clear: 'There is, then, only one acceptable system: that which has publicity and the speciality of mortgages at its heart'; in short, the Germanic system.

[16] Art 18 LH.

(b) *Registration of transactions relating to the property by abstracts ('inscription') not in full ('transcription').* The registered document is not copied out verbatim into the registration records, as it would be in a transcription system. Instead, those terms that have property-related legal impact are recorded in the form of an abstract.[17]

(c) *A property folio system.* Under article 243 LH, 'The Land Register shall be kept by opening a separate record for each property in the relevant book. All subsequent registration entries, annotations and cancellations relating to that property shall be made one after another, leaving no blank spaces between entries.' As a result, the legal history of the property can be reconstructed and is available to third parties and the Land Registrar.

(d) *Chain of title.* Each title holder except the first must have received good and sufficient title from the previous holder.[18] Therefore, the legal history of each property in the registration records must form a perfect, unbroken chain. This guarantees that the real situation is accurately reflected in the records. It is also a clear consequence of keeping the Register according to the principles of the property folio, legality and scrutiny.[19]

These are the organisational principles of the Spanish registration system, and they are what gives rise to the automatic legal presumption that its records are accurate, under the principle of conclusive title. In the following section, we shall turn our attention to the meaning of this principle of *fe pública registral* (public faith in the Register), which is seen as a cornerstone of the Spanish land registration system. We shall look into its requirements and its effects to ascertain whether it can lead to true *a non domino* acquisitions by third parties in good faith who purchase based on information disclosed by the Land Registry.

II. The Principle and Requirements of Conclusive Title through Registration[20]

The principle of conclusive title is established fundamentally in article 34 LH and forms the cornerstone of the Spanish registration system.[21] Under this provision, when a third party makes a purchase based on information published in the

[17] Lacruz Berdejo (n 7) 14.
[18] Art 20 LH.
[19] Espejo Lerdo de Tejada (n 5) 2.
[20] For detailed discussion, see JP Murga Fernández, 'La doble venta judicial y el artículo 34 de la Ley Hipotecaria: recepción de la doctrina uniforme sentada en 2007' in RCDI no 732, 2012, pp 1969–2044.
[21] The preamble to the Mortgage Act of 1944 itself stresses: 'Particular study has been devoted to the principle of conclusive title, a basic element of all mortgage systems.' Similarly, RM Roca Sastre, L Roca-Sastre Muncunill and J Berná i Xirgo, *Derecho Hipotecario*, Tome II, Vol 2 (Barcelona, Bosch 2008) 7 assert that 'the principle of conclusive title is the *raison d'être* of the registration system in its specific function of ensuring property transactions by means of protecting third parties in mortgage proceedings.'

Register and meets the other requirements set out in article 34, once he registers his right, his registration status becomes unassailable – at least under registry law; under civil law his position as regards his property may still be challengeable. We shall examine the 'other requirements' shortly. Article 34 reads as follows:

> Where a third party in good faith acquires a right for value from a person who appears in the Land Register as having the power to transfer it, the right shall be upheld once entered in the Register, even if thereafter the right of the transferor is annulled or cancelled for reasons not recorded in the Register.
>
> Third parties are always presumed to act in good faith, unless it is proved that they were aware of the inaccuracy in the Register.
>
> Parties acquiring property or rights gratuitously shall not enjoy greater protection by registration than that to which their predecessor or transferor was entitled.

For a fuller understanding of the contents and scope of article 34, we must pare down its internal architecture and examine the basics, ie, the requirements set by the article for the positive effectiveness of registered rights. Let us begin with the exact wording. There are fundamentally six conditions for the application of article 34: (1) The individual to be protected must be regarded as a third party, (2) who purchases a property right over immovable property, (3) in good faith, (4) for value, (5) from a person who is registered as the last holder of title to the right, and (6) the third party must ultimately have his right registered (this last condition is elementary, because conclusive title is an effect of registration). For conclusive title to become operational, an additional requirement must be added, too, implied from article 33 LH: the validity of the contract – which is the basis of the title of the third party to be protected. There has been enormous controversy over this point and the question of how it works in conjunction with article 34, as we shall see later.

We shall now analyse each of these requirements and highlight the main doubts about their interpretation.

A. Existence of a Third Party

The person protected by the principle of conclusive title must be a third party. To understand this, we must begin with the general concept of parties to the contract and add that third parties are persons who are not parties to a contract. In the context of registration, this means protecting a person who is not involved in the registered act or named in the registration entry. The third party must nevertheless be a purchaser whose purchase is, however remotely, predicated on the registered act and the registration entry. Let us suppose that A is the registered holder of title to a thing he has bought, and his title has actually been declared a nullity, but the Register does not reflect the causes of his title's nullity or the final court ruling declaring his title null. Under these circumstances, if A sells and delivers the thing to B, B qualifies as a third party with respect to the null act from which his purchase is remotely derived.

To understand this fully, we shall need to work out the correct relationship between article 34 LH and article 33 (which concerns the requirement that the instrument or contract which is the basis of the protected third party's right is itself valid). This is a difficult issue, discussed in Section II.G below. The registration system provides protection for third parties who trust in appearances as painted by the registration records, but this particular kind of protection does not extend to the parties to the contract. Registration leaves the registered situation unchanged between the parties to the contract, yet for third parties it creates an appearance on which they can legitimately rely.[22]

B. Acquisition of a Property Right Over Immovable Property

Article 34 LH does not specify the legal nature of the property right the third party must purchase in order to be considered a protected third party (*tercero hipotecario*), although this can be deduced from articles 1.1, 2.1, 2.2 and 5. Article 1.1 states, 'The purpose of the Land Register is to record or note instruments and contracts relating to ownership and other property rights over immovable property'. Paragraphs 1 and 2 of article 2 state that these things shall be registered: 'instruments of title transferring or establishing ownership of immovable or property rights imposed thereon'; and 'instrument of title constituting, recognising, transferring, modifying or extinguishing rights of usufruct, use, habitation, emphyteusis, mortgages, charges, servitudes and any other property rights'. And, according to article 5, 'Instruments of title referring to mere or simple possession shall not be eligible for registration'. We may conclude from all these provisions that the kind of publicity the Register provides concerns ownership and property rights over immovable property. So, a protected third party is a person who purchases a property right over immovable property.[23]

So far there do not seem to be many difficulties of interpretation, although the most authoritative scholars continue to ask: why is it that conclusive title enters the picture only in the acquisition of property rights, when the Mortgage Act also calls for and allows the registration of personal rights, such as leases of immovables[24] and cautions warning of attachment?[25] Without going into the various commentaries

[22] A Gordillo Cañas, 'El principio de fe pública registral (II)' ADC 2008, no 3, p 1101.

[23] L Díez Picazo, *Fundamentos de Derecho Civil Patrimonial*, III, 5th edn (Navarra, Civitas, 2008) 521 says, '[T]he third party to which article 34 LH refers is not just any person outside a legal relationship, as the purely civil law concept of "third party" might suggest, but a purchaser, and a purchaser of ownership of immovable property or of a property right limiting ownership'. Similarly, A Gordillo Cañas, 'El principio de fe pública registral (I)', ADC, 2006, no 2, pp 558–60.

[24] Art 2.5 LH.

[25] Art 42.2 LH. An *anotación preventiva de embargo* is a Land Registry entry recording a writ of attachment against the debtor's property, which has a transitory nature and serves to exclude the good faith of a third party.

in detail, we agree with Gordillo Cañas that the solution to the particular case of leases of immovables does not fall under article 34 LH.[26] With respect to cautions of attachment, we disagree with a certain minority of scholars[27] and believe the true nature and raison d'être of the caution of attachment is not to trigger conclusive title in the favour of the person entering the caution, but to avoid conclusive title from applying by preventing others from remaining innocently (in good faith) ignorant of attachments.[28] In short, a caution does not make an ordinary lender a protected third party, because he is not a third party who acquires a property right over immovable property. Once the attachment procedure is complete and the asset has been registered as belonging to its new owner, things change; the lender, now a purchaser/assignee, can enjoy the curative effects of conclusive title, provided that he meets the requirements set out in article 34 LH.[29]

C. The Purchaser's Good Faith

In addition to stipulating that the acquisition must be of a property right, article 34 requires – and this is the very foundation of conclusive title – that the buyer must

[26] Gordillo Cañas (n 22) 1060–61 asserts: 'In today's legislation it is blindingly clear and certain that things are not like that. The exceptional and very unusual example of *a non domino* acquisition of a lease of immovables does not run through the general channel laid by article 34 LH. Instead, it runs, under different conditions and with a different scope, through the specific channel established in article 13.3 of the Urban Lease Act'. Similarly, F Pantaleón Prieto (ed), *Comentario a la Ley de Arrendamientos Urbanos* (Madrid, Civitas, 1995) 30–31 says: '[H]is (the lessee's) right is not a property right that can be acquired *a non domino*. This is patently shown by paragraph 3 of article 13 itself: the only *a non domino* acquisition of tenants' rights is *a non domino* acquisition of a five-year residential lease. The need for a rule like article 13.3 arises precisely from the fact that conclusive title does not operation to acquire tenants' rights *a non domino*. And it is obvious that the new Lease Act has not attempted to change that'.

[27] The other group of scholars is headed by JA Álvarez Caperochipi, *Derecho Inmobiliario Registral* (Madrid, Civitas, 1986) 155–63; J Franco Arias, *El procedimiento de apremio* (Barcelona, Bosch, 1987) 360ff; and JM García García, 'El tópico de los efectos limitados de las anotaciones de embargo' in *Ponencias y comunicaciones presentadas al VII Congreso Internacional de Derecho Registral* (Madrid, Ilustre Colegio Nacional De Registradores de la Propiedad y Mercantiles de España-Centro de Estudios Hipotecarios, 1988). Their approach to an interpretation of the absolute real effect of cautions in the Spanish system is that an attachment is a kind of security interest very like a mortgage, in which the attaching lender acquires a property right. Accordingly, they regard the caution as a registry entry that can have, in the lender's favour, the same effect that article 34 attributes to registration itself. For further development of this position, see Gordillo Cañas (n 22) 1062ff.

[28] Gordillo Cañas (n 22) 1065–66. Supporting this same position, P De Pablo Contreras (gen ed), C Martínez de Aguirre Aldaz and MA Pérez Álvarez, *Curso de Derecho Civil (III), Derechos Reales* (Madrid, Colex, 2008) 376 state: 'A lender that has a caution relating to his attachment placed on the Register is not a third party: the efficacy of the attachment stems from its enforcement, and what the caution does is preclude the effects of conclusive title, thus preventing enforcement from being frustrated. It does not, however, attribute the effects of conclusive title to the lender who enters the caution'. Similarly, M Espejo Lerdo de Tejada, *Efectos Jurídico-reales del Embargo de Inmuebles en la Ley de Enjuiciamiento Civil* (Cizur Menor, Civitas, 2005) 89: 'Obviously, the reason for entering a caution relating to an attachment is precisely to keep any third parties protected under article 34 LH from gaining standing with respect to the attached property. A purchaser will not enjoy the protection of the Register if the attachment was already noted in a caution by the date of the transfer'.

[29] On the operation of conclusive title in purchases through judicial sales, see JP Murga Fernández, *Subasta judicial y transmisión de la propiedad* (Cizur Menor, Aranzadi, 2015) 383ff.

act in good faith. There are many questions about good faith, both as a general principle of law (under article 7.1 CC) and as a constitutive requirement for the application of conclusive title, which is the topic that interests us.

We shall begin, then, with the concept of good faith from the perspective of registration, and then look further into the main issues that good faith raises. Good faith has been defined by many authoritative Spanish legal writers and by many rulings in Spanish case-law, because, although it was not until the 1944–1946 reform that Spanish mortgage legislation expressly stipulated good faith as a requirement for protection through the mechanics of registration,[30] in practice good faith had long been required by both case-law and scholars. How can we define it? We can simply formulate the concept as phrased by Díez Picazo and the Spanish Supreme Court's judgment of 3 October 1963. According to Díez Picazo, good faith is

> the belief that the registered holder of title is the owner of the thing and has sufficient power of disposition over it to transfer ownership of it or to create a property right in it and, conversely, ignorance of non-existence of title to the property or any other circumstance that might render the title ineffective or limit it.[31]

STS 3 October 1963 says,

> [I]n its positive aspect, good faith consists in the belief, by someone who desires the protection of registration, that the person who created the property right in question owned the encumbered property and had manifest powers of disposition enabling him to create it, as we infer from article 1950 CC; and in its negative sense it is ignorance or unawareness of the existence of inaccuracies, flaws or defects affecting the owner's title as such.

As we can see from both definitions, good faith has two sides. One is positive, the other negative, and both must be satisfied in order for good faith to exist. The reasoning is logical: I have good faith (a) because, since I believe the information that appears in the Register, I believe that the person I am buying from is the true owner of title to the property right I wish to buy; therefore I believe he has the component powers that make up the property right (or at least he holds the power of disposition) under the conditions stated in the Register; and (b) because I am unaware of any unregistered flaws or defects that might invalidate the seller's apparent ownership.

However, there are two major issues regarding good faith in connection with conclusive title. First, whether good faith requires an additional degree of diligence beyond merely checking the Register.[32] Second, when does the third party have to be in good faith: when the purchasing mechanism is set in motion, or when the

[30] For a detailed analysis of the evolution of the good faith requirement in the various Spanish Mortgage Acts, see Gordillo Cañas (n 23) 572ff.

[31] Díez Picazo (n 23) 526–27.

[32] Díez Picazo (n 23) 527.

purchase is completed? The wording of article 34 LH provides no clear solution to these questions, which we shall now consider in turn.

i. *The 'Configuration' of Good Faith*

Authors generally support one or other of two conceptions – or 'configurations' (*configuraciones*) – of good faith.[33]

The first is known as the 'psychological' configuration of good faith. Reality as recorded in the Register prevails over the outside reality, and good faith is a state of mere ignorance of everything existing outside the Register.[34]

In the second or 'ethical' configuration of good faith, good faith is not just ignorance of reality. It also requires a certain element of excusability that makes that ignorance of reality justifiable and pardonable (at least ethically). In the ethical configuration, in order to have good faith, one must not only be unaware of reality, but also act diligently and in accordance with certain socially acceptable canons or criteria of behaviour.[35] This is the majority position unequivocally upheld in the case-law of the First Chamber of the Spanish Supreme Court.[36]

[33] On the configuration of good faith in the case of a protected third party, see detailed discussion by JP Murga Fernández, 'La configuración de la buena fe del tercero hipotecario. Breves notas en defensa de su concepción "ética"' in JP Murga Fernández and S Tomás Tomás, *Cuestiones actuales de derecho patrimonial desde una perspectiva italo-española* (Valencia, Tirant Lo Blanch 2013) 103–20.

[34] The main supporters of this position are Roca Sastre, Roca-Sastre Muncunill and Berná i Xirgo (n 21) 371ff; JM Miquel González, 'La buena fe y su concreción en el ámbito del Derecho Civil' in AAMN, vol XXIX (Madrid, 1990) 19–22; C Cano Tello, *Manual de Derecho Hipotecario*, 2nd edn (Madrid, Civitas, 1992) 302–03; JM García García in M Albaladejo and ST Díaz Alabart (eds), *Comentarios al Código Civil y Compilaciones Forales*, VII, vol 4 (Madrid, Edersa, 1999) 487ff; and A Pau Pedrón, *La publicidad registral* (Madrid, Centro de Estudios Registrales, 2001) 189–90.

[35] Díez Picazo (n 23) 527. The main supporters of the second position are: Díez Picazo (n 23) 527–28; De Pablo Contreras, Martínez de Aguirre Aldaz and Pérez Álvarez (n 28) 376–77; M Espejo Lerdo de Tejada, 'La buena fe requerida por el adquirente en remate *a debitore no domino*: comentario a la STS de 5 de marzo de 2007' RDP no 19, pp 412–13; Gordillo Cañas (n 23) 509ff; J-L Lacruz Berdejo, F de A Sancho Rebullida, A Luna Serrano, J Delgado Echeverría, F Rivero Hernández and J Rams Albesa, *Elementos de Derecho Civil, III bis, Derecho Inmobiliario Registral* (Madrid, Dykinson, 2001) 185–86; M Peña Bernaldo de Quirós, *Derechos Reales. Derecho Hipotecario*, Vol II, 3rd edn (Madrid, Centro de Estudios Registrales, 1999) 555–56; J Vallet de Goytisolo, 'La buena fe, la inscripción y la posesión en la mecánica de la fe pública' in *Estudios sobre derecho de cosas y garantías reales* (Barcelona, Nereo, 1962) 220ff.

[36] Several Supreme Court judgments embrace the ethical configuration of good faith, most notably the following: 8 March 2001 (RJ 2001\3975), 9 May 2003 (RJ 2003\3892), 29 September 2003 (RJ 2003\7006), 7 September 2007 (RJ 2007\5303), 7 December 2007 (RJ 2007\9057), 11 February 2011 (RJ 2011\2350), 12 January 2015 (RJ 2015\185) and 4 October 2017 (RJ 2017\4294). The judgment of 4 October 2017 comes down firmly on the side of the ethical definition:

> Case-law usually identifies good faith as the belief that the seller owns the thing he is selling or, alternatively, as unawareness that the thing has already been sold and effectively transferred to somebody else. However, judgments such as those of 25 October 1999, 8 March 2001 and 11 October 2006 also consider the presumption of good faith to be rebutted when the buyer's unawareness or ignorance of reality is a consequence of 'the negligence of the ignorant'. The 'ethical' conception of good faith – according to which the buyer must not merely act in ignorance of reality, but also diligently, which means doing more than just checking the Register – has been confirmed by the judgment of 12 January 2015. The ethical burden of diligence on the buyer's part

To explain these two positions further we should go back to their origins. Miquel González suggests the origin of the disagreement can be traced to Wächter and Bruns, who first started the debate around 1870 in relation to the good faith required in the *ius commune* for acquisitive prescription through continuous possession alone. Wächter was the standard bearer of the psychological configuration of good faith, whilst Bruns led the school supporting the ethical conception. In fact, the terminology 'psychological' and 'ethical' was coined by Bruns. Let us see what each of these authors had to say, to gain a better overview of the situation so we can then take our own position.

Wächter says good faith is the belief that one is doing no wrong to anyone; and that this belief is just a fact whose existence does not depend on the underlying cause of the belief and therefore does not depend on the excusability of mistakes. So, he reasons, the law cannot rule out good faith by reason of inexcusable mistakes, because, due to the way that belief in facts originates, good faith cannot be forced to depend upon the factual existence of a given circumstance. This is confirmed, according to Wächter, by passages in the *Digest* that also accept good faith in cases of error of law, which the Romans considered inexcusable error.

To counter these assertions, Bruns argues that Wächter's reasoning relies on the German concept and word *Glauben*, which means 'belief'. But the Roman word *fides* is not identical to *Glauben*; it does not mean 'belief', but 'faith', 'trust' or 'integrity'. So, according to Bruns, a person cannot be considered to be in good faith, according to a natural ethical feeling, if he believes something for his own benefit with blind selfishness. Only a person who holds an objectively-based belief reached by honest, thorough reflection can be considered to be in good faith. What one truly believes does not matter, says Bruns; what matters is what one could believe as an honest man, what an honest man could have or should have believed or known. The principle of good faith, then, is not psychological, but is a principle of ethics, law and business.[37]

That is the original approach in each school. Much can be said about them, and much has been written for and against each. But we regard the ethical configuration of good faith as the sounder, on the basis of the following arguments.

In the first place, as Gordillo Cañas says, the very term 'good faith' is already a reference to the moral dimension and a clue differentiating good faith from crass error or simple ignorance.[38]

does not mean the buyer should dispense with the Register; rather, under article 34 LH, which requires good faith, the registry's protection is limited when the buyer has not shown proper diligence in accordance with the circumstances to ascertain that the real situation and the Register agree. In other words, when the buyer 'had reasonable means and sufficient grounds to know, before the acquisition was completed, that the property or right was in the de facto possession of, and on the basis of a title as owner, by a person other than the person transferring the property' (argument under art 36 LH).

[37] JM Miquel González, 'Observaciones en torno a la buena fe' in *Homenaje al profesor Juan Roca Juan* (Murcia, Secretariado de Publicaciones de la Universidad de Murcia, 1989) 500–02.

[38] Gordillo Cañas (n 23) 587.

Indeed, it would make no sense for article 34 LH to refer to good faith if it were merely equivalent to simple ignorance. Good faith as a synonym of ignorance of reality outside the Register, and proved by the mere fact of learning what the situation is according to the Register, makes sense only in constitutive registration systems like the German,[39] where any investigation outside the land registry would be superfluous, because in matters of real estate it is impossible for there to be any difference between what the registry considers true and what actually exists. But this is not the case in legal systems, such as the Spanish, where registration is declaratory, where the establishment of ownership and other property rights (with a few controversial exceptions, such as mortgages and charges) takes place outside the Registry. In a system like ours, it does make sense for *ex lege* acquisitions[40] – and acquisition under the principle of conclusive title is an *ex lege* acquisition – to need an additional element, something that goes beyond reality-as-registered to justify such an exceptional acquisition. Support for this is to be found in German

[39] See § 892 BGB.

[40] Art 609.2 CC lists 'the law' as an autonomous mode of acquiring property rights. The meaning behind this mode of acquisition has been debated, particularly whether it makes any sense for this to be an autonomous mode, since the various modes of acquisition laid out in art 609 can all be classified as 'legal' because they are all in fact stated in some law. Leading scholars consider that it can be held to be an autonomous mode, one that encompasses all cases of acquisition occurring by operation of law regardless of the will of the parties involved. On this point JM Miquel González, 'Comentario al artículo 609 del Código Civil' in C Paz-Ares Rodríguez, L Díez-Picazo Ponce de León, R Bercovitz Rodríguez-Cano and P Salvador Coderch (eds), *Comentario del Código Civil* (Madrid, Ministerio de Justicia, Centro de Publicaciones, 1991) 1544 states, '[W]hen the Law is mentioned at the same level as the facts that the law must determine, that is flawed technique; but it can cover cases not mentioned or else allude to cases where the effect is not caused by the will of the parties or the purchaser, but instead is caused automatically, *ipso iure*, even without the purchaser's knowledge'. Similarly, MA Parra Lucán, 'Comentarios al artículo 609 del Código Civil' in R Bercovitz Rodríguez-Cano (ed), *Comentarios al Código Civil*, Vol IV (Valencia, Tirant lo Blanch, 2013) 4649 says, '[A] wide variety of events in which the acquisition of ownership or other property rights is not causally connected, or at least not pivotally connected, with a mechanism of negotiated agreement' can be included within the material scope of application of this mode of transfer. See A Domínguez Luelmo, 'Comentario al artículo 609 del Código Civil' in A Domínguez Luelmo (ed), *Comentarios al Código Civil*, 1st edn (Valladolid, Lex Nova, 2010) 713–14; M Cuena Casas, 'Comentario al artículo 609 del Código Civil' in A Cañizares Laso, P De Pablo Contreras, J Orduña Moreno, and R Valpuesta Fernández (eds), *Código Civil comentado*, Vol I, 1st edn (Navarra, Civitas, 2011) 27. Examples can be seen in cases where certain rights of first refusal are given to a particular series of persons (eg, co-owners, adjoining owners), in acquisition caused by natural phenomena or events (accession of everything produced by the property, or accession of everything incorporated in and attached to the property), acquisition through human acts that are not transactions (industrial accession, specification, intellectual creation), acquisition through juristic acts performed on indirect will (in spousal community property regimes, indirect acquisition of certain legal rights of first refusal), acquisition based on the rectification of a failed mechanism for negotiated agreement (acquisitions through *usucapio* and *a non domino* acquisitions), acquisition through constitutive registration when by law some legal authorisation is required before the right and its acquisition can exist (statutory mortgages, statutory rights of way, statutory succession), etc (see Parra Lucán, above, 4649–50). Many other cases could be mentioned, whose common denominator is that they are not transactions negotiated by the parties. For an exhaustive analysis of the various things that seem to fall under the system of transfer by operation of law, see R Sánchez Aristi, 'La adquisición por Ley de la propiedad y los demás derechos reales sobre los bienes' in *Revista Doctrinal Aranzadi Civil-Mercantil*, no 19, 2000.

law, where there is no public registration for movable property – and a purchaser in gross negligence of movables is not eligible for protection.[41]

This could be refuted, as Miquel González does, by arguing that third parties should be freed from the burden of investigating beyond the Register itself when the system's means of publicity are run by such highly qualified professionals and are so rigorously screened for due legal form.[42] We feel that the existence of a reliable means of publicity accessible to all third parties is indeed a basic element on which the protection of third parties in good faith should rest, but it does not entirely fulfil the good faith requirement on its own, for the very reason that, since the Spanish registration system is a declaratory system, some discrepancy between reality-as-registered and outside reality is inevitable. This extraordinary fall-back method for validating *a non domino* acquisitions of property and other property rights would need an extra element, to ensure that the mistake in question is excusable. As Vallet de Goytisolo says, when working miracles such as the miracle of the instrument of conclusive title, the law is not usually satisfied by ordinary good faith alone. It tends to require mistaken beliefs to have been based on some substantial, especially credible indication before it can pardon the mistake.[43]

Secondly, as Gordillo Cañas says, in article 36 LH there is a clear sign that good faith must consist in diligent behaviour on the part of the third party that goes beyond merely checking the Register.[44] Moreover, article 36 appears to be entirely applicable to our problem by analogy, since there are no particular reasons why the reasoning given there should be limited to *usucapio contra tabulas*.[45]

Miquel González disagrees. He says that the reasoning of article 36 applies exclusively to acquisitive prescription and therefore cannot be extended to the scope of article 34. In its second paragraph, article 34 seems to stipulate clearly the contents and configuration of the good faith requirement, identifying it with 'ignorance of inaccuracy in the Register'. Miquel González takes the view that the law sets a higher bar only for possession in the capacity of owner, and that this

[41] See § 932(2) BGB.

[42] Miquel González (n 37) 507.

[43] J Vallet de Goytisolo, 'La buena fe en las transmisiones inmobiliarias *a non domino*' in *Revista Jurídica del Notariado*, no 56, 2005, p 265.

[44] The point of art 36 LH is to regulate so-called *usucapio contra tabulas*, acquisitive prescription of a legal title to property or rights registered as belonging to another, in the particular case where the person who loses title qualifies as a protected third party under article 34. Art 36.1 provides:

> In the case of registered owners with third-party status within the meaning of article 34, acquisitive prescription which has already been completed or is completed within one year of acquisition shall prevail only in the following two cases: (a) when it is proved that the acquirer knew, or had reasonable means and sufficient grounds to know, before the acquisition was completed, that the property or right was in the de facto possession of, and on the basis of a title as owner by, a person other than the person transferring the property; (b) where, whilst not knowing of *or not being able to know* of such de facto possession in the above terms at the time of acquisition, the registered acquirer expressly or tacitly consents to such possession throughout the year after acquisition.

The words in italics underline the necessary excusability of ignorance that constitutes good faith.

[45] Gordillo Cañas (n 23) 587–88. For *usucapio contra tabulas* see n 44.

can be explained by the fact that possession as owner is something that cannot be checked through information that appears on the Register.[46]

So, does article 34.2, give any any guidance about what makes up the good faith requirement? The paragraph provides:

> Third parties are always presumed to act in good faith, unless it is proved that they were aware of the inaccuracy in the Register.

As can be seen, this paragraph only speaks of the presumption that the protected third party acts in good faith and how that presumption can be rebutted. Little is said about the exact contents and definition of good faith. Thus, it is both useful and necessary to look to article 36. Whilst article 36 does refer to *usucapio contra tabulas*, it nonetheless deals with a case of acquisition by operation of law, so we are justified in applying article 36 by analogy to acquisitions that fall under article 34.

Finally, from the ethical or moral standpoint that must justify, if not the actual existence of good faith, then at least its protective effects pursuant to the law (as recognised even by adherents to the psychological configuration of good faith),[47] Vallet de Goytisolo reasons that a farmer who farms his land, who makes it a productive part of the national economy and realises the social purpose of the land through his contact with it, deserves a thousand times more protection, even if he has not registered the land as his, than any speculator who has complied perfectly with all requirements of form but never deigned to take a look at the piece of Mother Earth that he was going to acquire.[48]

In summary, to meet the good faith requirement, a protected third party cannot merely check the Register. He must do more. He must find out who possesses the property, because if its actual possessor is not who the Register says it should be, that is the strongest possible sign of registry inaccuracy.[49]

ii. *The Timing of Good Faith under Article 34*

Another crucial issue is the time at which the purchaser must be in good faith in order to be protected. Depending on one's position on this question, the results may differ widely. The problem is nicely summed up by Clemente Meoro as follows:

> Under art 34 LH, the principle of good faith in registration only protects a third party who is in good faith … But, given that the transfer of property in our system works according to the theory of title and delivery (*titulus et modus*) (arts 609 and 1095 CC), only public instruments (*escrituras públicas*) qualify for registration, and the protected third party is required to have registered his title in order to get protection (art 34.1 LH). It is controversial whether his good faith needs to exist only at the time when instrument which is the basis of the transfer (ie the contract – the *titulus*) is made; or whether

[46] Miquel González (n 37) 504–06.
[47] Gordillo Cañas (n 23) 588.
[48] Vallet de Goytisolo (n 43) 255–56.
[49] Murga Fernández (n 29) 398ff.

> he must also have good faith at the time when his registrable public instrument of title is executed; or when both title and delivery are satisfied (ie, at the time of the acquisition); or even at the time of registration.[50]

In other words, there are four possible views:

(1) good faith must exist at the conclusion of the contract which is the basis of the transfer;
(2) good faith must exist at the excution of the registrable public instrument (*escritura pública*);
(3) good faith must exist at the moment of acquisition, when the transfer process takes place through the grant of both title and delivery; or
(4) good faith must exist when the title is registered.

There are scholars and case-law in favour of each of these four approaches, although the majority position, amongst scholars and courts alike, is that good faith must exist at the time when the acquisition is completed (when title has been transferred and delivery has been made). Let us look at some of the leading authors espousing each of the approaches and some of their main arguments.[51]

(1) *Good faith at the conclusion of the contract.* This position is fundamentally held by Lacruz Berdejo, for whom the purpose of the good faith requirement is fulfilled as soon as the contract is concluded. That is the time when the parties' wills set in motion the mechanism that creates registrable title, and that is when knowledge of an inaccuracy in the Register can influence the formation of their wills.[52]
(2) *Good faith at the execution of the registrable public instrument* (escritura pública). This is the position that García García supports. He says article 34 refers to third-party rights 'acquired in good faith', and, since article 34 is an item of mortgage legislation, we ought to look at 'acquired' in connection with the title for the acquisition (*titulus*) – the public instrument (*escritura pública*) – not the delivery (*modus*), because delivery is a concept foreign to the mortgage legislation, which refers only to public instruments. In addition, since what the Mortgage Act takes into account are registrable public instruments (*escrituras públicas*), not private contracts, it is the time when the *escritura pública* is executed, and no other, that must be considered when weighing the existence of the good faith necessary for the application of article 34.[53]

[50] ME Clemente Meoro, 'Sobre el momento en que ha de ser de buena fe el tercero hipotecario' in ME Clemente Meoro (ed), *Estudios de Derecho Inmobiliario Registral en Homenaje al Profesor Celestino Cano Tello* (Valencia, Tirant lo Blanch, 2002) 139.

[51] In this analysis we have followed the exhaustive study of the subject in TA Jiménez París, *El momento de la buena fe* (Madrid, Cuadernos de Derecho Registral, 2006) 13–98.

[52] Lacruz Berdejo, Sancho Rebullida, Luna Serrano, Delgado Echeverría, Rivero Hernández and Rams Albesa (n 35) 190–91.

[53] García García (n 34) 511ff.

(3) *Good faith at the moment of acquisition, ie, when the transfer process takes place through the grant of both title and delivery of the property.* The leading authors taking this position are Roca Sastre and Roca-Sastre Muncunill, who say that the time when the third-party purchaser is required to have good faith is when the juristic act of acquisition is completed according to the Civil Code. There is no point in taking any later time. They base their judgement on the literal wording of article 34, which speaks of 'third-party rights *acquired*.' As already mentioned, this also seems to be the majority position in case-law. Roca Sastre and Roca-Sastre Muncunill cite over twenty Supreme Court judgments taking this position.[54]

(4) *Good faith at the time of registration.* This position is led by Sanz Fernández, who argues that article 34 does not protect every derivative acquisition from a registered owner; it only protects acquisitions according to the Register, which require that the acquirer's title must be registered, there must be good faith, the transferor must have been registered before the acquisition and the acquisition must be derivative. When the registration entry in the transferor's favour is inaccurate but article 34 is used to remedy the inaccuracy and allow the *a non domino* acquisition to take effect, this happens only because the acquirer's title is registered. In that case, the time of acquisition is not the time when title is granted, but the time of registration. During the interval between the title date and the date of entry on the Register, the acquirer does not yet meet all the requirements for protection under article 34, because he has not yet registered his right. Therefore, during that time action can be taken against him, but as soon as he registers, the principle of conclusive title bars all action.[55]

Gómez Gómez is another supporter of this position. He accepts these two arguments and adds one further argument a fortiori: if the *a non domino* acquisition is a sort of immediate *usucapio*, and if in *usucapio* good faith needs to be held from the time when acquisition supposedly happens until the end of the required period of undisputed possession, why should good faith only at the beginning be enough for a registered *a non domino* acquisition? Why should good faith not have to last until end of the full period of time set by law for the acquisition to earn protection?[56]

[54] Roca Sastre, Roca-Sastre Muncunill and Berná i Xirgo (n 21) 294ff. This is also the position most widely embraced by scholars. Among them, Díez Picazo (n 23) 530 adds that this position follows from the underlying reason for protection under art 34, which is to provide conclusive title and security of transactions; and for that reason the matter crystallises at the point where the transaction or act of trade takes place. Other supporters include A De Cossío y Corral, *Instituciones de Derecho Hipotecario*, 2nd edn (Barcelona, Bosch Casa Editorial, 1965) 378; I De Casso Romero, *Derecho Hipotecario o del Registro de la Propiedad*, 4th edn (Madrid, Instituto de Derecho Civil, 1951) 378; L Martín-Ballesteros Hernández, 'La legitimación registral en la dinámica de las adquisiciones inmobiliarias a non domino' RCDI no 603, 1991, p 591; M González Enríquez, 'Momento en que es exigida la buena fe en la fe pública registral y otros problemas' ADC 1949, 1243.

[55] A Sanz Fernández, *Instituciones de Derecho Hipotecario*, I (Madrid, Reus, 1947) 466.

[56] M Gómez Gómez, 'Ámbito de aplicación del llamado principio de fe pública registral' RCDI, no 290–91, 1952, pp 571–72. Other supporters of this position include Clemente Meoro (n 50) 153;

These are the main positions and the arguments supporting them. In our view, the most appropriate is the position requiring good faith to last until registration. Although literally article 34 speaks of 'acquisition', and in the Spanish system of property transfer 'acquisition' occurs by title (*titulus*) and delivery (*modus*), article 34 is not referring to ordinary acquisition. It deals with *a non domino* acquisition by operation of law, where the acquisition is not completed until registration, because it is then that the principle of conclusive title comes into operation and bridges the defect in delivery. That is why good faith must be required right up to the very moment of registration.[57]

D. Acquisition for Value

Taking the requirements of article 34 in order, we now come to the fourth: that, in order to enjoy the protection of conclusive title, a third party acquiring a property right in good faith under civil law must also have acquired that right in return for value. What does it mean to acquire something 'for value'? Díez Picazo tells us that a title acquired for value – an 'onerous' title or a transaction with an 'onerous cause' – is 'that which has required the acquirer to provide some counter-performance, or sacrifice some asset or make some correlative allocation to the transferor'.[58]

This requirement that acquisition be onerous is also confirmed by the third paragraph of article 34, albeit in negative terms:

> Parties acquiring property or rights gratuitously shall not enjoy greater protection by registration than that to which their predecessor or transferor was entitled.

So, if the predecessor or transferor acquired the property rights for value, the gratuitous sub-acquirer is protected by the conclusive title. Therefore, it cannot be stated categorically that parties acquiring property rights gratuitously are left entirely without protection.

The requirement of Spanish law that acquisitions be onerous is unusual. None of our near European neighbours has exactly the same requirement.[59] What might the basis of the Spanish approach be? The words of the Preamble to the Mortgage Act are significant: 'It is preferable for a gratuitous recipient to cease to receive a

T Rubio Garrido, *La doble venta y doble disposición* (Barcelona, José María Bosch Editor, SA, 1994) 82; and Gordillo Cañas (n 23) 630ff.

[57] JP Murga Fernández, 'La doble venta judicial y el artículo 34 de la Ley Hipotecaria: recepción de la doctrina uniforme sentada en 2007' RCDI no 732, 2012, pp 2011–15.

[58] Díez Picazo (n 23) 531.

[59] In France, since the reform of 1953, the 'inopposibility' so characteristic of Latin-type systems (see above, text to n 13), and which underlies art 32 LH in Spain, is offered equally to all acquirers, regardless of whether their title is acquired for value or gratuitously. It is the same in Italy, with only a few exceptions. And the same may be said of Germany (§ 892 BGB) and Switzerland (art 973 ZGB), where the protective effect of genuine conclusive title by registration is extended to gratuitous and onerous acquisitions alike: Gordillo Cañas (n 22) 1083–84.

profit than for economic hardship to be inflicted upon others who, through legitimate acts of performance, can establish rights in the transferor's assets'. Or, as Gordillo Cañas puts it, the reason is that gratuitous acquisitions are foreign to the idea of the kind of transactions the land registration system is designed to protect.[60] Protection of acquisitions made gratuitously is not required in a system tailored to suit the needs of legal transactions.

E. The Transferor's Registered Ownership and Power of Disposition

Article 34 LH expressly states that, to receive the protection of registration, a third party who acquires a property right in good faith must do so 'from a person who appears in the Land Register as having the power to transfer it'. That is to say, the third party must have acquired the right from its registered owner. This requirement is a consequence of the registration system itself, first, because only the registered owner has the legal standing to dispose of registered rights,[61] and, secondly, because this is a vital corollary of the principle of chain of title stated in article 20 LH.[62]

The foundation of this requirement is the fact that protection can and should be given only to people who trust in the Registry's statements, in the presumption that the Register is accurate and in the legitimising force of a previous registration entry showing that the person registered as owner of a right can validly dispose of it, no matter what the real situation may be outside the Register.[63]

Various other issues concerning this requirement do exist, but we will only refer to the issue we consider most important: the time at which the entry registering the transferor's right must exist. Spanish legal scholars are basically of two views. The first is that the entry of the transferor's right must exist at the time when the third party to be protected concludes the contract with the transferor and

[60] Gordillo Cañas (n 22) 1084–85.

[61] See art 38 LH.

[62] Art 20 reads, 'To register or note instruments whereby ownership and other property rights are declared, transferred, encumbered, modified or extinguished, the right of the person effecting such acts or on whose behalf such acts are effected must already be registered or noted. In the case of rights entered under the name of persons other than the person effecting the transfer or encumbrance, the Registrars shall refuse the application for registration'. As correctly noted by García García (n 34) 457ff, 'The requirement of prior entry on the Register under art 34 must not be confused with the requirement of prior entry under art 20. Art 20 envisages a prior entry as a requirement before the next entry can be made. Art 34, however, envisages a prior entry as one of the requirements to trigger protection for a third party who acts on the basis of the registered owner's legal standing to dispose of the property'.

[63] Díez Picazo (n 23) 532. Similarly, Gordillo Cañas (n 22) 1068 asserts, 'what the principle of conclusive title purports to do is just to protect the trust the third party reposes in the Register when he allows himself to be guided by the information disclosed by the Register in pursuit of a secure, lawful acquisition'.

completes the acquisition transaction (this position is led by Roca Sastre).[64] The second holds that, in order for article 34 to confer its protection, the entry registering the transferor's right need not predate the third party's acquisition. If the entry is made before the third-party transferee submits his acquisition for registration, that is enough (this position is led by Sanz Fernández).[65] In our view, the first is undoubtedly the sounder thesis. The principle of conclusive title is based on the protection accorded to buyers and beneficiaries who in good faith trust in the appearance or legal picture painted by the Register. This would not work if there were no protected appearance in existence at the time when the third party enters into the contract. It is furthermore doubtful that good faith exists in the positive sense (belief that the registered holder of title is the owner of the thing and holds a sufficient power of disposition to transfer ownership of or create a property right over the thing), if, when the contract is made (which is the time up to which good faith must at least exist), the registry has no record of any ownership on which any belief at all can be based.

Finally, as a logical consequence of this requirement, the first person to apply to register an unregistered property can never be a protected third party. A protected third party by definition has to acquire his right from a person shown by the Register to have the power to transfer the right, and so, obviously, the first person to register a right can never qualify as a protected third party, because there is no previous entry of the right. However, a person acquiring a property right from the first registrant can benefit from the conclusive title provided by registration, as long as the two-year period set in article 207 LH has elapsed. Similarly, what we have said does not mean that the first registrant gains no protection whatsoever from registration. On the contrary, he is protected under article 32 LH, which establishes the typically Latin principle of 'inopposibility' – unenforceability of property rights that are registrable but not registered,[66] and so he cannot be subject to any right that is not recorded in the Land Register.[67]

[64] See Roca Sastre, Roca-Sastre Muncunill and Berná i Xirgo (n 21) 294–95: 'For the protection it establishes, art 34, paragraph 1, of the Mortgage Act requires the third party to acquire the registered property or right from its owner according to the Register. That means that, at the time of the acquisition by the third party, the owner must already be appear from the Register as the owner of the right'. Taking this same position, Gordillo Cañas (n 22) 1070–71 says: 'Nor can we share this (Sanz Fernández's) point of view … because it is in opposition to the reasoning behind the principle of conclusive title: prior registration is necessary inasmuch as it provides the necessary basis for the good faith that animates and qualifies the act of acquisition that the principle of conclusive title is going to protect'. Likewise, albeit rather more ambiguously, see Díez Picazo (n 23) 533.

[65] See Sanz Fernández (n 55) 430–31: 'The need for previous registration of the transferor should not be interpreted in the sense that the transferor of the right has to have already registered his right before the act or contract of conveyance is made, though that is what art 34 literally seems to require. It suffices for the disposing party to be the registered owner at the time when the act or contract is registered, so the chain of conveyances follows normally in compliance with art 20, and so the title giving the transferor his right can be traced back to a registered owner … Whether the previous entry is made before or after the act or contract therefore makes no difference. The entry just has to be made in the normal, conventional way'.

[66] See above, text to n 13.

[67] Díez Picazo (n 23) 533–34.

F. Title Registration

To obtain the protective healing effect of conclusive title through registration, it is not enough for a third party to fulfil the requirements stated so far. He must also register his new right. Article 34 LH expressly says so, affirming that the new right 'shall be upheld once entered in the Register'. The thesis is confirmed by, inter alia, article 36.1.b, which speaks of the 'registered acquirer',[68] referring to the third party in article 34.

The basis for this requirement is an entirely logical one. If the conclusive title gained through registration protects the trust a third party places in the appearance created by the information disclosed by the Register and makes the newly registered title prevail over all unregistered titles (even one purportedly acquired first), then the third party must necessarily continue trusting in the Register and consequently register his own new right. That is to say, trust in the appearance given by the Register is not full, is not complete, until the third party who wishes to benefit from that trust registers in turn his newly acquired right. Echoing the words of Roca Sastre, 'the demands of this requirement are logical; the system must protect acquisitions that embrace registration, not acquisitions that refuse it'.[69]

Once we know the reason behind this requirement for the operation of conclusive title, we naturally wonder what kind of controversy has arisen in its interpretation. Broadly, there are two issues: first, whether the *a non domino* acquisition that article 34 covers happens only as of registration of the acquired right, or whether it happens before the registration requirement is fulfilled, making registration an event subsequent to the actual acquisition; and second, how registration is characterised in this case: as declaratory (the ordinary value of registration in the Spanish system) or as exceptionally constitutive. We shall take up each issue briefly and give our opinion.

As for the first issue, as we have indicated, there are two major positions amongst Spanish legal scholars. The first, led by Roca Sastre and Vallet de Goytisolo, considers that the requirement of registering the newly acquired right

[68] See above, n 44.

[69] See Roca Sastre, Roca-Sastre Muncunill and Berná i Xirgo (n 21) 306, who continue, 'The advantages of the principle of conclusive title are so important, and the effort it signifies is so paramount, that of course its protection should not be wasted. It should instead hinge upon compliance with certain requirements, one of which is naturally that third parties who seek to preserve their acquisitions must accept the protection of the Register by having their acquisitions registered'. Similarly, see Gordillo Cañas (n 22) 1124–25: 'The registry is hardly going to offer its protection to a buyer who allows himself to be guided by the information the Register furnishes but is not interested in contributing to its accuracy by recording his own acquisition. Núñez Lagos was right to say the third party in art 34 LH is a twice-entered or "super-entered" third party: the entry before his, ie, his assignor's entry, generates it or conceives it; his own entry gives birth to it and nurtures it; he is a third party that only exists through and as of registration'. Likewise, Díez Picazo (n 23) 534 affirms, 'to obtain the protection of registration, it is not enough for the third party just to enter into his contract on the basis of trust in the Register. Once he has concluded his contract, he must keep trusting in registration as an institution and register his own acquisition'.

is the only requirement that can be fulfilled after the acquisition is finalised. In other words, that the *a non domino* acquisition happens before registration, and registration is therefore subsequent to the actual acquisition of the right in question. The second, led by Sanz Fernández and Núñez Lagos, holds that, on the contrary, *a non domino* acquisitions pursuant to article 34 do not effectively happen until the newly acquired right is registered.

Supporters of the first position say that their interpretation is more in tune with the literal wording of article 34 ('shall be upheld') and with the system of declaratory registration and acquisition through the mechanism of title and delivery (*titulus et modus*) adopted in Spain: acquisition takes place through grant of both title and delivery, which in this case is done instrumentally by means of executing the *escritura pública*. In short, registration of the acquisition is a simple legal condition for the maintenance of the acquisition, and its efficacy is retroactive to the moment of acquisition.[70]

Supporters of the second position say that, on the contrary, since article 34 does not protect just any acquisition but instead brings about an *a non domino* acquisition, whose effect occurs precisely at the registration of the newly acquired right, the time of acquisition in that case is not the time of execution of the *escritura pública*, but the time of registration.[71]

In our view, the position that best fits the system of protection under conclusive title through article 34 is the second. If article 34 covers anomalous acquisitions (and acquisition from a *non dominus* is decidedly anomalous) and cures the defect in the transferor's ownership (ownership being necessary to make the delivery valid, and delivery being in its turn a necessary ingredient for the derivative acquisition of property rights under the title-and-delivery system according to article 609 CC), then we cannot ignore the requirements set by article 34 for remedying the problem. In other words, the idea of invoking the requirements necessary to complete ordinary derivative acquisitions, and then asserting that the requirement of registration postdates the actual acquisition itself, is unconvincing.

[70] See Roca Sastre, Roca-Sastre Muncunill and Berná i Xirgo (n 21) 303–06:

> Unlike the other three requirements set by art 34, paragraph 1, for protection of the third party, this requirement can normally be fulfilled only after the acquisition has been made, except in the case of mortgages … Although conclusive title does not enter the picture until all four requirements are fulfilled, when registration occurs, conclusive title deploys its protective function with respect to the third party's acquisition, although it reaches back to the time when the act of acquisition took place. … In reality, we have to distinguish between the time of acquisition of ownership or of the property right and the start of the protection of registration under the mantle of conclusive title. The time of acquisition is referable to the time when the act of acquisition was performed, with the exception of cases of constitutive registration (mortgages, surface rights, acquisitions of immovable property by foreign citizens).

See similarly, Vallet de Goytisolo (n 43) 367–68. For an explanation of these arguments, see Gordillo Cañas (n 22) 1127ff.

[71] See Sanz Fernández (n 55) 466; R Núñez Lagos, 'Buena fe y fraude en el Registro de la propiedad' in *Revista General de Legislación y Jurisprudencia*, I, 1950, p 604; JL Lacruz Berdejo and F Sancho Rebullida, *Lecciones de Derecho Inmobiliario Registral* (Zaragoza, Artes Gráficas El Noticiero, 1957) 300; Gordillo Cañas (n 25) 1127–28.

The acquisitions addressed by article 34 are not ordinary acquisitions, but abnormal; acquisitions that need the curative effect of article 34. And that effect does not come about until the fulfilment of the last of the requirements expressly stated by the article, the requirement of subsequent registration of the right acquired by the third party. In conclusion, *a non domino* acquisitions pursuant to article 34 do not take place until each and every one of the requirements set by article 34 have been met, and those requirements include registration of the title. At that point, the acquisition takes effect, not before. True, article 34 itself uses the expression 'rights acquired … shall be upheld once entered', suggesting that acquisition has taken place before registration. Yet, the point of the article is to cure a defect and make an exception, so we ought to understand this expression to mean that 'the third party will truly acquire the right *a non domino* once he has registered his right'. Clearly, then, acquisition does not take place until the last requirement given by article 34 – registration of the newly acquired right – has been fulfilled.

The second of the controversial issues raised by the requirement of registration is whether in this case registration is declaratory or constitutive. This issue follows from the first, given the close relationship of the two. If we follow the trains of thought of the two fundamental positions with regard to the first issue, we might logically conclude that what we term the 'first position' (accepting acquisition prior to registration under article 34) would look on registration in this case as declaratory, just as registration ordinarily is under Spanish law;[72] whilst supporters of the 'second position' (*a non domino* acquisition does not take place until it is registered) would consider registration in this case to be constitutive, given that acquisition does not take place without registration.[73] This is, indeed, broadly the logic used. There are notable exceptions, however; certain authors who adhere to the second position think that registration is nevertheless still declaratory, not constitutive, because registration is still just as much a means of publicity as Spanish law normally holds it to be. Although registration is necessary for the acquisition to take effect, they say, registration still remains a necessary co-element of the normal mechanism for transferring property rights, and to argue otherwise is to lose one's focus on the technical concept of constitutive registration and confuse the effects of the principle of registration with the effects of the principle of conclusive title.[74]

In our view, however, the logic of these approaches suggests that registration under article 34 is constitutive, because registration is a decisive element without

[72] See RM Roca Sastre and L Roca-Sastre Muncunill, *Derecho Hipotecario* (Barcelona, Bosch, 1995) 216: 'We believe that it involves a deplorable confusion to take results that belong exclusively to the principle of conclusive title and apply them in a different context, that of constitutive registration in the strict sense, because the latter lies within the sphere of the principle of registration'.

[73] García García (n 34) 472; similarly, Peña Bernaldo de Quirós (n 35) 612.

[74] See Gordillo Cañas (n 22) 1129–30. When Gordillo Cañas refers to the principle of registration, he is underlining an essential characteristic of the Spanish registration system that contrasts with a transcription system. Instead of recording literally the contents of a registered instrument, the Registrar enters those portions that he has identified as having effect in rem and therefore qualifying for publicity.

which an *a non domino* acquisition cannot be 'constituted', ie, does not effectively happen. True, registration is still just an additional element that combines with the other elements we have already analysed to make for definitive acquisition. But the same also happens in mortgage registration. Registration in that case is said, with a certain unanimity amongst scholars and courts, to be constitutive, because without registration a mortgage does not even come into existence. Moreover, registration alone is not enough to bring a mortgage into existence;[75] a loan to be secured, an asset given as security, a necessarily registered property – all are necessary. In the same way, under article 34 a previously registered transferor, good faith and acquisition for value are all necessary in addition to registration, but without registration acquisition under article 34 does not take place. On the basis of this argument, we think that constitutive registration is the better position, precisely because without constitutive registration *a non domino* acquisition pursuant to article 34 does not come about.

G. Validity of the Title of a Protected Third Party

Finally, a third party acquiring a property right in good faith for value who subsequently registers his right in order to gain protection by way of conclusive title must also have acquired the property through a valid instrument or contract. This requirement is not expressly stated in article 34, but it follows from article 33, which reads, 'Registration does not validate instruments or contracts that are a nullity according to legislative enactments'. In other words, if the juristic instrument of acquisition is a nullity (and we shall look at what 'nullity' means presently), the protection of conclusive title ceases to take effect.

Why would such a rule be made? The words of Gómez de la Serna, echoed by Gordillo Cañas, are to the point: 'Registration does not cure instruments or contracts that are null, because the point of registration is not to lend force to instruments that have no force in themselves, but to publicise them so that people who were not party to them cannot be misled'.[76] That is to say, the efficacy of registration entries as a means of publicity operates separately from the validity of the instrument or contract being publicised, because that is the sole, exclusive role of the efficacy provided by the Spanish system of publicity by registration.

That said, the system for publicising land registration information is a unique, compound system, and the application of article 33 LH within that system has led to widely differing judgments, interpretations and problems.[77] This is not the place to dwell on each of these; it is sufficient to note the main problems, to the extent

[75] On the effects of unregistered mortgages and the controversial constitutive nature attributed by the majority to mortgages, see M Espejo Lerdo de Tejada, 'La hipoteca no inscrita y su valor jurídico: Comentario a la Sentencia núm. 368/2016 de 3 junio (RJ 2016, 2320)' RDP no 42, 2017, pp 287–308.

[76] Gordillo Cañas (n 22) 1100–01.

[77] Gordillo Cañas (n 22) 1098.

that each of them, as we shall see, has been a major source of misunderstandings in case-law (until the Spanish Supreme Court's leading case of 5 March 2007).[78]

There are primarily two problems. The first is, when article 33 speaks of instruments and contracts that are a nullity, is it referring only to the obligational element of acquisitions of immovables (the *titulus* for the transfer of ownership), or does it also extend to the act of delivery (the *modus*, or 'delivery' (*traditio*) element of the title-and-delivery system) which immediately produces the acquisition?[79] The second is, when article 33 refers to nullity, is it referring exclusively to total nullity, or does it also include all the different ways juristic acts can be ineffective or invalid (not just a total nullity, but also an instrument or contract which can be nullified)?

To settle the first of these debated issues requires a correct, systematic interpretation of articles 33 and 34 taken together. If we understand 'nullity' in article 33 as referring to both title and delivery, we severely curtail the sphere of application of article 34; whilst if, on the contrary, we understand 'nullity' to apply only to the title, the scope of operation of article 34 is much broader, because it includes also sales of things by a *non dominus* – a defect which is restricted to delivery, not title.[80] Indeed, if a contract of sale of a thing that does not belong to the transferor is held to be valid (since the power of disposition is a requirement pertaining to delivery, not title), then article 34 is applicable, because the very purpose of article 34 is to address such defects. Its application is not rendered invalid by article 33, because, we repeat, the title is fully valid. Therefore, we give the principle of conclusive title the curative value it truly has, and its correct relationship with article 33 LH.

Gordillo Cañas argues that nullity as referred to in article 33 cannot include the invalidity of instruments of acquisition due to defects in the title of the transferor, for two reasons. First, because the defect, as we have already made clear, does not affect the structural elements of the contract, as the title (*titulus*) for the transfer, and render it a nullity. Rather, the defect affects the legal basis for the effectiveness of the act of delivery or *traditio* (*modus*) that must follow the contract in order to complete the mechanism of acquisition. Second, because it is precisely that defect in ownership that conclusive title through registration seeks to remedy, in the interest of security of transactions entered into in good faith, if the third party meets the requirements in article 34.

In short, to apply article 33 to a case of *a non domino* acquisition by arguing that the acquisition is a nullity just adds confusion and ultimately undermines article 34, which is precisely the article that embodies the primary and most characteristic function of publicity by registration as providing security and protection.[81]

[78] STS 5 March 2007 (RJ 2007\723).

[79] Gordillo Cañas (n 22) 1107.

[80] See above, p 62 (Introduction to this Chapter).

[81] Gordillo Cañas (n 22) 1112–14. A majority of recent scholars agree that art 34 applies to *a non domino* acquisitions. Their understanding is that these are acquisitions whose defect concerns delivery, not title, and accordingly art 33 is applicable. See esp Díez Picazo (n 23) 535 ('scholars in general conclude that, in the situation envisaged by art 34, an *a non domino* acquisition is concluded in the

As for the controversy about the second issue (the scope of the term 'nullity'), we have to agree with the majority opinion that the term must be understood to include not only total nullity, but also every case in which a juridical act is rendered invalid. The main argument in favour of this is that all cases of ineffectiveness in transactions under Spanish law are regulated in Title II ('Contracts'), Chapter VI ('Nullity of Contracts') of the Civil Code.

III. The Fundamental Effect of Conclusive Title: Curing the Transferor's Lack of Power of Disposition and Establishing a True *A Non Domino* Acquisition

Article 34 LH provides that third-party rights 'shall be upheld once entered in the Register, even if thereafter the right of the transferor is annulled or cancelled for reasons not recorded in the Register'. Now that we have examined the principle of conclusive title, the requirements for its application and the main doubts about its interpretation, it can be concluded that the following situations are covered as a direct effect of conclusive title through registration.

(a) *A wholly a non domino acquisition by a protected third party*, when the inaccuracy in the Register consists in naming the wrong owner, either because the named person has never been an owner *(non dominus)* or because he used to be but is no longer at the time of the transfer *(ex dominus)*. This may occur in various situations.

First, the double sale of a property that is already registered. A sells the property to B, who takes possession of it. B thus becomes *verus dominus* – true owner – of the property, but he does not register his right. A therefore continues to be listed in the Register as the owner and takes advantage of this to sell the property again, this time to C. If C qualifies for conclusive title, C becomes the definitive, unassailable owner of the property. In this process a genuine *a non domino* acquisition is consolidated, in which the registration system makes up for the transferor's lack of power of disposition.

Second, the transferor is listed in the Register as the owner because a false or absolutely null title was registered, or because the registration authorities mistakenly entered the wrong name.

third party's favour. This conclusion seems correct, especially in those cases where the disponor or transferor is a *non dominus*'); De Pablo Contreras, Martínez de Aguirre Aldaz and Pérez Álvarez (n 28) 373–74 ('This substantial effectiveness of the land registration system, which structurally forms a case of *a non domino* acquisition, is known as conclusive title'); Espejo Lerdo de Tejada (n 35) 408 ('the problem that prevents the normal effectiveness of a transfer in these cases does not lie in the title, which is perfectly valid, but in the lack of power of disposition of the transferor, which means the delivery is not a true *traditio*. It is precisely that defect that the Register helps the purchaser overcome'); Lacruz Berdejo, Sancho Rebullida, Luna Serrano, Delgado Echeverría, Rivero Hernández and Rams Albesa (n 35) 408.

Third, the transferor is listed in the Register as the owner because he used to own the right but he lost it, either through some event like *usucapio contra tabulas*[82] or because his right was annulled, revoked or cancelled and the annulment, revocation or cancellation was never reported to the Registry.

(b) *Acquisition of a clean title from a transferor who holds a genuine but unstable or defective title, when the inaccuracy in the Register consists in not mentioning the instability or defect in the transferor's right.* Here too there is inaccuracy in registration, but this inaccuracy consists in defective publicity of the title, not absolute lack of title on the part of the person registered as the owner. A title that is in reality unstable or defective is portrayed to the public as stable or firm. A third party's protection in this case can be gauged in terms of his immunisation from the possibility of his own right being annulled or cancelled if the transferor's right collapses. Thus, the annulment or cancellation threatening the stability of the registered right for title-related reasons would not prevent that right from being acquired as a stable, firm right if the cause of the annulment or cancellation is not recorded in the Register; and an action for rescission, revocation or cancellation cannot be taken against a third party who has registered his own instruments of title in accordance with the Mortgage Act.[83]

(c) *Acquisition of an unencumbered title from an owner whose right is encumbered or restricted.* Let us suppose the registered owner, A, is the *verus dominus* – true owner – of a piece of land, but some unregistered, limited property right has been created over A's land. A sells the land to B, who acquires the land fully and definitively. Under the the principle of conclusive title, B acquires the land free of all charges and encumbrances, just as the Register describes it.

It should be stressed that the Spanish registration system follows a strong Germanic influence and establishes a new kind of acquisition *ex lege* – automatic, as a matter of law – that recognises and formally establishes the *a non domino* acquisition by a third party protected by conclusive title. This is in contrast to the mere 'inopposibility' – unenforceability – of unregistered property rights which would be the result more characteristic of Latin registration systems in general. The protective effect of conclusive title is not, then, gauged in terms of causing a subjective, personal, non-transferable protection against enforceability of rights, but as implementing the mechanism of an effective legal acquisition of property rights whose subject matter, once acquired, is therefore shielded from the possibility of being claimed by the previous owner and, as such, can be transferred to a third party. Proof of this is that even a person who acquires such a right gratuitously from a protected third party enjoys the same protection.[84] This *ex lege* acquisition takes place at the very moment of registration, since only at registration are the legal requirements satisfied for the change in the attribution of property rights.

[82] Art 36 LH; see above, n 44.
[83] Gordillo Cañas (n 22) 1133–73.
[84] Gordillo Cañas (n 22) 1157.

5

Contract and Conveyance: The Further Repercussions of Different Transfer Systems

BIRKE HÄCKER*

I. Introduction, or: On the Importance of Understanding Rules in Context

Legal rules and principles do not exist in isolation. They form part of a system. They are shaped by their legal environment and they, in turn, influence the environment around them. This is why context matters. However much we may try to compare individual rules in the abstract, they can only be fully understood and properly assessed as part of the broader system within which they operate.

Sometimes similar or similar-looking rules produce radically different outcomes on account of the national regime which flanks them. At other times, the practical outcomes produced by various systems evince a surprising resemblance, even though the applicable rules differ markedly from one another when looked at individually.

Comparative lawyers conventionally distinguish between the comparison of rules and the comparison of (actual or hypothetical) cases. Yet it has long been recognised that comparing either just specific rules or just the outcomes of concrete cases leaves part of the picture unaccounted for. A great deal of important and illuminating information lies in *how* precisely various rules within a given system interact to produce an outcome to a particular case, *whether* this interaction happens differently in another legal order, and *why* this leads to a similar or dissimilar outcome.

* I would like to thank John Cartwright, Olivier Deshayes, Geneviève Helleringer, Yves-Marie Laithier and Valentin Pinel le Dret for their comments and suggestions on a draft version of this chapter, particularly regarding the parts dealing with French law. All errors are my own.

It is unfortunate that traditional comparative law functionalism, which – though by no means uncontentious – is arguably still the dominant method and certainly a key benchmark with which any comparative project has to engage,[1] gives the impression of deliberately eschewing such contextual investigation. As espoused by Konrad Zweigert and Hein Kötz, whose seminal textbook is widely regarded as being at once *locus classicus* and authoritative restatement of the functional method,[2] functionalism requires the comparative researcher to adopt an external epistemic perspective rather than an insider's view of the different systems:

> [W]hen the process of comparison begins, each of the solutions [produced by national law] must be freed from the context of its own system and, before evaluation can take place, set in the context of all the solutions from the other jurisdictions under investigation. Here too we must follow the principle of functionality: the solutions we find in the different jurisdictions must be cut loose from their conceptual context and stripped of their national doctrinal overtones so that they may be seen purely in the light of their function, as an attempt to satisfy a particular legal need.[3]

This point is often underscored by the so-called 'black box' metaphor, according to which each legal system is an intricate piece of machinery into which, at one end, the functionalist feeds the 'social problem' under consideration and which spews out the 'solution' at the other end.[4] What goes on inside the 'black box' is either irrelevant or suppressed in the interest of ensuring maximum system neutrality and optimal comparability. Yet, as Kötz has acknowledged, finding 'solutions' as such is often less interesting than exploring the mechanisms by which they are produced.[5]

It is time we comparative lawyers uncloaked the 'black box' and allowed ourselves an inside view of different legal systems.[6] A glimpse is not enough. Only a detailed examination of the machinery operating within each of them, its complex system of rules and structures, can teach us to become good legal

[1] As has been aptly remarked by R Michaels, 'The Functional Method of Comparative Law' in M Reimann and R Zimmermann (eds), *The Oxford Handbook of Comparative Law*, 2nd edn (Oxford, Oxford University Press, 2019) 345, 346: 'The functional method has become both the mantra and the *bête noire* of comparative law. For its proponents it is the most, perhaps the only, fruitful method. For its opponents it represents everything bad about mainstream comparative law. The debate over the functional method is indeed much more than a methodological dispute. It is the focal point of almost all discussions about the field of comparative law as a whole …' (footnote omitted).

[2] K Zweigert and H Kötz, *An Introduction to Comparative Law*, 3rd edn (trans T Weir, Oxford, Oxford University Press, 1998) esp 32–47. An essentially functionalist approach to comparative law had already been advocated during the first part of the twentieth century by the likes of Ernst Rabel and Max Rheinstein.

[3] ibid 44.

[4] H Kötz, 'Abschied von der Rechtskreislehre?' [1998] ZEuP 493, 505.

[5] ibid.

[6] See already B Häcker, *Consequences of Impaired Consent Transfers* (Tübingen, Mohr Siebeck, 2009, and Oxford, Hart Publishing, 2013) 5–9.

mechanics and engineers. But we have to be modest in this endeavour, so as not to overextend ourselves. Limiting the number of systems covered is one precaution; using a particular rule as a focal point of the inquiry is another.

This contribution serves an avowedly didactic purpose.[7] It seeks to exemplify the contextual comparative analysis of legal rules and structures by reference to various different property transfer regimes.[8] More specifically, it undertakes to expose some of the repercussions that operating either a 'causal' or an 'abstract' property transfer system has for other parts of the national legal order. At the heart of the present inquiry therefore lies the relationship between 'contract' and 'conveyance'. To make the inquiry manageable, the term 'conveyance' is used to denote the transfer of full 'ownership' (in the civilian sense) or 'title' (in the common law sense of the word),[9] to the exclusion of lesser proprietary interests.[10] The main, but not exclusive, focus will lie on the transfer of movables in the form of – or pursuant to – a sale of specific goods. English, French and German law are to serve as the core legal orders being compared, though reference to other systems will occasionally be helpful to illustrate particular points.

After providing a brief overview of the different types of property transfer regimes (II),[11] the chapter will explore their implications for the passing of risk (III), the nature of the buyer's claim against the seller (IV), the parties' mutual protection against each other's insolvency (V), the interaction of 'causal' and 'abstract' property transfer regimes with the respective rules on rescission of contract (VI), the resulting size and structure of the law of unjust or unjustified enrichment (VII), and the scope of the so-called bona fide purchase rules governing the acquisition of property from a non-owner (VIII).

[7] As far as possible, the literature cited in footnotes is therefore in English.

[8] This is a field on which less comparative work has been done to date than in the areas of contract and tort law, presumably because legal systems here diverge more strongly and at a more fundamental level than in the law of obligations. However, over the past 20 years or so, property law has gradually started to capture the imagination of comparatists and now receives a good deal of attention. For some ambitious and significant recent work on the subject, see esp W Faber and B Lurger (eds), *National Reports on the Transfer of Movables in Europe*, vols 1–6 (Munich, Sellier, 2008); B Lurger and W Faber, *Acquisition and Loss of Ownership of Goods* (Munich, Sellier, 2011); M Graziadei and L Smith (eds), *Comparative Property Law: Global Perspectives* (Cheltenham, Edward Elgar, 2017). In German: C von Bar, *Gemeineuropäisches Sachenrecht*, vol 1 (München, CH Beck, 2015), vol 2 (München, CH Beck, 2019).

[9] For present purposes, 'ownership' can be equated with 'best possible title' and will be so equated unless otherwise specified. Another layer of complexity is added by the fact that common law systems tend to deal in relative 'titles' (being permanent rights to exclusive possession) of varying strengths, which may be acquired by the mere fact of possession, rather than employing an absolute notion of unique and indivisible 'ownership'. In so far as is possible, this aspect of the comparison will here be left to one side.

[10] Nor will this chapter deal with the transfer of other 'assets', such as the assignment of personal claims or IP rights.

[11] The term 'property transfer' is tricky, but not entirely avoidable. The word 'property' has a tendency to take on different meanings, especially so when looking at different systems. These meanings range from (physical?) things or assets to (particular kinds of?) *erga omnes* rights in respect of such things or assets.

II. Outline of the Different Property Transfer Regimes

A. Two or Three Basic Questions

The analysis of the way in which 'contract' and 'conveyance' interrelate in different legal orders can be broken down into two core questions.

Firstly, is the contract which creates one party's obligation to transfer property to another itself the vehicle which ultimately makes property pass, or is a (notionally) separate transaction required to effect the conveyance? In other words, is it the contractual consent of the parties which also brings about the transfer of property, such that both aspects are indivisibly rolled up into one, or are the two conceptually distinct, so that contract and conveyance are referable to different legal commitments? This is the question about the existence of a 'principle of separation'.[12] In our core example, it effectively asks whether or not the contract of sale concluded between the seller and the buyer of goods is alone enough to strip the seller of his[13] property rights and to make the buyer into their new owner (either immediately or after certain conditions have been fulfilled).[14] A system which envisages this can be described as 'unitary'.[15]

Secondly, *if* contract and conveyance are separate transactions, then does the validity of the latter depend on the validity of the former or is it to be assessed by entirely independent criteria? This second question determines whether a

[12] For a general discussion and assessment, see Lurger and Faber, *Acquisition and Loss of Ownership* (n 8) 444–52.

[13] In this chapter, all protagonists will be referred to in the masculine form, because this is how the relevant Codes are drafted and for ease of translation. The masculine should be understood in the generic sense and therefore as including the feminine (and any other) form.

[14] On this transaction- rather than time-centred understanding of the term 'separation', the fact that the full conveyancing effect of a transaction may depend on some additional element (eg, payment of the purchase price under a retention of ownership/title clause), thus causing a potential delay between the conclusion of the contract and the conveyance actually occurring, does *not in and of itself* mean that a system operates a principle of separation.

[15] The use of terminology in this chapter deliberately departs from that employed by the Draft Common Frame of Reference and some academic writers: cf C von Bar and E Clive (eds), *Principles, Definitions and Model Rules of European Private Law: Draft Common Frame of Reference (DCFR)*, Full Edition (Munich, Sellier, 2009) vol 5, 4379–80; Lurger and Faber, *Acquisition and Loss of Ownership* (n 8) 456–57 (paras [92]–[93]); L van Vliet, 'Transfer of Property inter vivos' in Graziadei and Smith (eds), *Comparative Property Law: Global Perspectives* (n 8) 150, 151. These authors speak of a 'unitary' approach where a system treats the passing of property as a question to be answered in an abstract, single step, with all the attendant consequences and repercussions in various parts of the law. They contrast the 'unitary' approach in this sense (which is very widespread and otherwise also known as the 'substantialist' approach) with the so-called 'functional' approach followed by Nordic legal systems. The latter answer every conflict-of-interest situation separately. For Nordic lawyers, the question when 'property' as such passes is therefore not central, and indeed meaningless: see J Sandstedt, 'Comparative Property Law and the Profound Differences between Nordic Functionalism and Continental Substantialism – The (Ir)Relevance of Ownership' in AH Persson and E Kristoffersson (eds), *Swedish Perspectives on Private Law Europeanisation* (Oxford, Hart Publishing, 2017) 53; M Lilja, 'National Report on the Transfer of Movables in Sweden' in Faber and Lurger, *National Reports on the Transfer of Movables in Europe* (n 8) vol 5, 1, 13–27; Jan-Ove Færstad, 'National Report on the Transfer of Movables in Norway and Denmark' in Faber and Lurger (ibid) 205, 214–22.

particular transfer system is described as 'causal' or 'abstract'.[16] In a causal system, the buyer (or would-be buyer) of goods cannot acquire ownership unless a valid contract of sale underlies and justifies the transfer. The contract functions as the indispensable legal basis or essential *cause* for the conveyance. In an abstract system, the lack of a legal basis may mean that the conveyance will subsequently have to be reversed, but the fundamental validity of the conveyance is unaffected by the absence of an underlying contractual obligation to bring it about.

As will be seen, abstraction presupposes separation. If a legal system is unitary and does not distinguish between contract and conveyance, it cannot treat the latter as valid where the former is invalid. On the other hand, it is perfectly possible to have separation without abstraction. Where contract and conveyance are distinct transactions, the effectiveness of the property transfer *can*, but *need not*, be made to depend on the existence of a valid legal basis. Which route a given legal order goes down will, however, have significant consequences and follow-on repercussions further down the line.

It is useful to add to these two key questions a third criterion which, though to some extent cutting across the basic scheme, will help us visualise it. It is a phenotypic inquiry: does the transfer of ownership or title in a given legal system occur by the parties' agreement and consent alone (*solo consensu*), or is something more required to perfect it, especially some outward manifestation of the property transfer such as a delivery of the goods sold by the seller to the buyer (*traditio*)?[17] As a rule of thumb, purely consensual transfer systems will typically[18] be unitary and causal, while those insisting on some additional act or element of publicity will often[19] operate a principle of separation; yet no reliable prediction is possible on whether the latter are likely to be causal or might not also accommodate the principle of abstraction.

B. France: A Pure Causal Consensual System

Of the three major legal orders considered here, France represents the clearest example of a unitary system at the causal consensual end of the spectrum.[20] Ownership passes by virtue of the very contract that envisages the transfer being made.

Article 711 of the French Code civil provides that ownership 'is acquired and transmitted by succession, by *inter vivos* or testamentary gift, *and by the effect*

[16] For a brief general discussion, see Lurger and Faber, *Acquisition and Loss of Ownership* (n 8) 452–55 (paras [82]–[89]).

[17] For a detailed discussion and assessment of the various options, see ibid 411–44 (paras [11]–[69]).

[18] But not necessarily! They could conceivably also incorporate an element of separation, as has been suggested for the English law governing the sale of goods: see text to n 69 below.

[19] Again, not necessarily: see comment in n 14 above.

[20] It is worth noting that the French commitment to a purely consensual transfer system was not nearly as strong at the inception of the Code civil as it is today. For a historical comparison of French law with Prussian, Austrian and Spanish law at the time, see F Danos, 'Étude sur les différents systèmes de transfert de la propriété: les exemples du Code prussien de 1794, du Code civil autrichien de 1811 et du Code civil espagnol de 1889' (2013) 91 *Revue historique de droit français et étranger* 659.

of obligations'.[21] For typical contracts of sale, this is fleshed out in article 1583,[22] which holds that a sale is 'complete as between the parties, and ownership is acquired … by the buyer with respect to the seller, as soon as the thing and the price have been agreed upon, although the thing has not yet been delivered nor the price been paid'.[23] It is possible for the parties to postpone the conveyancing effect of the obligatory contract by agreeing, for instance, a retention of title clause which delays the transfer of property until payment has been made in full.[24] Yet such a postponement merely inserts a suspensive condition into the contract (as regards its proprietary effect);[25] it does not distract from the purely consensual and causal nature of the transfer mechanism.[26]

Nevertheless, the reform of the French law of obligations in 2016 has brought about a slight shift in the way the transfer of property is conceptualised and thus shores up the commitment of French law to its purely consensual transfer system.[27] Drawing on the former distinction between obligations 'to give', 'to do' or 'not to do' something,[28] the old article 1136 Cc maintained that 'an obligation to give comprises an obligation to deliver the thing …',[29] with old article 1138 Cc specifying that '[t]he obligation to deliver the thing is performed [literally: 'perfected'] by the sole consent of the contracting parties' and that '[i]t makes the creditor the owner of the thing' without more.[30] The conveyance therefore used to be thought of as the result of a self-executing obligation to give. The relevant *traditio* was, it has been suggested, an intellectual rather than a physical act.[31]

[21] Art 711 Cc: 'La propriété des biens s'acquiert et se transmet par succession, par donation entre vifs ou testamentaire, *et par l'effet des obligations*' (emphasis added).

[22] The principle is not expressly repeated for most other types of contract, but it applies across the board. For gifts (*donations*), art 938 Cc contains a provision similar to art 1583 Cc: see below, comment at the end of n 31.

[23] Art 1583 Cc: 'Elle [la vente] est parfaite entre les parties, et la propriété est acquise de droit à l'acheteur à l'égard du vendeur, dès qu'on est convenu de la chose et du prix, quoique la chose n'ait pas encore été livrée ni le prix payé'.

[24] See art 2367 Cc. Such a clause has to be in writing (art 2368 Cc), which is primarily relevant for its third-party effect. For further discussion, see below, nn 149–51 and text thereto.

[25] There is some debate in France about the nature of a retention of title clause (*clause de réserve de propriété*) and the exact legal mechanism by which it operates, but the present reading most closely aligns with the wording of art 2367 Cc.

[26] See the comment in n 14 and text thereto.

[27] See esp G Helleringer, 'The Proprietary Effects of Contracts' in J Cartwright and S Whittaker (eds), *The Code Napoléon Rewritten: French Contract Law after the 2016 Reforms* (Oxford, Hart Publishing, 2017) 207, 208–09, 210–11. For the reform of French contract law in 2016/2018 generally, see also the references provided by Kwiatkowski, below, Ch 8, nn 1, 2.

[28] Old art 1101 Cc. Note that the obligation 'to give' was understood not (merely) as an obligation to deliver an object, but by definition implied an obligation to transfer ownership to the other party.

[29] Old art 1136 Cc: 'L'obligation de donner emporte celle de livrer la chose et de la conserver jusqu'à la livraison, à peine de dommages et intérêts envers le créancier'.

[30] Old art 1138 Cc:

> L'obligation de livrer la chose est parfaite par le seul consentement des parties contractantes.
>
> Elle rend le créancier propriétaire et met la chose à ses risques dès l'instant où elle a dû être livrée, encore que la tradition n'en ait point été faite, à moins que le débiteur ne soit en demeure de la livrer; auquel cas la chose reste aux risques de ce dernier.

[31] E Cashin Ritaine, 'National Report on the Transfer of Movables in France' in Faber and Lurger, *National Reports on the Transfer of Movables in Europe* (n 8) vol 4, 1, 75; P Chauviré, *L'acquisition*

The reformed French Code now establishes a more immediate link between contract and conveyance. In the section dealing with 'the effects of contracts between the parties', under the heading 'proprietary effect', new article 1196 Cc provides that '[a]s regards contracts whose object is to alienate property or the assignment of some other right, transfer takes place at the time of the conclusion of the contract', adding that '[t]his transfer may be deferred by the will of the parties, by the nature of the things in question or by the effect of legislation'.[32]

It remains to be flagged that although ownership therefore passes from one party to another by virtue of the obligatory contract and *solo consensu* (effectively *solo contractu*) under the French system, the physical delivery (transfer of actual possession or 'detention') in the case of movables, or the official registration of the transfer in the case of immovables, does play a role when it comes to asserting the resulting change of ownership via-à-vis third parties acting in good faith.[33] This so-called 'opposability' (*opposabilité*)[34] is closely connected with the rules on bona fide purchase which will be considered further below.[35]

C. Germany: A Fully-Fledged Principle of Abstraction

In sharp contrast with the pure causal consensual system of French law, German law is the epitome of a wholly abstract transfer system.[36] The conveyance is separate from the contract and in no way depends upon the obligation for its validity.

dérivée de la propriété: le transfert volontaire des biens (Issy-les-Moulineaux, LGDJ, 2013), emphasing – for the pre-2016 law – the centrality of the 'obligation to give'; F Danos, 'Obligation de donner, de livrer et de délivrer', in *Mélanges en l'honneur du Professeur Laurent Aynès. Liberté, justesse, autorité* (Issy-les-Moulineaux, LGDJ, 2019) 143. With respect to inter vivos gifts, note that art 938 Cc (still) speaks of ownership being transferred by a 'duly accepted' donation, 'without the need for any other [!] *traditio*'.

[32] New art 1196 Cc:

> Dans les contrats ayant pour objet l'aliénation de la propriété ou la cession d'un autre droit, le transfert s'opère lors de la conclusion du contrat.
>
> Ce transfert peut être différé par la volonté des parties, la nature des choses ou par l'effet de la loi.
>
> Le transfert de propriété emporte transfert des risques de la chose. Toutefois le débiteur de l'obligation de délivrer en retrouve la charge à compter de sa mise en demeure, conformément à l'article 1344-2 et sous réserve des règles prévues à l'article 1351-1.

[33] Cashin Ritaine (n 31) 77. Under the original Code civil of 1804, the provision governing 'opposability' of contracts was the former art 1165. A problem with applying the provision to conveyances was that, unlike contractual obligations with their relative effects, French law regards ownership as 'absolute', ie, as having *erga omnes* effect. The basic principle governing the effects of a contract on third parties has now been reformulated: cf arts 1199–1200 of the Code civil as reformed in 2016.

[34] Besides the 'validity' (*validité*) of a transaction, its 'opposability' (*opposabilité*) is a central concept of French private law, particularly of property law. Its exact meaning is, however, very hard to extract from the case law and literature. For an in-depth discussion of 'opposability', when juxtaposed to 'ownership' and 'possession', see F Danos, *Propriété, possession et opposabilité* (Paris, Economica, 2007).

[35] See the text to nn 246–47 below.

[36] Some scholars identify the French system with the Hegelian and the German system with the Kantian tradition, eg, S Sérafin, 'Transfer by Contract in Kant, Hegel, and Comparative Law' (2018) 31 Can J Law & Juris 151. For an in-depth comparison of the French and German transfer systems, see J Dubarry, *Le transfert conventionnel de propriété. Essai sur le mécanisme translatif à la lumière des droits français et allemand* (Issy-les-Moulineaux, LGDJ, 2014).

The sophisticated conceptual apparatus behind 'abstraction' lies in the painstaking dissection and analysis of Roman sources undertaken by proponents of the nineteenth-century Historical School of Jurisprudence and is usually attributed to its founder, Friedrich Carl von Savigny.[37] He developed the idea that every *traditio* (the dominant Roman method of conveyance) involved – in addition to the mere physical transfer of possession – an agreement between the parties to the effect that property was to pass. On Savigny's understanding, which has since found its way into the German Civil Code (*Bürgerliches Gesetzbuch*: 'BGB'), this agreement is of a truly contractual nature. It is concerned not with the creation or modification of obligations, ie, rights *in personam*, but is aimed solely at the transfer of rights *in rem*, particularly ownership. It is thus a 'real' (as opposed to an obligatory) contract. Being a distinct contract, its validity has to be determined separately from that of the underlying obligatory contract, by reference only to the general criteria for contractual validity. If the parties' matching declarations of intention to pass property are a genuine expression of their free will, then the conveyance is unaffected by any misapprehension impairing the obligatory contract and even by the complete lack of a recognised legal basis for the transfer (*iusta causa traditionis*). The latter concern mere (irrelevant) 'motives'. It has been said that the notion of a separate 'real agreement'[38] and the ensuing principle of abstraction are ultimately 'no more than the product of precise thinking'.[39]

In German law, the conveyance of both movables and immovables involves such a 'real agreement' and has to be coupled with an element of 'publicity': a physical delivery (or some recognised substitute)[40] in the case of movables or, in the case of immovables, registration of the proprietary interest to be acquired.[41] This element of 'publicity' is constitutive, not merely indicative of the transfer. Where a person has agreed to sell goods to another, the conveyance is normally effected in accordance with the general rule for movables contained in § 929, 1st sentence, BGB:[42]

> The transfer of ownership of a movable thing requires that the owner deliver the thing to the purchaser [ie, the physical delivery] and that both parties are agreed that ownership shall pass [ie, the real agreement].

[37] See esp FC von Savigny, *System des heutigen römischen Rechts*, vol 3 (Berlin, Veit & Co, 1840) esp 312–13, 354–58. It has been argued that Savigny's thinking on the matter was strongly influenced by Gustav Hugo: HH Jakobs, 'Gibt es den dinglichen Vertrag?' (2002) 119 ZRG (RA) 269, 280–94.

[38] In view of the fact that many legal systems do not share German law's broad conception of 'contract' (*Vertrag*) as any legal transaction (*Rechtsgeschäft*) effected by the mutual expression of consent of two or more parties, and instead associate the term 'contract' (or the translated national equivalent) with the creation or modification of *obligations*, the present contribution will speak of a 'real agreement' instead of a 'real contract', even when referring to German law.

[39] Jakobs (n 37) 300: 'nichts als das Produkt genauen Denkens'.

[40] §§ 929–931 BGB. In all these cases, possession (*Eigenbesitz*) passes to the transferee.

[41] §§ 873, 925 BGB.

[42] § 929 BGB: 'Zur Übertragung des Eigentums an einer beweglichen Sache ist erforderlich, dass der Eigentümer die Sache dem Erwerber übergibt und beide darüber einig sind, dass das Eigentum übergehen soll. Ist der Erwerber im Besitz der Sache, so genügt die Einigung über den Übergang des Eigentums'.

The notional separateness of contract and conveyance is not called into question by the fact that the obligatory contract of sale and the real agreement may be concluded at exactly the same time and that most people will typically not even realise that they are entering into a distinct real agreement for every single item to be disposed of.[43]

It is worth mentioning that it is possible for the parties to 'circumvent' the principle of abstraction if they wish, namely by making their real agreement expressly conditional on the existence and validity of the underlying obligatory contract.[44] This is an aspect of their contractual autonomy. However, German law will not lightly infer or imply such a condition so as not unduly to undermine abstraction and its effects.[45]

D. Austria: An Example of Separation without Abstraction

At this point, we should throw a side-glance at Austrian law, being a system that evinces a principle of separation without abstraction.[46] This half-way house position is also the product of an evolution in legal thinking.

Unlike the German BGB, which was only enacted in 1896 and came into force on 1 January 1900, the Austrian Civil Code of 1811 (*Allgemeines Bürgerliches Gesetzbuch*: 'ABGB') is premised on the then-contemporary understanding of the Roman transfer system.[47] § 380 ABGB requires both *titulus* and *modus* to effect a conveyance: 'It is impossible to obtain ownership without a title and a recognised mode of acquisition'.[48] The word 'title' here refers to a valid legal ground of acquisition, a *iusta causa traditionis*, such as a contract of sale.[49] The *modus* was originally conceived of as a purely factual act publicly attesting to the change of ownership,[50] namely physical delivery (*traditio*) in the case of movables (registration in the case of immovables followed only later).[51] However, under the influence of

[43] Every physical object ('thing') requires a separate real agreement, be it the individual goods bought or the notes and coins which the buyer uses to pay the seller.

[44] See § 158 BGB.

[45] Further references in Häcker (n 6) 61.

[46] There are a number of other such systems, including Swiss law (see text to nn 102–03) and Dutch law.

[47] The idea that every property transfer had to be supported by a *titulus* and *modus acquirendi* was a product of the period during the seventeenth and eighteenth centuries known as *usus modernus pandectarum*.

[48] § 380 ABGB: 'Ohne Titel und ohne rechtliche Erwerbungsart kann kein Eigenthum erlangt werden'.

[49] See § 424 ABGB. There is a question over quite how far the notion of 'title' extends, but this plays no role for present purposes. For a discussion, see H Koziol, R Welser and A Kletečka, *Grundriss des bürgerlichen Rechts*, 14th edn (Wien, Manz, 2014) vol 1, 339–40 (paras [955]–[956]).

[50] Ibid 340 (para [957]).

[51] See §§ 425–433 ABGB. § 425 ABGB expressly states that '[t]he mere title alone does not confer ownership' and decrees that, statutory exceptions apart, ownership and other property rights 'can only be acquired by legal delivery and receipt' ('Der bloße Titel gibt noch kein Eigenthum. Das Eigenthum und alle dingliche Rechte überhaupt können, außer den in dem Gesetze bestimmten Fällen, nur durch die rechtliche Uebergabe und Uebernahme erworben werden').

nineteenth-century German doctrine, Austrian lawyers came to regard the *modus* element as including a 'real agreement' distinct from the underlying contract. The obligatory contract and the ensuing conveyance were thus seen as notionally different legal transactions.

There is today little doubt that Austrian law accommodates a principle of separation of sorts, even though scholars and judges are deeply divided over whether the 'real agreement' is concluded at the same time as the underlying contract or at the (potentially later) time when delivery actually occurs.[52] Yet given that the Austrian Civil Code cannot dispense with a *iusta causa traditionis* in view of its expressly stipulated *titulus* requirement,[53] the conveyance is indisputably not 'abstract' in the German sense. Its validity instead depends on the validity of the underlying obligatory contract. In short, Austria has separation without abstraction. It operates a 'causal tradition system'.[54]

E. England: A Muddle?

English law is by far the hardest to place on the comparative map of property transfer systems. This is the result of a rather convoluted evolution of property law, with different forms of action historically shaping the law of 'real' and 'personal' property (a distinction which, for present purposes, roughly equates to that between immovables and movables) and with jurisdiction being more or less harmoniously shared for centuries between the ordinary 'common law' courts and the 'equitable' Court of Chancery. Although 'law' and 'equity' are nowadays dispensed by the same judges, the 'common law' and 'equitable' rules remain conceptually distinct.[55]

To facilitate the comparative discussion, we will have to concentrate primarily on the common law side of the matter, looking at equity only where, when and as far as this is necessary to avoid distortions of the picture. The first thing to note is that English law's answer to the three questions outlined above depends very much on the type of transaction under consideration and its subject matter.

As far as real property is concerned, it is clear that a contract for the sale of land, for instance, needs to be followed by a separate act of conveyance (consisting of the execution of a deed and a registration of the conveyance)[56] if the relevant estate is to become fully vested in the buyer. The obligatory contract as such has no

[52] For a brief discussion, see Koziol, Welser and Kletečka (n 49) vol 1, 355–57 (esp para [1010]); W Faber, 'National Report on the Transfer of Movables in Austria' in Faber and Lurger, *National Reports on the Transfer of Movables in Europe* (n 8) vol 1, 1, 81–86. But cf K Spielbüchler, *Der Dritte im Schuldverhältnis* (Wien and New York, Springer, 1973) 101–15; C Holzner, 'Dinglicher Vertrag im ABGB?' [2010] *Juristische Blätter* 674.

[53] See text to nn 48–49.

[54] Faber (n 52) 59–61, also pointing out (at 80) that, in the case of registered ships, transfers would exceptionally appear to be abstract.

[55] The Judicature Acts 1873–75 led to a procedural, not substantive, fusion of 'law' and 'equity'.

[56] LPA 1925, s 52 and LRA 2002, s 27.

proprietary effect at common law.[57] Once the formal conveyance has taken place, it alone sustains the transfer, regardless of the validity or fate of the underlying obligation. At common law, therefore, the conveyance is wholly abstract, whatever its legal basis.[58]

When we start looking at personal, movable property, the picture becomes much more complicated. For a start, many textbooks and other discussions make it appear as though all property transfers were either the result of a sale or a gift. Gift transactions, of course, are not classified as 'contractual' in a system which places the so-called doctrine of consideration at the very heart of contract law.[59] Only 'bargains' count as contracts under English law.

Inter vivos gifts of personalty can be either be made manually (from 'hand to hand'), by physical delivery of the relevant chattel to the donee, or by the donor executing a deed in the donee's favour.[60] In the first case, there is a big – and as yet unresolved – question over whether the 'gift' is anything more than a mere conveyance which is perfectly free and voluntary and therefore cannot later be impugned by the 'donor'.[61] In other words, it is hard to say whether or not any further underlying *cause* or *causa* is present or required, and what exactly its absence entails. Judging by the case law, the conveyance would at any rate *not* be treated as automatically 'void', even if it lacked a (further) legal basis. In the case of gifts by deed, English lawyers distinguish (though often not clearly enough) between deeds used to make a gratuitous promise enforceable and those that bring the gift about by effecting an actual transfer of property.[62] We might call the former 'obligatory' and the latter 'dispositive' deeds. Dispositive deeds used to make a gift raise much the same questions as gifts by hand. If there is a problem short of outright forgery, they are at most 'voidable'.[63] Where a 'gift' is made by obligatory deed, no property passes. Instead, the resulting obligation will have to be performed by a subsequent, separate transfer. This can be achieved either through a delivery or through the execution of another (now dispositive) deed. In neither case is the conveyance regarded as ineffective at common law merely because the underlying obligatory deed was non-existent or void.

We can learn from this that delivery and (dispositive) deeds are general conveyancing mechanisms in the realm of personalty, and that they are most likely

[57] On its effect in equity under the so-called doctrine in *Walsh v Lonsdale*, see below, n 138 and the accompanying text.

[58] On the position in equity, see below, in the text accompanying and following n 229.

[59] According to the common law doctrine of consideration, a contract is only valid (others would say: contractual claims are only enforceable) if each party to the contract has provided something of value in exchange for the other party's promise or performance. In a purely executory contract, each party's promise constitutes the consideration for the other party's counter-promise.

[60] For the formalities involved in a deed, see LP(MP)A 1989, s 1.

[61] See B Häcker, 'Mistaken Gifts after *Pitt v Holt*' (2014) 67 CLP 333, esp 340–45, 351–53.

[62] On gifts by deed, see ibid 369–71.

[63] The so-called doctrine of *non est factum* ('this is not my deed'), which allowed illiterate or disabled people to argue that they did not realise what they were doing is today only of marginal relevance.

'abstract' at common law.[64] They are, in fact, of considerable age and venerability – significantly older than the third vehicle of conveyance, on which the comparative discourse tends to focus, namely 'sale'. Everything is different in 'sale'. Under section 2 of the Sale of Goods Act 1979, an 'agreement to sell' becomes a 'sale' when the relevant transfer of property from seller to buyer takes place, and this happens *solo consensu*.

The modern rules governing contract and conveyance in 'contracts of sale'[65] originally developed sometime between the thirteenth and the fifteenth centuries.[66] They were first cast into statutory form by the Sale of Goods Act 1893, as part of the mini-wave of codification (or rather the wave of mini-codifications!) that swept through England during the latter part of the nineteenth century.[67] Under the heading 'Effects of the Contract – Transfer of property as between seller and buyer', what is now section 17 of the Sale of Goods Act 1979 provides:

> (1) Where there is a contract for the sale of specific or ascertained goods the property in them is transferred to the buyer at such time as the parties to the contract intend it to be transferred.
> (2) For the purpose of ascertaining the intention of the parties regard shall be had to the terms of the contract, the conduct of the parties and the circumstances of the case.

Title to the goods being sold therefore passes by consent alone as and when the parties want it to pass. In view of the fact that they will often not reach express agreement on the matter, section 18 provides a series of default rules for ascertaining intention, of which rule 1 is the most significant in the present context:

> Where there is an unconditional contract for the sale of specific goods in a deliverable state the property in the goods passes to the buyer when the contract is made, and it is immaterial whether the time of payment or the time of delivery, or both, be postponed.

Prima facie, the English sale of goods regime looks very similar to that expressed in article 1583 of the French Code civil.[68] However, while the conveyance by 'sale' is undoubtedly purely consensual under English law, it is by no means entirely

[64] Many issues are hardly discussed. For instance, although a conveyance by delivery must involve some sort of a 'real agreement' (see Häcker (n 6) 193) most English authors do not advert to it. For a commendable exception, see W Swadling, 'Property: General Principles', ch 4 in A Burrows (ed), *English Private Law*, 3rd edn (Oxford, Oxford University Press, 2013) 285–86 (paras [4.459]–[4.462]). As far as conveyances by deed are concerned, it appears that only the transferor's consent is required to effect the transfer of title, with the transferee subsequently having the opportunity to divest himself of it by repudiation: J Hill, 'The Role of the Donee's Consent in the Law of Gift' (2001) 117 LQR 127, 130, 133–35.

[65] This term denotes, according to SGA 1979, s 2, both 'agreements to sell' and 'sales'.

[66] For overview accounts of this development (with some variation in the detail), see SFC Milsom, 'Sale of Goods in the Fifteenth Century' (1961) 77 LQR 257, reprinted as ch 3 in SFC Milsom, *Studies in the History of the Common Law* (London, Hambledon Press, 1985); D Ibbetson, 'Sale of Goods in the Fourteenth Century' (1991) 107 LQR 480.

[67] See A Braun, 'The English Codification Debate and the Role of Jurists in the Development of Legal Doctrines' in M Lobban and J Moses (eds), *The Impact of Ideas on Legal Development* (Cambridge, Cambridge University Press, 2012) 404, esp 405–10.

[68] See above, text to nn 22–24.

clear that it is also part of a unitary and causal transfer system like the French. It may well be that the parties' agreement concerning the transfer of title as envisaged by section 17 of the Sale of Goods Act 1979 is notionally distinct from the underlying (obligatory) agreement to sell, ie, a kind of separate 'real agreement'.[69] It has further been argued that the English law on the sale of goods is wrongly regarded as causal and in truth accommodates a principle of abstraction.[70] This argument is based on the idea that, once the goods are delivered following a sale, the delivery becomes 'superadded' as a second mode of conveyance and that thereafter the transfer of title is independent of the underlying contract.[71] Whether the argument works will partly depend on the extent to which 'delivery and deed were impliedly abolished as means of passing title in sales transactions' when the Sale of Goods Act 1893 was enacted.[72] There are good reasons for thinking that they must have survived at least to cater for cases where the contract of sale is void *ab initio*.[73]

Finally, it is doubtful how far the *solo consensu* principle extends beyond sale. We know that the buyer's obligation to pay the purchase price is never self-executing, but this would appear to be no different in France. There are judicial dicta in England, both pre- and post-dating the Sale of Goods Act 1893, which suggest that any contract for valuable consideration can sustain a transfer by consent alone.[74] However, in Ireland (which has a Sale of Goods Act in all relevant respects identical to the English) the Supreme Court has held that the *solo consensu* principle does not apply in exchange transactions, so that title to a bartered chattel cannot pass without a delivery.[75]

III. The Passing of Risk

Before thinking about the connection between the passing of property and the passing of risk, it is worth pondering for a moment over what is meant by 'risk passing'.

[69] In this vein, L van Vliet, *Transfer of Movables in German, French, English and Dutch Law* (Nijmegen, Ars Aequi Libri, 2000) 110, 203–04.

[70] W Swadling, 'Rescission, Property, and the Common Law' (2005) 121 LQR 123.

[71] The argument is not without problems, albeit that these may be surmountable: B Häcker, 'Rescission of Contract and Revesting of Title: A Reply to Mr Swadling' [2006] RLR 106; B Häcker, 'Causality and Abstraction in the Common Law' in E Bant and M Harding (eds), *Exploring Private Law* (Cambridge, Cambridge University Press, 2010) 200, 210–12.

[72] See S Frisby and M Jones, 'National Report on the Transfer of Movables in England and Wales' in Faber and Lurger, *National Reports on the Transfer of Movables in Europe* (n 8) vol 2, 1, 72.

[73] Judging based on cases where the underlying contract was (described as) 'void' for infancy or illegality and property was nevertheless held to have passed: *Stocks v Wilson* [1913] 2 KB 235 (KBD), *Singh v Ali* [1960] AC 167 (PC); *Belvoir Finance Co Ltd v Stapleton* [1971] 1 QB 210 (CA). Yet Frisby and Jones (n 72) 72 are more cautious: 'Where the contract is void, however, it *might be* that title *may* pass by other means' (emphasis added).

[74] *Cochrane v Moore* (1890) 25 QBD 57 (CA) 70–71, 74–75; *Koppel v Koppel* [1966] 1 WLR 802 (CA) 811.

[75] *Flynn v Mackin* [1974] IR 101 (Irish SC) esp 111–12. It seems to have been important in this case that the contract did not envisage putting a specific monetary value to the parties' performances. cf *Aldridge v Johnson* (1857) 7 El & Bl 885, 119 ER 1476, and see EM Clare Canton, 'Sale of Goods and Barter' (1976) 5 MLR 589.

If a sale of specific goods has been agreed upon, then the buyer will necessarily bear the 'risk' (in one sense) of the seller not being able to deliver them because they have perished before delivery. Even legal systems that envisage specific enforcement as the primary remedy for non-performance make an exception where performance has become impossible, whether or not on account of the seller's fault.[76] German lawyers refer to this as the 'risk of performance' (*Leistungsgefahr*). But when we speak of 'risk passing' in sales transactions, we mean something different. We are then thinking of the buyer having to pay for the goods *even though* he never receives them. The relevant 'risk' is the economic one of losing the counter-performance without obtaining the expected consideration. The focus of the inquiry therefore lies on the 'price risk' (*Preisgefahr*).

Under normal circumstances, in all legal orders, the economic risk associated with a thing or other asset lies with its owner. The Latin maxim *res perit domino* or *casum sentit dominus* indicates that, unless the owner can point to somebody who has incurred a liability to compensate him (eg, a tortfeasor), he bears the loss himself. Typically, this will be the case where the asset has perished accidentally.

It is thus perhaps not surprising that some legal orders treat it as completely self-evident and axiomatic that the relevant risk should pass to the buyer as and when property passes. The new article 1196(3), 1st sentence, of the French Code civil, for instance, provides that '[t]he transfer of property entails the transfer of risk in the thing',[77] adding as riders only that the seller has an obligation to take reasonable care looking after it pending delivery[78] and that the risk may shift back to him once he is put on notice to perform.[79] Similarly, section 20 of the English Sale of Goods Act 1979 stipulates:[80]

(1) Unless otherwise agreed, the goods remain at the seller's risk until the property in them is transferred to the buyer, but when the property in them is transferred to the buyer the goods are at the buyer's risk whether delivery has been made or not.
(2) But where delivery has been delayed through the fault of either buyer or seller the goods are at the risk of the party at fault as regards any loss which might not have occurred but for such fault.
(3) Nothing in this section affects the duties or liabilities of either seller or buyer as a bailee or custodier of the goods of the other party.

[76] See, eg, art 1221 Cc; § 275 BGB. The fact that a legal system relieves the seller of the obligation to perform *in specie* where this is impossible, however, does not mean that the seller necessarily escapes all liability for the non-performance. A monetary (damages) claim will of course be available to the buyer in appropriate circumstances.

[77] Set out in n 32 above. An exception applies to certain consumer contracts. Art 20 of the Consumer Rights Directive 2011/83/EU requires the risk to stay with the trader until the consumer takes physical possession of the goods. This is implemented in France by art L216-4 of the Code de la consommation.

[78] Art 1197 Cc. See also the old art 1136 Cc (set out in n 29).

[79] Art 1196(3), 2nd sentence, Cc. See also the old art 1138(2) Cc (set out in n 30).

[80] Subsection (4) of SGA 1979, s 20, which is omitted here, contains the exception for certain consumer contracts motivated by the EU Consumer Rights Directive (see n 77 above). Under the national implementing provision, Consumer Rights Act 2015, s 29, the basic rule for relevant contracts is that the goods remain at the trader's risk until they come into the physical possession of the consumer. This special consumer protection provision remains in force (at least for the time being) despite Brexit.

However, as already pointed out by Ernst Rabel in his seminal monograph on the sale of goods, there is no inevitable connection between the passing of property and the passing of risk.[81] It is perfectly possible for the law – or the parties – to provide that the passing of risk shall be triggered by different criteria from those on which the passing of property turns.[82] Roman law is an example in point. While conveyances of goods sold were effected through a *traditio*[83] (most probably) supported by a *iusta causa traditionis*,[84] the 'price risk' already shifted to the buyer long before delivery occurred, namely as soon as the contract of sale was concluded. *Periculum est emptoris* was the maxim capturing this idea, and it constituted a deliberate departure from the basic rule that *casum sentit dominus*.[85] The Roman seller, while still owner of the goods sold, retained his claim to the purchase price if they were accidentally lost or destroyed before delivery.

It has been suggested that both the French and the English rules on the passing of property by consent alone may have been influenced by the Roman rule on the passing of risk. In *Cochrane v Moore*, for instance, Fry LJ said:

> This doctrine that property may pass by contract before delivery appears to be comparatively modern. It may … owe its origin to a doctrine of the civil law that the property was at the risk of the purchaser before it passed from the vendor.[86]

In fact, however, the historical evolution of the English *solo consensu* rule was a great deal more complicated than this statement suggests.[87] Nevertheless, we can observe that it became common as early as in Bracton's day to think of risk and property being intimately connected.[88] The original common law idea that the risk of a thing always lay with its possessor[89] thus merged into the idea that goods sold had to be delivered to the buyer for property to pass.[90] When English law later gave up the delivery requirement and allowed the buyer of specific goods to bring an

[81] E Rabel, *Das Recht des Warenkaufs*, vol 2 (Berlin and Tübingen, de Guyter and Mohr Siebeck, 1958) 296.

[82] As illustrated by the special consumer contract rule based on the EU Consumer Rights Directive mentioned in n 77 and n 80 above.

[83] *Mancipatio* and *in iure cessio*, special 'formal' modes of conveying *res mancipi* in the days when that category still existed, are here left to one side. See further López y López, above, Ch 2, n 5.

[84] A conveyance by *traditio* was thus (most likely) 'causal' in the modern sense, whereas the formal conveyances by *mancipatio* or *in iure cessio* were clearly 'abstract'.

[85] FH Lawson, 'The Passing of Property and Risk in Sale of Goods – A Comparative Study' (1949) 65 LQR 352, 358–62, 364, argues – following a theory first propounded by Bernhard Windscheid – that this was because property was considered already to have passed *inter partes*.

[86] *Cochrane v Moore* (n 74) 71.

[87] See the references in n 66 above.

[88] GE Woodbine (ed), SE Thorne (tr), Bracton *On the Laws and Customs of England (De legibus et consuetudinibus Angliae)*, vol 2 (Cambridge Massachusetts, Harvard University Press, 1968) 182–83. This was directly contrary to the Roman law of sale, but in line with the basic Roman principle that *casum sentit dominus*.

[89] See GDG Hall (ed), *The Treatise on the Laws and Customs of the Realm of England Commonly Called Glanvill* (Edinburgh, Nelson, 1965) 129–30 (chapter X, 14).

[90] T Rüfner, 'Traditio und Kaufpreiszahlung in Ius Commune und Common Law' in E Jakab and W Ernst (eds), *Kaufen nach Römischem Recht* (Berlin and Heidelberg, Springer, 2008) 233, 237–40; S Zwirlein, *Versprechen und Zufall* (Tübingen, Mohr Siebeck, 2017) 56–57.

action in 'detinue' as soon as the contract was concluded, thus implying that title had passed,[91] no one doubted that the necessary corollary was an earlier transfer of risk.[92]

The development of modern French law is linked much more directly than English law with the Roman law governing risk allocation in a contract of sale, along the very lines sketched by Fry LJ's dictum. Jurists in France, too, had become convinced that property and risk ought to go hand in hand, but here the application of the *periculum est emptoris* rule was so deeply entrenched in legal practice and thinking that it nudged the draftsmen of the Code civil towards adopting a unitary transfer system.[93] If the buyer of goods is to bear the risk of their accidental loss or destruction from the moment the contract of sale is concluded, so the reasoning went, then he also deserves to be treated as their owner.[94] As a result, the sale contract actually became the vehicle of conveyance under French law.

Given that legal systems differ with respect to the time when property passes from seller to buyer, their individual needs and practices for segregating risk from proprietary entitlement – where appropriate – also differ. We can observe that a number of systems link the transfer of risk to the transfer of possession (just as the common law did originally[95]), whether or not this is the moment where property also passes. Under § 446 of the German BGB, for instance, the buyer has to bear the risk of an accidental loss, destruction or deterioration of the object sold as soon as it is delivered to him.[96] Although this means that risk and property often pass together under the German *traditio*-based system,[97] they are in fact notionally independent. If, therefore, the parties agree on a reservation of title clause preserving the seller's real rights beyond the point of delivery, the passing of risk will precede the transfer of ownership (subject always to the parties' agreeing otherwise).[98] The Austrian ABGB expressly endorses the basic *casum sentit dominus* principle,[99]

[91] Initially on the basis of the fiction that the seller held the goods on a 'constructive bailment' for the buyer.

[92] Zwirlein (n 90) 57, also drawing attention (at 58–60) to the following statement by Blackburn J in *Martineau v Kitching* (1872) LR 7 QB 436, 453–54: 'As a general rule, res perit domino, the old civil law maxim, is a maxim of our law; and when you can shew that the property passed the risk of the loss, primâ facie, is in the person in whom the property is'.

[93] E Bucher, 'Die Eigentums-Translativwirkung von Schuldverträgen: Das „Woher" und „Wohin" dieses Modells des Code Civil' [1998] ZEuP 615, 651–59.

[94] ibid 652.

[95] See above, text to n 89.

[96] § 446, 1st sentence, BGB. Exceptionally, the risk can pass even before delivery where the buyer is *in mora* in accepting the goods, ie, where he is in default by delay (§ 446, 3rd sentence, BGB) or, in non-consumer cases, once the seller has dispatched the goods to the buyer (§ 447(1) BGB).

[97] See above, text accompanying nn 40–42.

[98] An account of the historical background is given by Zwirlein (n 90) 234–35. She also addresses the tricky question (at 231–33) of whether 'delivery' in § 446 BGB means only the transfer of actual physical possession or whether risk also passes to the buyer where the conveyance is achieved by what English lawyers refer to as a 'constructive delivery', namely a transfer of indirect possession, such as under a *constitutum possessorium* (§ 930 BGB). Zwirlein concludes that risk only passes when the buyer obtains immediate physical control over the goods sold (*unmittelbarer Besitz* or 'direct possession' as defined in § 854(1) BGB).

[99] § 1311, 1st sentence, ABGB.

but also contains specific provisions in its law governing sale contracts. These allocate the risks, the benefits and the burdens of 'having' an object to its buyer as from the agreed time of delivery and, failing this, from the moment of its actual delivery (again subject to a deviating agreement).[100]

By contrast, other civilian systems still stick with the old Roman *periculum est emptoris* rule. Swiss law is a case in point.[101] It operates a causal transfer system not dissimilar to the Austrian, so that the passing of property normally[102] depends not merely on a valid underlying contract, but additionally on a delivery of the goods by the seller to the buyer.[103] Yet article 185(1) of the Swiss Law of Obligations (*Obligationenrecht*: 'OR') provides that, from the moment a contract of sale is concluded, the benefits and risk connected with the thing sold are the buyer's, unless special circumstances or agreements warrant an exception.

For English and French law, as has been seen, the same early passing of risk already follows from the ordinary rules on the transfer of property in specific goods sold.[104] Where a reservation of title clause is agreed between the parties (as frequently happens), the natural consequence would be that the risk of the goods, too, only shifts to the buyer once the conditions set for the passing of property have been met. However, this may be impractical or inappropriate in certain circumstances, particularly where goods are handed over before they have been paid for. It is therefore common business practice to stipulate that the risk has to be borne by the buyer either while the goods are *in transitu*[105] or at any rate following their delivery. In English law, provisions making the passing of title dependent on full payment of the purchase price are commonly known as *Romalpa* clauses.[106] Even where these do not specifically allocate the risk of accidental loss or damage to the buyer, the seller is accorded a degree of protection by the fact that, following delivery of the goods, the buyer will be treated as his bailee with all the concomitant custodial duties.[107]

[100] §§ 1048–1051 ABGB. Note that a buyer who refuses to accept a proffered object without good reason when the agreed time for delivery comes would also bear the risk of their accidental loss, destruction or deterioration under German law on account of being *in mora* (see n 96 above).

[101] But see E Bucher, 'Notizen zu Art. 185 OR (Gefahrtragung durch den Käufer)' (1970) 89 *Zeitschrift für Schweizerisches Recht* 281, 285–89, arguing (at 288 f) that the Swiss rule is less a product of continued adherence to Roman principles than of French influence during the drafting process, mediated by the French-speaking regions in western Switzerland.

[102] There are exceptions, eg, where goods are sold by auction: art 235(1), 1st alternative, OR.

[103] Art 714(1) ZGB.

[104] See above, text surrounding nn 77–80.

[105] For an example where, in English law, such a separation of risk from proprietary entitlement gave rise to problems, see *Leigh & Sillavan Ltd v Aliakmon Shipping Co Ltd (The Aliakmon)* [1986] AC 785 (HL), where the goods had been negligently damaged by a third party employed to transport them. Compare § 447 BGB and German law's solution of allowing the seller-owner to recover the buyer's economic loss in such a situation (so-called *Drittschadensliquidation*).

[106] Named after the case of *Aluminium Industrie Vaassen BV v Romalpa Aluminium* [1976] 1 WLR 676 (CA). See SGA 1979, s 19. So-called 'title retention' clauses as security mechanisms are discussed further in the text to and following nn 143–44 below.

[107] Under SGA 1979, s 20(3), set out in the text to n 80 above. In this respect, s 20(3) is the mirror image of art 1197 Cc (see text accompanying n 78).

IV. The Nature of the Buyer's Claim against the Seller

Virtually all jurisdictions provide the seller with a personal claim against the buyer for payment of the agreed purchase price, and many add to this a positive obligation on the part of the buyer to accept the goods.[108] When it comes to the nature of the buyer's (main)[109] claim against the seller, however, legal systems necessarily differ, depending on the exact nature of their transfer system.

If property has already passed to the buyer *by virtue* of the contract of sale, then all that remains for the seller to do is physically to hand over the goods. Articles 1582 and 1603 of the French Code civil thus speak only of a 'delivery' (*délivrance*), defined in article 1604 as the 'transfer of the thing sold into the power and possession of the buyer'.[110] In English law, as we have seen, an 'agreement to sell' goods is one by which the seller undertakes 'to transfer the property in goods to the buyer', but this becomes a full-blown 'sale' as soon the property transfer takes place (typically *solo consensu* when the contract is concluded).[111] This is why the Sale of Goods Act 1979 treats in distinct parts the transfer of 'property' or 'title' on the one hand (under the heading 'Effects of the Contract')[112] and on the other hand the 'duty of the seller to deliver the goods … in accordance with the terms of the contract of sale' (under the heading 'Performance of the Contract').[113]

By contrast, legal systems which – like the German – separate cleanly between the conclusion of a purely obligatory contract and its performance by a notionally distinct act, will expressly require the seller to effect a conveyance to the buyer *in addition* to transferring possession of the goods, even if and where the conveyance itself involves a form of delivery.[114] Accordingly, the first sentence of § 433(1) BGB specifies that a seller's typical duties are 'to deliver the thing to the buyer and to transfer ownership of the thing to him'. A similar claim to a transfer of possession *plus* a conveyance exists in English law where the sale concerns real property rather than goods since contracts concerning dispositions of (interests in) land are not self-executing at common law.[115]

[108] See, eg, art 1650 Cc; § 433(2) BGB; SGA 1979, s 27, second part.

[109] The seller's duty to warrant against defects in the substance of the goods, defects of title, and/or against eviction will not be considered here, but see arts 1603, 1625 ff Cc; § 433(1), 2nd sentence, BGB; SGA 1979, ss 12 ff (non-consumer contracts); Consumer Rights Act 2015, ss 9 ff (consumer contracts).

[110] J Bell, S Boyron and S Whittaker, *Principles of French Law*, 2nd edn (Oxford, Oxford University Press, 2008) 351, point out for the pre-2016 law that the theoretical obligation to effect a conveyance (*obligation de donner*) – to the extent that it was self-executing – effectively boiled down to an obligation 'to do' (*obligation de faire*), namely to deliver the goods sold. But cf the comment to and in n 31 on the 'intellectual' nature of the *traditio* in normative terms, as distinct from the physical delivery.

[111] SGA 1979, s 2. See the text following n 64 above.

[112] Part 3 of SGA 1979.

[113] Part 4 of SGA 1979, esp s 27(1).

[114] The crucial issue then is that the delivery should not merely amount to a transfer of possession, but should be accompanied by the requisite intent to pass ownership (an aspect of the 'real agreement').

[115] See above, text accompanying nn 56–57, but cf the position in equity discussed in the text to nn 138–40 below.

Interesting comparative questions arise when it comes to the way in which the buyer's rights regarding the objects bought are asserted and enforced. In German law, where the buyer has no more than a personal claim under § 433(1) BGB, the matter is relatively straightforward. Cases of impossibility apart,[116] the right to demand performance of the seller's contractual obligation[117] can be specifically enforced. This may involve a court-appointed official taking goods away from the seller and handing them over to the buyer,[118] with the seller's agreement to the conveyance being substituted by a judicial decision.[119]

In French law, where property has already passed by virtue of the contract of sale, specific enforcement of the contractual obligation is necessarily confined to making the seller surrender the goods to the buyer. This can happen by means of a physical seizure on the part of the state,[120] but often takes the form of a so-called *astreinte* – a judicial order threatening the defendant with a fine for non-compliance.[121] However, it might well be asked whether, instead of seeking 'enforced performance in kind' of the contract of sale under article 1221 Code civil,[122] the buyer could instead stand on his ownership of the goods and demand their delivery up through a *vindicatio* (*action en revendication*). This scenario seems not to be considered much by judicial decisions or the relevant literature,[123] but neither does it appear to be ruled out by the type of *non-cumul* rule which in French law precludes a concurrence of contractual and delictual claims.[124]

[116] § 275 BGB. See already the text accompanying n 76.

[117] See § 241(1) BGB.

[118] § 883 ZPO (the German Code of Civil Procedure).

[119] § 894 ZPO.

[120] So-called *saisie-appréhension*.

[121] H Kötz, *European Contract Law*, 2nd edn (trans G Mertens and T Weir, Oxford, Oxford University Press, 2017) 201, referring in particular to Cass com, 12 December 1966, Bull civ III no 478. See also Bell, Boyron and Whittaker, *Principles of French Law* (n 110), 349–50, explaining how the primacy of monetary remedies in the original Code civil of 1804 was eroded by the courts and in practice turned into a primacy of specific performance (*exécution forcée en nature*), long before the 2016 reform of the French law of obligations formalised that position.

[122] Art 1221 Cc: 'A creditor of an obligation may, having given notice to perform, seek performance in kind unless performance is impossible or if there is a manifest disproportion between its cost to the debtor in good faith and its interest for the creditor'. Note that the provision therefore incorporates the kinds of defences which in German law are contained in § 275 BGB.

[123] But see the brief references to the *action en revendication* in J Huet, G Decocq, C Grimaldi and H Lécuyer, *Traité de Droit Civil: Les principaux contrats spéciaux*, 3rd edn (Paris, LGDJ, 2012) 223; D Mainguy, *Les contrats spéciaux*, 11th edn (Paris, Dalloz, 2018) 180; and the discussion by P Simler in JurisClasseur Civil Code, Art. 1221 et 1222: Contrat – Inexécution du contrat – Exécution forcée en nature, [2] and [53]. Compare and contrast the suggestion in some of the older literature that the *action en revendication* may actually be inappropriate in such a case given that the buyer had at no point prior to the contract been in possession of the goods: E von Caemmerer, 'Rechtsvergleichung und Reform der Fahrnisübereignung' (1938/39) 12 *Zeitschrift für ausländisches und internationales Privatrecht* 675, 686, referring to M Planiol, G Ripert and M Picard, *Traité pratique de droit civil français*, vol 3 (Paris, Librairie générale de droit & de jurisprudence, 1926) nos 378, 391 (pp 361–62, 375). This ties in with an understanding gleaned from what is now art 2276 Cc (see n 238), namely that the *action en revendication* is all about *re*-claiming goods that were previously in one's possession.

[124] Of course, if the goods sold were damaged by the seller while in his possession, the *non-cumul* rule may well prevent the buyer bringing a delictual claim for any loss sustained as a result. He would appear

In practical terms, the difference between the contractual claim and the proprietary *action en revendication* is probably small.[125] Where the goods have perished, the *vindicatio* fails as much as the enforcement claim under article 1221 Cc,[126] and a situation where there is a 'manifest disproportion' between the 'cost' to the seller of surrendering goods he has in his possession and the buyer's 'interest' in receiving them is unlikely to arise.[127] Yet whether or not the buyer needs to have given 'notice to perform' before seeking to enforce his claim to delivery is potentially relevant. If so, it may be that the notice requirement imposed by article 1221 Cc for enforced performance in kind would simply be transferred across to the 'proprietary' claim.[128]

English law faces the same theoretical question, but here the contractual and the proprietary regimes have been aligned. Given that damages are the common law's default remedy for breach of contract, specific enforcement of the buyer's contractual claim for delivery of the goods bought is an equitable remedy that will only be granted at the court's discretion. Its availability depends on a monetary award being inadequate to compensate for the breach, typically because the goods sold are unique and thus not available on the market. If, instead of suing for breach of contract, the buyer were to reframe his claim as one in the tort of conversion (a strict liability wrong which makes up for the fact that there is no *vindicatio* in English law), the seller's liability would arise from having interfered with the buyer's superior title to the goods following the passing of property under section 17 (and 18 rule 1) of the Sale of Goods Act 1979. The relevant legislation governing the remedial regime for all wrongful 'interference[s] with goods' provides for damages as the default remedy,[129] something which is in line with the old common law position. However, for the last 40 years statute has also allowed the court a discretion to order actual delivery up of the goods following a conversion,[130]

confined to the contractual route of seeking redress for non-performance of the contract (*inexécution du contrat*) or for its mal-performance (*exécution imparfaite*).

[125] I am very grateful to Olivier Deshayes for pointing out that there would be a jurisdictional difference in the case of immovables, for which the *action en revendication* lies in the exclusive competence of the *Tribunal judiciaire* (formerly *Tribunal de grande instance*).

[126] More specifically, in the case of sale, art 1121 Cc (governing 'enforced performance in kind' in general) has to be viewed in conjunction with art 1610 Cc (giving the buyer the right to insist on being 'put into possession').

[127] This is particularly so since the legislative revisions in 2018 of the 2016 reform, which inserted into art 1221 Cc a requirement that the debtor must be in 'good faith' in order to benefit from the provision.

[128] In practice, the bringing of an action in court seeking to enforce a buyer's claim would itself in all probability be enough to satisfy the notice requirement, as the defendant will at this point be reminded of the need to effect a delivery of the goods.

[129] As an alternative to a purely monetary order, the claimant can as of right also opt for 'an order for delivery of the goods, but giving the defendant the alternative of paying damages by reference to the value of the goods, together in either alternative with payment of any consequential damages': Torts (Interference with Goods) Act 1977, s 3(2)(b) and (c).

[130] Torts (Interference with Goods) Act 1977, s 3(2)(a) and 3(3)(b). Before this statute was passed, such an order was available only for the tort of detinue, not conversion. The Common Law Procedure Act 1854, s 78, granted common law courts a discretion to order specific delivery of detained chattels, something which thitherto had been the exclusive realm of equity. With effect of 1 January 1978, the Torts (Interference with Goods) Act 1977, s 2, abolished the tort of detinue and extended the tort of conversion to cover cases which previously would have been actionable as detinue.

and in practice the exercise of this discretion is guided by the same considerations as in the context of specific enforcement.[131]

V. Security Mechanisms and Protection against Insolvency

The extent to which parties to a contract are each protected against non-performance and the other's insolvency will depend on the nature of their mutual claims, at least in the first instance. While the seller's payment claim against the buyer is necessarily *in personam*, and therefore needs to be hedged about with special measures if it is to be 'secured', the point in time at which the buyer acquires property in the object sold – and thereby (potentially) a special status in the seller's insolvency – differs between the various jurisdictions and accordingly entails different challenges. We will look first at the buyer's position vis-à-vis the seller and then at the mechanisms securing the seller in the event of the buyer's non-performance or insolvency.

A. The Buyer's Position

Generally speaking, systems like the French or English, which allow the transfer of property to take place when the underlying contract of sale is concluded, are capable of bestowing on the buyer a relatively secure position at an early stage of the transaction. Although the goods may not yet have been delivered to him, his proprietary interest in them will provide him with a measure of protection[132] against the seller's non-performance or insolvency. Quite how far this protection reaches in the latter case, however, depends on the extent to which the seller's trustee in bankruptcy is bound by the terms of the contract which is not yet fully executed. Generally speaking, the trustee in bankruptcy stands 'in the debtor's

[131] See M Bridge, *Personal Property Law*, 4th edn (Oxford, Oxford University Press, 2015) 120, speaking of the pre-1978 position in relation to detinue: 'courts proceeded on the same basis as that governing the award of specific performance in contract actions'; cf also S Green and J Randall, *The Tort of Conversion* (Oxford, Hart Publishing, 2009) 208, referring to a statement by Sir Robert Megarry VC in *Howard E Perry & Co Ltd v British Railways Board* [1980] 1 WLR 1375 (ChD) 1382–83: 'A principle on which the court has long acted is not to order delivery of goods which are ordinary articles of commerce with no special value or interest, whether to the plaintiff or others, when damages will fully compensate … If a plaintiff can easily replace the goods detained by purchasing their equivalent on the market, then the payment of damages out of which the price of the equivalent may be paid is adequate compensation to the wronged plaintiff, and there is little or no point in making an order for the delivery of the goods. Far better to let the plaintiff fend for himself with the defendant's money'.

[132] Always subject to the rules governing, in the terminology of French law, the *inopposabilité* ('non-opposability') of this interest vis-à-vis third parties acting in good faith or, in the more common English terminology, the relevant bona fide purchase rules, on both of which see above, text to nn 33–35, as well as below, text to nn 246–48.

shoes'; he is not considered a 'third party'.[133] While he may have the option of calling off the whole transaction,[134] in which case the purchase price would not fall due, if he decides to keep the contract afoot, the delivery will have to be effected. The buyer's economic risk is therefore limited. Where the buyer has in the contract agreed to a reservation of title clause pending payment, thus ousting the basic rule and accepting a delayed conveyance, there is of course similarly no real risk on him. It is then up to him to ensure that that the purchase price is paid, at which point the conveyancing effect of the contract will automatically be activated.

By contrast, systems which adopt a principle of separation and operate a *traditio*-based system of conveyance, such as German or Austrian law, tend to place greater reliance on the buyer securing himself against the seller's insolvency. He will normally be able to refuse payment until the seller offers to perform his side of the bargain.[135] If, however, the buyer decides to pre-perform and pays up without receiving the goods, he takes the risk of subsequently having to line up with the seller's unsecured creditors for *pari passu* distribution.

It will be recalled that the English transfer system resembles the French only in respect of the sale of goods. Outside this context, it looks more like the German.[136] As a result, the (intended) transferee's protection is less pronounced in these areas or has to be brought about by other means.[137] An intriguing purchaser protection mechanism may be found in the law relating to sales of land, ie, 'real property'. Where a binding and specifically enforceable contract for the sale of land has been concluded, but the conveyance has yet to take place, English law treats the seller as holding the land on trust for the buyer on the basis that 'equity regards as done that

[133] Yet note that, historically, there used to be a widespread idea in both England and France that a person's (here the seller's) 'reputed' or 'apparent ownership' should be taken into account in the case of bankruptcy, such that trustees in bankruptcy were under certain circumstances authorised to sell goods not belonging to the bankrupt (and in our example belonging to the buyer) for the benefit of the bankrupt's creditors. See, eg, Bankruptcy Act 1825, s 72; Bankruptcy Act 1914, s 38(2)(c), as far as English law was concerned. In France, the doctrine of apparent ownership was closely connected with the principle that *possession vaut titre* (on which see the text to n 238 below). However, the notion that a merely 'reputed' or 'apparent' ownership should entail such drastic consequences in insolvency is now in steady decline and the doctrine is gradually disappearing throughout Europe: EM Kieninger, 'Evaluation: A Common Core? Convergences, Subsisting Differences and Possible Ways For Harmonisation' in EM Kieninger (ed), *Security Rights in Movable Property in European Private Law* (Cambridge, Cambridge University Press, 2004) 647, 652–54.

[134] For France: Cashin Ritaine (n 31) 110, referring to art L 622-13 II Code de commerce. For England: Insolvency Act 1986, ss 178, 315 (treating unprofitable contracts as 'onerous property' which may be disclaimed by the trustee in bankruptcy).

[135] See §§ 320–322 BGB; §§ 1052, 1062 ABGB. For French law, cf arts 1219–1220 Cc, but note that this will affect only the seller's obligation to deliver, not the transfer of ownership as such (see above, text preceding n 110, as well as below, text accompanying n 145).

[136] See the discussion in section II.E above.

[137] Interestingly, a delivery can occasionally be crucial even if it is *not* the vehicle of conveyance. Where title to goods is transferred by means of a deed, without a transfer of possession taking place (typically where the transfer is made so as to provide the transferee with a security), the transferor's trustee in bankruptcy will not be bound by the instrument – known as a 'bill of sale' – unless it has been registered: Bills of Sale Act 1878. Note that the law governing bills of sale has recently been reviewed by the Law Commission, *Bills of Sale* (Law Com No 369, 2016).

which ought to be done'.[138] In other words, although at common law the estate sold does not vest in the buyer until the formal conveyance (by deed and registration) is completed, the conscience-orientated system of equity[139] imposes a so-called 'vendor-purchaser constructive trust' on the seller, requiring him to hold the land for the buyer's benefit pending the outright transfer of property.[140] Were the seller to become bankrupt in the interim, the buyer would be protected by virtue of his 'equitable interest' in the land,[141] even (and particularly!) if he has already paid the full purchase price.[142]

B. The Seller's Position

The most obvious way for a seller to protect himself against the risk of the buyer's insolvency in any system is to make the passing of property conditional on full payment of the purchase price. Such 'reservation of title' or 'title retention' clauses[143] have already been mentioned.[144] The exact point at which they operate depends on how and when the relevant property rights are transferred. In systems envisaging a conveyance at the moment the underlying contract is concluded, such

[138] The leading cases in this area are *Lysaght v Edwards* (1876) 2 Ch D 449 (ChD) and *Walsh v Lonsdale* (1882) 21 Ch D 9 (CA). It is commonly thought that no similar vendor-purchaser constructive trust can arise in the context of the sale of personal property, ie, goods. This is usually because full (unencumbered) common law title will already pass to the buyer *solo consensu* when the contract of sale is concluded or as soon the goods are appropriated to it. Where the parties have agreed a reservation of title clause, on the other hand, a vendor-purchaser constructive trust would be inconsistent with the parties' carefully balanced rights and interests under the Sale of Goods legislation. In *The Aliakmon* (n 105) 812, Lord Brandon said: 'I do not doubt that it is possible … for equitable interests in goods to be created and to exist. It seems to me, however, extremely doubtful whether equitable interests in goods can be created or exist within the confines of an ordinary contract of sale. The Sale of Goods Act 1893 … is a complete code of law in respect of contracts for the sale of goods'. See also *Re Wait* [1927] 1 Ch 606 (CA) 635–36 (per Atkin LJ, *obiter*). This argument would seem to apply irrespective of the question of specific enforceability. However, it has recently been argued that the vendor-purchaser constructive trust should, in principle, be recognised by analogy with land law where goods are unique or scarce: M Pawlowski and J Brown, 'Sale of Land and Personal Property: The Purchaser as Beneficial Owner?' (2020) 34 TLI 63.

[139] On the distinction between the common law and the equitable jurisdiction of English courts, see text accompanying n 55 above.

[140] For more details, see Cartwright, below, Ch 6.

[141] Insolvency Act 1986, s 283(3)(a). Critical of the vendor-purchase constructive trust for this (and other) reasons: W Swadling, 'The Vendor-Purchaser Constructive Trust' in S Degeling and J Edelman (eds), *Equity in Commercial Law* (Sydney, Lawbook Co, 2005) 463, esp 467, 485–87.

[142] See *Jerome v Kelly (Inspector of Taxes)* [2004] UKHL 25, [2004] 1 WLR 1409, [32], where Lord Walker commented that it would be 'wrong to treat an uncompleted contract for the sale of land as equivalent to an immediate, irrevocable declaration of trust (or assignment of beneficial interest) in the land' and said: 'If the contract proceeds to completion the equitable interest can be viewed as passing to the buyer in stages, as title is made and accepted and as the purchase price is paid in full'.

[143] French: *clause de réserve de propriété*; German: *Eigentumsvorbehaltsklausel*. In England also known as a *Romalpa* clause (see n 106 and the text thereto).

[144] The relevant provisions are art 2367 of the French Code civil; s 19 of the English Sale of Goods Act 1979; § 449 of the German BGB; and (*e contrario*) the dispositive provision in § 1063 of the Austrian ABGB (on which see the text accompanying n 154 below).

as the French and English, they will *flank* the seller's ability to withhold delivery of the goods to the buyer until the latter proffers the agreed purchase price.[145] In *traditio*-based systems, such as the German and Austrian, the same principle of simultaneous exchange[146] ensures that *both* ownership and possession are normally transferred to the buyer only when he pays up.

In all of the legal orders considered, the main practical relevance of title reservation clauses therefore lies in the time *after* delivery. They enable the seller to retain a proprietary interest in the goods while at the same time already letting the buyer into physical possession. This is why the seller's right *in rem* is widely regarded as a form of security interest.[147] Some jurisdictions – in particular many common law jurisdictions other than England, but also a number of civilian systems – draw from this recognition the conclusion that the seller's reserved property right is not enforceable in the buyer's insolvency unless it[148] is registered and thereby publicised to third parties dealing with the latter.[149] Concern about the false appearance of solvency created by title retention clauses is what initially also led French courts to deny their ability to withstand bankruptcy proceedings,[150] a position which only changed through legislative intervention in 1980.[151]

Interestingly, a strong historical pedigree links the transfer of property in goods sold to the payment of their purchase price. Justinianic Roman law propagated a kind of 'retention of title by operation of law'.[152] Unless the sale was one on credit, the buyer did not acquire ownership of the goods delivered until he had paid the price or provided the seller with a security for it (a personal security such as a surety, or a real security such as a pledge).[153] This rule lingered on through the medieval *ius commune* and well into the early modern period. It explains why the Austrian Civil Code of 1811 approaches title retention from what to modern eyes may appear the wrong end of the stick. It provides as the dispositive basic rule that if the seller delivers the thing sold to the buyer without receiving the purchase

[145] See arts 1219–1220, 1583, 1602 Cc; SGA 1979, ss 27–28.

[146] See §§ 320–322 BGB; §§ 1052, 1062 ABGB.

[147] Expressly classified as such by art 2329 Cc (no 4).

[148] Or the retention of title clause itself – registration practices vary.

[149] Statutory registration regimes (so-called Personal Property Security Acts or PPSAs) exist in Australia, Canada, and New Zealand. See also article 9 of the US Uniform Commercial Code. Amongst European civil law jurisdictions, Italy and Spain operate registration systems. In France nowadays, writing is prescribed as far as movables are concerned.

[150] Seminal: Cass req 21 July 1897, DP 1898.I.269.

[151] So-called *loi Dubanchet* (no 80-335) of 12 May 1980, subsequently followed by a number of further reforms. For a discussion of title retention clauses in France, see Cashin Ritaine (n 31) 141–45, M Saint-Cène, 'France' in I Davies (ed), *Retention of Title Clauses in Sale of Goods Contracts in Europe* (Abingdon, Routledge, 1999) ch 5, and cf text to n 24 above. See also arts 2367 ff Cc; arts L624-16 ff Code de commerce.

[152] Thus described by Rabel (n 81) 40.

[153] Inst 2.1.41. See T Honoré, 'Sale and the Transfer of Ownership: The Compilers' Point of View' in PG Stein and ADE Lewis (eds), *Studies in Justinian's Institutes in Memory of J.A.C. Thomas* (London, Sweet & Maxwell, 1983) 56. It is not entirely clear whether or how far the same position already pertained in classical Roman law.

price, then the sale is *deemed to be one on credit*, so that property passes to the buyer immediately.[154] In France, prior to the enactment of the Code civil, the seller's ability to 'pursue' the goods (in the sense of revindicating them) if the buyer failed to pay up was expressly recognised, for instance, by the sixteenth-century *Coutume de Paris*.[155] English law was influenced by similar ideas. Although it had dispensed with the need for a delivery as a vehicle of conveyance following sale,[156] judicial opinion between the fifteenth and eighteenth centuries wavered over whether the passing of title might depend on payment of the purchase price.[157] It was not until the appearance of Colin Blackburn's influential treatise on sale in 1845 that such doubts were finally laid to rest.[158]

Yet in both English and French law, the 'retention of title by operation of law' lives on in a different shape. Having dispelled the notion that title to goods sold only passes when they are delivered or paid for, Blackburn mentions that the unpaid vendor under English law is in the 'peculiar' position of having a lien to secure payment of the purchase price while the goods are in his possession, and indeed a right to stop goods 'in transitu' while they are on their way to the buyer.[159] The unpaid vendor's rights, described by Blackburn as an 'anomalous sort of property springing up upon the insolvency of the owner',[160] are today codified in the Sale of Goods Act 1979.[161] In France, where the compilers of the Code civil decided to adopt the consensual transfer system outlined above, under which the obligation to 'give' was to be self-executing at the very moment it was undertaken (partly motivated by the desire to align the passing of property with the passing of risk),[162] they decided to preserve the seller's secured position by implementing a regime of vendor's privilege.[163] This protects the seller against the buyer's insolvency while he is still in possession of the goods, and even for some time after delivery if the

[154] § 1063 ABGB.

[155] Art 176 of the *Coutume* (first compiled in 1510, re-enacted in 1580) provided: 'Qui vend aucune chose mobiliaire sans iour & sans terme esperant estre payé promptement, il peut sa chose poursuivre en quelque lieu qu'elle soit transportée, pour estre payé du prix qu'il l'a venduë'. That this was understood to be not merely as a security right, but a form of retained ownership, can be seen from Pothier's commentary on the provision: RJ Pothier, *Traité du droit du domaine de propriété*, vol 1 (Paris and Orléans, Debure Père and Veuve Rouzeau-Montaut, 1772) [242] (at 236–37): 'demeure toujours sa chose jusqu'à ce qu'il ait été payé'.

[156] See above, text accompanying nn 66, 90–91, as well as the references mentioned there.

[157] Milsom (n 66) 123–25; Rüfner (n 90) 245–49, referring to a disagreement between Judges Choke and Brian in the late fifteenth century.

[158] C Blackburn, *A Treatise on the Effect of the Contract of Sale* (London, Benning & Co, 1845) 195–96.

[159] ibid 199–200. Note that rights of stoppage *in transitu* are not unknown in civilian jurisdictions, though they are less practically relevant where the passing of property depends on a *traditio*. In Austria, § 45 of the Bankruptcy Code (*Konkursordnung*: 'KO') expressly provides for a so-called *Verfolgungsrecht*. A similar provision in the old German Bankruptcy Code (§ 44 KO) was deliberately not replicated in the new Insolvency Code (*Insolvenzordnung*) which came into force in 1999.

[160] Blackburn (n 158) 200.

[161] SGA 1979, ss 39, 41–48.

[162] See above, text accompanying nn 28–31 and nn 93–94.

[163] A historical account is given by LD Cromwell, 'Vendor's Privilege: *Adheret Visceribus Rei*' (2015) 75 *Louisiana Law Review* 1165, 1169–71.

sale was not on credit.[164] As a result, it can be said that both French and English law counter-balance the economic risks involved in the early transfer of property by providing the seller with a (limited) security interest in the buyer's insolvency. To some extent, this mirrors the buyer's secured position in the seller's insolvency when it comes to ascertained goods after property has passed *solo consensu*.

VI. The Effects of Rescission of Contract

Where an obligatory contract underlying a transaction is avoided with retroactive effect, one would expect to find property that has passed in pursuance of it revesting (retroactively) in the transferor if a given transfer system is causal, but not if it is abstract. The present discussion is confined to cases of what English lawyers call 'rescission', such as in particular for fraud,[165] yet the basic logic also holds for systems that treat terminated contracts as if they had never been validly concluded in the first place.[166] (It is worth noting that although termination is by-and-large retrospective in the theory of the civilian tradition, many legal orders acknowledge that the contract has certain 'after-effects', thus indicating that it is regarded as dissolved rather than completely non-existent.[167] On the received common law understanding, termination operates prospectively only, even though English lawyers sometimes confusingly call it 'rescission for breach'.[168]) We will discount in our discussion the exact mechanism of avoidance, which is in some systems perceived as a right of self-help exercisable by mere declaration,[169] and which requires a court order in others.[170]

The basic contrast between the effect of rescission in causal and abstract transfer systems is nicely illustrated by comparing French and German law. Where a contract, eg, of sale, is 'annulled' under article 1178 Cc because it does not satisfy all the conditions required for its validity, it is 'deemed never to have existed'.[171]

[164] Art 2332 Cc (no 4).

[165] Note that the grounds of rescission vary greatly as between systems, as outlined in n 183 below.

[166] Such as, in particular, Spanish or Italian law.

[167] In German law, *Rücktritt* necessarily only affects the obligatory contract and leads to the parties' relationship being turned into a special restitutionary regime (§§ 323 ff, 346 ff BGB). In French law, *la résolution* used to be thought of as retroactive in theory, but it had long been recognised that this was not to be taken at face value. The recent reform acknowledges this theoretical reorientation and expressly provides that certain clauses such as those concerning dispute resolution, confidentiality and non-competition, are unaffected by a *résolution* of the contract (arts 1224 ff Cc, esp arts 1229 and 1230). It is worth noting that the Code civil does not allow a clear inference on the proprietary consequences of *la résolution* either way since the envisaged restitutionary regime applies independently of any particular allocation of property rights: see the text to nn 207–15 below, especially that surrounding n 212.

[168] Lord Wilberforce famously warned against the use of this terminology in *Johnson v Agnew* [1980] AC 367 (HL) 392–93; *Photo Production Ltd v Securicor Transport Ltd* [1980] AC 827 (HL) 844–45.

[169] See § 143 BGB. This is how rescission is widely thought to operate in English law.

[170] See arts 1131, 1178 ff Cc. Some older English equity cases also subscribe to this view.

[171] Art 1178(2) Cc: 'Le contrat annulé est censé n'avoir jamais existé'.

As a result, doctrinal analysis dictates that it cannot have functioned as a vehicle for the transfer of property in any goods supposedly sold. Barring some other means of loss and acquisition of these rights (such as by operation of law and/or by a third party's bona fide purchase),[172] the would-be-transferor still holds them and has – as we now know – actually retained them all along.[173]

Contrast the same situation in German law. Since contract and conveyance are separate transactions and since the latter is 'abstract' vis-à-vis the former,[174] a rescission of the obligatory contract of sale alone has no bearing on the allocation of property rights. Provided the conveyance has been validly executed by the conclusion of a 'real agreement' coupled with the requisite element of publicity, the transferee remains – on the proprietary level – fully entitled to the objects of the sale. This is the very gist of 'abstraction'. However, there is a twist: if the situation happens to be such that the defect of consent on which rescission of the obligatory contract was based can at the same time also be said to have induced the 'real agreement' in a legally relevant way, then the transferor may avoid the conveyance in just the same manner as the underlying contract of sale. The principle of abstraction is effectively circumvented, but not undermined. It is not undermined *in theory* because two notionally separate acts of rescission (*Anfechtung*) are necessary; and it is not undermined *in practice* because cases where it is possible to avoid both contract and conveyance are rare. A textbook example of a so-called 'identity of defect' situation (*Fehleridentität* or *Doppelmangel*) is of a transaction induced by fraud.[175] Where the buyer has deliberately misled the seller of goods, his misrepresentation will typically have caused the seller *both* to enter into the contract of sale *and* to deliver the goods with the intention of passing property to the buyer. Both agreements – the obligatory and the 'real' contract – suffer from the same defect. Yet in the far more common kind of case the seller will want to escape from the transaction on account of having made a unilateral mistake (something which is in principle perfectly possible under German law).[176] He may, for instance, have mistyped the price at which he was willing to offer the goods,[177] or he might have laboured under a misapprehension about some quality that impacts their market value.[178] Under German law, this kind of error goes to the

[172] See the discussion in section VIII below.

[173] Although the would-be-transferor should thus in theory be able to assert his ownership right by means of a *vindicatio* (*action en revendication*), art 1178(3) Cc actually points claimants to the special restitutionary regime in arts 1352 ff Cc. This does not appear to be premised on the claimant's proprietary interest subsisting: see the text accompanying nn 207–15 below. In practice, therefore, the claimant will pursue what is technically an action *in personam* rather than *in rem*.

[174] See section II.C above.

[175] Fraud and duress give rise to a right to rescind: § 123 BGB.

[176] By contrast with English law and the common law more generally, civilian systems generally tend to allow rescission for (certain types of) unilateral mistake: see n 183 below and text thereto.

[177] Relevant under § 119(1) BGB.

[178] Relevant under § 119(2) BGB. Note that the value of an object is not in and of itself an 'essential quality'.

heart of the exchange transaction and allows the contract of sale to be avoided.[179] Yet as far as the conveyance is concerned, the seller's mistake was purely 'motivational' and does not provide a valid ground for rescission.[180] The point becomes even clearer if one imagines the buyer as the mistaken party. He can set aside the bargain if he failed to appreciate its terms (eg, the contract price), and if fraud was in play he may even be able to set aside the real agreement(s) by means of which payment was effected; but none of this undoes the seller's conveyance of the goods or provides anyone with the power unilaterally to avoid that conveyance.

We have seen that English law – properly analysed – operates a mix of different conveyance mechanisms, some of which are comparable to the German 'abstract' model (especially real property transactions) and others of which broadly resemble the French causal consensual system (especially sale of goods transactions).[181] The matter is complicated further by the fact that certain grounds of rescission (such as fraud and duress) have their historical roots in the ordinary jurisdiction of the common law courts, while others (most notably avoidance of a contract for non-fraudulent misrepresentation and undue influence) are based on the principles of equity and the jurisdiction of the Court of Chancery. It is already worth noting in this context that English law does *not* permit contracts to be rescinded for one party's unilateral mistake, however fundamental that mistake may be.[182] In contrast to the civilian approach, the grounds of rescission under English law are always process- and never content- or substance-orientated.[183]

Despite all this complexity, there is a widely held view amongst English lawyers that when contracts (of whatever kind) are rescinded, any property which has passed 'under' them automatically 'revests' in the party from whom it came.[184]

[179] Note that § 119 BGB allows rescission only for certain types of mistakes, especially mistakes about the content of a transaction, identity mistakes, and mistakes about an essential quality of a person or a thing.

[180] This is controversial for rescission under § 119(2) BGB (see n 178), but the preferable view is that a mistake about essential qualities that affect an object's value do not normally impinge on the transferor's intention to convey that particular object: Häcker (n 6) 62–63.

[181] See section II.E above.

[182] Unilateral mistakes may in certain circumstances prevent the contract being concluded in the first place (if they are sufficiently fundamental: *Cundy v Lindsay* (1878) 3 App Cas 459), or they may lead to the rectification of a written instrument embodying the contract (if the mistake related to terms of the contract and the other party knew of it: *Riverlate Properties Ltd v Paul* [1975] Ch 133 (CA) 140; *Thomas Bates & Son Ltd v Wyndham's (Lingerie) Ltd* [1980] 1 WLR 505 (CA) esp 515–16). For further discussion, see J Cartwright, *Misrepresentation, Mistake and Non-Disclosure*, 5th edn (London, Sweet & Maxwell, 2019) chs 13–15.

[183] Häcker (n 6) 22–24. In broad outline: While virtually all legal orders recognise that affected parties may escape from contracts induced by fraud and (at least certain forms of) duress, systems diverge on what is otherwise required. Civilian systems tend to focus on 'substantive' grounds for avoidance which invoke the nature and gravity of the defect in a party's consent (see § 119 BGB; arts 1132–1136 Cc), whereas English law looks – 'procedurally' – at how a defect came about and whether the other party was responsible for it (the law of 'misrepresentation' is effectively the law of induced mistakes, whether the inducement happened fraudulently, negligently or even wholly innocently).

[184] As just one typical example amongst many, see the statement by A Burrows, 'Judicial Remedies' in A Burrows (ed), *Principles of the English Law of Obligations* (Oxford, Oxford University Press, 2015) 323, [4.11]: 'While one can regard [rescission] as always being a contractual remedy in the sense that

On this surprisingly undifferentiated account, the exact mechanisms of conveyance or the specific ground(s) of rescission in play appear to matter little. It may be that the former is not as big a problem for English law as it would be for a civilian system. After all, having a purely process-orientated law of rescission means that, even where contract and conveyance are notionally separate and subject to a principle of abstraction, the same ground for rescission will typically allow a transferor to impugn both the obligatory and the real agreement. Structurally, 'identity of defect' is not an exception under English law; it is the norm.[185] However, it is puzzling that English lawyers also pay such scant attention to the distinction between the effect of rescission at common law and in equity. For it is hard to see how an avoidance of both contract and conveyance based on equitable principles could ever lead to 'title' (or any other common law property right) 'revesting' in the rescinding party. It must be the case that rescission in equity generates at most an equitable interest under a trust in favour of the rescinding transferor.[186] And there are, in fact, no precedents seriously suggesting otherwise.

What we do find in the case law are precedents dealing with the 'revesting' of common law title in cases of fraudulently induced sales.[187] The most well-known is *Car & Universal Finance Co Ltd v Caldwell*.[188] The facts (slightly simplified for exposition purposes) were as follows: Caldwell had been induced by a rogue to sell and hand over his Jaguar car in exchange for a cheque which later bounced. As soon as he discovered the fraud, he informed the police and the Automobile Association and asked for their help in finding the vehicle. It was later located in the hands of an innocent third party purchaser. The Court of Appeal held that, under all the circumstances, Caldwell's actions in contacting various agencies had been sufficient to avoid his contract of sale (even in the absence of any direct communication with the rogue), and that as a result of this 'rescission without notice',[189] Caldwell had 'recovered his title to the car before the purported sale [to

it wipes away and allows escapes from a contract, it is also a restitutionary remedy reversing unjust enrichment where a contract has been wholly or partly executed and where the effect of the rescission is therefore to restore benefits to the contracting parties. The rescission may effect personal restitution (eg, by entitling the payer to the repayment of a purchase price); but *it is also commonly a proprietary restitutionary remedy in that it revests the proprietary rights to goods or land transferred under the contract*' (emphasis added; footnotes omitted). Other authors do not even enter the caveat concerning money paid under the contract, even though it is beyond doubt that title to notes and coins never 'revests' upon rescission (unless, of course, the notes or coins are the very goods being 'sold', eg, as collectors' items).

[185] See Häcker (n 6) 198–201.

[186] As was stated by the High Court of Australia in *Alati v Kruger* (1955) 94 CLR 216 (HCA) 224: 'Of course, a rescission which the common law courts would not accept as valid cannot of its own force revest the legal title to property which had passed, but if a court of equity would treat it as effectual the equitable title to such property revests upon the rescission'.

[187] In such a scenario, equitable interests tend only to come into play where the claimant seeks to 'trace' from the asset in question (particularly through a mixed fund) or where the formalities of land registration stand in the way of an estate in land 'revesting' at common law.

[188] *Car & Universal Finance Co Ltd v Caldwell* [1965] 1 QB 525 (QBD and CA).

[189] As it came to be called – the term is not actually used in the judgments.

the first innocent third party]'.[190] At least as far as the sale of goods is concerned, therefore, English law reaches a result which is consistent with the causal consensual model.

Yet why did it matter in *Caldwell* whether – and when – an innocent third party purchaser came into the picture? By contrast with French law, which relegates the question of protecting innocent third parties to the realm of bona fide purchase,[191] English law deals with the matter within the law of rescission itself.[192] The basic rule is (said to be)[193] that contracts can no longer be rescinded once innocent third parties have intervened and provided valuable consideration in order to acquire title or some other common law interest from the transferee.[194] This so-called 'third party rights bar to rescission' hence prevents the contract of sale being avoided. It does so in order to protect the innocent third party who would – so the reasoning goes – otherwise be deprived of the proprietary interest he or she has 'bought' in good faith.

Interestingly, although rescission (where it is possible) avoids the contract *ab initio* under English law, it is not at all clear whether this means also that, looking back, title can be said to have remained with the transferor all along. Quite the contrary. The very language of 'revesting' suggests an operation *ex nunc*, and it may be that the same 'prospective' understanding of title reverting to the transferor in fact underpins the 'third party rights bar to rescission'. Retroactivity is, of course, primarily an issue as regards a potential liability for wrongfully meddling with the goods in the period between the conclusion of the contract and its rescission. In so far as English cases address this question at all, they indicate that the transferor cannot sue in conversion for an interference which took place at a time when title had not *yet* 'revested' in him.[195]

VII. The Size and Structure of the Law of Unjust(ified) Enrichment

The different transfer systems outlined above and the proprietary (or, as the case may be, non-proprietary) consequences of rescission just discussed go a long way

[190] *Car & Universal Finance Co Ltd v Caldwell* (n 188) 549 (Sellers LJ).

[191] See section VIII below, esp the text to n 263.

[192] It is not untypical of English law to incorporate into its law of rescission rules which in other systems would be found in different parts of the law. The so-called '*restitutio in integrum* bar' to rescission, to give another example, performs some of the functions which in German law are catered for by the so-called *Saldotheorie* within the law of unjustified enrichment: see Häcker (n 6) 109–13.

[193] For a critical analysis, see B Häcker, 'Rescission and Third Party Rights' [2006] RLR 21.

[194] Or from any successors in title who are volunteers or have notice of the fraud.

[195] In *Bolton Partners v Lambert* (1889) 41 Ch D 295 (CA) 307, Cotton LJ stated, albeit in the slightly different context of (in principle retroactive) ratification: '[A]n act lawful at the time of its performance [cannot] be rendered unlawful … by the application of the doctrine of ratification.' For a while, there was talk in Australia of a doctrine described as 'conversion by relation back' (*Hunter BNZ Finance Ltd v CG Maloney Pty Ltd* (1988) 18 NSWLR 420), but this has since been disapproved: *Perpetual Trustees Australia Ltd v Heperu Pty Ltd* [2009] 76 NSWLR 195 (NSWCA) [79]–[81].

towards explaining something which causes private lawyers puzzlement at first sight. Why is the law of unjust/unjustified[196] enrichment of such disparate size, structure and importance in various national legal orders?

Before exploring this further, a terminological clarification is apposite. When French lawyers speak of *l'enrichissement injustifié* (the heading under which the judicially developed doctrine of *l'enrichissement sans cause* was codified in the 2016 reform of the law of obligations),[197] they do not have in mind the kind of cases that English or German would regard as core to their law of 'unjust enrichment' or, respectively, *ungerechtfertigte Bereicherung*. The central case with which English and German lawyers – and we here also – are concerned is that of a mistaken payment or some other performance rendered in the erroneous belief that it is owing when in fact it is not. In Latin terminology, we are in the realm of the Roman *condictio indebiti*, that which some writers of the *ius commune* period later subsumed under the *condictio sine causa (generalis)*. To French lawyers, this central case is not, however, caught by the rules on *l'enrichissement injustifié*, but by those governing *le paiement de l'indu* (literally 'undue payment').[198] Where a performance is rendered without being due, or where a contract is annulled with the consequence of performance retroactively becoming undue, the Code civil orders the recipient to make restitution (*restitution*).[199]

The puzzling thing from a comparative perspective is that French lawyers – courts and commentators alike – tend to pay scant attention to *le paiement de l'indu* and the remedial regime governing *les restitutions*. The whole area is noticeably underexplored by comparison with the great importance that German law has accorded to unjustified enrichment (§§ 812 ff BGB) since the enactment of the BGB and the increasing interest English lawyers have shown over the past 50 years in discovering, emancipating and developing their own law of restitution for unjust enrichment. Yet the reason why *condictio indebiti*-type claims are of such great practical significance in German law is that they are typically the only remedy available to a person who has made a transfer without a valid legal basis. Teleologically speaking, the whole point of abstraction is to prevent every defect in the parties' obligatory legal relationship automatically 'infecting' property (or other) transfers made in pursuance of it.[200] However, if conveyances are usually *un*affected by problems pertaining to the underlying legal basis, then

[196] The present chapter does not seek to explore the fundamental conceptual distinction between the common law's so-called 'unjust factor' approach to restitution for unjust enrichment and the civilian understanding of unjustified enrichment as being premised on the absence of a legal basis. For an overview and comparative discussion, see B Häcker, 'Unjust Factors Versus Absence of Juristic Reason (Causa)' in E Bant, K Barker and S Degeling (eds), *Research Handbook on Unjust Enrichment and Restitution* (Cheltenham, Edward Elgar, 2020) 290–313.

[197] See arts 1303 ff Cc.

[198] See arts 1302 ff Cc. The relevant action was previously known as *l'action en répétition de l'indu* and governed by arts 1376 ff of the original Code civil. For a comparative account and assessment in English of the old and new French law, see E Descheemaeker, 'The New French Law of Unjustified Enrichment' [2017] RLR 77.

[199] See the reference to arts 1352 ff Cc in art 1302-3(1) and art 1178(3), respectively.

[200] Whether or not this was the original intention behind abstraction: text to nn 264–66 below.

the legal system cannot rely on its rules of property law – especially the *vindicatio* or *vindicatio*-like claims[201] – to put the parties as far as is possible back into their original position. What is then needed is a dedicated claim that allows the mistaken transferor to seek a re-conveyance from the transferee. In the words of Barry Nicholas:

> [T]he more readily a system gives abstract effect to a conveyance or other transaction (i.e., allows it to be effective although its accompanying cause is vitiated by mistake or other defect), the more prominent will be the need for a remedy in terms of unjust enrichment.[202]

In German law, this remedy is provided by the *condictio indebiti* set out in the first sentence of § 812(1) BGB:

> A person who, without juristic reason [also referred to as *causa*], obtains something by way of another person's performance ... is obliged to surrender to that person what he has so obtained.

Since the transferee has typically obtained ownership of the object in question from the transferor, this is what he will have to return under the law of unjustified enrichment. If, exceptionally, ownership has for whatever reason not actually passed to the transferee as a result of the transferor's performance,[203] then the latter will have both a *vindicatio* and a so-called *condictio possessionis* (a claim in unjustified enrichment aimed at recovering 'mere' possession). Under a causal transfer system, such as French or Austrian law, by contrast, one would expect such a competition of claims between the 'proprietary' *vindicatio* and an 'obligatory' *condictio* to be the norm. This is indeed the case in Austria, where it is recognised that the transferor can choose freely either to rely on a claim in unjustified enrichment[204] or to bring a *vindicatio*,[205] and that one or the other may be preferable depending on the circumstances of the case.[206] In France, by contrast, the relationship between the *action en revendication* and the new rules governing *les restitutions* in articles 1352 ff Cc is not widely explored and is thus to an extent shrouded in obscurity.[207] The provisions on *les restitutions* appear to be prima face indifferent as to the underlying allocation of property rights.

[201] Such as the (strict liability) tort of conversion in English law, which to some extent functions as a *vindicatio*-substitute.

[202] B Nicholas, 'Unjustified Enrichment in the Civil Law and Louisiana Law' (1962) 36 *Tulane Law Review* 605 (Part I) 608.

[203] For example, due to a retention of title clause (see section V.B), or because the transfer of ownership was made expressly conditional on the validity of the underlying contract (see the text accompanying n 44), or in the rare case of the identical defect invalidating both contract and conveyance (see the text accompanying and following n 175).

[204] Under § 877 ABGB (rescission scenario) or § 1431 ABGB (liability mistake scenario).

[205] § 399 ABGB.

[206] See Faber (n 52) 74–75; OGH, 29 February 1984, SZ 57/44.

[207] But note the illuminating discussion (with further references) by C Simler, 'L'action en revendication et le régime des restitutions issu de l'ordonnance du 10 février 2016' [2018] D 1923.

This does not mean, however, that the two kinds of actions – one *in rem*, the other *in personam* – are conceptually indistinct. Being inspired by the old regime for recovering undue transfers (*répétition de l'indu*),[208] articles 1352 ff Cc were clearly never envisaged to apply to the *action en revendication* as such.[209] The provisions on *les restitutions* are technically triggered by 'undue payments' and the annulment of contracts (eg, for mistake),[210] and additionally also by the 'lapse' of contracts[211] or their termination.[212] Yet the question nevertheless arises whether, in the context of contractual annulment scenarios and (other) 'undue payment' situations at least,[213] the action for *la restitution* may be regarded as simply the specific form the French *vindicatio* takes, rather than competing with it side-by-side.[214] If so, then it is an action which can survive the loss of ownership of the goods in question if needs be and will subsequently function as a follow-on personal claim to restitution in monetary terms.[215]

Three further observations are warranted in respect of the interaction of property transfer systems and the law of unjust(ified) enrichment. One concerns the so-called 'proprietary' theory of restitution for unjust enrichment. This theory nowadays has most of its proponents in the common law world,[216] though in the

[208] Old arts 1235, 1376 ff Cc.

[209] Simler (n 207) 1924, pointing out, however, that while the 'juridical nature' of the *vindicatio* (a 'real' action) and the *condictio* (a 'personal' action) differed, their effects were very similar.

[210] See n 199 and text thereto.

[211] Art 1186–1187 Cc, esp art 1187(2). The so-called *caducité* of a contract is triggered where one of its essential elements (see art 1128 Cc) disappears.

[212] See the reference to arts 1352 ff Cc in art 1229(4) Cc.

[213] Perhaps it is even possible to see the regime governing *les restitutions* more generally as a specific template for the *action en revendication*, as Simler (n 207) makes clear, without ultimately deciding.

[214] I am very grateful to Valentin Pinel le Dret for discussing with me the idea originally conceived when writing this chapter that the *action en restitution de l'indu* (ie, the French version of the *condictio indebiti* or, perhaps more accurately, of the *condictio sine causa*) may be a species of the *rei vindicatio* and for encouraging me to believe that there may be something in it. Historically at least, it is conceivable that this is how the fathers of the Code civil may well have thought about the matter, as Valentin Pinel le Dret will go on to explore in his forthcoming thesis. The well-known presumption of ownership in favour of the current possessor of movables ('possession vaut title' rule) in art 2276 Cc does not necessarily stand in the way of such an analysis, if – but only if(!) – one allows the claimant 'transferor' of goods to rebut the presumption of the defendant possessor's ownership by demonstrating that the latter obtained them without a valid legal basis. Regarding this particular aspect, cf M Costa and W Faber, 'Past, Present, and Future of the French "possession vaut titre"-Rule' (2014) 3 EPLJ 147, 156–58.

[215] It is worth noting that, as far as cash payments are concerned which turn out not to have been due, French lawyers would more or less immediately resort to the personal action because it is (allegedly) impossible to 'revindicate' money on account of its fungible nature: see references in n 237 below. The potential competition between the provisions governing *les restitutions* and the *action en revendication* therefore in practice only exists with respect to 'undue payment' situations concerning specific, identifiable goods, and – perhaps confusingly for the English reader – not payments of money!

[216] See SJ Stoljar, *The Law of Quasi-Contract*, 2nd edn (Sydney, The Law Book Co, 1989) 5–10, 13, 250; S Stoljar, 'Unjust Enrichment and Unjust Sacrifice' (1987) 50 MLR 603; P Jaffey, *The Nature and Scope of Restitution* (Oxford, Hart Publishing, 2000) esp ch 9; P Jaffey, 'Two Theories of Unjust Enrichment' in JW Neyers, M McInnes and SGA Pitel (eds), *Understanding Unjust Enrichment* (Oxford, Hart Publishing, 2004) 139, 146–51; Dan Priel, 'The Justice in Unjust Enrichment' (2014) 51 *Osgoode Hall Law Journal* 813, 837–42; C Webb, *Reason and Restitution: A Theory of Unjust Enrichment* (Oxford, Oxford University Press, 2016) esp chs 3 and 4.

past similar theories also surfaced in the civilian sphere.[217] The basic idea is that the law of unjust enrichment marks out situations in which the claimant has a form of continuing 'proprietary' interest in the asset supposedly transferred to the defendant, such that – properly analysed – the defendant actually received something 'belonging' to the claimant.[218] It is clear that, at its purest, the proprietary theory is at most compatible with a causal transfer system; it cannot account for the fact that, in an abstract system, title or ownership undisputedly passes quite regardless of the accompanying unjust factor or lack of underlying legal basis.[219] However, a more nuanced version of the theory maintains that even though the claimant may have lost his legal interest through the prima facie valid conveyance, 'normatively' the law still ascribes the proprietary interest to him, and it is this interest which the law of restitution for unjust enrichment vindicates.[220]

A second theory about the way in which the law of unjust enrichment interacts with property law, and one which is entirely common-law-centred, makes what is essentially the opposite case, namely that the ability unilaterally to undo what is prima facie a valid conveyance (through 'rescinding' the transfer) is itself based on unjust enrichment.[221] In other words, the argument is that the transferor's power to avoid a conveyance, where it exists, is a proprietary response to the transferee's unjust enrichment at his expense – and not the other way around. It is a form of 'proprietary restitution' even before the power to 'revest' title is exercised! Some authors go further still and argue that unjust enrichment explains not only the power *in rem* to 'rescind' a conveyance if appropriate, but also the mistaken transferor's power *in personam* to rescind the underlying contract.[222]

[217] Savigny (n 37) 358–62, for instance, regarded the Roman *condictio* as a special action by which a dispositive transaction could be 'rescinded … *as invalid*' (emphasis added: '*als ungültig* durch besondere Klagen angefochten …') on account of a party's (the transferor's) motivational mistake concerning the existence or validity of the underlying *causa*. In other words, he saw the *condictio indebiti* as reflecting the fact that the conveyance or other disposition entered into without a proper legal basis was somehow defective *inter partes* or at any rate not fully and finally 'valid'.

[218] Stoljar, 'Unjust Enrichment and Unjust Sacrifice' (n 216) 603 summarises his theory thus: 'The point is … that the recovery of anything, whether money or land or chattels, rests on the claimant (P) being able to show that what he seeks to recover in fact "belongs" to him, having a better "title" to it than the person (D) from whom recovery is sought'.

[219] This is the essence of a frequent criticism of the proprietary theory: see, eg, A Burrows, *The Law of Restitution*, 3rd edn (Oxford, Oxford University Press, 2011) 29–30; G Virgo, *The Principles of the Law of Restitution*, 3rd edn (Oxford, Oxford University Press, 2015) 52.

[220] Priel (n 216) 838, for instance, puts it thus: 'Unjust enrichment is needed as a doctrinal corrective for cases of mismatch between legal title and what may be termed "moral title," an assessment of who really should own a particular piece of property. This implies that at the justificatory level the law recognizes that legal title is not the ultimate determinant of property rights, that it is moral notions of property and rightful ownership that explain unjust enrichment, not the other way around. It is because of our views of what it takes to earn or lose property that we conclude that the defendant has been unjustly enriched in a particular instance but not in another'.

[221] P Birks, *An Introduction to the Law of Restitution* (Oxford, Clarendon Press, 1985) 163, 171–72; P Birks, *Unjust Enrichment*, 2nd edn (Oxford, Oxford University Press, 2005) 173–76; Burrows (n 219) 172 under (iv); C Mitchell, P Mitchell and S Watterson, *Goff & Jones: The Law of Unjust Enrichment*, 9th edn (London, Sweet & Maxwell, 2016) [40-01]–[40-30].

[222] See the discussion in Häcker (n 6) 107. Critical: L Smith, 'Unjust Enrichment: Big or Small?' in S Degeling and J Edelman (eds), *Unjust Enrichment in Commercial Law* (Sydney, Lawbook Co, 2008) 35, 40–43.

Translated into the civilian sphere, this theory means that the principle against unjust(ified) enrichment is in fact much broader than might be suggested by the compartmentalised headings within existing codifications.[223] It could be seen as the normative reason *behind* a given legal system's rules for rescission of contracts and/or other transactions.[224] Wherever a party has obtained a right by virtue of another's consent, whether that right be purely personal or proprietary, if that consent was in a relevant way defective,[225] the law allows the transaction to be reversed on account of the right having been unjustly obtained at the other's expense.[226] The only difference then between causal and abstract transfer systems is that, at the proprietary level, abstract systems usually require the enriched party to participate in this reversal process (by effecting a re-conveyance), while causal systems provide for automatic or unilateral divestment without his participation.

The third and final observation adds another layer of complexity generated by the common law discourse. The concept of 'proprietary restitution' has already been mentioned.[227] It denotes rights[228] generated by unjust enrichment which consist of more than an *in personam* claim by one party against another, more than a chose in action needing to be asserted in court if necessary. Beside the rescission example outlined above, English lawyers also discuss other forms of proprietary restitution. In our context, the most significant of these relates to whether trusts can function as mechanisms for reversing unjust enrichments. The whole debate cannot be rehearsed here. Yet it is worth noting that there is a view according to which transfers under English law are for the most part 'abstract' at common law, but effectively 'causal' in equity.[229] This, proponents maintain, is because a transferee who has unjustly and without legal ground obtained title to an object from the transferor (eg, in a mistaken payment case) ought to make restitution *of that very right* by effecting a re-conveyance of the object whence it came. And since 'equity regards as done that which ought to be done' (so one main strand of the argument runs), it follows that there arises by operation of law a trust in favour of the original transferor.[230] The transferee will hold the title on trust from the very moment he acquires it. This 'resulting' trust (which is at the same time 'constructive' since it does not depend on consent) ensures that the equitable interest in the property right which was transferred unjustly and without a legal basis

[223] Such as, eg, §§ 812 ff BGB and arts 1302 ff (or at any rate arts 1303 ff) Cc.

[224] Such as, eg, §§ 119 ff BGB and arts 1130 ff Cc.

[225] See n 183 and the accompanying text.

[226] The argument is pursued further in Häcker (n 6) 171–74; B Häcker, 'Fog on the Channel? Six Comparative Lessons in Unjustified Enrichment' [2017] RLR 61, 75–76.

[227] See the text between n 221 and n 222 above.

[228] Most people assume that what is meant are *in rem* rights or powers, but 'proprietary restitution' can occasionally relate to *in personam* rights/powers as well, as shown by the examples of contractual rescission (discussed above) and the subrogation to contractual claims.

[229] Further explanation and discussion in Häcker (n 6) 127–29; B Häcker, 'Causality and Abstraction in the Common Law' in E Bant and M Harding (eds), *Exploring Private Law* (Cambridge, Cambridge University Press, 2010) 200, 212–17.

[230] See, eg, R Chambers, 'Resulting Trusts in Canada' (2002) 16 *Trust Law International* 104, 138, 146–47; R Calnan, 'Imposing Proprietary Rights' [2004] RLR 1, 12.

automatically 'jumps back' to the claimant-transferor, thus securing his right to restitution against the risk of the defendant-transferee's insolvency.

It will have become evident from the foregoing overview that the rules governing property transfers within a given system are inextricably linked to the significance, structure and size of that system's law of unjust(ified) enrichment. Neither can be properly understood without the other.

VIII. The Rules on Bona Fide Purchase

The final area to consider is the law relating to what is generally known as good faith acquisition or bona fide purchase. Here we have to distinguish two different ways in which the bona fide purchase rules link up with the rules on property transfers. For exposition purposes it will be useful to address them one by one.

A. The First Connection: Bona Fide Purchase Rules and Derivative Acquisition

The first connection is obvious. On a widespread understanding of the term,[231] bona fide purchase necessarily involves a transfer since it is triggered by a derivative (act of) acquisition. If someone sells and delivers goods he does not own,[232] such as goods he has found or stolen, then a system's bona fide purchase rules determine whether or not the buyer nevertheless becomes their owner on account of his good faith. Systems take different views on when to prefer the innocent purchaser's interest to that of the original owner. As Denning LJ observed in *Bishopsgate Motor Finance Corp v Transport Brakes*, there is a tension between two competing principles:

> The first is for the protection of property: no one can give a better title than he himself possesses. The second is for the protection of commercial transactions: the person who takes in good faith and for value without notice should get a good title.[233]

His Lordship went on to explain that English law historically preferred the first principle, but had come to accept certain modifications made 'by the common law itself and by statute so as to meet the needs of our own times'.[234] These modifications are sometimes referred to as 'exceptions' to the basic principle that

[231] But note that the exact conceptual basis of bona fide purchase varies as between different systems: see below, text to nn 243–45, 260–62.

[232] On the common law's relative conception (see n 9), what is meant is that the seller purports to transfer a better title to the goods than he himself holds.

[233] *Bishopsgate Motor Finance Corp v Transport Brakes* [1949] 1 KB 322 (CA) 336–37.

[234] ibid 337.

nemo dat quod non habet. Their remit is quite limited. Perhaps the most well-known one is the rule that a person who acquires title to money[235] in good faith and for valuable consideration, without notice of the fact that it is not the payer's, thereby obtains an indefeasible common law title, even where the payer had previously stolen the money.[236]

The French Code civil adopts exactly the opposite starting point when compared with English law. For movables at least, it contains an exceptionally broad principle of bona fide purchase. Article 2276(1) provides that, with respect to movables,[237] 'possession is equivalent to [literally: "worth"] title'.[238] Subject to certain qualifications pertaining to lost or stolen goods,[239] this means that it is generally possible for someone who in good faith[240] acquires (mere) possession of goods from a non-owner also to acquire ownership of the goods, and that the giving of value per se is not an express precondition.[241]

It is worth pondering for a moment the requirement that the bona fide purchaser should acquire actual possession of the goods in question.[242] As will be recalled, French law normally operates a pure causal consensual principle, according to which ownership passes by virtue of the contract alone. However, it will be immediately evident that a system under which bona fide purchase from a non-owner is possible by dint of mere agreement, without anything to justify the assumption that the goods belong to the transferor, would not be sensible or indeed workable in practice. This is one reason why the Code civil insists on 'super-adding' the *appearance* of ownership created by possession and underpinned by its physical transfer before bona fide purchase can occur. The other, more formal reason derives from the fact that article 2276 Cc is technically

[235] More specifically: cash (notes and coins) used as currency.

[236] The leading case is *Miller v Race* (1758) 1 Burr 452, 97 ER 398.

[237] Note that not everything that is movable actually counts as a 'movable' for this purpose (see arts 527 ff Cc, esp art 533). In particular, money in all forms – including cash – would appear to be outwith the remit of art 2276 Cc. Yet this exclusion does not prejudice innocent acquirers in the end result since it is (widely considered to be) impossible to 'revindicate' money in France: see Cass com 4 February 2003, [2003] D 1230, noted R Libchaber, 'L'impossible revendication des sommes d'argent' [2003] *Répertoire du notariat Defrénois*, art 37810, p 1163, but cf the preceding discussion by DR Martin, 'De la revendication des sommes d'argent' [2002] D 3279. Query to what extent the French (alleged) rule against applying the *action en revendication* to money depends on identification problems caused by mixing (either typically or in the specific case).

[238] The provision, which was previously (until 2008) contained in art 2279(1) Cc, reads: 'En fait de meubles, la possession vaut titre'.

[239] See arts 2276(2), 2277 Cc, outlined in n 281 below.

[240] This requirement is read into art 2276(1) Cc, with good faith being rebuttably presumed (cf art 2274 Cc).

[241] Yet specifically on this latter point, see the comment in n 257 below and especially the comparative discussion by Costa and Faber (n 214) 204–08, who conclude that gratuitous acquisitions ought ideally to be excluded from the remit of art 2276 Cc.

[242] Interestingly, it has been suggested that in the case of a *constitutum possessorium* being agreed, possession mediated through the transferor might be enough as far as the 'opposability' of ownership vis-à-vis third parties is concerned, but not in order to exclude an original owner's ability to 'revindicate' the goods: Cashin Ritaine (n 31) 96 (text to fn 611) by contrast with 123 (text to fn 771).

a rule about the acquisitive prescription of movables (as can be seen from its location in the Code),[243] not their derivative acquisition.[244] From this perspective, it is an immediately effective acquisitive prescription, one without any time lag.[245] That the acquirer's actual possession of the goods should be required is therefore unsurprising.

Delivery, it will be recalled, is a touchstone for determining when a transfer of movables under French law is 'good' in the sense of being fully effective, or 'opposable', as against third parties acting in good faith.[246] We have just seen that the publicity function of possession also explains why a transferor who never owned the object in question is nevertheless able to bestow ownership on a good faith purchaser under article 2276(1) Cc. Both ideas – that of 'opposability' on the one hand and that underlying bona fide purchase on the other – become closely aligned in situations where the transferor *was* originally the owner of a movable, but has purported to dispose of the object to two successive purchasers (such as in a double sale scenario). Here the Code civil expressly provides that the 'opposability' or effectiveness of the conveyance vis-à-vis the outside world is determined not by the chronology of contracts (as the consensual principle would seem to dictate), but by who first in good faith acquires possession of the object.[247] It is, incidentally, worth noting at this point that the English Sale of Goods Act contains a similar double sale rule which also turns on delivery.[248]

[243] The original Code civil contained only a single title on prescription, dealing with both extinctive and acquisitive prescription in a relatively undifferentiated manner. The former art 2279 Cc (now art 2276 Cc) featured within this title as a particular prescription period. Following a wholesale reform of the French law governing prescription in 2008, the Code civil now distinguishes more clearly between the two forms: see B West Janke and F-X Licari, 'The French Revision of Prescription: A Model for Louisiana?' (2010) 85 Tul LR 1, 31–33.

[244] For a discussion of the conceptual basis (bases?) and different functions of art 2276(1) Cc, see Costa and Faber (n 214) 151–59.

[245] This perspective also leads to a question about the way art 2276(2) Cc (set out in n 281 below) ought best to be conceptualised. Does the provision extend the prescription period from zero to three years for lost or stolen goods, or does acquisitive prescription happen immediately in all cases, with only the original owner's ability to 'revindicate' the goods in question being (exceptionally) preserved for three years where the goods are lost or stolen? cf also the third possible view outlined in n 280 below.

[246] See above, text accompanying nn 33–35.

[247] The relevant provision is now contained in art 1198 Cc:

> Where two persons successively acquire the same physical movable thing and hold their right from the same person, the person who has taken possession of this movable thing first is to be preferred, even if his right is later, provided that he is in good faith.
>
> Where two persons acquire rights over one and the same immovable property in turn and hold their right from the same person, the person who first published his title of acquisition made in an authenticated instrument on the land register [*fichier immobilier*] is preferred, even if his right is later, provided that he is in good faith.

cf the former arts 1140 (for immovables) and 1141 (for movables) Cc. The recent reform lays to rest an old question on which judicial practice had thitherto shifted to and fro regarding immovables, namely whether a third party's ability to rely on the registered position should be absolute or depend on his state of mind, ie, good faith.

[248] See SGA 1979, s 24 (entitled 'Seller in Possession after Sale').

On the spectrum ranging from the *nemo dat* starting point to a full-blown principle of bona fide purchase, modern German law comes down somewhere in the middle, yet much nearer the French position than the English. The BGB sets out in some detail the bona fide purchase rules applicable to particular modes of conveyance.[249] The principal provisions are contained in § 932 BGB:

> (1) By virtue of a transfer under § 929 the purchaser becomes owner even if the thing does not belong to the transferor, unless he [ie, the purchaser] is not in good faith at the moment when he would, according to these provisions, acquire ownership. …
>
> (2) The purchaser is not in good faith if he is either aware, or as a result of gross negligence unaware, that the thing does not belong to the transferor.

However, § 935(1) BGB makes clear that bona fide purchase cannot take place where the original owner had lost possession involuntarily, such as where the object was stolen from him.[250] This means that German law effectively operates an 'entrustment' principle: the owner will only lose out against the purchaser where he has voluntarily parted with possession, thereby enabling someone else to appear as the goods' owner.[251] A counter-exception is made for money and certain other cases where ease of commerce trumps the original owner's interest in being protected against the loss of his rights.[252]

With respect to the topic here under consideration, three points are worth making. The first is that, since § 929 BGB requires both a real agreement and a delivery (transfer of possession) for the conveyance of movables to be effective even under ordinary circumstances,[253] there is nothing special about insisting on a delivery where the conveyance is made by a non-owner to a prospective good faith purchaser. German law does not therefore face the same obvious questions as French law. Nevertheless, where the transfer of possession would normally occur only 'indirectly', without a physical handing over, through according the intended transferee a claim against the immediate or 'direct' possessor,[254] there the bona fide purchaser will acquire ownership only at a later point in time, namely when the non-owner transferor has relinquished all possession to him.[255] This means, for example, that the good faith acquisition of goods by means of constructive delivery

[249] §§ 932–934 BGB.

[250] § 935(1), 1st sentence, BGB: 'No acquisition of ownership under §§ 932 to 934 occurs if the thing was stolen, lost or otherwise separated from its owner without his consent'. The second sentence contains a qualification for cases of indirect possession.

[251] Entrustment is also relevant in French law, albeit less directly, as will be evident from art 2276(2) Cc: see n 281 below and already n 245 above.

[252] Besides money, § 935(2) BGB mentions bearer instruments as well as things transferred at public auction. For money, cf the position in English law (nn 235–36 and text thereto) as well as French law (n 237). For transactions in a specific public setting, cf the old English 'market overt' rule, formerly contained in SGA 1979, s 22 (now abolished) as well as the French art 2277 Cc (set out in n 281).

[253] See section II.C above, especially text to nn 40–43.

[254] See §§ 930, 931 BGB.

[255] See §§ 933, 934 BGB. The purchaser's good faith then needs to persist until the relevant later point in time.

(*constitutum possessorium*) is delayed until there is an actual physical delivery of the goods by the transferor to the transferee.[256]

The second point to note is that, just as (arguably) in French law,[257] but in stark contrast with the relevant provision in the Austrian ABGB and the English common law position,[258] the giving of value is not a requirement for good faith purchase under German law. §§ 932 ff BGB operate whether or not the transfer is gratuitous. This is not a coincidence, but a conceptual necessity. Looking closely at the interaction between the bona fide purchase rules and the BGB's property transfer regime, one finds that it cannot be otherwise. Since abstraction presupposes a strict separation between an obligatory transaction and a subsequent conveyance, and since each transaction is to be assessed purely on its own terms, it would be virtually impossible to make the validity of the conveyance *to the third party recipient* depend on the performance *by him* of an obligation arising from an underlying contract with the person making the unauthorised disposition. This does not, however, mean that good faith purchasers who gratuitously acquire ownership of goods from non-owners will be allowed to keep these goods. The German law of unjustified enrichment ensures that ownership is subsequently retransferred to the person who lost it on account of the bona fide acquisition.[259]

Thirdly, following on seamlessly from the previous two points, the BGB deals with bona fide purchase as part and parcel of the provisions governing derivative acquisitions. It has separate rules for the acquisitive prescription of movables,[260] and does not run the two regimes together as the French Code civil does. In contradistinction to English law, where the '*nemo dat* exceptions' are of course also triggered through an act of derivative acquisition, but where it is (in most cases) enough to protect the purchaser by extinguishing any relevant superior titles,[261] German law would seem to envisage an actual 'transfer' of ownership happening between the original owner and the acquirer in good faith.[262] In this respect, of the three main systems considered here, it displays the closest direct connection between the conveyancing rules and those on good faith acquisition.

[256] cf the comment in n 242 as regards French law.

[257] Cashin Ritaine (n 31) 121. Note, however, that the question of whether there is a 'value' requirement under French law is hardly discussed and far from settled: see reference in n 241 above.

[258] See § 367 ABGB as well as Lord Denning's quote in the text to n 233 above.

[259] § 816(1) BGB: 'If an unauthorised person disposes of an object in such a way that the disposition is effective vis-à-vis the person entitled, he is obliged to surrender to the person entitled what he has obtained by virtue of the disposition. *If the disposition is made gratuitously, the same obligation applies to the person who obtains an immediate legal advantage through the disposition*' (emphasis added).

[260] §§ 937 ff BGB.

[261] This is due to the English system of relative titles (cf n 9) above. The exact way in which the bona fide purchase rules operate differs as between the different '*nemo dat* exceptions'. In the case of money, all superior titles are extinguished under the rule in *Miller v Race* (n 236). In other situations, only certain titles are affected: see, eg, *National Employers Mutual General Insurance Association v Jones* [1990] 1 AC 24 (HL).

[262] This is not, however, undisputed. Some authors regard the bona fide purchaser's acquisition as *original* and have strong arguments for doing so, despite the supposedly derivative triggering act.

B. The Second Connection: Protecting Third Parties in Conveyance Chains

The above outline of the three systems shows that it would in principle be possible to couple the system-specific rules of conveyance with any bona fide purchase regime (either having a broad general rule or starting from the *nemo dat* rule). However, once we look at the *second* way in which the relevant rules are linked, it becomes clear that the choice of bona fide purchase regime closely interacts with the mechanisms of conveyance at a different level. To see this, we need to shift our focus from the transfer involving the innocent third party purchaser to an earlier transfer that will often have taken place between the original owner and the person who purports to effect the onward conveyance to the third party. In short, the core example now is that of a *fraudster rather than a thief* disposing of goods wrongfully obtained, and our attention must be on the first in a chain of two or more conveyances if we are fully to appreciate the connection. It is best illustrated by reference to French law: since the causal principle makes the first conveyance 'vulnerable' to rescission by the original transferor,[263] an innocent third party purchaser from the fraudulent transferee can only be protected through a broad principle of bona fide purchase. The same would be true if the contract underlying the first conveyance had been invalid for other reasons, such as on the ground of illegality or following avoidance for unilateral mistake, or if the original transferor had been trying to fulfil a merely putative obligation that did not in fact exist.

One argument often advanced in favour of the German principle of abstraction is that, within a chain of several transactions, it 'shields' purchasers further down the line from problems occurring in transactions higher up.[264] Although such an instrumental understanding may not have been foremost in Savigny's mind when developing the principle,[265] there is no denying that abstraction promotes security of transactions and ease of commerce.[266] Yet an obvious question arises as to why German law should choose to 'shield' third party purchasers through both abstraction *and* a set of entrustment-orientated bona fide purchase rules.[267]

A conceptual answer might be that the bona fide purchase rules protect some third parties who are otherwise 'insufficiently' protected by abstraction. Take the case of a person who is induced by another's fraud to conclude a contract for the

[263] See the text to nn 171–73 above.

[264] See already text to n 200 above.

[265] See n 39 and the text thereto.

[266] The element of 'transactional security' (*Verkehrsschutz*) entailed by abstraction was and remains an important teleological factor in the acceptance and application of the principle over the years: see, eg, R von Jhering, *Geist des römischen Rechts auf den verschiedenen Stufen seiner Entwicklung*, vol 3/1, 4th edn (Leipzig, Breitkopf & Härtel, 1888) 178–241, esp 210–15; A Stadler, *Gestaltungsfreiheit und Verkehrsschutz durch Abstraktion* (Tübingen, Mohr Siebeck, 1996).

[267] For an in-depth discussion of German law, with detailed comparative reference to the French and Spanish systems, see B Rodríguez-Rosado, *Abstraktionsprinzip und redlicher Erwerb als Mittel zum Schutze des Rechtsverkehrs* (Frankfurt/Main, Peter Lang, 2009).

sale of goods and, in pursuance of it, to effect a conveyance passing possession to the fraudster. The fraudulent buyer will typically dispose of the goods to an innocent third party and disappear as quickly as possible. As seen above, fraud is a case where the identical defect usually allows the seller to avoid both the obligatory contract and the real agreement underlying the conveyance.[268] Here the bona fide purchase rules are of independent value to the third party. Since the seller has parted with possession voluntarily, the goods are not treated as lost or stolen, and any person who acquires them in good faith, believing the rogue to be their owner, will thus prevail against the original owner-transferor.

However, there are also situations in which such a two-tiered system of third party protection produces what might be regarded as more problematic outcomes.[269] If, for example, the seller of goods makes a mistake which allows him to avoid the obligatory contract of sale, but not the ensuing conveyance of the goods to the buyer, then a third party purchaser who subsequently acquires the goods from the buyer obtains them *from their owner*. This is an ordinary derivative acquisition under §§ 929 ff BGB. It therefore does not matter at all whether the third party purchaser knew of the problem besetting the underlying contract, ie, whether or not he was 'in good faith' with respect to the buyer's right to retain the goods.[270] In fact, the third party purchaser would be 'protected' by the abstract nature of the original transfer even if he were the one who had caused the whole problem in the first place by inducing the original seller's mistake.[271] German law therefore arrives at different outcomes from causal systems, where the third party's 'immunity' vis-à-vis rescinding vendors further up the chain depends solely on the operation of bona fide purchase rules. If, under French law, the third party purchaser knew of the problem besetting the original transfer, and especially if he himself had caused it, he would be precluded from relying on article 2276(1) Cc by his bad faith.[272]

The reason why German law has a 'double-layered' safety-net is actually historical rather than conceptual.[273] When the principle of abstraction was first conceived

[268] See the text to and following n 175 above.

[269] This aspect is also highlighted by Rodríguez-Rosado (n 267) chs 4 and 7 (at 115–31 and 165–68), arguing that a causal *traditio* transfer system regarding movables, such as that operated by Spanish, Austrian or Swiss law, when coupled with a robust principle of bona fide purchase, produces the most appropriate overall balance between the competing interests of the various parties involved.

[270] If the acquisition was gratuitous, the third party would under certain circumstances be exposed to a *personal* claim by the original transferor. This is a 'leapfrogging' claim based on unjustified enrichment: § 822 BGB. In other cases, however, a *mala fide* third party purchaser acquiring the goods (for value) directly benefits from the effect of abstraction between his predecessors in title. This is also noted by Rodríguez-Rosado (n 267) 116, who criticises the result as being out-of-sync with the value judgements underlying §§ 892, 932 BGB and very hard to justify in ethical terms.

[271] Note that, if the third party acted as the buyer's *agent* in the first transaction, then any fraudulent misrepresentation made by him would count as the buyer's fraud. If the third party was *not* the buyer's agent, then the seller would only be able to rescind (both transactions) on account of fraud if the buyer knew of the fraudulent misrepresentation or ought to have been aware of it: § 123(2) BGB. Any wrongs-based claims by the original seller which may be available directly against the third party misrepresentor are, of course, unaffected.

[272] See n 240 and the text thereto.

[273] Suggestions for reforming the law without embracing a wholesale 'abolition' of abstraction, thus respecting the existing conceptual framework, are provided in Häcker (n 6) 250–55.

by Savigny and subsequently propounded by his followers, it was premised on the old Roman maxim that *nemo dat quod non habet*.[274] Like classical Roman law, the tradition of the European *ius commune* did not recognise a principle of bona fide purchase. Barring exceptional circumstances,[275] anyone who was owner (*dominus*) of an object could recover it from its current possessor by means of the *vindicatio*. Yet various of the codifications which began to emerge from the late eighteenth century onwards started incorporating rules based on the rival Germanic tradition. This only offered protection to people who had involuntarily lost possession of an object,[276] not to those who had willingly parted with it.[277] As a result, there was greater transactional security for third party purchasers, who were not vulnerable to claims by the original 'owner' unless they had acquired something which was lost or stolen. While the Prussian General State Law of 1794 incorporated a limited number of specific exceptions to the *nemo dat* rule,[278] the Austrian ABGB of 1811 went further and provided for a general entrustment principle.[279] By far the broadest rule, however, is the French rule already outlined above. It will be recalled that, according to the French approach, 'possession is equivalent to title', and the (original) owner's *vindicatio* is excluded,[280] except where the goods in question were lost or stolen from him.[281]

[274] More precisely, according to Dig 50.17.54 (Ulpian), 'nemo plus iuris ad alium transferre potest, quam ipse haberet' ('no-one can transfer to another more in terms of rights than he himself might have' or, in the better-known and oft-cited translation by Alan Watson, 'no one can transfer greater rights to someone else than he possesses himself').

[275] In particular, the owner of a *res mancipi* who had sold it and conveyed it to the purchaser by a simple *traditio* instead of the requisite formal mode of conveyance, would be met by a defence (*exceptio rei venditae et traditae*) enabling the purchaser to keep it. The latter is therefore often referred to as 'bonitary owner'.

[276] Technically, what was at issue was not the Roman notion of 'possession', but a protected relationship between a person and a thing under his control (*gewere*), equivalent to the old common law notion of *seisin*.

[277] We can here see the origins of the entrustment principle. The maxims *Hand wahre Hand* and the saying that 'you must look for your faith where you have reposed it' express the idea that the owner who voluntarily gives up goods to another has to bear the consequences where his trust subsequently turns out to have been misplaced.

[278] Part I, Title 15, §§ 1, 42 ff of the *Allgemeines Landrecht* ('ALR'), pertaining to things acquired at public auction, from merchants belonging to a guild, cash or bearer instruments. Note additionally Part I, Title 15, § 25 f ALR, providing that, even where no bona fide purchase had occurred, innocent purchasers for value could reclaim the purchase price from the owner. There is a resemblance here with the French *droit de remboursement* (outlined at the end of n 281 below).

[279] §§ 367 f ABGB. These provisions were redrafted with effect from 2007, but as far as is relevant here, their core remains the same.

[280] If one regards art 2276(1) Cc as a genuine case of acquisitive prescription (see text to nn 244–45), then the exclusion of the original owner's *vindicatio* is a logical consequence. The wording of the provision, however, also allows for an alternative view. On this view, the owner's *vindicatio* is excluded *although* his rights remain theoretically unchanged, and the acquirer in good faith is merely fictitiously treated henceforth *as if* he were the owner.

[281] Under art 2276(2) Cc (formerly art 2279(2)), a person who has lost a thing or from whom it has been stolen 'can reclaim [literally: revindicate] it within three years, counting from the day of the loss or the theft, against the person in whose hands he finds it', leaving the defendant third party purchaser to seek an indemnity from the person who sold it to him. However, there is an immediate qualification in art 2277 Cc (formerly art 2280). In certain circumstances, particularly where the defendant

The French and Austrian provisions became influential during the deliberations leading up to the enactment of the BGB.[282] They had already inspired the General German Commercial Code of 1861 (*Allgemeines Deutsches Handelsgesetzbuch*: 'ADHGB') to adopt a basic entrustment principle, hedged about with special privileges – irrespective of loss or theft – for the good faith purchase of bearer instruments.[283] Although the preliminary draft of the book on property law within the BGB had stuck to the basic Roman *nemo dat* rule,[284] the first drafting commission took the view that the general private law rules on movables about to be codified should ideally align with those in the ADHGB and indeed the law governing immovables, where the possibility of good faith acquisition in reliance on the land register had already been approved.[285] Its members thus decided to change direction and to include within the BGB a *bona fides* regime based on entrustment.[286] The functional overlap with the principle of abstraction thereby created seems not to have commanded much attention at the time.[287]

One might expect a system like the English, whose conveyancing rules are neither wholly 'causal' nor wholly 'abstract', but a weird-and-wonderful mixture of both,[288] to have bona fide purchase rules befitting this state of affairs. That is indeed what we find on closer inspection. It will be recalled that English law's basic starting point is the idea that no-one can give more or better rights than he himself has, yet with a range of common law and statutory 'exceptions' carved out of the basic *nemo dat* rule.[289] And while one may well criticise English law for

possessor bought the lost or stolen thing at a fair, market, in a public sale or from a shop selling items of the relevant kind, the success of the owner's *vindicatio* will be conditional on reimbursing the purchase price the defendant paid for it, thus effectively shifting the economic risk onto the claimant (former?) owner.

[282] The legislative process is traced by W Schubert, *Die Entstehung der Vorschriften des BGB über Besitz und Eigentumsübertragung* (Berlin, de Gruyter, 1966) 149–54, 157–60, 165–69.

[283] §§ 306 ff ADHGB.

[284] See § 135 of the draft (*Teilentwurf*: 'TE') by Reinhold Johow, which allowed for good faith purchase only in a very limited range of circumstances, namely for the case of money, bearer instruments and things sold at public auction. Yet note that the innocent third party purchaser was in all other cases afforded at least *economic* protection through being able to claim reimbursement of the purchase price from the claimant owner: § 186 TE (so-called *Lösungsrecht*, comparable to French law's *droit au remboursement* now contained in art 2277 Cc).

[285] *Protokolle der 1. Kommission zur Ausarbeitung des BGB*, 26 May 1884, Prot I 4003–6, published in HH Jakobs and W Schubert (eds), *Die Beratung des Bürgerlichen Gesetzbuchs, Sachenrecht I: §§ 854–1017* (Berlin, de Gruyter, 1985) 598–99; *Motive zu dem Entwurfe eines Bürgerlichen Gesetzbuches für das Deutsche Reich*, vol 3 (Berlin and Leipzig, Guttentag, 1888) 344–50.

[286] The first drafting commission nevertheless wanted to retain the right to claim reimbursement that had featured in § 186 TE (see n 284). The claim would effectively have been confined to the situation where lost or stolen goods are vindicated. As such, however, it entailed a real danger of undermining the security of ownership. The second drafting commission thus scrapped the *Lösungsrecht*: A Achilles, H Gebhard and P Spahn (eds), *Protokolle der Kommission für die zweite Lesung des Entwurfs des Bürgerlichen Gesetzbuchs*, vol 3 (Berlin, Guttentag, 1899) 367–69.

[287] Despite the fact that the drafters were well aware of the close interaction between the French causal consensual transfer system and the Code civil's broad principle of good faith acquisition: see *Motive* vol 3 (n 285) 334.

[288] See section II.E above.

[289] See text to nn 234–36 above.

lacking an overarching principle of bona fide purchase based on coherent value judgements,[290] it is worth recognising that its law on bona fide purchase governing second and subsequent transactions in conveyance chains is broadly attuned to the 'causal' or 'abstract' nature of the first transfer within the chain.[291]

This statement needs some fleshing out. It was demonstrated above that there are only a very limited number of scenarios in which English law can be said to be fully 'causal' in the French sense, namely where a contract for the sale of goods is rescinded for fraud or duress.[292] In this case, as demonstrated by *Car & Universal Finance Co Ltd v Caldwell*, title 'revests' in the original transferor at common law. However, in all other situations, including the case where a seller of goods delivers them to a buyer under a void contract, English law is either fully 'abstract' or – depending on one's view of resulting trusts – at most 'causal' in equity.[293] Assuming the latter, the original transferor would have a vested equitable interest under a trust or a power *in rem* to bring such an interest into existence. In either event, his interest is 'killed off' by a subsequent common law conveyance of the asset in question to a bona fide purchaser for value without notice. This means that a third party who qualifies as 'equity's darling'[294] and in good faith acquires title to the affected goods for valuable consideration from the transferee will be 'immune' as regards any proprietary interest of the original owner.[295] This equitable bona fide purchase rule applies generally and across the board. Within its remit, the *nemo dat* principle is ousted.

What remains are (for the most part)[296] cases of the type in which the original transferor purports to avoid a contract at common law and at the same time to 'revest' title to the goods conveyed under or in pursuance of it. Considering its basic commitment to the *nemo dat* principle, English law here provides quite a remarkable measure of protection to innocent third party purchasers from the transferee. The so-called 'third party rights bar to rescission' has already been mentioned.[297]

[290] A Tettenborn, 'Transfer of Chattels by Non-Owners: Still an Open Problem' (2018) 77 CLJ 151, for instance, argues in favour of a default rule based on entrustment.

[291] The present chapter does not seek to address ordinary cases where a bailee of goods or the borrower to whom the 'owner' has entrusted an item (without a conveyance being envisaged at any point) purports to effect an unauthorised conveyance. Here there does indeed appear to be an evident lacuna in English law, which is only insufficiently plugged by the estoppel-principle mentioned at the end of s 21(1) SGA 1979.

[292] See text to nn 65–75 as well as to nn 184–90.

[293] See the discussion in the text to nn 227–30 above. A trust is also the maximum a transferor of goods can hope to achieve where he rescinds the underlying contract and/or the conveyance for the other party's non-fraudulent misrepresentation or undue influence: n 186 and text thereto.

[294] This term, though widely used, is somewhat misleading. As pointed out by J Hackney, *Understanding Equity and Trusts* (London, Fontana Press, 1987) 24–25, 'Equity shows him no affection at all, he has simply shown himself to belong to that large class of common law owners with whom Equity has nothing to do'.

[295] See, eg, *Cave v Cave* (1880) 15 Ch D 639 (ChD). The case nicely illustrates the difference between good faith purchasers of legal and equitable interests.

[296] Leaving aside cases such as *Cundy v Lindsay* (n 182), where a 'fundamental' mistake, especially an identity mistake, prevents title passing both under the contract of sale *or* by a subsequent delivery.

[297] See text to n 194 above.

It is best understood as a version of the bona fide purchase defence,[298] and its statutory incarnation is to be found in section 23 of the Sale of Goods Act 1979:

> When the seller of goods has a voidable title to them, but his title has not been avoided at the time of the sale, the buyer acquires a good title to the goods, provided he buys them in good faith and without notice of the seller's defect of title.

In the days before *Caldwell*, this would typically have been all the protection third parties required. Either a rogue still had the goods when found, in which case there was no problem about rescinding the sale; or he had already passed them on, in which case innocent third party purchasers for value were protected, but not bad faith purchasers or donees. Innocent third parties would rarely suffer.[299] Yet *Caldwell* changed the landscape. By facilitating rescission without giving notice to the rogue,[300] the decision created – or significantly enlarged – a lacuna in the English bona fide purchase regime. This was evident from the very start. Shortly after it had decided *Caldwell*, the Court of Appeal handed down a second decision, in a case called *Newtons of Wembley Ltd v Williams*.[301] The facts were similar to those in *Caldwell*. A rogue had defrauded the claimants into selling and delivering a car to him. When the cheque tendered in payment bounced, the claimants took all available steps to disaffirm the contract, but failed to locate the car. The villain later sold it on Warren Street market (a second-hand car market in London) to an innocent purchaser, who in turn sold it on to the defendant. Had the case been decided solely on the 'rescission without notice' principle recognised in *Caldwell*, the claimants' action in conversion[302] against the defendant should have succeeded. Yet both the trial judge and the Court of Appeal felt uncomfortable with this result and found an ingenious solution to avoid the conundrum. They relied on a special bona fide purchase rule in section 9 of the Factors Act 1889. This governs dispositions by parties who have bought or agreed to buy goods and are in possession of them with the consent of the seller despite not (yet) having acquired full title. There is a parallel provision in section 25(1) of the Sale of Goods Act 1979 entitled 'buyer in possession after sale'.[303] So far as is relevant here, section 25(1) reads:

> Where a person having bought or agreed to buy goods obtains, with the consent of the seller, possession of the goods or the documents of title to the goods, the delivery or transfer by that person … of the goods or documents of title, under any sale, pledge, or

[298] See Häcker (n 193) esp 22–24, 33–40.

[299] A potential problem could and still can arise with bona fide donees who no longer have the goods they innocently converted. They would be left out of pocket if they had to pay the claimant 'owner' the full value of the goods or even to compensate him for consequential losses. It has been tentatively suggested that they may at any rate not need to do the latter: *Kuwait Airways Corp v Iraqi Airways Co (Nos 4 & 5)* [2002] UKHL 19, [2002] 2 AC 883, per Lord Nicholls at [79].

[300] See n 189 and text thereto.

[301] *Newtons of Wembley Ltd v Williams* [1965] 1 QB 560 (CA).

[302] The claim was actually based on detinue and conversion. As noted above (n 130), the tort of detinue was subsequently abolished by means of the Torts (Interference with Goods) Act 1977, s 2.

[303] It is what might be described as the mirror image of the provision in s 24 SGA 1979 (already mentioned), dealing with a 'seller in possession after sale': see n 248 and text thereto.

> other disposition thereof, to any person receiving the same in good faith and without notice of any lien or other right of the original seller in respect of the goods, has the same effect as if the person making the delivery or transfer were a mercantile agent in possession of the goods or documents of title with the consent of the owner.

When first enacted in the Factors Act 1889 and the Sale of Goods Act 1893,[304] this provision was intended to cover cases where goods purchased under a reservation of title clause were disposed of by the purchaser before they had been paid for, or where an unpaid seller's lien exceptionally persisted despite the temporary release of the goods to the buyer. In *Newtons of Wembley*, however, it was made serviceable for cases in which the original seller's title had 'revested' on account of a timely act of rescission. The trial judge (just about) managed to distinguish *Caldwell* on the facts.[305] While in *Caldwell*, the immediate purchaser from the rogue had had notice of the defect in his seller's title, the first purchaser in *Newtons* did not. This meant that the sale by the rogue in *Newtons* (on our scheme the *second* sale in the entire conveyancing chain) would have – in the words of the statute – 'the same effect as if the person making the delivery or transfer were a mercantile agent in possession of the goods or documents of title with the consent of the owner'.[306] And since a second-hand car sale on Warren Street market was perfectly compatible with a mercantile agent's ordinary course of business,[307] the bona fide purchaser from the rogue obtained a title which was good as against the defrauded claimants and which he was thus able to pass on to the defendant (in the ensuing third sale).

These kinds of subtle distinctions between good faith purchasers directly from the rogue and innocent third parties acquiring goods further down the line are undeniably less than ideal.[308] Nonetheless, they must not obscure the fundamental point at issue here, namely that English courts have responded to an increased likelihood of the *first* conveyance in a chain being impugned by an act of rescission without notice through expanding the scope of bona fide purchase when it comes to a *second* transaction further down the line. Once again, the takeaway message is that the conveyancing regime and the bona fide purchase rules interrelate very closely indeed.

IX. Conclusion

Just as animals and plants are adapted to their natural habitat, so legal rules and concepts exist in a normative environment to which they will typically adjust and which they, in turn, influence and shape in various respects. This chapter

304 What is now s 25(1) SGA 1979 was previously contained in s 25(2) SGA 1893.

305 *Newtons of Wembley Ltd v Williams* [1964] 1 WLR 1028 (QB) 1033.

306 On the meaning of this rather obscure phrase, see *National Employers Mutual General Insurance Association v Jones* (n 261).

307 *Newtons of Wembley v Williams* (n 305) 1034.

308 Häcker (n 6) 233, 255–56.

has focused on the way in which different systems' conveyancing rules (primarily those concerning the transfer of movables) interact with a series of other legal issues, from the question about the passing of risk, via the law governing rescission and unjust(ified) enrichment, to the respective bona fide purchase regimes.

There is, however, a broader comparative lesson to learn. Studying the similarities and differences between individual rules across two or more systems is not enough; nor is it enough to focus solely on the 'outcome' of actual or hypothetical cases solved within each 'black box'. We should instead strive for a holistic approach and understand *how* and *why* whole sets of rules (and, where appropriate, practices) together function as part of an intricate legal machinery. It is unlikely we will ever be able to see the complete picture across even a modest number of systems. But, staying with the machinery metaphor, our aspiration as comparative lawyers must be to become the best possible engineers – with no less competence in the minutiae of fine-mechanics than visions for outcome or grand design.

6

The Creation and Transfer of Property Rights by Contract in English Law

JOHN CARTWRIGHT

I. Introduction. Contract and Property: Independence and Interdependence

We learn early in our legal training that contract and property are fundamentally different categories within the structure of private law. Contracts belong within the law of obligations, and create rights which, in principle, are personal to those involved in the creation of the obligations (the parties to the contract). Property is an entirely separate category of right which, in principle, is not limited to those involved in its creation but is able not only to be transferred for the benefit of third parties but also to burden third parties. The core distinction, expressed by Roman law, is between rights *in personam* and rights *in rem*,[1] and the categoric separation of contract and property is also recognised in English law.[2] The distinction in nature between contract and property leads our legal systems also to develop different procedures by which such rights can be created (and, where so permitted, transferred). For example, the requirements for the formation of a contract are different from the requirements for the creation or transfer of property rights, and in many situations requirements within the law of property are stricter than within the law of contract – such as in the formalities required for the creation or transfer of rights to certain forms of property.

Each of the chapters in this book explores some aspect of the nature of contractual rights and/or property rights, in one jurisdiction or comparatively between

[1] B Nicholas, *An Introduction to Roman Law* (Oxford, Clarendon Press, 1962) 99–103; P Birks, 'Five Keys to Land Law' in S Bright and J Dewar (eds), *Land Law Themes and Perspectives* (Oxford, Oxford University Press, 1998) 472–73.

[2] *National Provincial Bank Ltd v Ainsworth* [1965] AC 1175 (HL) 1247–48 (Lord Wilberforce: 'Before a right or an interest can be admitted into the category of property, or of a right affecting property, it must be definable, identifiable by third parties, capable in its nature of assumption by third parties, and have some degree of permanence or stability').

jurisdictions. In this chapter, I want to consider one particular aspect of the relationship *between* contract and property: the way in which property rights can be created or transferred *by* contract. The focus here is English law rather than comparisons with the civil law because, as we shall see, English law has developed some solutions which are peculiar to the common law's way of thinking. The chapter will also focus, at least in the first instance, on property rights in land, and contracts relating to land, since it is in this context that a particular link between contract and property has been developed, although later we shall see some general points that can be made about contracts to transfer property generally (including therefore contracts for goods as well as for land). In essence, the common theme of the chapter is when (and why) English law sees the contract to transfer a right of property as in itself having the effect of transferring the property right (or, at least, creating *a* property right); and the extent to which the strength or validity of the property right that is thereby created or transferred can be related back to the validity of the contract – the interdependence of the contract by which the property right is created or transferred, and the property right itself.

II. Contracts to Transfer Rights in Land: The Creation of Property Rights in Equity

First, contracts to transfer rights in land – and here, the starting-point is the independence of the contract and property. We can take the simplest case of a transaction involving the sale of land, which is commonly effected in two stages. First, the contract of sale of the land is entered into as soon as the parties have come to an agreement as to the terms of the transaction (and, in particular, the price), in order to take the property off the market and to impose mutual obligations on the parties to proceed with the transaction – the obligation on the vendor to transfer his rights in the land,[3] and the obligation on the purchaser to pay the price and take the transfer.[4] At some later time, fixed by the contract, the

[3] In English law, the subject-matter of the transfer is not 'ownership' in the sense understood by a civil lawyer in the Roman tradition: the legal title that is sold is either the freehold estate (an 'estate in fee simple absolute in possession': LPA 1925, s 1(1)(a); this approximates to the civil law notion of ownership, but is technically the right to possession of the land without limitation of time, and which is transferable and continues until the current estate owner dies without any heir to whom it can be transmitted) or a leasehold estate (a 'term of years absolute': LPA 1925, s 1(1)(b); this is the right to exclusive possession, granted by a person with the right to possession (the freeholder or another leaseholder) for a defined period of time). See EH Burn and J Cartwright, *Cheshire and Burn's Modern Law of Real Property*, 18th edn (Oxford, Oxford University Press, 2011) 12–14, 20 and (for more detail and history) 48–59, 123–24; S Bridge, E Cooke and M Dixon (eds), *Megarry & Wade, The Law of Real Property*, 9th edn (London, Sweet & Maxwell, 2019) [7-002]–[7-013].

[4] The contract will normally contain other obligations, too: a contract which simply contains the minimum express agreement (the parties, the property and the price) will contain certain limited implied terms as to proof of title by the vendor, but in practice contracts for the sale of land are entered

transaction is 'completed' by the transfer of the property rights themselves. In principle, the contract and the transfer are independent, with separate requirements set by the law to make them effective: a contract for the sale of land must be in writing, containing all the expressly agreed terms of the contract and signed by both parties;[5] but the transfer ('conveyance') of land or of an interest in land must generally be by 'deed'[6] – a written instrument which must make clear on its face that it is intended to be a deed and, in the case of a deed executed by an individual, must be signed by the person(s) entering into it, and the signature must be attested (witnessed by a person who confirms on the document that they have witnessed the signature).[7] In order for the transfer to be fully effective, the transfer must be completed by registration at the Land Registry.[8]

The validity of the transfer does not depend on the validity of the contract;[9] indeed, there is no requirement for a contract at all: the parties may proceed directly to the transfer without having first entered into a separate contract. However, the more interesting question for our purposes is what happens where the parties fail to execute a transfer in accordance with the legal requirements for a deed of transfer. They may fail altogether to execute the deed, or they may make an attempt to do so but in a way which fails properly to comply with the formality requirements for the deed, and so the deed is void. In either case, as long as there is a contract for the sale,[10] we shall see that the contract itself can have proprietary consequences,

into on detailed terms contained in standard forms: *Cheshire and Burn's Modern Law of Real Property* (n 3) 950–54.

[5] LP(MP)A 1989, s 2. Before this Act came into force, a contract for the sale of land could be created without writing, but generally it could be enforced only against a party who had signed a written memorandum creating or acknowledging the contract: LPA 1925, s 40, re-enacting a provision of the Statute of Frauds 1677. In practice, contracts for land were therefore already entered into in writing.

[6] LPA 1925, s 52(1). There are certain exceptions, set out in s 52(2).

[7] LP(MP)A 1989, s 1. Before this Act came into force, a deed had to be *sealed* rather than witnessed; but now only corporations can seal a deed (and do not need to do so, but can execute a deed by witnessed signatures). It should be noted that English law does not use the formality of notarisation for the transfer of land: although the execution of a deed requires a third-party witness, this formality is private, and significantly less onerous than attending before a notary. cf J Cartwright, '"Authenticity" and "Authentic Instruments": The Perspective of English Law' in L Aynès (ed), *L'authenticité* (Paris, La documentation Française, 2013) 183–208.

[8] LRA 2002, s 27, which set out a list of dispositions of registered land which are required to be completed by registration before they 'operate at law'. This is a reference to the distinction between 'legal' and merely 'equitable' title: see below, section II.C. The entry of the person in the register as the proprietor of the legal estate conclusively vests the title in him: LRA 2002, s 58.

[9] The transfer is therefore 'abstract' in the sense discussed generally in this book; see also Häcker, above, Ch 5, esp text to n 58.

[10] This will usually be a contract of sale which was intended by the parties to be followed by a deed (but the deed has not been executed), but it may sometimes be where there is no contract of sale but there is an instrument which was intended to take effect as a deed to transfer the property, which fails to satisfy the legal requirements for a deed: if it fulfils the legal requirements for a contract of sale between the parties (above, n 5), it can take effect as if it had been intended to be a contract: eg *Bank of Scotland plc v Waugh* [2014] EWHC 2117 (Ch), [2015] 1 P & CR DG3 (a purported grant of a mortgage was not effective as a deed because it was not attested, but it satisfied LP(MP)A 1989, s 2, and so took effect as a contract for a mortgage and therefore as an equitable mortgage under the doctrine of *Walsh v Lonsdale*, below, section II.B).

even without the deed having to be executed. It does not have the same effect as a deed, of course, otherwise the requirement of a deed would be superfluous. However, although the contract does not transfer the full ('legal') property, it can create in the intended transferee a lesser ('equitable') interest in the property.

A. The Distinction between Legal and Equitable Rights in Land: Historical Context

We cannot here discuss in detail the distinction between legal and equitable property rights, and their historical development,[11] but a brief overview is necessary in order to understand the discussion which follows.

The King's courts (the 'common law' courts), developing land law within a feudal structure from the early middle ages onwards, recognised certain rights in land – estates in land (freehold and leasehold) and interests in or over those estates (such as easements, our equivalent of servitudes in civil law systems) – which operated in a way similar to the civil lawyer's notions of ownership and of limited rights over the ownership of property:[12] in effect, as rights *in rem*, binding all those who come to the land. However, from the fifteenth century onwards, a separate regime was developed by the King's Chancellor into what became the (separate) Court of Chancery – a court of 'equity': and the Court of Chancery came to recognise (equitable) estates and interests in land separately from the estates and interests recognised by the common law courts. Today, there are no longer separate courts of common law and of equity in England: the old courts were united into a single court structure by the Judicature Act 1873. However, the substantive rules of common law and equity remained distinct, but were (and still are now)[13] administered by the unified court. So the modern courts – the High Court, the Court of Appeal and the Supreme Court – still recognise the old distinction between legal (common law) property rights and equitable property rights.[14]

The courts of equity recognised certain rights which are different from those recognised by the common law: the most significant – not limited to land – is the interest of the beneficiary under a trust.[15] They also recognised rights which

[11] *Cheshire and Burn's Modern Law of Real Property* (n 3) ch 3; *Megarry & Wade, The Law of Real Property* (n 3) ch 4.

[12] See above, n 3; Birks (n 1) 472–75.

[13] Senior Courts Act 1981, s 49(2).

[14] The 1873 Act provided, however, that 'conflict or variance between the Rules of Equity and the Rules of the Common Law with reference to the same matter [on matters not specifically regulated by the Act], the Rules of Equity shall prevail': s 25(11), now contained in the Senior Courts Act 1981, s 49(1).

[15] Another is the covenant which restricts the use of land in favour of a neighbour, and which therefore has the potential to benefit and bind successive owners of the benefited and burdened property: *Tulk v Moxhay* (1848) 2 Ph 774, 41 ER 1143 (ChD); *Cheshire and Burn's Modern Law of Real Property* (n 3) ch 19; *Megarry & Wade, The Law of Real Property* (n 3) ch 31.

could have been created as legal rights, but which had not been properly created as such – in effect, therefore, creating equitable estates and interests in parallel to the estates and interests recognised by the common law. But the force given by the courts of equity to such (equitable) interests was not a strong as that given by the common law courts to legal estates and interests:

> An equitable estate was not, however, as strong as a legal estate; and an equitable interest was not as strong as a legal interest. A legal estate and interest operated as a property right in the full sense – as a right *in rem*, which would bind any person who came to the land over which the estate or interest had been created. An equitable estate or interest, however, was not so fully effective. It had the main characteristic of a property right in that it was capable of enduring through successive changes of ownership of the land, so as to both benefit and bind parties who were not involved in its original creation. But it was defeated if a legal estate in the burdened land passed into the hands of a bona fide purchaser for value who had no notice of the prior equitable estate or interest. This 'bona fide purchaser' (as he was – and is – commonly known) took priority over the equitable owner.[16]

In relation to land, in particular where the title to the land has been registered, we no longer formally use the test of the 'bona fide purchaser', which has been replaced by statutory tests based on registration (and, in some cases, occupation of the land by the holder of the interest).[17] But this is still the general test outside the context of land law; and in all cases the core distinction between legal and equitable interests remains as it was developed by the old courts: a legal property right in principle binds all who come to the property; an equitable interest binds all except a person who purchases a legal estate or interest in the property without notice of the equitable interest.

B. The Creation of Equitable Interests by Contract: The Doctrine of *Walsh v Lonsdale*

There are a number of closely-related situations in which the courts have recognised that an (equitable) interest in property can arise in spite of the fact that the formalities, normally required for the creation of a (legal) interest to be recognised at common law, have not been complied with.[18] Amongst them is that with which

[16] *Cheshire and Burn's Modern Law of Real Property* (n 3) 15 (footnotes omitted); further detail is set out in chapter 3 of that work.

[17] Below, section II.C.

[18] J Cartwright, 'Equity's Connivance in the Evasion of Legal Formalities' in E Koops and WJ Zwalve (eds), *Law & Equity: Approaches in Roman Law and Common Law* (Leiden, Martinus Nijhoff, 2014) ch 5, esp 112–21, discussing the doctrines of *part performance* (to avoid the requirement under LPA 1925, s 40 of a signed written memorandum to render an oral agreement for the sale of land enforceable); *secret trusts* (to avoid the requirement under Wills Act 1837 of testamentary dispositions being contained in a duly executed will); *constructive trusts* and *proprietary estoppel* (to avoid the requirement

we are concerned, sometimes referred to as the doctrine of *Walsh v Lonsdale* (after the case of that name), under which a general principle has been established: that a contract to transfer or create a legal estate or interest in land is treated, in equity, as itself transferring or creating the equivalent estate or interest, on the basis that 'Equity treats as done that which ought to be done'.[19] As long as the contractual promise to transfer or create the legal estate or interest would be enforced by the court, Equity will already give effect to it.

Walsh v Lonsdale[20] involved a contract to create a seven-year lease, where the deed required to create the legal lease had not been executed. Jessel MR in the Court of Appeal said:

> The tenant holds under an agreement for a lease. He holds, therefore, under the same terms in equity as if a lease had been granted, it being a case in which both parties admit that relief is capable of being given by specific performance. That being so, he cannot complain of the exercise by the landlord of the same rights as the landlord would have had if the lease had been granted. On the other hand, he is protected in the same way as if the lease had been granted …[21]

In this case, therefore, a contract to create a (legal) lease was held to create an equivalent equitable lease. Similarly, it has been held in other cases that a contract to transfer the legal fee simple (the freehold title) already creates an equivalent equitable title;[22] a contract to create a legal easement creates an equitable easement;[23] and a contract to create a legal mortgage creates an equitable mortgage.[24] This was not a new principle when *Walsh v Lonsdale* was decided in 1882; in an earlier case in which the owner of a freehold estate in land had entered into a contract to sell the land, but had not yet completed the sale, Jessel MR had said:

> What is the effect of the contract? It appears to me that the effect of a contract for sale has been settled for more than two centuries; certainly it was completely settled before the time of Lord Hardwicke,[25] who speaks of the settled doctrine of the Court as to it. What is that doctrine? It is that the moment you have a valid contract for sale the vendor becomes in equity a trustee for the purchaser of the estate sold, and the beneficial ownership passes to the purchaser, the vendor having a right to the purchase-money, a charge or lien on the estate for the security of that purchase-money, and a right to retain possession of the estate until the purchase-money is paid, in the absence of express contract as to the time of delivering possession …[26]

under LPA 1925, ss 52 and 53 of a deed and/or writing for the express creation of rights in property). See also J McGhee (ed), *Snell's Equity*, 34th edn (London, Sweet & Maxwell, 2019) ch 24.

[19] *Snell's Equity* (n 18) [5-015], doubting whether it is really a useful basis for the operation of the doctrine of *Walsh v Lonsdale*; J Glister and J Lee, *Hanbury and Martin: Modern Equity*, 21st edn (London, Sweet & Maxwell, 2018) [1-032].

[20] (1882) 21 Ch D 9 (CA).

[21] Above, n 20 at 14–15.

[22] *Lysaght v Edwards* (1876) 2 Ch D 499 (ChD).

[23] *McManus v Cooke* (1887) 35 Ch D 681 (ChD).

[24] *Tebb v Hodge* (1869) LR 5 CP 73 (ExCh); *Bank of Scotland plc v Waugh* (n 10).

[25] [Lord Hardwicke was Lord Chancellor from 1737 to 1756.]

[26] *Lysaght v Edwards* (n 22) at 505–06.

According to this analysis, the legal owner of land, having contracted to sell, has created a *trust* of his legal title to the land in favour of the purchaser – commonly seen as a 'constructive trust' (one imposed by the law, rather than expressed directly by the parties) between vendor and purchaser.[27] Whether the purchaser's interest is properly regarded as that of the beneficiary under a (constructive) trust has been debated by academic writers in recent years,[28] but the details of that debate do not concern us here. It is sufficient to note that the contract of sale is seen as creating not merely a personal relationship between the parties – mutual rights *in personam*, including the purchaser's (contractual) right to call for the completion of the transfer – but an equitable proprietary right in the hands of the purchaser. To understand the nature of this (proprietary) right, we should consider its strength, but also its origin in the link to the remedy of specific performance of the contract of sale by which it is created.

C. The Strength Against Third Parties of the Purchaser's Equitable Interest Arising under a Contract of Sale of Land

The vendor retains the legal title until he executes the deed of transfer (and until, in the case of registered land, the transfer is completed by registration).[29] So the purchaser does not yet become the (full) owner of the title to the land. But from the moment the contract is entered into, the purchaser acquires an equitable interest in the land which has proprietary characteristics: it has the capacity to bind not only the vendor but also other parties into whose hand the land comes. If, therefore, having contracted to sell the land to P1, the vendor (V) instead transfers the land to P2, P2 may in certain circumstances take the land subject to the prior right of P1 – who may therefore be able to enforce his right and deprive P2 of the title to the land. Under the system of unregistered conveyancing, which was the normal form of land ownership and transfer before the introduction of registration of the title to land by the Land Registration Act 1925, the equitable interest created by the contract in P1's favour would bind P2 unless he was a bona fide purchaser of

[27] *Hanbury and Martin: Modern Equity* (n 19) [12-008]–[12-009]; *Snell's Equity* (n 18) [24-002]–[24-004].

[28] *Hanbury and Martin: Modern Equity* (n 19) [12-009] ('No doubt it is too late now to say that the relationship between vendor and purchaser is not that of trustee and beneficiary … Yet there will remain considerable controversy over this issue and the terminology must be treated carefully'). PG Turner, 'Understanding the Constructive Trust Between Vendor and Purchaser' (2012) 128 LQR 582 is strongly in favour, and gives a very helpful analysis of the arguments; cf WS Swadling, 'The Fiction of the Constructive Trust' (2011) 64 CLP 399. For recent discussion of some of the issues by the Supreme Court, see *Re North East Property Buyers Litigation* [2014] UKSC 52, [2015] AC 385 at [55]–[79], [104]–[114] (the purchaser of land cannot create a proprietary (sub-)interest in the land which is capable of being an overriding interest (see below n 36) and binding on the purchaser's mortgagee, until his contract is completed and he acquires the legal title).

[29] Above, text to nn 6–8.

the legal estate without actual or constructive notice of P1's interest;[30] this means that a donee of the land is bound by P1's prior interest, but a purchaser of land can take free of it as long as he had no notice of it: his 'conscience is clear'.[31] And since 1926, even the question whether a purchaser of unregistered land has notice of the prior interest depends not on the general facts of the case, but on whether P1 has placed an entry in the register of land charges, so that P2 can discover it by searching the register.[32] Under the system of registered conveyancing, where the title to the land itself is registered,[33] the starting point is the same: the prior equitable interest will bind a donee of the registered title to the land,[34] but a purchaser for value may take free of it. But in that case the question is no longer, in principle, whether P2 has 'notice' of P1's equitable interest, but whether the interest is protected,[35] either by being entered on the register of the title (so that P2 will see it when he inspects the register to see the title that he is buying) or where P1's interest is an 'overriding interest' – one of certain categories of interest that will bind purchasers even if they are not entered on the register. The relevant category of overriding interest here is the interest of a person in 'actual occupation' of the land in question, since a purchaser ought to make inquiries of anyone in occupation of the land he is buying.[36] If, therefore, P1 is not yet in occupation of the land, and has not protected his interest under the contract by an entry on the vendor's title, P2 takes free of it when he is registered as the new proprietor of the land. Otherwise, he takes his legal title subject to P1's equitable interest under the contract.

What, though, does it mean to say that P2 takes the legal title subject to P1's equitable interest? In simple terms, it means that P1's rights, as they were enforceable against V under (and by virtue of) the contract, are equally enforceable against P2. So as long as P1 could have required V to complete the transfer in his favour had V remained owner of the legal title, this is the claim which P1 can now make against P2. So, in a sense, what is enforceable against P2 is the contractual rights, and the remedy of specific performance of those rights.[37] But this means that the

[30] Above, n 16.

[31] AH Chaytor and WJ Whittaker, *Maitland's Equity* (Cambridge, Cambridge University Press, 1929) 118–19.

[32] LCA 1972 (replacing the original LCA 1925) ss 2(4) (class C(iv) land charge, an 'estate contract'), 4(6).

[33] The current system of registration of title to land dates from the LRA 1925, but it was introduced slowly, across different areas of the country, and requiring the title to land to be registered only when it was sold or a long lease was granted. Only in 1990 was this form of compulsory registration extended to the whole of England and Wales (SI 1989/1347), and although the triggers for compulsory registration were extended when the 1925 Act was replaced by LRA 2002, the register is still some way from being a complete record of titles to land: the *HM Land Registry Annual Report and Accounts 2019/20*, published in July 2020, said (pp 4–5) that 87.4 per cent of land had been registered (25.8m registered titles) and that it is aiming to achieve comprehensive registration by 2030.

[34] LRA 2002, s 28.

[35] LRA 2002, s 29.

[36] LRA 2002, Sched 3 para 2. The interest does not override if P1 did not disclose it if asked by P2 or if P1's occupation would not have been obvious on a reasonably careful inspection of the land (and as long as P2 did not actually know of the interest).

[37] The nature of the 'equitable interest' under the contract of sale (cf above n 28) might, therefore, be better seen as an *equity* – the right to enforce an equitable remedy against a third party into whose

nature of the right as it can be enforced against a third party – the proprietary effect of the right – depends on the contract and the availability of the remedy of specific performance.

D. The Basis of the Purchaser's Equitable Interest in the Remedy of Specific Performance

The operation of the doctrine of *Walsh v Lonsdale* requires not merely a valid contract to transfer or create the estate or interest in question, but also a contract *of which the court would grant specific performance if so requested*. This is a key to the operation of the doctrine, according to the case law,[38] although it is important to see that the availability of specific performance is relevant in two distinct ways – at two distinct times.[39]

According to the doctrine, an interest arises in equity at the moment that the contract is entered into, but only if the contract is one of which the court would grant specific performance. Even though the contract does not require the legal transfer of the land until a date in the future, and so specific performance of the transfer itself could not yet be obtained, still the duty to make the transfer is already anticipated, and the contract is seen as creating an equivalent equitable interest from the very beginning. At this stage, the question is therefore whether the contract is one of which, in principle, the court would order specific performance. A second question is whether, when the claimant (P1 in the example used above) seeks to enforce the right to the transfer, he will in fact be able to obtain an order of specific performance. It may be that, by this time, there is some obstacle to the award of the remedy of specific performance, such as misconduct by the party seeking to assert an equitable interest. In *Coatsworth v Johnson*,[40] for example, the intended tenant under a contract for a 21-year lease lost the right to specific performance when, having been allowed to go into occupation of the land, he broke covenants of the intended lease: he could therefore no longer claim in equity

hands property, to which the equitable remedy was attached, has passed. The same analysis, however, applies, since an equity can also bind a transferee: in registered land, see LRA 2002, s 116(b).

[38] *Howard v Miller* [1915] AC 318 (PC) 326 (Lord Parker of Waddington: 'It is sometimes said that under a contract for the sale of an interest in land the vendor becomes a trustee for the purchaser of the interest contracted to be sold subject to a lien for the purchase-money; but however useful such a statement may be as illustrating a general principle of equity, it is only true if and so far as a Court of Equity would under all the circumstances of the case grant specific performance of the contract. The interest conferred by the agreement in question was an interest commensurate with the relief which equity would give by way of specific performance'). See also *Ezair v Conn* [2020] EWCA Civ 687, [2020] BCC 865 at [47], [54] (Patten LJ: 'It is … dependent upon the contract remaining specifically enforceable and … remains at all times subject to the terms of the contract. … [T]he trust which arises is one to give effect to the contract and, it must follow, is governed by its terms').

[39] Turner (n 28) 589–92.

[40] (1886) 54 LT 520 (CA).

to be treated as if he had a 21-year lease.[41] Although this case did not involve a claim against a third-party transferee of the legal estate, it shows that, even though an equitable interest can arise by virtue of the contract, by reason of the availability in principle of the remedy of specific performance to enforce the interest, it can later be lost if the right to specific performance is lost. This reinforces the point made above: that the nature of the equitable interest under the contract is dependent on the (continuing) enforceability of the contract; and that if a claim to the equitable remedy of specific performance would not be available against the original contracting party, it should not be available against a transferee.

Given that the basis of the equitable (proprietary) interest – its creation and its continuing validity – is in the fact that the contract is one of which the court would order specific performance, we must be clear about the scope of this remedy within the English law of contract. It is well known that we here find a significant difference from the approach taken by civil law systems: typically, the civil law sees enforced performance of the contract as the creditor's right, subject only to certain limitations such as impossibility of performance, or where the nature of the obligation is too personal.[42] By contrast, the common law sees damages as the primary remedy for breach of contract, and specific performance is available only where damages would not provide an adequate remedy.[43] The effect is that specific performance is awarded only where the claimant could not obtain substitute performance from a third party in the market – and in the context of a contract of sale, this means where there is in practice no alternative market for the subject-matter of the sale because it is in a literal, or commercial, or practical sense 'unique'.[44] For our purposes, it is significant that the English courts characterise every plot of land (and therefore of every right to, or over, such a plot of land) as inherently unique – therefore the most common category of contract for which specific performance is in practice available is the contract relating to land.[45] One

[41] Specific performance is a discretionary remedy; and the court will not order it where the claimant's conduct has been such that he does not 'come to equity with clean hands': *Hanbury and Martin: Modern Equity* (n 19) [1-028], [27-035]; *Snell's Equity* (n 18) [5-010], [17-039].

[42] For the traditional view in France, for example, see B Nicholas, *The French Law of Contract*, 2nd edn (Oxford, Clarendon Press, 1992) 216–20. However, the recent reform of the French Civil Code has introduced a new definition (with a new economic limitation): art 1221 Cc 'A creditor of an obligation may, having given notice to perform, seek performance in kind unless performance is impossible or if there is a manifest disproportion between its cost to the debtor in good faith and its interest for the creditor'; see also Y-M Laithier, 'Exécution Forcée en Nature' in J Cartwright and S Whittaker (eds), *The Code Napoléon Rewritten: French Contract Law after the 2016 Reforms* (Oxford, Hart Publishing, 2017) 257.

[43] J Cartwright, *Contract Law: An Introduction to the English Law of Contract for the Civil Lawyer*, 3rd edn (Oxford, Hart Publishing, 2016) 272–80.

[44] *Falcke v Gray* (1859) 4 Drew 651, 62 ER 250 (two china jars: 'articles of unusual beauty, rarity and distinction, so that damages would not be an adequate compensation for non-performance': Kindersley VC at 658, at 252); cf *Cohen v Roche* [1927] 1 KB 169 (eight Hepplewhite chairs: 'ordinary articles of commerce and of no special value or interest, and no grounds exist for any special order for delivery': McCardie J at 181).

[45] G Jones and W Goodhart, *Specific Performance*, 2nd edn (London, Butterworths, 1996) 32. Specific performance is granted not only to the purchaser of land (which therefore protects his interest in acquiring the unique asset which it constitutes) but also to the vendor.

might wonder whether land is really always unique – in commercial terms, at least, such as where the purpose of the purchase is as an investment where any similar plot of land would serve equally well. The Supreme Court of Canada has taken a less firm view about the uniqueness of land (and therefore of the right to specific performance).[46] But, as long as the basis of the equitable property right under the doctrine of *Walsh v Lonsdale* is in the specifically-enforceable contract, this may be a case where we need to allow the property tail to wag the contractual dog: even if we might be inclined to take a more case-by-case view of the test of the adequacy of damages for the purpose of the contractual remedy, it would destabilise the certainty of proprietary rights which arise from a contract for the sale of land.[47] The English courts' unwillingness to relax the rule that land is unique is therefore understandable.

E. The Operation of the Principle Outside the Context of Land

Although the equitable interest arising under a contract for the sale of land is the most common context in which this principle is encountered, the logic is not limited to contracts relating to land. Equitable interests can be created in other property: and where there is a contract to transfer another asset which is unique, in the sense understood within the remedy of specific performance of the contract, the contract can similarly be treated in equity as already having the effect as if the remedy had been awarded – such as a contract to transfer shares in a private company of which the court would order specific performance.[48] However, such an analysis is not generally necessary,[49] especially in the case of movable property, since there is generally no formality required to transfer the property in movables and, indeed, the contract of sale can itself transfer the full title to the movable. To this we now turn.

[46] *Southcott Estates Inc v Toronto Catholic District School Board* 2012 SCC 51, (2012) 351 DLR (4th) 476 (refusing specific performance for a contract to purchase land which was merely an investment, where the claimant, a single-purpose company incorporated solely for the purpose of the specific land purchase, could find other property), building on the earlier decision in *Semelhago v Paramadevan* (1996) 136 DLR (4th) 1 (SCC).

[47] See also Turner (n 28) 603; PS Davies, 'Being Specific About Specific Performance' [2018] Conv 324, arguing that (contrary to the developments in Canada) the traditional position that specific performance of contracts for the sale of land will be granted as a matter of course, should be maintained in English law.

[48] *Oughtred v Inland Revenue Commissioners* [1960] AC 206, HL.

[49] There are even arguments that it is normally undesirable to apply the doctrine of *Walsh v Lonsdale* too widely to contracts for the sale of goods, because it is undesirable to create equitable interests which could affect creditors' rights in case of insolvency: E Peel (ed), *Treitel: The Law of Contract*, 15th edn (London, Sweet & Maxwell, 2020) [21-026].

III. Passing the (Legal) Property in Movables by Contract

As we see in other chapters of this book,[50] legal systems take different approaches to the significance of the contract of sale in relation to the transfer of movables. Some keep the contract of sale and the (contract of) transfer of property separate, to the point that they not only operate independently, but any defect in one does not in principle affect the other. This is traditionally identified with the abstract transfer system of the German model.[51] Others – identified traditionally with the unitary causal consensual system of the French model[52] – see the contract as itself automatically transferring the property. The thing (the subject-matter of the contract) must of course exist and be capable of transfer for the property in it to transfer at the time the contract is formed; and the parties may choose to defer the transfer,[53] but in principle the contract effects the transfer. In English law, by contrast, the contract of sale of goods can pass the property (and, in very many cases, will do so – and so in practice the result is close to the French solution),[54] although the test is the intention of the parties:[55]

> Where there is a contract for the sale of specific or ascertained goods the property in them is transferred to the buyer at such time as the parties to the contract intend it to be transferred.

However, as generally in English contract law, the parties' intention is tested objectively[56] and in this context the intention is ascertained having regard to the terms of the contract, the conduct of the parties, and the circumstances of the case.[57] Moreover, statute provides default rules for ascertaining the parties' intention as to

[50] See Ch 2 (López y López: Spanish law); Ch 7 (Oliva Blázquez: DCFR); Ch 5 (Häcker: general comparative discussion).

[51] See Häcker, above, Ch 5, esp section II.C.

[52] See Häcker, above, Ch 5, esp section II.B.

[53] Art 1196 Cc (2016 revision: see above, n 42): 'As regards contracts whose object is the alienation of ownership or the assignment of some other right, transfer takes place at the time of the conclusion of the contract. This transfer may be deferred by the will of the parties, by the nature of the things in question or by the effect of legislation …'

[54] This applies to the contract *of sale of goods* in English law, but may not apply more widely: see Häcker, above, Ch 5, esp section II.E.

[55] SGA 1979, s 17(1). The 1979 Act replaced similar provisions in the SGA 1893. The same rules apply at present for all contracts of sale, including contracts between a trader and a consumer, but the Law Commission has proposed a Bill which, if enacted, would provide for consumer sales contracts to include a (mandatory, non-excludable) term as to the time at which ownership transfers to the consumer: Law Commission Report No 398, *Consumer sales contracts: transfer of ownership* (2021). In the case of transfer of legal title to movables other than by a contract (eg by gift, which is not a contract in English law) the *transferor's* intention must be shown, but must also be accompanied by delivery of possession, or a deed (above, n 7); and the equitable interest may be passed by a declaration of trust: see generally M Bridge, *Personal Property Law*, 4th edn (Oxford, Oxford University Press, 2015) ch 5. See also Häcker, above, Ch 5 section II.E.

[56] Cartwright (n 43) 67–69.

[57] SGA 1979, s 17(2).

the passing of property – to be used where no different intention is apparent. The most significant rule is that

> Where there is an unconditional contract for the sale of specific goods in a deliverable state the property in the goods passes to the buyer when the contract is made, and it is immaterial whether the time of payment or the time of delivery, or both, be postponed.[58]

This therefore seems straightforward. Unlike the contract for the sale of land, discussed in the previous section, the contract for the sale of goods can effect the transfer of the full title, and all that is required is a valid contract of sale[59] – not a contract of a kind which will be enforced by a court order of specific performance. The remedy of specific performance does not therefore appear in the analysis here – which is just as well, since the courts will not normally order specific performance of most contracts for the sale of goods, even contracts for specific and ascertained goods. Such an order will be made only where the goods are unique – where there is no market into which the disappointed purchaser could take his damages in order to buy a substitute.[60] In this, the law treats even specific goods as generally replaceable in the market, unless they have some special characteristic that merits protection for the buyer, such as an antique.[61] A contract for the sale of a car, for example, will generally not be enforced – even a second-hand car, of a particular make, model, age, colour, mileage and general quality that attracted the purchaser to agree to the contract: he must be satisfied with an award of damages, unless there is something objectively special about the particular car.[62]

However, even where the full legal title passes by the contract of sale of goods, we may ask how strong is the purchaser's right to the goods. There are two separate points here. First, can the vendor (V), having transferred the property in the goods to a purchaser (P1), still transfer title by a later sale to another (P2)? In the case of a contract for the sale of land,[63] this question arose because the contract did not transfer legal title to the land to P1, but only created an equivalent interest in equity, and therefore left V with the legal title which he could still transfer to P2; the question there was therefore whether the transfer of the legal title to P2 was subject to the prior contract in favour of P1. In the case of a contract for the sale

[58] SGA 1979, s 18, Rule 1.

[59] In the modern law, the contract of sale of goods has no formality requirement. Until it was repealed by the Law Reform (Enforcement of Contracts) Act 1954, s 2, SGA 1893, s 4 provided (continuing a rule first set out in the Statute of Frauds 1677, s 17) that, in the absence of part performance or a deposit, a contract for the sale of goods of the value of £10 or more could not be enforced without a written memorandum signed by the defendant or his agent.

[60] Above, section II.D.

[61] *Falcke v Gray* (n 44).

[62] No doubt specific performance could be obtained of a contract to sell a rare vintage car; or one which has some special characteristic such as having been owned by the Queen, or being the Aston Martin DB5 used in an early James Bond film.

[63] Above, section II.C.

of goods, however, the contract transfers the legal title to P1, and so V retains no title that he can later transfer to P2 – and English law adheres to the basic rule that, although a person may be able to enter into a valid contract to sell something he does not own,[64] he cannot transfer property that he does not have: *nemo dat quod non habet*.[65] However, the analysis does not stop here: although V cannot transfer *his title* to the goods to P2 once he has parted with it by transfer to P1, he can still transfer *P1's title* to P2 if he is authorised by P1 to act as his agent. This might seem unlikely. But, using this analysis, the law assumes that, if P1 has left V in possession of the goods, he has given V implied authority to continue to deal with the goods (and therefore V retains a power to transfer (P1's) title to P2) – but only where P2 takes actual delivery, and does not know of the defect in V's title. This is set out in section 24 of the Sale of Goods Act 1979:

> Where a person having sold goods continues or is in possession of the goods, or of the documents of title to the goods, the delivery or transfer by that person, or by a mercantile agent[66] acting for him, of the goods or documents of title under any sale, pledge, or other disposition thereof, to any person receiving the same in good faith and without notice of the previous sale, has the same effect as if the person making the delivery or transfer were expressly authorised by the owner of the goods to make the same.

Until he takes possession of the goods, therefore, the purchaser under a contract of sale of goods remains at risk of losing title to a second purchaser. The contract effects a technical legal transfer of the title, but the purchaser is more secure once he has received possession – not surprising, since the basis of title to goods in English law is the right to possession,[67] and so an owner out of possession is naturally in a weaker position than one in possession.

This leads on to the second point in relation to the strength of the purchaser's right to the goods. If the contract of sale is not specifically enforceable (because the goods are not unique), can the purchaser none the less rely on the title that he has acquired under the contract in order to vindicate his right to the property? The answer again is peculiar to English law: there is no *vindicatio* for the assertion of rights *in rem* to goods.[68] The way in which the person with title to movable property – or, rather, the person with the right to possession of the property – can assert his title against another is through the law of tort: the tort of conversion.[69] And the principal remedy for the tortious interference with the property is damages

[64] *Vehicle Control Services Ltd v Revenue and Customs Commissioners* [2013] EWCA Civ 186, [2013] STC 892 at [22] (Lewison LJ: 'There is no legal impediment to my contracting to sell you Buckingham Palace. If (inevitably) I fail to honour my contract then I can be sued for damages').

[65] Bridge (n 55) 197, but going on to discuss exceptions to the rule.

[66] '"mercantile agent" means a mercantile agent having in the customary course of his business as such agent authority either – (a) to sell goods, or (b) to consign goods for the purpose of sale, or (c) to buy goods, or (d) to raise money on the security of goods': SGA 1979, s 26.

[67] Bridge (n 55) 43–46.

[68] Bridge (n 55) 79. See Häcker, above, Ch 5 section IV.

[69] Bridge (n 55) 86–89; for detail, see M Jones (ed), *Clerk & Lindsell on Torts*, 23rd edn (London, Sweet & Maxwell, 2020) ch 16.

to reflect the value of the property.[70] The court has the power to order specific delivery of the goods to the claimant whose right to possession has been interfered with – thus appearing in its operation like a *vindicatio*. However, in practice the circumstances in which the courts will make such an order are limited to those where damages cannot adequately compensate the claimant for the loss of his goods.[71] This means that the very situation in which the purchaser cannot obtain specific performance of the contract of sale to obtain delivery of the goods is that in which he cannot, either, obtain an order for specific delivery of the goods to vindicate the title to the goods which he has acquired by the contract.

IV. Conclusions

The approach taken to the relationship between the contract of sale and the transfer of property in English law varies significantly depending on whether the subject-matter is an interest in land, or movables.

In the case of land, the contract does not transfer the legal title, but can have the effect of creating an equivalent equitable title, which is not as secure as the legal title and can be defeated by a sale to a third-party purchaser where the beneficiary of the contract has not registered his right and is not in actual occupation of the land. In other respects, however, it can operate as a full proprietary right, and because its origin is in the fact that the contract is specifically enforceable, the right itself is also generally specifically enforceable, against third parties as well as against the original vendor.

In the case of movables, by contrast, the contract can (and very often does) transfer the legal title. This sounds more secure for the purchaser – and, indeed, he does acquire the title which he can in principle exploit. But he still risks losing the title if he allows the vendor to remain in possession after the sale, since any subsequent delivery of the goods by the vendor to a third party who acquires the goods in good faith and without notice of the vendor's defect in title will be treated as being with his authority. The problem for the purchaser of goods is that in practice he cannot generally enforce the vendor's contractual duty to deliver, nor can he obtain specific delivery of the goods by way of vindication of his title to the goods, because of the limitations of the remedy of specific performance in the case of goods.

There is therefore something of a paradox: the contract of sale can operate to transfer or to create property rights to both land and goods. The apparently stronger right which arises from the contract – the transfer of legal title – is in the case of goods; yet, by contrast with the purchaser of land, the purchaser of goods has in practice a weaker claim to the property itself, and is generally expected to

[70] Bridge (n 55) 113–17.
[71] Bridge (n 55) 120–21; *Clerk & Lindsell on Torts* (n 69) [16-91].

be satisfied with an award of damages. Underlying this difference in outcome are the different approaches of the courts to the remedy of specific performance in the cases of land and goods. And this is itself a reflection of the higher respect and protection that is generally given to the interests of purchasers of land over the interests of purchasers of movables.

7

The Transfer of Ownership of Goods in the Draft Common Frame of Reference

FRANCISCO OLIVA BLÁZQUEZ

I. Introduction

One of the most important and complex issues in patrimonial private law relates to the moment at which the transfer of ownership of movable property – goods – normally acquired in the framework of a contract (most commonly a contract of sale), occurs. Its importance lies in the fact that the transfer of ownership (not only of possession) of goods is essential for the proper functioning of the market, for otherwise the purchaser may be obliged to deal with the claims of third parties (claims for recovery of the goods sold) which would end up undermining the functional utility of the business concluded. In the words of Drobnig, 'market economies depend upon such changes of attribution to facilitate the optimal use of assets by citizens and professional market participants'.[1]

In turn, as already stressed, it is a particularly thorny issue in which contract law (dynamic patrimonial private law) interacts with the specific doctrines of property law (static patrimonial private law).[2] We can turn to comparative law to see how historically the transfer of ownership has been tackled in very different ways in different legal systems around the world, which shows how little certainty this problem has always given rise to in legal science.[3]

[1] U Drobnig, 'Transfer of property' in A Hartkamp, M Hesselink, E Hondius, C Joustra, E du Perron and M Veldman (eds), *Towards a European Civil Code* (The Hague, Kluwer Law International, 2004) 725.

[2] 'The crossroads of contract and property': C von Bar and U Drobnig, *The Interaction of Contract Law and Tort and Property Law in Europe* (Munich, Sellier, 2004) 324.

[3] For a very instructive and clear explanation, see F Ferrari, 'Transfer of Title (Movable Goods)' in J Basedow, KJ Hopt, R Zimmermann and A Stier (eds), *The Max Planck Encyclopedia of European Private Law*, Vol I (Oxford, Oxford University Press, 2012) 1678–81. Similarly, but briefer: JH Beekhuis, 'Civil Law' in *International Encyclopedia of Comparative Law, Vol VI, Property and Trust, ch 2, Structural Variations in Property Law* (Tübingen, JCB Mohr, 1976) 14.

Indeed, in the first instance, some legal systems inspired by the Roman *traditio*[4] require *modus*, or effective transfer of possession of goods (transfer by delivery, or the 'split approach'),[5] while in others it is sufficient to enter into an underlying contract (*solo consensu*),[6] that is, with the consent of the contracting parties (transfer by consent, or the 'unitary approach'). Furthermore, transfer can also be theoretically determined by the time of payment, although this solution is envisaged as such in hardly any European legal system.[7]

Moreover, the legislation of the majority of European countries requires the existence of a prior valid right or obligation (the causal system),[8] except for the BGB in Germany,[9] which devised its own theory of 'abstract' transfer. This can be explained by the fact that in German law the transfer of ownership is based on a second legal act of delivery (*Trennungsprinzip*) grounded in a 'real agreement' (*dinglicher Vertrag*),[10] which is no more than a contract with real legal effectiveness (*Verfügunsgeschäft*), whose validity is not linked to the existence of an underlying contract (*Abstraktionsprinzip*).[11]

On the other hand, the majority of legal systems are based on the so-called 'unitary transfer approach', by virtue of which, once the moment of transfer of ownership (eg, the delivery of the goods or a simple agreement) has been established by means of a concrete rule, all the powers and rights linked to ownership are automatically transferred to the owner (the right to transfer the goods, to establish limited rights in rem over them, to use and consume them, to repossess them, etc). In Scandinavia, on the contrary, the 'functional approach' is applied, which, in contrast to the unitary system, considers that the different elements constituting ownership can be transferred at different moments and in a totally independent fashion.[12]

[4] 'Traditionibus et usucapionibus dominia rerum, non nudis pactis transferuntur' (the ownership of things is transferred by *traditio* and *usucapio*, not by agreement alone) (C 2.3.20).

[5] Austrian, Spanish, Dutch and Swedish law require *titulus* (title) and *modus* (delivery). The German system also requires delivery (the 'abstract tradition system'): see LPW van Vliet, 'Transfer of property *inter vivos*' in M Graziadei and L Smith (eds), *Comparative Property Law, Global Perspectives* (Cheltenham, Edward Elgar, 2017) 151. For discussion of the *titulus et modus* system in Spanish law, see Espejo Lerdo de Tejada, above, Ch 3 section I, esp n 1, and generally Cartwright and López y López, above, Ch 1 section II.

[6] France and Italy champion the consensual system, which is also implemented in, eg, Belgium, Portugal, Luxemburg, Malta, Poland, Bulgaria, and England and Wales.

[7] Payment can, however, be decisive if so agreed by the parties – which in fact is very common, by means of a retention of title clause.

[8] eg, Austria, Holland, Spain, Slovenia, Switzerland, the Czech Republic, Slovakia, Lithuania, Latvia and Hungary.

[9] And countries, such as Greece and Estonia, that have adopted this model.

[10] Curiously, the Austrian system also requires a 'real agreement' subsequent to the initial binding contract, as is also the case in the Dutch and Swiss systems, although none of them recognise the mechanism of abstraction ('causality and separation'): S Zogg, *Effects of Mistake and Other Defects on the Passage of Legal Title* (Cambridge, Intersentia, 2019) 28.

[11] For a clear explanation of these complex concepts, see JT Füller, 'The German Property Law and its Principles' in W Faber and B Lurger (eds), *Rules for the Transfer of Movables: A Candidate for European Harmonisation or National Reforms?* (Munich, Sellier, 2008) 200–01.

[12] 'For one aspect, the conclusion of the underlying contract may be decisive, for another one, delivery or payment of the price may be', B Lurger and W Faber, *Principles of European Law: Acquisition and Loss of Ownership of Goods (PEL Acq Own)* (Munich, Sellier, 2011) 407.

Faced with this highly complex regulatory reality, it should come as no surprise that the drafters of the Vienna Convention on Contracts for the International Sale of Goods (CISG), currently the most successful uniform private law text in the world for contracts, expressly decided to exclude from its scope of application the determination of the moment at which, or the conditions under which, the transfer of ownership of sold goods is to be taken to have occurred (Article 4 (b) CISG). As the Secretariat stated in its comments on the 1978 Draft, this was due to the fact that, in light of the disparity between existing transfer systems, 'It was not regarded possible to unify the rule on this point nor was it regarded necessary to do so'.[13] Accordingly, it was left to private international law to identify in each case which system should be applied to determine the moment at which the ownership of sold goods is transferred.[14]

II. The Proposal for Harmonising the Transfer of Ownership of Goods: The Work of the Study Group on a European Civil Code

But is it really impossible to propose a universal and common solution to this problem?[15] Although legal scholars have long been sceptical in this regard,[16] the DCFR has attempted to break this taboo, regulating for the first time the necessary requirements for the transfer of ownership of goods in Article VIII–2:101.[17]

To begin with, the fact that the DCFR has endeavoured to regulate an issue that goes beyond the scope of the strictly contractual sphere – the raison d'être and ultimate purpose of most of the European Union's harmonisation efforts in the field of private law – is quite remarkable. But the truth is that the European Commission itself, in its 2004 Communication on European Contract Law, recommended extending research to other fields related to contract law, expressly mentioning the transfer of title to goods.[18]

[13] Text of Secretariat Commentary on Article 4 of the 1978 Draft: see http://www.cisg-online.ch/index.cfm?pageID=644#Article%204.

[14] The Convention on the Law Governing Transfer of Title in the case of International Sale of Movables, of 15 April 1958, drawn up by the Hague Conference on Private International Law, intended to regulate the issue in a uniform manner, although the project never passed the planning stage.

[15] See F Ferrari, 'Abstraktionsprinzip, Traditionsprinzip e Consensualismo nel Trasferimento di Beni Mobili. Una Superabile Divaricazione?' *Rivista di Diritto Civile*, 1993, 729–57.

[16] Ferrari (n 3) 1680 ('It has often been stated that the various principles that govern the relationship between the contract of sale and the transfer of property are incompatible with each other, which is why it is unsurprising that unification in this area has not occurred, at least not on a substantive level').

[17] To be fair, art 46 of the European Contract Code, drafted by the so-called 'Pavia Group', the Academy of European Private Lawyers (Gandolfi Project), also addressed this issue, linking the transfer of ownership, as does the DCFR, to the moment of delivery: G D'Amico, 'Contratto di compravendita, effetto traslativo e problemi di armonizzazione' in E Navarreta (ed), *Il Diritto europeo dei contratti fra parte generale e norme di settore* (Milano, Giuffrè, 2007) 528.

[18] Communication from the Commission to the European Parliament and the Council, *European Contract Law and the revision of the* acquis: *the way forward*, 11 October 2004, COM (2004) 651 final.

In this connection, it should be recalled that the Study Group on a European Civil Code[19] (SGECC) created a specific working group, initially called 'Transfer of Movables', whose mission was to analyse this issue in depth.[20] This group, working from Graz and Salzburg (Austria), was led by Professors Brigitta Lurger (team leader) and Wolfgang Faber (co-leader). Although at first it was primarily concerned with the transfer of ownership of movables, it later extended the scope of its research to other areas, such as acquisition by continuous possession (*usucapio*), good faith acquisition, the protection of ownership and possession and, broadly speaking, other matters relating to the acquisition and loss of rights to movables. For this reason, it came as no surprise when, in 2005, the working group changed its name to 'Acquisition and Loss of Ownership in Movables', which gives a much better idea of the real purpose of the research conducted by the Graz and Salzburg group within the network of excellence – funded by the European Commission – known as 'Common Principles of European Contract Law' (CoPECL Project).

This group's working methods were grounded in the orthodoxy of the most classical (theoretical) comparative approach. Accordingly, a series of national reporters were first commissioned to draft a comprehensive and exhaustive report on the way in which their own legal systems addressed the issues described above. All these reports (28 in total) were published in six separate volumes, thus constituting a very valuable source of legal information which, above all, highlights the fact that this work has a solid comparative basis.[21] In other words, unlike what has happened in other parts of the DCFR, the rules included in Book VIII are the result of a serious, rigorous, methodical and exhaustive legal comparison.

The report that Professors von Bar and Drobnig drew up for the European Commission, in which they expressly recommended that this matter be addressed in the DCFR, primarily in order to bridge the gap between the consensual systems and those based on delivery, undeniably influenced this decision: see von Bar and Drobnig (n 2) 467ff. However, the authors themselves recognise that for the stakeholders that were consulted, 'the division between the unified and the split approach is not regarded as a practical obstacle to intra-EU border-crossing trade' (p 468).

[19] The Study Group, which (together with the Acquis Group) prepared the DCFR, and a number of other commentaries on the Principles of European Law (see, eg, Lurger and Faber (n 12)), was the successor (from 2008) to the Commission on European Contract Law (the 'Lando Commission') which had prepared the PECL. For details of the Study Group and its activities, see C von Bar and E Clive (eds), *Principles, Definitions and Model Rules of European Private Law: Draft Common Frame of Reference (DCFR)* (Munich, Sellier, 2009) vol 1, 17–18, 25–28; Lurger and Faber (n 12) vii–ix (Foreword by C von Bar).

[20] The creation of this working group was first proposed by Professors Michael Rainer (Salzburg) and Willibald Posch (Graz) in 2001. On the origin and evolution of this group's research, see B Lurger, 'Introduction to the Project "Transfer of Movables": Organisational Framework, Basic Issues and Goals' in Faber and Lurger (n 11) 1ff.

[21] W Faber and B Lurger (eds), *National Reports on the Transfer of Movables in Europe* (München, Sellier, 2008–11). Similarly, other national reports on the subject can be consulted in the volumes published by M Rainer and I Filip-Fröschl (eds), *Transfer of Title Concerning Movables* (Frankfurt am Main, P Lang, 2006).

Once the information had been received, analysed and studied in detail, the working group tried to pinpoint the most habitual or common solution to each issue (the 'common core'), with a view to incorporating it as a general rule. Nevertheless, as Professor Lurger has explicitly acknowledged, the number of functionally similar solutions in this field is considerably fewer than in contract law and, therefore, they were often obliged to choose only one of the possible options.[22] To focus on the issue with which we are concerned in this chapter: it is clear that in the European Union there is – as has been seen – no single solution shared by all as to the moment at which the ownership of goods is transferred. It is therefore necessary to adopt one of them at the expense of the rest (or to give up any attempt at harmonisation).

And the crux of the matter is: what criterion should be employed when choosing which solution to adopt? According to the project's drafters, they tried to streamline the selection process by making allowances for the following three aspects: (i) the impact of the proposed rule on the parties directly involved in the transaction (in this case, the transferor and the transferee); (ii) its impact on other indirectly involved parties (such as creditors, heirs and other market participants); and (iii) its impact on the market and society as a whole (economic efficiency, expectations, transparency, justice, etc).[23] The logic of these criteria is both compelling and unquestionable and, in terms of our object of study, we shall see below how the second criterion has been decisive in determining the moment of, and requirements for, the transfer of ownership of goods.

Following this approach, the working group, suitably advised by the esteemed members of its advisory council (Hugh Beale, Michael Bridge, Torgny Håstad, Matthias Storme and Anna Veneziano), submitted different drafts and proposals at a number of meetings, which were then discussed by the Co-ordinating Group of the Study Group on a European Civil Code.[24] Finally, all those years of work were brought to fruition in Book VIII of the DCFR, whose first complete edition was published in 2009.[25] Two years later, the working group published a second version, extended and improved, with further notes of comparative law, entitled *Principles of European Law, Study Group on a European Civil Code. Acquisition and Loss of Ownership of Goods (PEC Acq Own)*. This is the version generally used in this chapter.[26]

[22] Lurger (n 20) 7.

[23] ibid 7.

[24] The working group's endeavours were discussed at the following meetings: Oporto (December 2002), Leuven (December 2003), Warsaw (June 2004), Berlin (June 2005), Oslo (June 2006), Lucerne (December 2006), Budapest (June 2007), Prague (December 2007) and Athens (June 2008): see Lurger and Faber (n 12) xiii.

[25] von Bar and Clive (n 19) Vol 5.

[26] Lurger and Faber (n 12).

III. The Basic Structure of Article VIII–2:101 DCFR

After having presented the necessary historical background and having explained the process of preparing and drafting Book VIII of the DCFR, the time has now come to focus on the object of our study: Article VIII–2:101 DCFR, which sets out the necessary requirements for the transfer of ownership of goods.

It can be argued that this article is the most important rule of all in Book VIII of the DCFR and, in all likelihood, in view of its practical significance and doctrinal importance, one of the most symbolic. The fact that the full commentary on this article (including the notes on comparative law) – which will be analysed below – runs to over 100 pages, something unprecedented when compared with the rest of the DCFR, is evidence of the importance that the drafters gave this text.[27] It is evident that the working group, with a rigour and integrity worthy of unstinting praise, wanted to justify and explain fully all its decisions and, thanks to this process, has ultimately bequeathed to the legal community a priceless monograph on the transfer of ownership of goods that deserves to be studied in depth.

The text of Article VIII–2:101 DCFR, entitled, 'Requirements for the transfer of ownership in general', reads as follows:

(1) The transfer of ownership of goods under this Chapter requires that:
  (a) the goods exist;
  (b) the goods are transferable;
  (c) the transferor has the right or authority to transfer the ownership;
  (d) the transferee is entitled as against the transferor to the transfer of ownership by virtue of a contract or other juridical act, a court order or a rule of law; and
  (e) there is an agreement as to the time ownership is to pass and the conditions of this agreement are met, or, in the absence of such agreement, delivery or an equivalent to delivery.

(2) For the purposes of paragraph (1)(e) the delivery or equivalent to delivery must be based on, or referable to, the entitlement under the contract or other juridical act, court order or rule of law.

(3) Where the contract or other juridical act, court order or rule of law defines the goods in generic terms, ownership can pass only when the goods are identified to it. Where goods form part of an identified bulk, VIII–2:305 (Transfer of goods forming part of a bulk) applies.

(4) Paragraph (1)(e) does not apply where ownership passes under a court order or rule of law at the time determined in it.

This wording is certainly complex and over-detailed (unfortunately, a very common shortcoming throughout the DCFR), but three basic rules that serve to regulate the transfer of ownership of goods can be gleaned from its content.

First and foremost, it is recognised that the parties can establish the moment at which ownership should be transferred: 'there is an agreement as to the time

[27] Lurger and Faber (n 12) 405–528.

ownership is to pass and the conditions of this agreement are met, or, in the absence of such agreement, delivery or an equivalent to delivery' (Article VIII–2:101(1)(e)). Therefore, it is clear that party autonomy, the cornerstone of the DCFR, is the fundamental governing principle of the transfer of ownership. In other words, its drafters consider that the parties involved can freely decide the exact moment at which the ownership of goods is to be transferred, all legal systems having the obligation to respect that expression of common intention.

Secondly, in the absence of such an agreement (the default rule), the transfer of ownership requires 'delivery or an equivalent to delivery' (Article VIII–2:101 (1)(e)). Therefore, the DCFR is clearly committed to the rule of *modus* or delivery, ruling out that the mere will emanating from the contract is in itself sufficient for the automatic transfer of ownership (the consensual system).

Thirdly, in both of the above two cases, it is essential that 'the transferor has the right or authority to transfer the ownership' (Article VIII–2:101(1)(c)). Furthermore, it is established that the transferee must be 'entitled as against the transferor to the transfer of ownership by virtue of a contract or other juridical act, a court order or a rule of law' (Article VIII–2:101(1)(d)). And, finally, it is recalled that 'the delivery or equivalent to delivery must be based on, or referable to, the entitlement under the contract or other juridical act, court order or rule of law' (Article VIII–2:101(2)). Interpreting these rules as a whole, we can enables us to deduce a third rule: a sufficient and suitable title (agreement) is required for transferring ownership and the causal principle is adopted rather than the principle of abstraction.

If we had to summarise in a nutshell the final outcome of the comparative analysis carried out and reflected in the DCFR, we could say that both the French and German systems have lost out, while the Austrian[28] and, notably, the Spanish systems have won hands down, for all of their key elements are faithfully reflected in the proposed rule: *titulus* (agreement), *modus* (delivery) and cause. But beyond this summary, which is as simplistic as it is probably striking, it is necessary to explain in some detail why these last two criteria were adopted (that of agreement does not pose any particular problem), as well as the reference to autonomy of will.

IV. Autonomy of Will and Transfer of Ownership

As has just been observed, the DCFR confers the greatest possible effectiveness on the principle of the autonomy of the will and, therefore, grants the parties the right

[28] Unsurprisingly, it has been observed that, at first sight, the drafters could be accused of a certain degree of 'home bias' (since, as we have seen, the leaders of the working group are Austrian), although the thoroughness of the comparative analysis performed, together with the large number of arguments that were deployed, encourages us to disregard that false impression: LPW van Vliet, 'Acquisition and Loss of Ownership of Goods' in *A Factual Assessment of the Draft Common Frame of Reference* (Munich, Sellier, 2011) 296.

to determine when and under what circumstances ownership is to be transferred.[29] It seems to have been a fitting decision, especially when taking into consideration that European legal systems tend to grant autonomy of will the broadest scope of operation in this context.[30]

Indeed, the legal systems based on the Roman principle of *traditio* recognise dematerialised forms of transfer of ownership, without the need for physical delivery – ie, through a simple contract – as is the case with the *constitutum possessorium*[31] (an agreement through which the transferor undertakes to retain control of the goods on behalf of the transferee, this being deemed sufficient for the transfer of ownership). And, conversely, there is nothing to prevent parties who enter into a contract under a consensual jurisdiction from postponing the transfer of ownership until the moment when delivery takes place. In this sense, in section 17 of the UK Sale of Goods Act 1979 it is clearly established that the ownership of the sold goods will be transferred to the purchaser 'at such time as the parties to the contract intend it to be transferred'. Even the BGB allows the parties to depart from the principle of abstraction and link the validity of the real contract to the underlying obligational agreement.[32]

Therefore, there is absolutely no doubt that the parties can agree that transfer will take place before the delivery of the goods, at the time of entering into the contract, at the same moment that delivery takes places or even afterwards when final payment is made. Nonetheless, the freedom of choice recognised in the DCFR is not absolute, inasmuch as it must always comply with any fundamental mandatory requirements. For instance, it is essential that the goods exist (Article VIII–2:101(3)) or, should generic goods be involved, that these be specified before their ownership can be transferred (Article VIII–2:101(3)).

V. The Principle of Delivery and the Greater Protection of the Interests of All the Parties Involved (Creditors)

The most controversial and debated issue among the members of the working group doubtless had to do with the crucial choice between the principle of delivery and its consensual counterpart. Indeed, in the commentaries on the provision in question it is recognised that a considerable number of the members of the Study Group's Co-ordinating Committee were more in favour of adopting the

[29] Lurger and Faber (n 12) 455.

[30] See K Kullerkupp, 'Private Autonomy in Property Law: Can the Parties Design their Transfer?' in Faber and Lurger (n 11) 57.

[31] With the exception of Sweden, whose legal system requires delivery in order that the purchaser of the goods should be fully protected from the transferor's ordinary creditors: Lurger and Faber (n 12) 409.

[32] For further details, see Ferrari (n 3) 1680–81.

consensual system than that based on delivery.[33] According to the drafters of Article VIII–2:101(3) DCFR, the final selection process took the following course.[34]

At first, it was suggested that the most common system in the EU, quantitatively speaking, be adopted (ie, the common core approach). But this idea was immediately discarded for two reasons: firstly, because it was impossible to reach a consensus on this point; and, secondly, because the result might have been ambiguous in light of recent trends in legal systems evolving in their own peculiar way. For instance, in Sweden, where the system of delivery prevails, in the legislation on consumer sales contracts the consensual principle is adopted, while in France the principle of delivery is steadily gaining ground in both commercial practice and in legislative texts, essentially to protect the interests of the seller in the event of non-payment.[35]

Also, it was suggested that account be taken of 'citizen's expectations' (the 'natural solution'), namely, what people (and particularly commercial parties) expect from a rule intended to regulate the exact moment at which ownership is transferred. However, this criterion was also rejected since, apart from the fact that citizens' expectations are more often than not linked to their own personal interests (thus, the buyer will normally want to acquire ownership of the goods as soon as the contract is concluded), as well as the economic and legal practices prevailing in each country, the truth is that there are no reliable empirical studies that can be used as a basis for taking these aspects into account.

The drafters of the DCFR, faced with the ineffectiveness of the criteria discussed above, finally opted for a technical or academic solution (the 'better law approach') grounded in the general criterion anticipated above: the rule must take into account the interests of all the parties involved, thus including not only those of the transferee and transferor, but also those of their ordinary creditors.[36] This approach is essential insofar as the principle of relativity, inherent to contract law (article 1257 CC), yields when we abandon the realm of strictly obligational relationships (*inter partes*) and enter that of proprietary relationships (in this case, the acquisition of ownership), whose effects are declared *erga omnes*. That is, from the moment at which the ownership of the goods is transferred the situation of third parties, indirectly involved, can be affected, and the legal system has the unavoidable duty to make allowances for the interests of all parties ('interested third parties')[37] before making a decision that may affect them.[38]

[33] Lurger and Faber (n 12) 410.

[34] Further details of the arguments set out here can be consulted in Lurger and Faber (n 12) 412–13.

[35] This is also currently the case in Belgium where it is argued that the purchaser should only be protected once the goods have been delivered.

[36] Lurger and Faber (n 12) 422.

[37] von Bar and Drobnig (n 2) 328.

[38] Lurger and Faber (n 12) 430–31.

Going a step further, it should be recalled that the heart of the matter is to contrast the functioning of the system of delivery with that of the consensual system in the following scenario: the appearance of the transferor's creditors who intend to make claims on the transferred goods in the event of insolvency proceedings.[39] Against this background, we must ask ourselves whether the transferee has the right to have the goods excluded from the transferor's estate or, on the contrary, whether his ordinary creditors (ie, those without special security) can attach those goods and share their value among themselves.[40] The consensual system clearly corresponds to the first case, since ownership is transferred once the contract has been entered into, the goods automatically being excluded from the transferor's estate. By contrast, if the transfer of ownership is linked to the effective delivery of the goods, the creditors can exercise their credit claims on the transferor's full estate, including the goods that, despite having been sold, were not delivered (article 1911 CC).[41]

So, at first sight, everything would seem to indicate that the system of delivery better protects the interests of creditors than its consensual counterpart. However, the working group was not content with this hasty conclusion and, subsequently, performed a detailed and exhaustive analysis on all the pros and cons of each of the possible solutions. Given the limits of our study, it is impossible to set out, even briefly, each and every one of the arguments deployed. So, only those that we believe to be the most important will be discussed here.

Before all else, it is essential to bear in mind the possible insolvency of the transferor of the goods, which in turn requires taking into account the fundamental principles governing European insolvency law.[42] There is an old aphorism that regulates this matter in all legal systems: *par conditio creditorum*. From this axiom the conclusion necessarily follows that the buyer who has not taken possession of the purchased goods should be regarded as just another creditor (equality of treatment for creditors), lacking any special preference to be able to demand full performance of the contract from the debtor (ie, delivery and transfer of ownership).[43] Obviously, the system of delivery is perfectly adapted to this principle.

For that matter, we should ask ourselves why the purchaser of existing and specific goods should receive preferential treatment (as is the case in the consensual

[39] The working group also envisaged the opposite situation, namely, the possible protection of the transferor against the transferee's creditors. However, this scenario is less controversial, since both systems basically coincide in their solutions. As one would expect, the system based on the Roman principle of *traditio* protects the transferor until the moment of delivery, while in those countries in which the consensual system applies (and where the solution should be vice versa) the transferor is also generally protected insofar as he has physical control over the goods (through a right of retention, a statutory lien, or another similar instrument): Lurger and Faber (n 12) 435–37.

[40] Lurger and Faber (n 12) 416.

[41] See V Sagaert, 'Consensual versus Delivery Systems' in Faber and B Lurger (n 11) 40–41.

[42] E Beltrán and R Sebastián (eds), *European Insolvency Regulations* (Cizur Menor, Thomson Reuters, Aranzadi, 2010).

[43] Lurger and Faber (n 12) 423.

system), but not so the purchaser of generic goods; and why the purchaser of a specific object who has paid in advance should be given preference over other creditors who have also granted the transferor unsecured loans (such as a service provider who lacks protection, even when he has rendered the performance in advance).[44] It should also be recalled that, according to the consensual system, the purchaser of movable goods is given preference over other creditors who do not even have a contractual relationship with the bankrupt debtor (such as one claiming maintenance or damages in tort), when it is more logical that those who have voluntarily entered into a legal business relationship with the insolvent party should assume the risk of insolvency. It is evident that the principle of delivery makes it possible to curtail this unjustified preferential treatment by regarding the mere purchaser of movable goods as just another creditor.

Another question, inextricably linked to the *par conditio creditorum* principle, is that of the purpose of contracts pending performance in the context of insolvency proceedings. Again, the majority of the EU Member States coincide in granting the insolvency administrator broad powers to decide whether to continue contracts or terminate them.[45] The former case does not pose any further problems (the purchaser is still able to demand delivery of the goods). But in the latter case, it is imperative to consider that if the purchaser has paid the price of the goods, he has become an ordinary creditor who will have to enter into an arrangement with the rest of the creditors in order to receive, where appropriate, his fair share (pro rota). That said, it is quite apparent that a transfer system based on delivery adapts perfectly to this principle of insolvency law, for until the *traditio* occurs the goods will continue to form part of the estate of the now-insolvent transferor and, consequently, the administrator may elect to terminate the contract, thus converting the purchaser into a mere creditor for the monetary counter-performance.[46]

Finally, in all these cases our reasoning is based on the fact that since the purchaser has paid for the acquired goods, it is only reasonable that he should be deemed their owner. However, it should be borne in mind that the purchaser has personally assumed a risk, ie, that of the non-compliance of the other party and, therefore, should suffer the possible consequences, as with the rest of the creditors who have granted unsecured loans (or even the seller himself, should he decide to deliver the goods before being paid in full the agreed price).[47]

[44] Lurger and Faber (n 12) 424.

[45] As is the case in Spain where Insolvency Law (*Ley 22/2003, de 9 de julio, Concursal*, as amended) art 61.2 stipulates that the declaration of insolvency will not, by itself, affect the validity of contracts with reciprocal obligations pending performance, although the insolvency practitioner or the insolvent debtor himself may request the termination of the contract, should this be deemed appropriate in the interests of the insolvency proceedings.

[46] In legal systems that implement the consensual model (eg, France, Belgium and Italy), the administrator's power of election is not usually recognised, since ownership is transferred at the moment when the contract is entered into. Nevertheless, in England and Wales the administrator is indeed given the option of refusing to perform the contract: Lurger and Faber (n 12), 423.

[47] Lurger and Faber (n 12) 424.

For these reasons and many others that have not been set out here, the drafters of the DCFR concluded that the rule of delivery is the only one that really guarantees the full application of the general principle of equality of treatment in similar situations.[48] In other words, it is doubtless the one that best safeguards the interests of creditors, ensuring that everyone is treated fairly.

VI. Abstract Transfer versus Causal Transfer

We have already observed that the DCFR rejected the abstract system of the BGB and expressly opted for the causal system. The *Abstraktionsprinzip*, the result of the dogmatic elaboration of Savigny,[49] was justified by the need to increase the confidence of purchasers of movable goods in light of the many defects that can affect the contract (nullity, annulment, termination, etc), and by the consequent desire to favour and foster the system of exchange of goods in the modern economy (security of legal transactions).[50] For the joint application of the principles of *nemo plus iuris ad alium transferre potest quam ipse haberet*[51] and *iusta causa traditionis*[52] can indeed lead to the transfer of ownership being considered as ineffective, even when delivery has taken place, in all those cases in which the agreement entered into is invalid, and this can lead to undesirable distortions in the normal functioning of the market. So, considering that one of the stated aims of the DCFR is precisely to reinforce the protection of the right to ownership and to promote market efficiency,[53] the question is self-evident: why was the abstract system not chosen (the 'better law approach')?[54]

The drafters of Article VIII–2:101 DCFR justified their decision with a powerful and irrefutable argument: the application, in addition, of the principle that possession of movables is equivalent to ownership (*possession vaut titre*)[55] provides the necessary legal certainty. Indeed, it should be recalled that, from a practical point of view, the problem arises above all when the purchaser, whose original contract with the seller is invalidated by a legal defect, has in turn transferred the goods to third parties who, according to the abstract system, should be protected provided that the 'real agreement' that they have entered into is valid. Thus, the

[48] Lurger and Faber (n 12) 424.

[49] In his famous work entitled, *System des heutigen Römischen Rechts*: see S Bartels, 'An Abstract or Causal System', in Faber and Lurger (n 11) 61.

[50] Ferrari (n 3) 1678.

[51] Dig 50.17.54: 'No one can transfer greater rights to someone else than he possesses himself'.

[52] See also López y López, above, Ch 2 section II.

[53] C von Bar, H Beale, E Clive and H Schulte-Nölke, 'Principles' in von Bar and E Clive (n 19) Vol 5, 61.

[54] Van Vliet proposed a middle way between the causal and abstract systems, called the '*animus* theory', according to which the transfer of ownership depends on the existence of a genuine will to transfer, without there having to be any valid contract: LPW van Vliet, *Transfer of Movables* (Nijmegen, Ars Aequi Libri, 2000) 205.

[55] In French law, see art 2276 Cc: 'En fait de meubles, la possession vaut titre'. In Spanish law, art 464 CC provides for this principle.

security and protection of legal transactions that the abstract model provides for in these cases can be similarly achieved with the general principle that possession of movables in good faith is equivalent to ownership, a situation expressly provided for in Book VIII, Chapter III of the DCFR. Article VIII–3:101 stipulates that in the event that the person purporting to transfer the ownership of goods has neither the right nor the authority to do so, the purchaser nonetheless acquires them (and the former owner loses his ownership) provided that the transaction has been made for value and in good faith. Thus, the sub-purchaser's good faith acquisition of the goods will be automatically protected, and so the security of legal transactions will be fully safeguarded. Moreover, as the commentaries on Article VIII–2:101 incisively note, the principle of abstraction grants an excessive and unprecedented level of protection, insofar as it does not even require the good faith of the affected party, for which reason the text of the DCFR is much fairer, more ethical and more coherent.[56]

To our mind, the decision made by the drafters of the DCFR is very sound. Beyond the arguments deployed, it should be noted that German doctrine itself recognises the extreme complexity, artificiality and lack of realism of the principle of abstraction. Indeed, it should be borne in mind that, according to Kronke, any transfer of ownership of movable goods always involves three transactions (the binding or causal transaction – *Verplifchtungsgeschäft* – the transaction involving the goods and, lastly, the transaction involving the monies paid in exchange) and two real transfers (the delivery of the goods and the payment of the monies).[57] It is evident that this complex legal structure is contrary to reality, overshadowed by the general perception that there is only one economic fact.[58] Furthermore, it should not be forgotten that the 'real agreement' can be voided by any one of the causes applicable to legal transactions and when this happens, the transfer will be invalid. Therefore, legal certainty is not as absolute as might have been expected in the abstract system.

VII. Conclusion

The DCFR, as a set of rules designed with the purpose of harmonisation, has been bold enough to tackle one of the most complex issues in patrimonial private law: the transfer of ownership of goods. And, curiously enough, it has achieved this by championing a solution that is very familiar: an agreement (*titulus*), delivery (*modus*) and cause (*causa*) are necessary for transfer of ownership. Spanish jurists, who are well known for their compulsive criticism of their own Civil Code, should

[56] Lurger and Faber (n 12) 454.

[57] H Kronke, 'Il trasferimento della proprietà nel diritto tedesco' in F Galgano (ed), *Atlante di Diritto Privato Comparato* (Bologna, Zanichelli 1992) 112.

[58] See van Vliet (n 54) 205.

congratulate themselves that article 609 CC, in its interpretation by courts and by scholars, has served as a model for European legal comparison (the 'better law approach'). Even more so when article VIII–2:101 DCFR, as already noted, is the undeniable result of a rigorous and exhaustive comparative analysis and legal reflection that, regrettably, are conspicuous by their absence in other parts of the DCFR. Of course, one may agree with the proposal studied here, or criticise it; but in no way can it be described as the product of a frivolous, incomplete, hasty or premature effort.

However, readers may legitimately wonder about the true purpose of the article examined here, since it is to be found in a mere soft law text without any mandatory effectiveness. It is undeniable that the DCFR has seen better days, which, in our view, is more a consequence of the crisis in which the EU's identity and project are currently immersed than of its own shortcomings and defects (of which it has plenty). The idea of using the DCFR as the basis for the adoption of an 'optional instrument' having now been abandoned, at least for the time being,[59] all that remains is for it to serve as a tool box for improving the *acquis communautaire* or as a model for national legislations. Notwithstanding this, since its impact in this respect has also been very limited, realistically its scope should be reduced to a purely academic one, namely, teaching and legal research. And it is no trivial or minor issue, especially in a field like the one analysed here in which comparative studies have been few and far between, at least by comparison with what has happened in other spheres of private law, such as contract and tort.[60] Article VIII–2:101 DCFR, with its commentaries and notes on comparative law, constitutes an unprecedented comparative analysis for both its quality and thoroughness, and we jurists would do well to acknowledge its inestimable contribution to contemporary learning within private law. By doing so, the effort will have been worthwhile.

[59] For the development of proposals for a European Contract Law from the PECL, through (inter alia) the DCFR to the draft Common European Sales Law (CESL) as an optional instrument, and its ultimate withdrawal at the end of 2014, see R Schulze and F Zoll, *European Contract Law*, 2nd edn (Baden-Baden, Nomos, 2018) 24–34.

[60] 'Unlike the law of obligations, until two decades ago comparative lawyers seem to have avoided property law': S Van Erp, 'Comparative Property Law' in M Reimann and R Zimmermann (eds), *Oxford Handbook of Comparative Law*, 2nd edn (Oxford, Oxford University Press, 2019) 1032.

8

The Assignment of Contract

Some Comparative Reflections on French and English Law

AGNÈS KWIATKOWSKI

I. Introduction. The Assignment of Contract: An Intriguing Recognition

'Modernising the rules relating to the assignment of the benefit of rights, …; recognising the assignment of the burden of rights and the assignment of contract'.[1] This was one the objectives of the French reform of contract law which entered into force in October 2016.[2] This recent and quite sudden concern for assignment is particularly intriguing, not only because now this mechanism clearly manifests itself in different forms (assignment of benefit, of burden and of the contract), but also because the objective of modernisation of the law of assignment, including the introduction of assignment *of the contract*, appeared to be so important for the French reform to recognise it formally. This raises many questions, both theoretical and practical. Practice may justify the recognition of the mechanism of assignment of contract, but there is a particular enthusiasm that characterises this recognition. It is this enthusiasm, along with the new recognition of assignments both of the burden of rights and of contract, that is puzzling.

[1] 'Moderniser les règles relatives à la cession de créance, …; consacrer la cession de dette et la cession de contrat': *Rapport au Président de la République relatif à l'ordonnance no 2016-131 du 10 février 2016 portant réforme du droit des contrats, du régime général et de la preuve des obligations*, JORF no 0035 du 11 février 2016, texte no 25 (Report to the President of the Republic, by the Minister of Justice, explaining the text of the *ordonnance* by which the Code Civil was reformed in 2016), available also at www.legifrance.gouv.fr/eli/rapport/2016/2/11/JUSC1522466P/jo/texte.

[2] *Ordonnance no 2016-131 du 10 février 2016 portant réforme du droit des contrats, du régime général et de la preuve des obligations*: JORF no 0035 du 11 février 2016, texte no 26. The *ordonnance* was ratified by a *loi* in 2018: *Loi no 2018-287 du 20 avril 2018 ratifiant l'ordonnance no 2016-131 du 10 février 2016 portant réforme du droit des contrats, du régime général et de la preuve des obligations* JORF no 0093 du 21 avril 2018, texte no 1. This *loi* also made some (generally minor) amendments to the text as originally reformed by the *ordonnance*. The text referred to in this chapter is the final version, in force since 1 October 2018.

Assignment is an economically very important operation; however, its interpretation can be more or less efficient and pragmatic. This can be demonstrated in particular by the different understandings of the mechanism by French law and English law. They will reveal, each in their own way, that the object of the assignment must be understood in a very particular way; and the transfer that is involved in an assignment combines both contract law and property law. This is where we must be particularly cautious. As Cartwright says 'we learn early in our legal training that contract and property are fundamentally different within the structure of private law'.[3] In other words, contract law is one thing but property law is supposed to be something else. In his chapter, he explains that property may be created or transferred by contract. But the connection could be pushed even further: if the assignment of contract can effect the transfer of the instrument, contract law and property law may be mixed to the point of assimilating the contract not to property itself, but at least to a form of property.

At first sight, the assimilation of the contract to a form of property does not seem impossible, in so far as the new French provisions talk about the mechanism of assignment of contract, apparently used to transfer the whole contract. But perhaps this is to jump to a hasty conclusion: saying that a contract is assigned may not mean that the instrument itself is assigned, but that something else is transferred.[4] In any event, we need to consider very carefully the provisions relating to the assignment of contract, as now recognised by the French legislator; and here comparative law can be particularly useful, placing the law of two systems (France and England) together to reveal similarities and differences. First, however, it will be helpful to consider briefly the main notions involved in the new French law, and the context in which they are written.

A. General Definition of Assignment

In very broad terms, assignment involves a transmission, a transfer; the transfer of rights, obligations,[5] assets.[6] In French law, assignment – *cession* – can be defined as 'the transmission of a right inter vivos';[7] and transferability – *cessibilité* – as 'the

[3] Above, Ch 6 section I.

[4] According to Aynès, it is a 'misguided phrase' ('une expression malencontreuse'): L Aynès, 'La cession de contrat' *Droit et Patrimoine* no 249, 2015, p 73.

[5] Obligations represent a burden, a legal duty. Duties arising from contract are assignable in French law, but not generally in English law. An apparent exception is the lease, where the benefit and burden of the landlord's and/or the tenant's covenants pass on assignment of the premises and/or the reversion; but '[a] lease is a hybrid, part contract, part property. So far as rights of alienation are concerned a lease has been treated as a species of property': *Linden Gardens Trust Ltd v Lenesta Sludge Disposals Ltd* [1994] 1 AC 85 (HL) 108 (Lord Browne-Wilkinson).

[6] Assets can be 'physical like ships and aircraft' or 'intangible … like shares, debt securities, receivables, insurance policies, intellectual property rights and investment products': M Bridge and L Gullifer, *The Law of Personal Property*, 2nd edn (London, Sweet and Maxwell, 2018) [1-001].

[7] 'Transmission d'un droit entre vifs': *Lexique des termes juridiques*, 27th edn (Paris, Dalloz, 2019) 170.

character of intangible property (shares, securities, goodwill) allowing its transfer'.[8] In English law, 'assigning a chose in action involves the transfer of that chose from the assignor to the assignee'.[9] Without going into too much detail for the moment, it should be borne in mind that the central idea is the transfer, either of rights or of 'choses [things][10] in action', which is allowed because of the seemingly proprietary nature of the object of the transfer. In the case of an assignment of contract, it is easy to imagine that what will be assigned is either the rights arising under the contract or possibly, as its name suggests, the contract itself. In any case, it is the particular character of the transferred object that will allow its assignment, and it is this character that will have to be explored.

B. A Specific Context in French law: The Reform of Contract Law

The reform of contract law (and, more broadly, the law of obligations) has been greatly discussed in France in recent years. After a succession of reform projects,[11] a governmental decree (*ordonnance*)[12] reforming the French law of contract and the general regime of obligations was finally published in February 2016 and entered into force on 1 October 2016; this reform was ratified with certain amendments by parliamentary legislation (*loi*) in 2018.[13] This reform was necessary, in particular, because the general rules of the French law of contract had never been reformed since the Napoleonic Code in 1804. Its main aim was therefore to modernise and simplify the law and to make it more accessible to citizens. However, since it came into effect, this reform has been much written about and some provisions remain, in some respects, debatable – including the new provision on the assignment of contract. In order to fulfil its purpose of modernity and clarity, the 2016 reform has created not only a definition of the assignment of the burden of obligations (a 'debt')[14] but also a definition of the assignment of contract, to coexist alongside

[8] 'Qualité d'un bien incorporel (part sociale, titre, fonds de commerce, etc) permettant sa cession': *Lexique des termes juridiques* (n 7) 170.

[9] M Smith and N Leslie, *The Law of Assignment*, 3rd edn (Oxford, Oxford University Press, 2018) [11.02].

[10] In this chapter we generally use the term 'chose in action' (see further below, n 59), except where quoting from a text which refers to 'thing in action': see, eg, Law of Property Act 1925, s 136 (n 69).

[11] See esp P Catala (ed), *Avant-projet de réforme du droit des obligations et de la prescription: Rapport remis au garde des Sceaux* (Paris, La Documentation française, 2006: the 'Avant-projet Catala'); F Terré (ed), *Pour une réforme du droit des contrats* (Paris, Dalloz, 2009); F Terré (ed), *Pour une réforme du droit de la responsabilité civile* (Paris, Dalloz, 2011); F Terré (ed), *Pour une réforme du régime général des obligations* (Paris, Dalloz, 2013). The French Ministry of Justice produced draft reform proposals for the reform of the law of obligations in 2008, 2009 and 2013; and the *ordonnance* of 2016 (see above, n 2) was preceded by a draft proposal in 2015. The reform of civil liability is still underway, following the publication of a reform bill by the Minister of Justice on 13 March 2017.

[12] Above, n 2.

[13] Above, n 2.

[14] The terminology in French law of 'debt' [*dette*] (and 'debtor' [*débiteur*]) and 'credit' [*créance*] (and 'creditor' [*créancier*]) is very different from the usage in English law, where these words are generally

the assignment of the benefit of rights arising from obligations, assignment by operation of legislation and novation. This multiplicity is astonishing, especially when it is put in parallel with the English model, where there is only one form of assignment – of the benefit of rights – clearly and logically differentiated from novation, which involves a new contract.

C. A Bit of History

Recent disquiet around the concept of assignment in French law has not been felt by English law. The contemporary French debate raises questions about the origins of this movement, as well as the roots of the concept of assignment. Originally, although it was clearly of great economic and practical utility, the idea of assignment inspired mistrust, especially its speculative aspect.[15] This is also why the drafters of the Code civil of 1804[16] defined its rules very carefully. English lawyers, just as suspicious, came to the more radical decision that contractual rights could not be assigned at common law.[17] Thus, in English common law, before 1875, the only way to achieve 'the equivalent of an assignment of contractual rights'[18] was to use the mechanism of novation – also recognised by the Napoleonic Code of 1804, which similarly differentiated it from assignment. The only alternative in English law was Equity, which had already recognised the assignment of a trust.[19] On both sides, tortuous paths were therefore taken to fulfil an economic necessity, even though assigning the benefit of a debt seemed to be useful 'to enable someone else to collect it on his behalf and in his absence' but also 'to enable the assignor to pay the debt owed by him'.[20] But it was mainly the prohibition of maintenance[21] which

used only to describe someone with a duty or right relating to the payment of money: see J Cartwright and S Whittaker, 'Introduction to the English Translation' in F Ancel and B Fauvarque-Cosson, *Le Nouveau Droit des Contrats: Guide Bilingue à l'Usage des Praticiens* (Paris, LGDJ, 2019) 435–39. To provide clarity for the English reader, in this chapter the French concepts of *dette* and *créance* will generally be translated as (respectively) the burden of an obligation, and the benefit of (rights arising under) an obligation.

[15] Assignment could be made for value – the assignee pays the assignor for the transfer of the benefit of the rights arising under the obligation – but the value of those rights may be uncertain, and the assignee may have no recourse against the assignor if it should later turn out that the rights have little (or even no) value.

[16] Arts 1689–1701 Napoleonic Code (1804). This group of articles formed Chapter VIII ('The transmission of rights under obligations and other incorporeal rights' [*Du transport des créances et autres droits incorporels*]) of Title VI (Sale) within Book III ('The different ways by which ownership is acquired' – the Book which also included the Titles on contracts and consensual obligations in general, non-contractual obligations, and various particular types of contract).

[17] H Beale (ed), *Chitty on Contracts*, 33rd edn (London, Sweet & Maxwell, 2018) [19-001].

[18] ibid.

[19] *Warmstrey v Tanfield* (1628) 1 Ch Rep 29, 30; 21 ER 498.

[20] M Holden, *The History of Negotiable Instruments in English Law* (London, Athlone Press, 1955) 11.

[21] ie, the support of litigation by a person who has no legitimate concern in it: Beale (n 17) [16-078]. Maintenance was a crime, and therefore (for the purposes of contract law) contrary to public policy: ibid [16-076], [16-077].

led to the impossibility of assignment; the main barrier was that it would involve a third party who had no legitimate interest in the debt. Besides, 'the perception that rights of action are personal',[22] deriving from Roman law, was very strong. So, until 1875, even though this rejection by the English common law was criticised,[23] the common law – unlike French law and Equity – did not acknowledge the need to recognise assignment alongside novation. However, the first formal acceptance of assignment into the English common law appeared in the Judicature Act 1873,[24] in provisions which were later re-enacted by the Law of Property Act 1925[25] and are still in force today. Thus, assignment entered into English law, in a form quite similar to the French assignment of the benefit of rights of 1804. From then until the later 20th century, the approach of the two systems seemed quite comparable: only the benefit of rights was transferable, and only under certain conditions, although these were rather different. It was then the French case law, inspired first by practice and then by academic writing,[26] which made significant developments, marking a clear separation of the paths of French law and English law. French law alone moved in the direction of accepting the assignment of the burden of obligations and of contract; English law has remained impervious to such a development. As a result, the two models have become different: one has continued to develop the debate incrementally to create operations in which the status as party has an important role to play, the other has remained focused on the economic purpose and the practical effect of the operation. While the initial design of assignment, as it came from the Napoleonic Code, could be compared with English assignment until the French reform, recent debates[27] have shifted the perspective towards a potential assignment of the contractual instrument itself.

D. The Idea of Transfer

As already stated, in the mechanism of assignment the central idea is to transfer[28] something to another, which immediately involves a third party in the contractual

[22] J Edelman and S Elliott, 'Two Conceptions of Equitable Assignment' (2015) 131 LQR 228.

[23] *Master v Miller* (1791) 4 TR 320, 340; 100 ER 1042, 1053.

[24] Supreme Court of Judicature Act 1873, s 25(6).

[25] LPA 1925, s 136; see below, n 69.

[26] C Lapp, *Essai sur la cession de contrat synallagmatique à titre particulier* (doctoral thesis, University of Strasbourg, 1950); C Larroumet, *Les opérations juridiques à trois personnes en droit privé* (doctoral thesis, Université Montesquieu Bordeaux IV, 1968); J Ghestin, C Jamin and M Billiau, *Traité de droit civil, Les effets du contrat*, 3rd edn (Paris, LGDJ, 2001) 1113; O Maira Lamas, *La cession de contrat en droit comparé* (doctoral thesis, University of Paris, 1960); P Malaurie, *La cession de contrat, Cours de Doctorat Paris II, 1975–1976* (Paris, les Cours de droit, 1976); C Vilar, *La cession de contrat en droit français* (doctoral thesis, University of Montpellier, 1968); L Aynès, *La cession de contrat et les opérations juridiques à trois personnes* (Paris, Economica, 1984).

[27] Above, n 26.

[28] 'Transfer' means 'To convey or take from one place, person, etc. to another; to transmit, transport; to give or hand over from one to another', or (in a more specialist legal sense) 'To convey or make over (title, right, or property) by deed or legal process': 'transfer, v.' *OED Online*, Oxford University Press, March 2021.

relationship, modifying in consequence the relational aspect of the operation. Essentially, following the Roman conception, the obligation is a legal relationship between two (or more) individuals,[29] so this relational dimension to the obligation should defeat any transmission. But apparently this is not the case. The practice of assignment in business shows the opposite, and legislation corroborates this. Indeed, the contract has not only a relational dimension but also a strong economic dimension. Hence, the justification for having an interest in transmitting an obligation is what a French lawyer would refer to as a *valeur patrimoniale* – 'patrimonial value' – meaning an exchange value, an economic value, a tradable interest. This could be more or less related to the concept of bargain in English law. The reference to the notion of patrimony[30] is central in French law but is not used in English law. *Patrimonial*, in French law, 'characterises what is appreciable in money, as part of the patrimony, conceived as a mass of goods and which, therefore, is susceptible of assignment and transmission',[31] which is thus distinguished from the *extrapatrimonial*, which means 'excluded from legal trade'.[32] In other words, being *patrimonial* means having a pecuniary value, being exchangeable, being owned – since what is owned is inside the *patrimoine*, the patrimony. This can easily be related to concepts such as property or assets, also marked by an economic imprint, all the more so when we remember that, in English law, property law 'deals with the relations between persons with regard to things'.[33] Nevertheless, 'when used in a legal sense the word property describes a relationship between a person and a thing, and not the thing itself'.[34] It therefore describes a relation of possession or ownership, either absolute or divided, with a thing that can be owned. Yet, if it is owned, it has a certain value, it holds an interest. Assets, which represent 'an item of value owned',[35] can be proprietary as far as they represent 'physical property and/or rights that have a monetary value and are capable of being those of a juristic person or a natural person … A distinction can be made

[29] Inst 3.13 pr: 'Obligatio est iuris vinculum quo necessitate adstringimur alicuius solvendae rei secundum nostrae civitatis iura' ('an obligation is a tie of law, by which we are bound to fulfil something in accordance with the laws of our state').

[30] 'Patrimony' (*le patrimoine*) means all of a person's goods, rights and obligations, considered together as a legal right, within which the assets and liabilities cannot be dissociated, although benefits offset burdens in assessing its totality: see *Lexique des termes juridiques* (n 7) 783 (Patrimoine: 'ensemble des biens, droits et des obligations d'une personne, envisagé comme une universalité de droit, c'est-à-dire comme une masse mouvante dont l'actif et le passif ne peuvent être dissociés'). This patrimony can be possessed by either an individual person or a legal entity. The concept was taken up and developed by Aubry and Rau, who were inspired by Zachariae. It was not exported to English law, so English lawyers do not refer to it in the contexts in which it is used in French law, although the closest equivalent in English is a person's 'estate'.

[31] Patrimonial 'caractérise ce qui est appréciable en argent comme faisant partie du patrimoine conçu comme une masse de biens et qui, par conséquent, est susceptible de cession et de transmission': *Lexique des termes juridiques* (n 7) 785.

[32] 'exclu du commerce juridique': *Lexique des termes juridiques* (n 7) 409.

[33] FH Lawson and B Rudden, *The Law of Property*, 3rd edn (Oxford, Oxford University Press, 2002) 5.

[34] Bridge and Gullifer (n 6) [1-002].

[35] 'asset, n.', *OED Online*, Oxford University Press, March 2021.

between tangible assets (such as land and buildings) and intangible assets (such as goodwill)'.[36] So something that has a pecuniary value can be designated as an asset or as a *patrimonial* item. If it has a *patrimonial* value, it can be exchanged and if it can be exchanged, it is in the patrimony. What is in patrimony is owned and what is owned is *patrimonial*. Consequently, if this idea is transposed to the context of an assignment, it is clear that the object of the operation, in the French vision, goes from one patrimony to another and in the English vision, goes from one party to another as an asset. In both cases, even though the concepts used may be different, the object of assignment is owned by one party, then transmitted and owned by another. Of course, there are peculiarities specific to the application and scope of these concepts in both systems, but this chapter will use only these general ideas.

In 2016 French law formally created within the Code civil a mechanism called 'assignment of contract'.[37] This makes it necessary to examine the fate of the object of this transfer operation – the contract – when the mechanism is put into action. The first task will therefore be to understand how (or, indeed, whether) the contract itself can be transferred, and here we shall consider the answers given by both French law and English law. Moreover, since the question is whether what is transferred is an interpersonal link (the contractual relationship) or an asset, the notion of assignment (transfer) of contract will necessarily raise questions about the contract itself.

II. Opposing Visions of the Mechanism of Assignment

The mechanism of assignment is seen differently by the two legal systems. Their construction has gradually been differentiated over time and the distinction between the two models has been confirmed and reinforced by the 2016–18 French reform. This mechanism is not only technically different, it is also conceptually different.

A. Technically Different

i. A Problematic Construction in French Law

In French law, a distinction must be made between the law before the 2016 reform, and the law after the reform.

Before the reform, there was no article in the Code civil defining the assignment of contract.[38] It is fundamentally an instrument that resulted from practice.

[36] J Law (ed), *Oxford Dictionary of Law*, 9th edn (Oxford, Oxford University Press, 2018) 53 ('assets').
[37] Art 1216 Cc (*la cession de contrat*).
[38] There was a provision for the assignment of the benefit of rights arising from obligations (*créances*). The assignment of the benefit of rights was governed by the provisions of articles 1689–1701 in the old

It could be found in some cases,[39] but could not be explained within the theory of French contract law. The Cour de cassation (the French Supreme Court) tried from time to time to lay down some rules, but these were not certain or settled. All we knew was that assigning a contract meant transferring 'all the rights and obligations arising from the contract'[40] and that, for this, it was possible to 'refer to the contractual stipulation of substitution';[41] yet the court decided that 'substitution does not have the character of an assignment'.[42] So what was clear was that the assignment of contract involved the transfer of both benefits and burdens which arose from the contract, but the definition of the operation itself was not clear. The only clue was that apparently it could not be assimilated to a *substitution*.[43] Writers therefore took up the question and proposed different theoretical explanations. Two main conceptions were put forward. First, given that a contract is composed of rights and obligations that are linked by a contractual relationship, the dualistic conception advocated in favour of a divided vision of the contract. Following this logic, these different elements of the contract must be transferred separately.[44] At that time, however, it was impossible to assign the burden of a debt in French law.[45] Second, the monistic or unitary conception held that the contract as a whole, the totality of its elements, must be assigned in a single operation, given that it is impossible to consider benefits and burdens separately because they are indissolubly linked.[46] Some writers were hostile and rather reluctant to accept assignment of contract (strictly understood), on the basis that we cannot assign an interpersonal relationship[47] and in particular we cannot assign a contract as we would assign

Code Civil, which were placed within the section on the contract of sale: see above, n 16. This mechanism was therefore understood as a contract of sale for a special good, the benefit of the right.

[39] Cass civ (3) 12 December 2001, no 00-15.627, D 2002, 984; RDI 2002, 230; RDI 2002, 49; Cass com 6 May 1997, no 95-10.252, D 1997, 588; RTD civ 1997, 936; Cass civ (1) 14 December 1982, no 81-15.455.

[40] 'L'ensemble des droits et obligations nés du contrat': Cass civ (1) 14 December 1982 (n 39).

[41] 'Se référant à la stipulation contractuelle de substitution': Cass com 6 May 1997 (n 39).

[42] 'La faculté de substitution n'a pas le caractère d'une cession': Cass civ (3) 19 March 1997, no 95-12.473, RJDA 7/1997 no 945.

[43] A substitution can be defined as the transaction whereby a person (A) carries out an obligation which was created between two other persons (B), the person whose obligation is carried out and (C), whose obligations are unchanged without B disappearing entirely from the legal relationship, and with the result that (A) and (C) are directly linked to each other: E Jeuland, 'Proposition de distinction entre la cession de contrat et la substitution de personne' D 1998 chron 356.

[44] Lapp (n 26); Larroumet (n 26); Ghestin, Jamin and Billiau (n 26), 1113; Maira Lamas (n 26); Vilar (n 26).

[45] It was, however, considered by case law: see eg Civ (1) 30 April 2009, no 08-11.093, although the consent of the creditor must be obtained.

[46] Aynès defended this idea in his doctoral thesis (n 26). According to him, the contractual relationship postulates the unity of the contractual relationship. Put another way, if the economic purpose pursued by the parties is the same, then the assignee may pursue the same objectives as the assignor did, and then the unity of the contract is not affected by the assignment (before the 2016 reform this could be explained by reference to the doctrine of *la cause*: the new parties are pursuing the same *cause*, the same objective, so it is still the same contract). Following this reasoning, the assignment of the whole contract becomes possible.

[47] Ghestin, Jamin and Billiau (n 26) 1113.

tangible property such as a car or a house[48] because the contract cannot be understood as a *thing*.[49] Yet the assignment of contract was a commercial reality, and all the more so given that legislation recognised the assignment of certain contracts, such as a lease,[50] an insurance contract[51] or an employment contract.[52] Thus, the practice existed, but no general definition nor rules applicable to a general assignment of contract could be found in the legislative texts. Besides, theory could not explain how an interpersonal relationship, linking rights and obligations arising from the contract, could be assigned. Only limited answers were given by the case law. There was therefore an ambiguity that needed to be resolved. It was only in 2016 that the legislator took the matter in hand.

A new provision on the assignment of contract has been created by the reform in articles 1216 to 1216-3 Cc, in the chapter on 'the effects of contracts'. This is in addition to a new provision in articles 1327 to 1328-1 on the assignment of the burden of obligations in the chapter dealing with 'transactions relating to obligations', where it sits with the well-established provisions on the assignment of rights arising from obligations in the new articles 1321 to 1326.

According to the new definition in article 1216, 'a contracting party, the assignor, may assign his status as party to the contract to a third party, the assignee, with the agreement of his own contractual partner, the person subject to assignment'.[53] A number of observations can be made. First, the assignment of contract is not in the chapter on 'transactions relating to obligations'. Therefore, it is not understood as a transfer operation – *une opération translative* – such as the assignment of the benefit of rights arising from obligations, but more as a substitution of a party to the contract. When a status is assigned, one person takes the place of the other. The positioning of the article in a chapter entitled 'the effects of contracts' not only shows that this assignment of contract has an impact on the effect of the contract but also that the unitary conception[54] has clearly been chosen, since the assignment of contract is an operation on the contract itself. It therefore appears that this process involves the transfer of the entire contract,[55] the contract as a whole, comprising both benefits and burdens. Finally, it is clear that this definition mixes an economic aspect, the transfer itself, with a more personal aspect, reflected by the assignment of the 'status as party'. In other words, a personal position in the contract becomes the object of the economic transfer. The description of the operation itself is very peculiar.

[48] P Berlioz, *La notion de bien* (Paris, LGDJ, 2007) 1042, 1054.

[49] L Aynès, 'La cession de contrat' *Droit et Patrimoine* no 260, 2016.

[50] Art 1743 Cc.

[51] Art L121-10(1) Code des assurances.

[52] Art L1224-1 Code du travail.

[53] 'Un contractant, le cédant, peut céder sa qualité de partie au contrat à un tiers, le cessionnaire, avec l'accord de son cocontractant, le cédé'.

[54] Above, n 46.

[55] G Chantepie and M Latina, *Le nouveau droit des obligations*, 2nd edn (Paris, Dalloz, 2018) 545.

There is therefore an obvious collision of the contract as an interpersonal relationship with patrimonial aspects normally attached to property, embodied in a single mechanism, which reveals its complexity.

ii. A Comparison with English Law

There has been no such debate about assignment in English law, at least not recently.[56] The rules relating to assignment are much more refined and fit within English contract law's overall logic of pragmatism and economic efficiency. In English law, assignment refers to the transfer of a right.[57] It represents the mechanism by which 'choses in action can be transferred voluntarily by one person to another'[58] – by an assignor to an assignee. A chose in action is 'a known legal expression used to describe all personal rights of property which can only be claimed or enforced by action, and not by taking physical possession'.[59] The assignment is therefore understood only through a transfer of rights. It is thus clear that English law has not chosen a unitary conception of assignment, by contrast with French law.[60] The English vision of assignment is much more like the assignment of rights arising from obligations in French law, or at least closer to the dualistic conception contemplated by legal writers.[61] But in English law it is simply impossible to assign the burden of an obligation. The operation of assignment does not require any consent, and transferring a burden without consent is on principle unthinkable. 'It would be a curious principle that allowed the two parties to a contract to agree to impose an obligation on a third party not involved in the contract, without that party's consent'.[62] French law took the same position until the French legislator created assignment of the burden of an obligation – but accompanied by consent.[63] It is then the very notion of what is meant by assignment – or at least what it should technically imply – that is challenged. Is assignment a mechanism requiring consent or not? In English law, '[a]s a general rule, liabilities cannot be assigned without the consent of the party to whom the liability is owed'.[64] And the assignment 'only transfers an existing right',[65] it does not create a new one. Therefore, in English law there is

[56] There was a debate long ago about the recognition of assignment by the common law and whether or not choses in action should be transferable: see *Master v Miller* (n 23).

[57] cf 'assignment, n.', *OED Online*, Oxford University Press, March 2021 ('legal transference of a right or property').

[58] Smith and Leslie (n 9) [1.02].

[59] *Torkington v Magee* [1902] 2 KB 427 (KB) 430.

[60] Above, nn 37, 46.

[61] Above, n 44.

[62] Smith and Leslie (n 9) [5.06].

[63] Art 1327(1) Cc: 'A debtor may assign his debt [the burden of his obligation] to another person with the agreement of the creditor' ('Un débiteur peut, avec l'accord du créancier, céder sa dette').

[64] E McKendrick, *Contract Law: Text, Cases and Materials*, 9th edn (Oxford, Oxford University Press, 2020) 962.

[65] J Cartwright, *Contract Law: An Introduction to the English Law of Contract for the Civil Lawyer*, 3rd edn (Oxford, Hart Publishing, 2016) 256.

no such thing as the assignment of a contract as a whole, implying the transfer of both benefit and burden, even though the phrase 'assign this contract' is sometimes used. As Lord Browne-Wilkinson declared in *Linden Gardens Trust Ltd v Lenesta Sludge Disposals Ltd*:

> Although it is true that the phrase assign this contract is not strictly accurate, lawyers frequently use those words inaccurately to describe an assignment of the benefit of a contract since every lawyer knows that the burden of a contract cannot be assigned.[66]

Thus, the only way to picture the assignment of a contract as a whole is through novation, which is also a known mechanism of French law.[67] The multiplicity of French models is also interesting. The clean and simple English model makes the French approach all the more debatable, and the existence of novation may call into question the urgency of establishing a new mechanism of transfer of the contract in French law. Novation has a different definition: it is (art 1329) 'a contract which has as its subject-matter the substitution of one obligation (which it extinguishes) with a new obligation (which it creates)'. Although both mechanisms now exist in French law, English law confines the replacement of an entire contract to novation. Therefore, introducing an assignment of contract does not seem to be obvious. The English assignment is more similar to the French assignment of the benefit of rights arising from obligations than its idea of an assignment of contract.

It should be noted that the legal basis of assignment is dual in English law. As already mentioned, assignment was previously not allowed under the common law rules, subject to certain exceptions such as assignments to or by the Crown.[68] Essentially, there are two types of assignment, one 'legal' – ie, recognised by the common law, and found in statute – the other equitable. The common law was sometimes very strict, which prompted the courts of equity to allow some assignments to take effect even if they did not meet the conditions required for a legal assignment. The definition of legal assignment and the conditions required to perform this operation and to assign the benefit of a debt can be found in Law of Property Act 1925, section 136. Under this provision, the assignment of 'any debt or other legal thing in action' is effective if it is absolute, 'not purporting to be by way of charge only', written by the assignor, and if the debtor was notified about it.[69] There is no requirement for the debtor to consent to the assignment, just that he should have notice of it. This allows the operation to be immediately effective, and the assignee is then allowed to exercise the assigned rights in his own name. These same operating rules can also be found in the French assignment

[66] *Linden Gardens Trust Ltd v Lenesta Sludge Disposals Ltd* (n 5) 103.

[67] Arts 1329–35 Cc (arts 1271–81 before the 2016 reform).

[68] Smith and Leslie (n 9) [10.11].

[69] 'Any absolute assignment by writing under the hand of the assignor (not purporting to be by way of charge only) of any debt or other legal thing in action, of which express notice in writing has been given to the debtor, trustee or other person from whom the assignor would have been entitled to claim such debt or thing in action, is effectual in law (subject to equities having priority over the right of the assignee) to pass and transfer from the date of such notice': LPA 1925, s 136.

of the benefit of rights arising from obligations.[70] These rules must, however, be contrasted with those of the assignment of contract, which require consent[71] – which can be easily understood since the contract contains the burden of rights arising from obligations, as well as benefits. The parallel is therefore relevant, bearing in mind that in English law 'an absolute assignment is one that transfers the assignor's entire interest to the assignee unconditionally'.[72]

B. Conceptually Different

Assignment in French law and English law are also conceptually different. To discuss the assignment *of contract*, it is necessary to understand how the contract, the object of the operation, is perceived by the two legal systems. This distinction will also be found in their perception of the transfer that is involved in an assignment.

i. The Contract as Object of the Assignment

In French law, a contract is defined as 'a concordance of wills of two or more persons intended to create, modify, transfer or extinguish obligations'.[73] Put another way, a contract represents the meeting of the wills of two (or more) parties, and so an interpersonal link is created. The French contract is obviously subjective since the contract is considered from a relational perspective. The meeting of minds and its subjectivity overrides the objectivity attached to the perception of the instrument. There is an agreement when – and only when – the parties had the subjective intention to enter into a contract with each other and on the same terms. Consequently, according to this theory, the meeting of subjective wills is required to form a contract. In English Law, the spirit in entirely different. 'The first requirement for the formation of a contract is that the parties should have reached agreement' and 'the law regards an agreement as having been reached when an offer made by one of the parties (the offeror) is accepted by the other to whom the offer is addressed (the offeree or acceptor)'.[74] But the agreement is

[70] Arts 1321–26 Cc.

[71] Art 1216(1) Cc: 'A contracting party, the assignor, may assign his status as party to the contract to a third party, the assignee, with the agreement of his own contractual partner, the person subject to assignment' ('Un contractant, le cédant, peut céder sa qualité de partie au contrat à un tiers, le cessionnaire, avec l'accord de son cocontractant, le cédé'). Art 1216-1 requires *further* consent if the assignor is to be discharged. Without this consent, the assignor and the assignee are jointly and severally liable: art 1216-1: 'If the person subject to assignment has expressly consented to it, assignment of contract discharges the assignor for the future. In its absence, and subject to any term to the contrary, the assignor is liable jointly and severally to the performance of the contract'.

[72] *Oxford Dictionary of Law* (n 36) 54 ('assignment').

[73] Art 1101 Cc ('un accord de volontés entre deux ou plusieurs personnes destiné à créer, modifier, transmettre ou éteindre des obligations').

[74] Beale (n 17) [2-001].

not perceived subjectively: even though there must be an intention to create legal relations, this is tested objectively:[75] 'the parties' intentions are to be determined by reference to their external manifestation: it is the declared intention, rather than the internal, subjective intention, which counts'.[76] French law and English law have fundamentally opposite visions on this point. But since it is a mechanism of assignment of contract that French law has attempted to create, the perception of the contract, as the object of the operation, is significant. So, we should ask whether the subjectivity of a contract constitutes an obstacle to the mechanism of assignment of contract.

ii. The Transfer

This same contrast is found in the mechanism of assignment. The operation described in article 1216 Cc consists of assigning a status as party, and therefore in replacing one person with another,[77] and not in assigning the contractual instrument itself, understood as a whole. English law knows no such transaction, since it rejects the assignment of a burden, and recognises only the assignment of certain choses in action. Given that French law, before the reform, was in line with English law on the assignment of the benefit of a right – *cession de créance* – one might expect the two systems to agree on the definition of assignment and what it technically involves. But it appears that the 2016 reform has changed things. French law, it seems, has given a new meaning to the mechanism of assignment, and has subjectivised it. By emphasising the personal aspect of the contractual relationship between the parties, French law has significantly reduced the economic aspect of the operation. Of course, the contract is undeniably an interpersonal relationship, but assignment remains a business transaction. It seems therefore difficult to claim that there is an 'assignment of contract' when only a substitution of a party to the contract – ie, replacing one party with another – is involved. Yet, following this logic, French law now considers that the replacement of one person by another constitutes an assignment of contract.[78] In this, the true meaning of assignment as a *transfer*[79] is brushed aside.

There is therefore a real question about whether the operation described in article 1216 should have the name of 'assignment'. Moreover, there seems to be a paradox: the contract is seen as an interpersonal link that cannot itself be assigned; so what is chosen to be transferred is something even more subjective, but also

[75] *RTS Flexible Systems Ltd v Molkerei Alois Müller GmbH* [2010] UKSC 14, [2010] 1 WLR 753 [45].

[76] Cartwright (n 65) 96.

[77] The 'substitution of a party to the contract' is a concept that already existed before the reform: but the Cour de cassation had declared that substitution does not have the character of an assignment: Cass civ (3) 19 March 1997 (n 42).

[78] Above, n 37.

[79] Above, section I.A.

unclear, a 'status as party'.[80] However, given that the transferred object can be as personal as a *status*, is it really impossible to conceive of the transfer of *the contract itself* as an interpersonal link that is transferred? Or should the contract itself – objectively understood as an economic instrument, ie, an asset – be conceived of as the object of transfer? The recognition of an operation entitled 'assignment of contract' describing the assignment of a *status as party* brings about confusion. Perhaps there was no need to confuse the definition of assignment, but just to explore the potentialities of the contract itself as an object of the transfer. The contract, in spite of having a personal dimension, is an economic instrument which, in practice, may pass from one hand to another, from one party to another, from one patrimony to another. This reveals a contract behaving in some ways like property – as an economically significant asset. This is very important since assignment is 'an important feature of commercial practice'.[81]

III. A Mechanism Revealing the Proprietary Character of the Contract

The mechanism of assignment of contract created by the 2016 reform is questionable, not only because it does not match the concept nor the understanding of assignment, but also because it does not conform to the reality of practice. English law has a more accurate approach, consistent with the classic meaning of assignment, which helps us to challenge the new French 'assignment of contract', and perhaps to suggest a new approach.

A. The Nature of Contractual Rights

i. Contract and Property: A Difficult Line to Draw in the Context of Assignment

The creation of the mechanism of assignment of contract is controversial.[82] Since the name of the mechanism indicates that the contract itself is the subject of the

[80] See A Chabalier, *La patrimonialité de la position contractuelle* (doctoral thesis, University of Montpellier 1, 2000).

[81] McKendrick (n 64) 962.

[82] Aynès (n 4); Aynès (n 46); Berlioz (n 48) 1038 ff; Lapp (n 26); Larroumet (n 26); Ghestin, Jamin and Billiau (n 26) 1113; Maira Lamas (n 26); Malaurie (n 26); Vilar (n 26); Aynès (n 26); G Pillet, 'La cession conventionnelle de contrat du Code civil: une consécration en demi-teinte' RDC 2017, 392; M Billiau, 'Le point sur la cession conventionnelle du contrat' *Les petites affiches* 1998, 46; C Juillet, 'Le sort des sûretés du cédé dans la cession de contrat de droit commun' RDC 2017, 382; O Deshayes, 'Proposition de modification des articles 1216-3, 1328-1 et 1334 du Code civil : le sort des sûretés en cas de cession du contrat, de dette et de novation' RDC 2017, 189; P Crocq, 'Sort des sûretés et cession de contrat ou de dette' D 2016, 1958; O Deshayes, T Genicon, Y-M Laithier, *Réforme du droit des contrats,*

transfer, this questions the very notion of contract, and its nature, as well as the relationship between contract and property. If the contract itself is to be transferred, it appears to be treated as an item of property; and even in a legal system, such as English law, which recognises only assignment of rights arising from obligations, 'assignment demonstrates, quite acutely at times, how difficult it is to draw the line between matters of contract and matters of property'.[83] Although the notion of contract is based on an interpersonal relationship between the parties, contract is a much more complex instrument with many facets. This interpersonal relationship gives birth to an economic instrument oscillating between purely contractual aspects and others that are more proprietary. Assignment clearly reveals this feature. 'Where an assignment has been validly effected, the chief consequence is that the intangible property passes from the assignor to the assignee; this is the point of an assignment'.[84] When a right is transferred by assignment, the right held by one party passes into the hands of another party, which can be compared to a transfer of property. The French vision of assignment *of the contract* would therefore imply that the contract itself has travelled from one patrimony to another. Thus, the distinction between 'what I own and what I am owed'[85] loses relevance, especially when a 'bare contractual claim is also a form of property'.[86]

The assignment of contract therefore involves contractual elements transferred in a similar way to the transfer of property. French law seems reluctant to recognise the links between contract law and property law, but in assignment these links appear stronger because of what could be called the *patrimonial* dimension of the operation or, in other words, its proprietary effect. However, English law adopts a different general view of assignment which tends to bring closer the links between contract and property. Even though the assignment can be only of the benefit of an obligation, the assigned personal right is turned into a chose in action – property. To this end, what is chosen to be the object of assignment and its conception will be revealing.

ii. A Chose in Action as the Central Element in English Law

The chose in action is a central element to understand since in English law it constitutes the object of assignment. English law seems to allow a rapprochement between contract law and property law through assignment, and it is the nature

du régime général et de la preuve des obligations, 2nd edn (Paris, Lexis Nexis, 2018) 517; Chantepie and Latina (n 55) 545ff; L Gratton, 'Le contrat de cession, instrument de sécurisation de la cession de contrat' RDC 2017, 370; A Hontebeyrie, 'Quelques observations sur la délimitation temporelle de la cession de contrat' RDC 2017, 378; A Bénabent and L Aynès, 'Réforme du droit des contrats et des obligations, un aperçu général' D 2016, 434.

[83] Bridge and Gullifer (n 6) [21-007].

[84] Smith and Leslie (n 9) [1.22].

[85] E McKendrick, *Goode on Commercial Law*, 5th edn (London, Lexis Nexis, 2016) [2-012].

[86] *Belmont Park Investments Pty Ltd v BNY Corporate Trustee Services Ltd* [2011] UKSC 38, [2012] 1 AC 383 [167].

of the chose in action that enables this. As already mentioned above, in English law assignment can be defined as the transfer of a chose (or 'thing') in action.[87] However, finding the meaning and the content of this notion is not easy since 'the chose in action as comprising all rights which can only be claimed or enforced by action is an unhelpfully wide one'.[88] For essentially historical reasons, the term 'chose in action' encompasses a wide variety of rights that differ fundamentally from one another. But what matters for our purposes is to understand the place given to the contract, or at least to contractual rights, in the content of this notion. A classification, usually considered satisfactory, has been established.[89] Thus, choses in action can be arranged in six main categories, namely rights or causes of action, debts, rights under a contract, securities, intellectual property, and leases. Therefore, both debts[90] and rights under a contract are considered to be choses in action and therefore assignable. Those choses in action are also considered to be interests in intangibles since 'the essence of a chose in action is that it is a right or interest in an intangible'.[91] They are also pure intangibles[92] because they are just rights in intangible things, that do not need to be embodied in a document.[93] If they have a monetary value, they are receivables. The interest is therefore to understand how we pass from the receivable to the asset, given that a contractual right is a right *in personam*. However, 'rights under a contract clearly embrace an enormous range of rights',[94] some of which are considered as transferable, in spite of their personal aspect. Therefore, it becomes clear that the law of assignment connects contract law and property law because 'the law of assignment is concerned with intangible property'.[95] And, as pointed out earlier, the title *chose in action* was – and still is – used to describe this type of intangible property. Indeed, choses in action are still 'characterized by the fact that they consist of private property rights in intangible property'.[96] Hence, the law of assignment, allowing the transfer of choses in action, clearly shows that contract law is fraternising with property law. Nonetheless, as stated in *National Provincial Bank Ltd v Ainsworth*

> before a right or an interest can be admitted into the category of property, or of a right affecting property, it must be definable, identifiable by third parties, capable in its nature of assumption by third parties, and have some degree of permanence or stability.[97]

[87] *Torkington v Magee* (n 59) 430.
[88] Smith and Leslie (n 9) [2.55].
[89] Smith and Leslie (n 9) [2.69].
[90] 'Debt' is here used in the traditional sense of English law, to refer to a monetary obligation: cf above, n 14; and what is assignable is of course only the benefit of the debt, not its burden.
[91] Smith and Leslie (n 9) [2.72].
[92] M Bridge, *Personal Property Law*, 4th edn (Oxford, Oxford University Press, 2015) 16.
[93] This is contrasted with documentary intangibles, such as a bill of lading, or a bill of exchange: Bridge (n 92) 19.
[94] Smith and Leslie (n 9) [5.01].
[95] Smith and Leslie (n 9) [1.01].
[96] Smith and Leslie (n 9) [1.07].
[97] *National Provincial Bank Ltd v Ainsworth* [1965] AC 1175 (HL) 1247–48.

Besides, since the proprietary character can ensure the transferability of the object, an opportunity factor could be found in determining what should or should not be considered as proprietary. What represents an economic value should be transferable and therefore considered as property. As Lawson and Rudden noted,

> the law of property also determines the types of interests which will be treated as proprietary, that is as being more than merely personal, familial, or contractual, and it spells out the consequences of a finding that a particular interest is proprietary.[98]

Then, if there is a specific interest, in particular an economic one, it can be property because 'the physical and economic characteristics of particular things naturally exert an influence on their legal treatment, especially when the thing comes to be transferred'.[99]

iii. Contractual Rights as Property

Contractual rights are included within choses in action. It may be reasonable to expect that, since the mechanism of assignment mixes contract law and property law, some rights marked with a strong personal character[100] benefit from special treatment. In any case, it is above all the bilateral or personal nature of the contractual right that must be emphasised. Whether we consider the benefit or the burden of contractual obligations, they are essentially bilateral, which means that they are effective between the parties to the agreement, following the logic of privity of contract. Yet, there is a distinction between what is property and what is personal, according to the differentiation of what is *in rem* and what is *in personam*, the first referring to the relations between people and things and the second to those between persons, in this case the parties to a contract. This has been criticised, in particular by Hohfeld,[101] since in the event of a dispute over a thing in relation to a right *in rem*, the right will be exercised against a defendant and not literally against a thing. There is always a person involved. Thus, the main difference would lie in what a French lawyer would call *opposabilité* – against whom the right will be exercisable: 'against the world' – therefore, universal – or against one or more designated persons. Contractual rights are bilateral by nature, created between designated persons, the parties to the contract. But this does not mean that they are not transferable. So this personal aspect, attached to the contract, does not really prevent the involvement of property law concepts in contractual matters – and

[98] Lawson and Rudden (n 33) 4.

[99] Lawson and Rudden (n 33) 19.

[100] French law generally refers to these by the phrase '*intuitu personae*'. For examples in English law, see below, n 108.

[101] W Hohfeld, *Fundamental Legal Conceptions as Applied in Judicial Reasoning: and Other Legal Essays* (New Haven, Yale University Press, 1923) 99ff.

interpersonal relationships. In any event, as seen previously, the object of an assignment under English law is to transfer only contractual rights, and not the contract itself, since only the benefit of the contract can be assigned,[102] so the contract is made up of a multitude of choses in action that are transferable. But these choses, while they affect the contract and its personal aspect, will also have a property aspect.

'Intangibles, or choses in action, are a form of property'.[103] Since contractual rights are considered to be choses in action, potentially they are considered as property. Although contractual rights are prima facie a private matter between the parties, the transfer and the introduction of a third party to the contract changes the situation. This is the reason why, according to Bridge, 'a central element in the law of assignment of things is that the added third-party dimension can convert a personal right into a proprietary right'.[104] Therefore contractual rights, being choses in action, can be property. Likewise, 'a right can be proprietary in character even if its exercise converts it into a commensurate or even greater liability'.[105] Furthermore, in *Wilson v Secretary of State for Trade and Industry*[106] contractual rights have been interpreted to benefit from the protection of 'possessions' under article 1 of the First Protocol to the European Convention on Human Rights, and therefore within the Human Rights Act 1998. Of course, this does not mean that everything has to be generalised and that all contractual rights are like that:[107] some rights are too personal and untransferable.[108] Nevertheless, many contractual rights do fit the model. And since a chose in action or a pure intangible is considered as 'a valuable piece of property because of its exchange value',[109] and given that some contractual rights can be transferable and therefore choses in action, then such contractual rights can logically be pieces of property.

Contractual rights can be assignable, they are considered as choses in action and can therefore have a proprietary aspect.

[102] *Linden Gardens Trust Ltd v Lenesta Sludge Disposals Ltd* (n 5) 103: 'The burden of a contract can never be assigned without the consent of the other party to the contract in which event such consent will give rise to a novation' (Lord Browne-Wilkinson).

[103] Smith and Leslie (n 9) [2.01].

[104] Bridge (n 92) 3–4.

[105] Bridge and Gullifer (n 6) [4-007]. See *JSC BTA Bank v Ablyazov* [2013] EWCA Civ 928, [2014] 1 WLR 1414 where the question was whether a contractual right to draw down under an unsecured loan facility qualifies as an 'asset' for the purposes of a freezing order.

[106] *Wilson v First County Trust Ltd (No 2)* [2003] UKHL 40, [2004] 1 AC 816.

[107] *Murungaru v Secretary of State for the Home Department* [2008] EWCA Civ 1015 at [30] (Sedley LJ: 'The fact that possessions can include contracts does not mean that all contracts are possessions').

[108] Such as an insurance policy: *Peters v General Accident and Life Assurance Corp Ltd* [1938] 2 All ER 267 (CA); or where the parties have a personal relationship: *Kemp v Baerselman* [1906] 2 KB 604 (CA) where a contract to supply eggs was held, on the facts, to be personal and not assignable.

[109] Bridge (n 92) 16.

B. The Contract as an Asset

i. The Contract Behaves Like Property

The observations that have been made above allow us to propose a more general hypothesis. Given that the contract is a set of rights (and corresponding duties), the contract is a container that houses these rights and duties within a single entity. If these contractual rights can – in certain circumstances and provided that they are not *intuitu personae* – be considered as choses in action, and therefore transferable, could it be possible to contemplate the assignment of the whole entity holding those rights – that is, the assignment of the contract itself? And could the contract then take on a proprietary effect and character? The French legislator must have considered this, since it decided to create a provision for the 'assignment of contract'. However, it is clear that the question is very delicate and mixes issues of contract law and property law, which tends to make the legislator uncomfortable. Moreover, it is clear that in its attempt to construct the assignment of contract, the French legislator distorted the notion of assignment in order to keep contract law separate from property law. It is understandably difficult to mix notions of property with the fundamentally personal elements of contract law, and for a French lawyer to talk about the *patrimonialisation* of such personal elements. However, the legislator felt the need to create the new provision in article 1216 Cc because the possibility to transfer contracts is, in practice, an essential business tool.[110] Thus, a general provision may genuinely be timely. There are other established legislative provisions on the assignment of contract which result in the transfer of the instrument, such as a transmission of an employment contract to a new employer,[111] or an assignment of the contracts of a company in judicial liquidation.[112] It is therefore clear that the contract, by its transfer, can behave like an item of property – not as property in the strict sense but adopting a similar position. The contract represents a certain economic value that cannot be denied and that could be expressed in this way, which would actually be closer to the reality of practice. For instance, a loan agreement between two parties[113] allows the holder of the right (the creditor) to act against the property of the debtor if he defaults. What must be understood, as Lawson and Rudden explained, is that the creditor owns the right against the debtor, just as he owned the money before lending

[110] 'Translating the desire of this *ordonnance* to modernise the law of contracts by drawing on the contributions of practice, assignment of contract makes its first appearance in the Code civil' ('Traduisant le souhait de la présente ordonnance de moderniser le droit des contrats en s'inspirant des apports de la pratique, la cession de contrat entre dans le code civil'): *Rapport au Président de la République* (n 1).
[111] Art L1224-1 Code du travail.
[112] Art L642-7 Code de commerce.
[113] Lawson and Rudden (n 33) 36.

it. 'That amount of cash in his assets has been replaced by a claim for the same sum'.[114] Thus, this money claim clearly holds value. The creditor owns it and can do whatever he wants with it. Therefore, this receivable, this right, behaves clearly as an object of property held by the creditor. The right to be paid has an economic value that makes it behave like property and therefore as an asset. So, in a way, 'a right arising out of an obligation is the property of the person to whom it is due and may be transferred as such'.[115] But of course, this cannot be generalised and cannot apply to all personal obligations.

Taking these observations into account, the idea is therefore the following: if the contract is a set of rights that can be assigned and if the possibility of assignment of the contract is considered, why should we not see the contract itself as a transferable asset? An asset represents rights that have an economic value. This perceptible property aspect could turn some contracts into assets.

ii. Recognising a Real Assignment of 'the Contract'

In seeking to create an assignment of contract, the reform of French law seems to have created more questions than it has answered. It is clear that assignment is an economic mechanism that necessarily involves a transfer of the right to the thing, which is property. But when it applies to the contract, the question becomes more delicate, mixing issues of personal rights and property rights. But this does not mean that the idea of an assignment of contract must be completely rejected. It is certain that what appears today in article 1216 Cc, referring to the assignment of the 'status as party', does not constitute a genuine assignment of contract, transferring the instrument as an asset. But constructing the notion of assignment of contract – properly so-called – and overcoming the challenges involved in such a construction, does not seem to be a wholly impossible task.

'The law of personal property, or moveable wealth, is both developed and sophisticated … any new item of wealth or other resource which is clearly not an interest in land falls within the scope of this category'.[116] Yet any item that does not fall into a predetermined category cannot be strictly classified. In the same vein, something pictured as being partly personal and partly property cannot be completely one or the other. It simply does not fit. Equally, it appears difficult to try to remove the property aspect of an instrument that behaves as such. It could therefore correspond to a *sui generis* category of personal property, adapted to the specificity and the essential nature of the contract. If human bodily products can be recognised to have a proprietary nature,[117] why would it be impossible for some contracts? After all, 'the list of personal property is an open-ended one: any

[114] Lawson and Rudden (n 33) 37.
[115] Lawson and Rudden (n 33) 37.
[116] Bridge and Gullifer (n 6) [1-013].
[117] *Yearworth v North Bristol NHS Trust* [2009] EWCA Civ 37, [2010] QB 1.

novel phenomenon that is recognised as property will in practice be classified as personal property'.[118]

A practical example demonstrates that it would not be unthinkable for the burden of a contract to be assigned at the same time as the benefit of it. Following the model of assignment of leases, in English law both benefits and burdens of the landlord's and tenant's obligations can be transferred by assignment of the lease[119] or of the reversion.[120] A lease represents both an estate in land – ie, the right to possession of the land, entitling the lessee to exercise proprietary rights over the land for the period of the lease – and a contract. Historically the lease was considered as solely a contract, conferring rights *in personam*. Gradually over time, it came to be understood as an attribute of the law of real property in the sense that it guaranteed the lessee to recover possession of the leased land.[121] Thereby 'leases acquired the proprietary characteristics of an estate',[122] finding their roots in contract law but benefiting from the protection granted to property rights. This led Lord Browne-Wilkinson in *Linden Gardens Trust Ltd v Lenesta Sludge Disposals Ltd*[123] to state that 'a lease is a hybrid, part contract, part property'. And that 'so far as rights of alienation are concerned a lease has been treated as a species of property'. Consequently, a lease of land, though being a contract between a landlord and a tenant, can also be considered as a chose in action, assignable in law. Thus, through assignment, the tenant assignor can transfer his whole interest in land to an assignee. That being so, the assignor falls out of the picture and a new contractual relationship takes place between the assignee and the landlord in relation to the leased land, granting both contractual rights and property rights to the new lessee. In any case, as an interest in land is transferred, it cannot be purely contractual.[124] This duality of character could be found more generally in a contract going through the process of assignment. The example of the lease shows that contractual roots should not stand in the way of a more property-oriented vision of the object of assignment.

IV. Conclusion

English lawyers may be surprised by the recent French formal recognition of assignment of contract, but Spanish lawyers may be less so: reasoning within the Roman law tradition, they can even adopt a similar vision to the French.[125]

[118] AP Bell, *Modern Law of Personal Property in England and Ireland* (London, Butterworths, 1989) 1.
[119] Landlord and Tenant (Covenants) Act 1995 s 5.
[120] Landlord and Tenant (Covenants) Act 1995 ss 6, 7.
[121] Smith and Leslie (n 9) [8.05].
[122] ibid.
[123] *Linden Gardens Trust Ltd v Lenesta Sludge Disposals Ltd* (n 5) 108.
[124] *Milmo v Carreras* [1946] KB 306 (CA) 312.
[125] A Cristóbal Montes, 'La cesión de contrato' ADC 1968, 851–90.

This demonstrates how further comparative analysis could give a better understanding of the models and help to refine them.

Recognising the proprietary behaviour of the contract and considering it as an asset will open new perspectives, ensuring the economic efficiency of contractual transactions, whilst still protecting the most personal aspects involved. It will involve challenging, as sensitively as possible, deep-rooted concepts and ideas. After all, some situations[126] in which *extrapatrimonialisation* of *patrimonial* elements are recognised reveal that the lines drawn between what is exclusively personal or non-personal no longer align with contemporary practice. This does not mean that all the lines should be completely erased. On the contrary, they must only be moved and redesigned, using a more global vision, closer to contemporary business practice. The French attempt at recognition of the assignment of contract is itself an acknowledgment of the need to ensure the efficiency of the model. The focus will then be on this necessity, and how to achieve it. But the work has just begun. There is more to come.

[126] Such as the 'patrimonialisation of image rights': Cass civ (1) 11 December 2008, no 07-19.494, RTD civ 2009, 295; JCP G, 2009, 10025; RTD civ 2009, 342; Cass civ (1) 28 January 2010, no 08-70.248, *Dalloz Actualité* 2010, 15.

9

Mistakes in Wills

SIMON DOUGLAS

I. Introduction

A will is a formal document executed by a testator in order to dispose of assets on death.[1] If a person leaves no will, or leaves a will that fails to dispose of their entire estate, there is an intestacy under which certain individuals will take the estate in an order determined by law.[2] A will, therefore, is the normal means by which a testator directs how their estate is to be divided on their death.[3]

Whilst homemade wills are not uncommon, the technical nature of the document means that many (particularly those with valuable estates) will instruct lawyers to draft their wills. Notwithstanding this, errors invariably arise from time to time. Commas can be misplaced, clauses left out, and entire documents executed by mistake. The purpose of this chapter is to consider the different remedies available when a will is affected by a mistake.

Mistakes in legal documents can raise several difficult issues including the tension between the subjective and objective intention of the author,[4] the admissibility of parol evidence,[5] standards of proof and the effect on third parties. Wills pose special problems. For one, as a will only takes effect on the testator's death, the testator will not be present to give evidence on their intended meaning. For the same reason, there is no opportunity for the testator to start again once the mistake comes to light: the beneficiaries are largely stuck with the document left by the testator.[6]

[1] A document must comply with the formality requirements set out in Wills Act 1837, s 9 to count as a will. Broadly speaking, this requires the testator to sign the document and for two witnesses to attest his signature.

[2] The entitlements of intestacy beneficiaries are set out in Administration of Estates Act 1925, s 46.

[3] Increasing importance is now attached to 'will substitutes', such as pension nominations and joint tenancies. See A Braun and A Röthel, *Passing Wealth on Death: Will-Substitutes in Comparative Perspective* (Oxford, Hart Publishing, 2016).

[4] See PS Davies, 'Rectification versus Interpretation: The Nature and Scope of the Equitable Jurisdiction' [2016] CLJ 62.

[5] See R Stevens, 'Objectivity, Mistake and the Parol Evidence Rule' in A Burrows and E Peel (eds), *Contract Terms* (Oxford, Oxford University Press, 2007) 101.

[6] The beneficiaries under a will have a power to vary their entitlements, and the varied will is treated (for Inheritance Tax purposes) as having been effected by the testator: Inheritance Tax Act 1984, s 142.

This contrasts with the position in relation to lifetime gifts, where the law allows a donor to escape unforeseen consequences, such as an unknown tax charge.[7] There is no easy escape route in the case of a will, which often puts pressure on the available remedies.

This chapter will begin by considering the different types of error that can affect a will. The following section will then discuss the three principal methods by which mistakes can be cured, namely, the doctrine of knowledge and approval, construction and rectification.

II. Mistakes

A mistake is a false belief or erroneous assumption.[8] In *Pitt v Holt* Lord Walker distinguished mistakes from mere ignorance: 'Forgetfulness, inadvertence or ignorance is not, as such, a mistake, but it can lead to a false assumption which the law will recognise as a mistake'.[9] A lack of awareness of some fact or rule is not a mistake in and of itself, but it may lead a person into a conscious belief that something is true when in fact or law it is not.

A testator's mistake may relate to a factual state of affairs, such as where a testator leaves a gift to a beneficiary in the false belief that the beneficiary is poor and in necessitous circumstances;[10] or the mistake may relate to a legal rule, such as an erroneous belief that a disposition will not attract inheritance tax.[11] The causes of a mistake vary from case to case. It may result from the testator receiving poor advice; it may be caused by the testator's misunderstanding of a technical word or phrase; or it may result from careless drafting and the testator's failure to check the document properly before executing it.

When analysing mistakes, a distinction can be drawn between what may be termed 'content errors' and 'meaning errors'. The former describes those cases where a word, phrase or clause is accidentally included or omitted from a will. Take the following example:

> (1) A testator instructs his solicitor to draft a will which leaves the testator's property, 'no 17 Brookside Close', to his wife. The solicitor drafts the will which leaves 'no *19* Brookside *House*' to the testator's wife. The testator fails to read the draft carefully and executes it.[12]

However, this requires the consent of all of the parties, so is unsuitable when their interests are adverse to each other.

[7] eg under the doctrine of 'equitable mistake' as set out in *Ogilvie v Littleboy* (1897) 13 TLR 399 (CA).

[8] See J Cartwright, *Misrepresentation, Mistake and Non-Disclosure*, 5th edn (London, Sweet and Maxwell, 2019) [12-02]–[12-06].

[9] *Pitt v Holt* [2013] UKSC 26, [2013] 2 AC 108 [105].

[10] eg *Re Belliss* (1929) 45 TLR 452 (PDA); *Goss-Custard v Templeman* [2018] EWHC 2476 (Ch), [2018] WTLR 893.

[11] eg *Martin v Nicholson* [2004] EWHC 2135 (Ch), [2005] WTLR 175.

[12] *Guthrie v Morel* [2015] EWHC 3172 (Ch), [2016] WTLR 273.

This is a 'content error' in that the testator is mistaken as to the contents of his will. He believes it contains a particular term (a gift of 'no 17 Brookside Close'), when in fact it contains a different one (of 'no *19* Brookside *House*').

By contrast, a 'meaning error' arises in cases where a testator has intentionally used a particular word or clause, but is mistaken as to its meaning or effect. Take the following example:

> (2) A testator leaves his entire estate to his 'issue', mistakenly believing that the word 'issue' will include his step-children, when in fact it means lineal descendants.[13]

Unlike in the previous example, the problematic word in this case ('issue') was deliberately chosen by the testator. The mistake relates to its meaning, not its presence in the will.

To correct errors in wills, the law has developed three remedies: the doctrine of knowledge and approval, construction and rectification. There may be some merit in the claim that 'meaning errors' are primarily remedied by construction, and 'content errors' remedied by knowledge and approval and rectification. Unfortunately, as we will see in the following sections, the picture is not always so clear.

III. Remedies

A. Knowledge and Approval

The doctrine of 'knowledge and approval' arose from the process of confirming the validity of a will. This is known as 'entering the will into probate', a formal process whereby the executor[14] submits the document purporting to be the final will of the testator to a probate registry, along with an oath stating that, in his belief, the document represents the final will and testament of the testator.[15] The effect of obtaining a grant of probate is that it is conclusive evidence of the validity of the will,[16] giving the executor a degree of protection when he applies the testator's estate in accordance with the terms of the will.[17]

To obtain a grant of probate there are two requirements. First, the document must be in the nature of a will. Whilst there is no universally accepted definition

[13] *Reading v Reading* [2015] EWHC 946 (Ch), [2015] WTLR 1245.

[14] The 'executor' is the person appointed by the testator to administer the estate. If the testator's will contains no executorship clause, a person can apply for a grant of 'administration with the will annexed'.

[15] See RR D'Costa, P Teverson and T Synak, *Tristram and Coote's Probate Practice*, 32nd edn (London, LexisNexis Butterworths, 2020) for detailed commentary on the procedure.

[16] In *Re Berger* [1990] Ch 118 (CA) 133 Buckley LJ said: 'The function in English law of a probate court is to ascertain and determine what testamentary paper or papers is or are to be regarded as constituting the last will of the testator, and who is entitled to be constituted his legal personal representative'. See also *Barrance v Ellis* [1910] 2 Ch 419 (Ch).

[17] Administration of Estates Act 1925, s 37.

of a will, generally speaking it is a written document[18] concerning the disposition of the testator's property. It must be evident from the document or the surrounding circumstances that the testator had *animus testandi*, that is, an intention that that the document be an ambulatory and revocable disposition of the testator's property on his death.[19] As such, a letter of instructions to draw up a will,[20] or a memorandum setting out the testator's intention to execute a will,[21] will not normally be admitted to probate as a testator will rarely intend for such documents to be binding on their death. Second, the document must comply with the formality requirements set out in section 9 of the Wills Act 1837. Whilst the details of these requirements are complex, broadly speaking section 9 requires the document to be signed by the testator, and his signature to be made or acknowledged in the presence of two witnesses. Importantly for present purposes, section 9(2) specifically provides that it must appear that the 'testator intended by his signature to give effect to the will'. These twin requirements mean that a document submitted to a probate registry should represent the testamentary intention of the testator.[22]

It is implicit in these two requirements that the testator must be aware of the contents of his will and intend that the clauses contained therein take effect on his death. The traditional way of expressing this has been to say that the testator must have 'knowledge and approval' of the will when executing it.[23] As Chadwick LJ said in *Fuller v Strum*:

> It is not, and cannot be, in dispute that, before admitting the document to probate, the judge needed to be satisfied that it did truly represent the testator's testamentary intentions; or, to use the traditional phrase, that the testator 'knew and approved' its contents.[24]

A 'knowledge and approval' plea is made by a person challenging the validity of a will. In essence, the claim is that the testator was unaware of the contents of the will and, hence, lacked the necessary *animus testandi* for a grant of probate. It is not only possible to claim that the testator was unaware of the contents of the entire document, but also to claim that the testator had not read or had his attention

[18] In certain cases the law permits informal wills. Such privileged wills are limited to soldiers and mariners: Wills Act 1837, s 11.

[19] See *Re Berger* [1990] Ch 118 for discussion of the basic requirements of a will.

[20] *Guardhouse v Blackburn* (1866) LR 1 PD 109.

[21] *Whyte v Pollok* (1882) 7 App Cas 400 (HL(Sc)).

[22] *Re White* [1991] Ch 1 (Ch).

[23] *Gill v Woodall* [2010] EWCA Civ 1430, [2011] Ch 380 [14]. As Parry and Kerridge point out, the formalising of this plea might be due to the Contentious Probate Rules 1862, r 40a, which made clear that if a party wished to challenge a testator's capacity to make the will, then the plea must allege (i) lack of capacity, (ii) undue influence, (iii) fraud or (iv) lack of knowledge and approval: see R Kerridge (assisted by AHR Brierly), *Parry and Kerridge: The Law of Succession*, 13th edn (London, Sweet and Maxwell, 2016) [5-33].

[24] [2001] EWCA Civ 1879, [2002] 1 WLR 1097 [59].

drawn to a particular word, phrase or clause. Again, as Chadwick LJ said in *Fuller v Strum*:

> Nor is it in dispute that, if satisfied that the testator knew and approved of part only of the contents of the document, the judge was bound, before admitting the document to probate, to require that those parts with respect to which he was not so satisfied be struck out.[25]

The result of a successful plea is that the words which the testator had no knowledge of are not entered into probate, and they are effectively deleted from the will. In *Fuller v Strum* the plea of want of knowledge and approval was made by the defendant, the testator's adopted son, who was described as 'that Irish bastard' by the testator in the will. It was argued (unsuccessfully) that the words were so out of character that the testator could not have had knowledge of them, and that it was more likely that they had been inserted by the claimant, the testator's other son, who then procured the testator's signature. The case is typical in that it involved an elderly testator whose capacity was in question, especially in the presence of an over-bearing party who 'helps' the testator prepare their will. A similar case is *Gill v Woodall*[26] where a testatrix had left the majority of her estate to the RSPCA (the Royal Society for the Prevention of Cruelty to Animals), largely to the exclusion of her daughter, the claimant. The will had been prepared at the testatrix's husband's behest and it was alleged that the testatrix suffered from an anxiety condition that prevented her from fully understanding the meaning and nature of the document.

Whilst there is some uncertainty as to the scope of the doctrine,[27] most 'knowledge and approval' claims involve suspected fraud, where it is argued that the testator's signature is procured by a person who benefits under the will.[28] In such cases the plea is similar to that of *non est factum*, in that it alleges a complete lack of intention on the part of the testator to give any testamentary effect to the document.[29]

The doctrine of knowledge and approval has also been used (albeit less regularly) in cases involving mistake. Unlike the fraud and capacity cases, in mistake cases there is an intention on the part of the testator to give testamentary effect to the document, but that intention is impaired, or vitiated, by a false belief as to the contents of the document. Take the case of *Re Morris*[30] where a testatrix had instructed her solicitor to draft a codicil which would revoke the legacies contained in clauses '3 and 7(iv)' of her will. The solicitor prepared a draft that provided for

[25] ibid.

[26] [2010] EWCA Civ 1430, [2011] Ch 380.

[27] See R Kerridge, 'Suspicious Wills' [2000] CLJ 310 and P Reed, 'Capacity and Want of Knowledge and Approval' in B Häcker and C Mitchell (eds), *Current Issues in Succession Law* (Oxford, Hart Publishing, 2016) 169.

[28] See eg *Re R* [1951] P 10 (PDA), *Griffin v Wood* [2008] WTLR 73 (Ch) and *Burgess v Hawes* [2013] EWCA Civ 94, [2013] WTLR 453.

[29] *Saunders v Anglia Building Society* [1971] AC 1004 (HL).

[30] [1971] P 62 (PDA).

the revocation of clauses '3 and 7'. The testatrix failed to notice the mistake and executed the codicil. The effect was that all of the legacies contained in clause 7, not just that at clause 7(iv), were revoked. The mistake led Latey J to conclude that the testatrix could not have known and approved of the contents of her will:

> The introduction of the words 'clause 7' instead of 'clause 7(iv)' was per incuriam. The solicitor's mind was never applied to it, and never adverted to the significance and effect. It was a mere clerical error on his part, a slip. He knew what the testatrix's instructions and intentions were, and what he did was outside the scope of his authority and he did it, of course, without knowing and approving what he himself was doing. How can one impute to the principal the agent's knowledge and approval which the agent himself has not got?[31]

A similar case is that of *Re Schott's Goods*[32] in which the testator had instructed his solicitor to draft a will which left the 'residue' of the estate to his sister. A typographical error crept in during successive drafts of a will, whereby the word 'residue' was replaced with 'revenue', which had a dramatic effect on the sister's entitlement. Whilst it is clear that the testator intended the document to have testamentary effect, he did so in the false belief that it reflected his earlier instructions to his solicitor. The mistake was sufficient to have the affected parts excluded from probate.

These cases are examples of content errors: a word or clause is accidentally included in or omitted from the will, such the that the testator is mistaken as to the contents of the document they have executed. In some cases the testator can be mistaken as to a single word, in others to the entire contents of a document, as happened in the case of *Re the Estate of Fanny Deborah Meyer*[33] where two sisters each executed the other's will by accident.[34] If it can be demonstrated that the testator did not intend any of the words to have testamentary effect, they are excluded from probate in their entirety and have no validity at all.

Where knowledge and approval cannot be used, however, is where a word or clause has been deliberately included within a will, albeit that its meaning or effect misunderstood. As explained above, these are sometimes referred to as 'meaning errors'. The best example is the case of *Re Horrocks*,[35] where a will was drawn up leaving the testator's residuary estate to 'charitable or benevolent' objects. As a matter of authority, a bequest to 'charitable *and* benevolent' objects has been construed as a charitable gift, and therefore valid under the rule that a gift to charitable purposes is permitted. However, a gift to 'charitable *or* benevolent' purposes is not exclusively charitable and therefore fails under the rule against non-charitable purposes trusts. It was held that it was not possible to delete the word 'or' from the

[31] ibid, 81.
[32] [1901] P 190 (PDA).
[33] [1908] P 353 (PDA).
[34] As seen below, this is now dealt with under rectification, as exemplified by the similar case of *Marley v Rawlings* [2014] UKSC 2, [2015] 1 AC 129.
[35] [1939] P 198 (CA).

will on the basis that it had frustrated the testator's intention. The words had been deliberately chosen by the testator, even though their meaning, or legal effect, had been misunderstood. As Greene MR said:

> If the testator himself approved the words to which he put his signature (and the presumption is that he approved them), those words must stand. If the words were selected by a draftsman to whom the testator confided the task of drafting his will, similarly the words so selected must stand, even if the testator was ignorant of the actual words used. The mistake of the testator or of the draftsman employed by him as to the legal effect of the words used is immaterial.[36]

'Meaning errors' are ill suited to the plea of want of 'knowledge and approval'. As the testator in *Re Horrocks* had deliberately included the problematic word in the will, it was impossible to claim that he had not 'approved' of it.[37] The result, therefore, is that only 'content errors' can be excluded from a will under this doctrine. Other forms of error can be corrected, if at all, under the doctrines of construction and rectification.

There are other significant limitations to the doctrine of knowledge and approval as a means of correcting errors in wills. The main issue is that if the plea is successful, its effect is wholly negative. It will be recalled that the purpose of the plea is to prevent a will, or part of it, from being entered into probate. The only possible outcome of a successful plea, therefore, is the exclusion of the words from the will. In this sense the doctrine operates like partial rescission for equitable mistake, whereby a clause can be deleted from a trust or other unilateral transaction where the intention of the party is vitiated by a serious mistaken belief.[38] However, unlike an inter vivos declaration of trust, the author of the will does not have the opportunity to start again, and execute new documents that better reflect their intention. Rather, the executors are stuck with the document entered into probate, minus the excluded words and clauses. This often leads to arbitrary results, as illustrated by the case of *Wightman v Reynette-James*.[39] The testatrix gave detailed instructions to drawn up a will which, at clause 10, made an absolute gift of the capital to her son, subject to a life interest to her sister and friend. It was also to include a reversionary gift for the testatrix's grandchildren, should the son not survive the testatrix. In the event, the document drafted by the solicitors omitted any mention of the gift to the son, and this was not noticed by the testatrix when she executed the will. A plea of want of knowledge and approval succeeded, but it had the wholly negative effect of excluding everything from clause 10 other than the life interests for the sister and friend. It was not possible to import the intended words into the will, meaning that the son and grandchildren took nothing, and the residuary beneficiaries received a windfall. This unsatisfactory result can now be avoided by bringing the claim as one for rectification rather than knowledge and approval.

[36] ibid 216.
[37] *Re Beech's Estate* [1923] P 46 (CA) 53–54.
[38] *Kennedy v Kennedy* [2014] EWHC 4129 (Ch), [2015] WTLR 837.
[39] [1976] 1 WLR 161 (Ch).

B. Construction

Once a will has been admitted into probate, the executor will then need to administer the deceased's estate and distribute its contents according to the will. In order to do this, it will be necessary to ascertain the meaning of the will. This is the process of construction. As *Williams on Wills* states:

> The first and great rule to which all others must bend is that effect must be given to the intention of the testator; but the intention here in question is not the intention in the mind of the testator at the time he made his will, but that declared and apparent in his will.[40]

If the will has been carefully drafted, its meaning should be clear. It should be apparent to the executor who the legatees are, the identity of the residuary beneficiary, the order of the payment of the legacies, and the administrative powers of the executor. However, this is often not the case and executors (or their legal advisors) will need to turn to the principles of construction in order to ascertain the meaning of the will.

i. The Traditional Approach to Construction

Historically the construction of wills was characterised by two general approaches. The first was to place what might be seen as undue weight upon the literal or grammatical meaning of the words contained in a will, even when that would lead to constructions that were obviously not intended by the testator. An example of this approach is found in *Re Rowland*,[41] a case in which a husband and wife had made mirror wills, each disposing of their estates to the other, except that their estates would go to another person if their deaths 'coincide'. In the event, both husband and wife were aboard a ship that sunk with no survivors. The majority of the Court of Appeal held that the word 'coincide' in the will referred to deaths at a simultaneous time, and there was no evidence that they had died at precisely the same moment, it being possible that one would have survived the other for a short period. Lord Denning MR, in the minority, criticised this approach as being overly-literal, saying: 'I decline, therefore, to ask myself: What do the words mean to a grammarian? I prefer to ask: What did Dr. Rowland and his wife mean by the word "coincide" in their wills?'[42]

The second characteristic of construction was the general reluctance to admit any extrinsic evidence of the meaning of the will. While there was never a complete exclusion of such evidence (or 'parol evidence'),[43] a court would

[40] RFD Barlow and others, *Williams on Wills*, 10th edn (London, LexisNexis, 2014) [49.1].

[41] [1963] Ch 1 (CA).

[42] ibid 11. See also *Higgins v Dawson* [1902] AC 1 (HL).

[43] For instance, courts would apply the so-called 'arm chair' principle, whereby they would put themselves in the position of the testator, and hence admit evidence of matters that the testator was aware of when making the will: *Boyes v Cook* (1880) 14 Ch D 53 (CA) 56.

generally confine itself to the document in question. The influence of Sir James Wigram's book, *An Examination of the Rules of Law Respecting the Admission of Extrinsic Evidence in the Aid of Interpretation of Wills*, published in 1831, has been noted by commentators.[44] Wigram's book listed a number of exceptional cases in which parol evidence might be admitted, but otherwise advocated its exclusion.

The literalist approach, reinforced by restrictive rules on the admission of parol evidence, meant that mistakes contained in wills were often embedded, not remedied, by construction. An example is the case of *In the Goods of Peel*,[45] where a testator had appointed 'Francis Courtney Thorpe' to be his executor. There was such a person, but he was twelve years old, and his father, one 'Francis *Corbet* Thorpe', was a longstanding friend of the testator. Despite the clear mistake in the will, evidence of the testator's intended meaning was extrinsic to the will and was not admissible. The mistake, therefore, could not be remedied.[46]

The way in which courts construe wills has developed significantly in recent years. For one, parol evidence is now admissible in certain cases. Second, there has been a move to align the principles of will construction with that of other commercial documents, where courts take a far less literalist approach. As we will see, these developments mean that errors in wills are now routinely corrected by construction.

ii. Parol Evidence

In 1973 the Law Reform Committee published a report[47] that declared the traditional approach to construction of wills unsatisfactory, and argued that the continuing exclusion of parol evidence was unjustified. Their recommendations resulted in section 21 of the Administration of Justice Act 1982, which provides:

> (1) This section applies to a will—
>
> (a) in so far as any part of it is meaningless;
> (b) in so far as the language used in any part of it is ambiguous on the face of it;
> (c) in so far as evidence, other than evidence of the testator's intention, shows that the language used in any part of it is ambiguous in the light of surrounding circumstances.
>
> (2) In so far as this section applies to a will extrinsic evidence, including evidence of the testator's intention, may be admitted to assist in its interpretation.

The effect of this section is that parol evidence is admissible whenever there is some ambiguity, either on the face of the will or in the surrounding circumstances.

[44] See Law Reform Committee Nineteenth Report (n 47) [4]; Parry and Kerridge (n 23) [10-17].

[45] (1870) LR 2 P & D 46.

[46] This is sometimes described as a 'latent' (as opposed to 'patent') error, where extrinsic evidence was traditionally inadmissible as a guide to interpretation. See L Tucker, N Le Poidevin and J Brightwell (eds), *Lewin on Trusts*, 20th edn (London, Sweet & Maxwell, 2020) [7-012]–[7-016] for discussion.

[47] Law Reform Committee Nineteenth Report: *Interpretation of Wills* (Cmnd 5301, 1973).

As the Law Reform Committee explained, extrinsic evidence should not be admissible in each and every case, but only where there is 'a legitimate dispute about the language of the will'.[48]

Section 21 did more than bring wills into line with other types of legal documents, where extrinsic evidence has long been admissible.[49] The section goes further by permitting the admission of evidence of the 'testator's intention' as an aid to construction. Take, for instance, a testator who executes a will leaving the residue of his estate to 'my dear Sarah', and confusion arises because it is not clear whether the testator was referring to his sister or his daughter, as both are called 'Sarah'. Let us also say that the testator kept a diary, in which he noted that he had executed a will and left his residue to 'my dear *sister*, Sarah'. Although this document evinces the testator's subjective intention, it would be admissible as an aid to the construction of the will under section 21(2). This is an unusual feature of the rules of will construction: a similar document would be inadmissible as an aid to the construction of a contract or a trust. This can be seen in the Australian case of *Byrnes v Kendle*[50] where the claimant, Mr Byrnes, had executed a trust deed declaring that he held his house 'on trust' for himself and his former wife. He pleaded that, notwithstanding his declaration, he meant no more than an undertaking to split the proceeds of the sale should the house be sold in the future. Rejecting the claim, Heydon and Crennan JJ said that although trusts give effect to intention, 'the "intention" referred to is an intention to be extracted from the words used, not a subjective intention which may have existed but which cannot be extracted from those words'.[51] Where there is a disparity between what a person means by his words, and what meaning is reasonably conveyed to others, the law gives primacy to the latter. Mr Byrnes' intention, in the subjective sense, was wholly irrelevant.

Wills, however, are different. Whilst the approach to construction is still objective, what a testator intended his words to mean is admissible as an aid to construction. It is conceivable, therefore, that when a testator makes a 'meaning mistake' – ie, he deliberately uses the word *x* when he meant *y* – his intended meaning (*y*) might be admitted as an aid to the construction of the word he actually used (*x*).

iii. Modern Approach to Construction

Following the statutory changes on the admissibility of parol evidence, it was perhaps inevitable that the courts would move away from the 'literalist' approach to construction. Whilst this has happened over several years,[52] the modern

[48] ibid [56].

[49] eg under the approach to the construction of contracts taken in *Investors Compensation Scheme Ltd v West Bromwich Building Society* [1998] 1 WLR 896 (HL) 912, evidence of the surrounding context is an essential component.

[50] [2011] HCA 26, (2011) 243 CLR 253.

[51] ibid [114]. To similar effect is Lord Wright's statement in *Commissioners of Inland Revenue v Raphael* [1935] AC 96 (HL) 135: '[The] court, while it seeks to give effect to the intention of the parties, must give effect to that as expressed, that is, it must ascertain the meaning of the words actually used'.

[52] See, eg, *Re Williams* [1985] 1 WLR 905 (Ch); *Re Segelman* [1996] Ch 171 (Ch).

approach to construction was confirmed in the landmark decision of *Marley v Rawlings*.[53] The case, which is important for both construction and rectification of wills, concerned mirror wills that had been prepared for a married couple, Mr and Mrs Rawlings. Other than the clause identifying the testator and the beneficiaries, the wills were drafted in identical terms, with both testators leaving their entire estate to the other should they survive them and, if not, to their adopted son, Terry Marley (the appellant in the case). The mistake arose because the solicitor handed the wrong drafts to the testators, with Mr Marley executing Mrs Marley's will, and vice versa. As such, neither document, on its face, made much sense and led to the prospect that both had died intestate.

It was argued that that the error in the case could be corrected by construction. As Mr Rawlings' will was meaningless on its face, counsel argued, it was possible to admit extrinsic evidence, which obviously included the document executed as a will by Mrs Rawlings; and when these two documents were read side by side Mr Rawlings' intention was obvious.[54] This argument, which implicitly rejects the literalist approach to construction, was entertained as a serious possibility by the Supreme Court, although ultimately the Court chose not to express a conclusion on this issue (as the remedy of rectification was found to be available). Lord Neuberger did, however, state that wills should be interpreted in the same way as other documents, such as contracts:

> When interpreting a contract, the court is concerned to find the intention of the party or parties, and it does this by identifying the meaning of the relevant words, (a) in the light of (i) the natural and ordinary meaning of those words, (ii) the overall purpose of the document, (iii) any other provisions of the document, (iv) the facts known or assumed by the parties at the time that the document was executed, and (v) common sense, but (b) ignoring subjective evidence of any party's intentions. …
>
> When it comes to interpreting wills, it seems to me that the approach should be the same. Whether the document in question is a commercial contract or a will, the aim is to identify the intention of the party or parties to the document by interpreting the words used in their documentary, factual and commercial context.[55]

In the context of contract law it has long been established that a court, when construing the document, is not bound by the grammatical or literal meaning of its words.[56] Rather, the aim is to ascertain the meaning of the document when read against the relevant background information.[57] It is open to the court to conclude that the meaning conveyed by a document differs from the literal construction of the words used in it. A well-known example is the case of *Mannai Investment Co Ltd v Eagle Star Assurance Co Ltd*,[58] where a clause in a notice

[53] [2014] UKSC 2, [2015] AC 129.
[54] ibid [34]–[42].
[55] ibid [19]–[20].
[56] *Chartbrook Ltd v Persimmon Homes Ltd* [2009] UKHL 38, [2009] 1 AC 1101 [99].
[57] *Investors Compensation Scheme Ltd v West Bromwich Building Society* (n 49) 912–13.
[58] [1997] AC 749 (HL).

to quit on '12th January 1995' was construed as meaning a notice to quit on '13th January 1995'. It was held by the House of Lords that the landlord's mistake was obvious when the document was read in its context.

By aligning the construction of wills with the construction of contracts, it must now be the case that a court, when interpreting a will, should ask what meaning is conveyed by the document when it is read against the relevant background information (which can include evidence of the testator's subjective intention).[59] When approached in this way, it is open to the court to conclude that, as in *Mannai Investment*, there is an error in the drafting of the will, and that what the document means is something different to what it actually says. There are examples of this new approach to construction in the few years since *Marley v Rawlings*. In *Slattery v Jagger*[60] a testator instructed his solicitor to draft a will in which he would leave his share in his home to his wife. The relevant clause failed to name his wife or any other beneficiary, the clause simply stating:

> I give devise and bequeath my beneficial share [in my property] …

This is an example of a content error, as words had been accidentally omitted from the will. It was held that the mistake could be cured by construction. There was a clear ambiguity on the face of the will, meaning that parol evidence (including the testator's letter of instructions) was admissible. When read against this the intended meaning of the will was clear.[61]

A second example is provided by the case of *Reading v Reading*,[62] where the testator executed a will dividing his estate between his 'issue' in equal shares. The word 'issue' is normally understood to mean a testator's natural and adopted children, not his step-children. However, the testator had not realised this, and deliberately selected the word in the false belief that it would include his step-children. The court allowed the parties to introduce a letter of wishes which was evidence of the testator's subjective understanding of the word 'issue', and the will was construed accordingly.[63] This was an example of a 'meaning error', where the mistake relates to the meaning or effect of a word. It could be corrected by construction as the court was willing to introduce evidence of the testator's subjective intention.

The implications of this new approach to construction is still to be worked out. In particular, it appears to have caused construction to move into an area traditionally occupied by rectification, the remedy for the correction of errors in legal documents. This will be explored in the next section.

[59] See section III.B.ii above.

[60] [2015] EWHC 3976, [2017] WTLR 321. See also *Guthrie v Morel* (n 12).

[61] See also *Blech v Blech* [2002] WTLR 483 (Ch). For older examples, see *The National Society for the Prevention of Cruelty to Children v The Scottish National Society for the Prevention of Cruelty to Children* [1915] AC 207 (HL(Sc)) and *Shore v Wilson* (1842) 9 Cl & Fin 355, 8 ER 450.

[62] Above, n 13.

[63] The court accepted that there was some ambiguity in the testator's usage of the word 'issue', thus triggering s 21(1)(b) of the Administration of Justice Act 1982. A similar case is *Brooke v Purton* [2014] EWHC 547 (Ch), [2014] WTLR 745.

C. Rectification

The remedy of rectification allows a court to correct a legal instrument which fails to give effect to the intention of the parties to the document.[64] Whereas construction is the attempt to ascertain the meaning of a document, the aim of rectification is to re-write it so that it better reflects the intention of the parties. As Lord Walker said in *Pitt v Holt*:

> Rectification is a closely guarded remedy, strictly limited to some clearly-established disparity between the words of a legal document, and the intentions of the parties to it.[65]

Whilst the courts of chancery have long exercised this jurisdiction[66] in cases involving contracts, conveyances, trusts, patents and other legal documents, it was always assumed that there was no power to rectify a will. To re-write a will is to give testamentary effect to words never executed as a will by the testator, something which courts were very reluctant to do. As Sir John Leach said in *Earl of Newburgh v Countess Dowager of Newburgh*:[67]

> [To rectify a will] would, in effect, be to repeal the Statute of Frauds in all cases where a devisor failed to comply with the statute by mistake or accident, and to operate this repeal by permitting parol evidence of the devisor, which it was the very object of the statute to avoid.[68]

The fallacy in this reasoning is that rectification (in the context of contracts, trusts and other documents) always involves giving effect to terms proved by parol evidence. There was no particular reason to treat wills any differently. The Law Reform Committee recognised this in its Nineteenth Report, and recommended that rectification be extended to wills. This was enacted as section 20(1) of the Administration of Justice Act 1982:

> If a court is satisfied that a will is so expressed that it fails to carry out the testator's intentions, in consequence—
>
> (a) of a clerical error; or
> (b) of a failure to understand his instructions,
>
> it may order that the will shall be rectified so as to carry out his intentions.

[64] *Marley v Rawlings* (n 53) [27].

[65] Above (n 9) [131].

[66] In *Sieff v Fox* [2005] EWHC 1312 (Ch), [2005] 1 WLR 3811 [33] Lloyd LJ helpfully described the jurisdiction in the following terms: 'As a general proposition, English law affords relief against the consequences of a mistake on the part of the person who executes a document as to the nature, terms or effect of that document, but only in circumstances which are strictly limited'.

[67] (1820) 5 Madd 364, 365–66; 56 ER 934, 935.

[68] ibid 366–67. In *Wightman v Reynette-James* [1976] 1 WLR 161 (Ch) 166 Templeman J said: 'Any document other than a will could be rectified by inserting the words which the secretary omitted, but in this respect the court is enslaved by the Wills Act 1837. Words may be struck out but no fresh words may be inserted'.

Whilst this statutory change was well overdue, a difficult question, alluded to above, is whether it has been overtaken by developments in construction.

i. Construction versus Rectification

When the Law Reform Committee recommended the introduction of rectification it acknowledged that there would be overlap between rectification and construction, noting that 'interpretation and rectification merge indistinguishably into the fundamental problem of the proper extent of the court's power to decide on the effect of a will'.[69] Yet in light of the developments detailed above, the concern is not so much of overlap, but that construction will make rectification largely redundant as a remedy.[70] Errors can, and routinely are, corrected by the process of construction. A mis-spelling, wrong name, or incomplete sentence might be obvious, and the intended meaning clear, when a document is read against the relevant background information. Indeed, as Lord Hoffmann famously said in *Chartbrook Ltd v Persimmon Homes Ltd*, when construing a document 'there is not, so to speak, a limit to the amount of red ink or verbal rearrangement or correction which the court is allowed'.[71] In analysing the remedy of rectification, therefore, the first question to consider is its relationship with construction.

The language in section 20(1) is not particularly helpful in drawing the line between rectification and construction. A 'clerical error' clearly covers the case of an accidental inclusion or omission of a word or clause, ie a content error. As Lord Neuberger said in *Marley v Rawlings*,

> If, as a result of a slip of the pen or mistyping, a solicitor (or a clerk or indeed the testator himself) inserts the wrong word, figure or name into a clause of a will, and it is clear what word, figure or name the testator had intended, that would undoubtedly be a clerical error which could be rectified under section 20(1)(a).[72]

It could also refer to the case where a testator has deliberately chosen a word or a phrase in the mistaken belief as to its meaning, ie a meaning error. Both kinds of mistake, as we saw above, can be corrected by construction. Nor does the other basis of rectification, a 'failure to understand instructions', provide clear guidance on the scope of the respective remedies. A 'failure to understand instructions' could refer to a literal disparity between words dictated by the testator and those used by the solicitor; or it might refer to a deliberate choice of words by the drafter in the false belief that they will give effect the testator's intention. Again, there seems to be no reason why errors of both kinds cannot be corrected by construction.

[69] Law Reform Committee Nineteenth Report (n 47) [15].
[70] A Burrows, 'Construction and Rectification' in Burrows and Peel (eds), *Contract Terms* (n 5) 77.
[71] *Chartbrook Ltd v Persimmon Homes Ltd* (n 56) [25].
[72] Above, n 53 [72].

Furthermore, the courts appear to be willing to rely on construction to re-write significant parts of a will. For instance, in *Brooke v Purton*[73] the testator had instructed his solicitors to draft a will in which he would pass his entire estate, 90 per cent of which was comprised of company shares, on a discretionary trust for his children. The solicitors used the wrong will precedent, essentially a will template, which was only effective to dispose of the testator's chattels and goods. After admitting evidence of the testator's intention, the court was able to construe the will as passing the testator's entire estate. In so doing, the court was effectively re-writing the will, by replacing the will precedent used by the solicitors with a more appropriate one. If errors of this nature can be corrected by construction, it might be asked what role is left for rectification. Construction also has procedural advantages over rectification: it does not require an application to court,[74] nor are there any time limits.[75] What need, it might be asked, is there for rectification?

I would suggest that there is still a need for rectification as a separate remedy for correcting errors in wills. In particular, there are two types of mistake which cannot be remedied by the process of construction and require an application to rectify the will. These are set out in the following two sections.

ii. Meaning Errors

We saw above that a 'meaning error', where a testator deliberately adopts a word or clause but misunderstands its meaning, can be corrected by construction. Take the following example:

> A testator's will includes the clause: '*All my money to Charles*.' As well as bank savings, the testator's estate includes investments in bonds. There is extrinsic evidence (from a letter sent to Charles) that the testator intended to give his bonds to Charles.

The word 'money', whilst obviously covering the testator's bank savings, is not particularly apt to dispose of the testator's bonds.[76] However, as it is an ambiguous term[77] it will be possible, under section 21(2) of the Administration of Justice Act 1982, to introduce evidence of Charles' subjective intention when construing the word. When read in light of this evidence, it may be possible to construe 'money' so that it reflects the testator's intended meaning. In this way 'meaning errors' can be corrected by construction.

[73] [2014] EWHC 547 (Ch), [2014] WTLR 745.

[74] If the parties are unable to reach an agreement as to the meaning of the will, it is possible to make an application to court for the construction of the will, a step executors often take in order to protect themselves from claims from disappointed beneficiaries.

[75] A rectification claim must be brought within six months of a grant of probate: Administration of Justice Act 1982, s 20(2).

[76] *Re Gates* [1929] 2 Ch 420 (CA).

[77] *Perrin v Morgan* [1943] AC 399 (HL).

There are, however, limits to this technique. Section 21(2) merely makes evidence of the testator's subjective intention admissible as an aid to construction. Construction remains the process of ascertaining the *objective* meaning of the testator's will. As such, when the language used by the testator in his will has a clear meaning, the court is not free to construe it otherwise notwithstanding that the testator meant something else. Consider the following example:

> A testator's will provides: '*All income from my bonds to Charles.*' There is extrinsic evidence (from a letter sent to Charles) that the testator intended to gift his bonds to Charles outright.

'Income' (unlike 'money') has a clear meaning, in that it disposes of the income generated by the bonds, not the bonds themselves. As there is no ambiguity in the words in the will, it is not possible to construe them in a way that is consistent with the testator's intended meaning. The testator's mistake in his choice of words, therefore, can only be cured by making an application to rectify. This point was highlighted in the case of *Re Williams*[78] where a testatrix had left a will which merely listed the names of 25 beneficiaries, whom she had divided into three groups. She subsequently wrote a letter to her solicitors in which she expressed a wish that the £2,000 be paid to those in the first group, £1,000 to those in the second group and £500 to those in the third group. Although the testatrix's subjective intention was clear, it was not possible to construe her will, such as it was, to give differing amounts to the three groups. As Nicholls J said:

> But if, however liberal may be the approach of the court, the meaning is one which the word or phrase cannot bear, I do not see how carrying out a process of construction … the court can declare that meaning to be the meaning of the word or phrase. Such a conclusion, varying or contradicting the language used, would amount to re-writing part of the will, and that is a result to be achieved, if at all, under the rectification provisions of section 20.[79]

To conclude, where there is a meaning error, the mistake might be cured by construction provided the words used are ambiguous and capable of bearing the testator's intended meaning. In other cases, especially those where the words used in the will are clear, the mistake can only be cured by rectification.

iii. Parol Terms

The second function of rectification in the context of wills lies in giving effect to what we might call 'parol terms'. It is sometimes the case that a settlor executes a will in the false belief that it reflects the terms contained in an earlier 'parol' document[80] such as an earlier will, a draft, memorandum or detailed written

[78] [1985] 1 WLR 905 (Ch).
[79] ibid 911.
[80] Confusingly 'parol' means 'oral', but 'parol evidence' refers to any evidence (written or oral) outside of the will.

instructions to draft a will. Correcting the error involves re-writing the will so that it is consistent with the earlier parol document. Consider the following example:

> In 2012 a testator executes a will (the 2012 Will) which contains a legacy of '*£10,000 to Charles*'. In 2015 the testator instructs his solicitor to update the 2012 Will in certain minor ways but to leave the legacies unchanged. By reason of a drafting error the new will (the 2015 Will) omits any reference to the legacy to Charles. The testator fails to notice the omission and executes the 2015 Will.

This is an example of a 'content error', in that the testator was mistaken as to the terms contained in the 2015 Will, believing that it included a £10,000 legacy to Charles. It might be argued that the error in this example can be corrected by construction: if the 2012 Will is admissible as an aid to the construction of the 2015 Will,[81] might a court not conclude that the testator intended to give a legacy to Charles? I would suggest that this type of argument, which was attempted by counsel in *Marley v Rawlings*,[82] is mistaken, and that such an error cannot be cured by construction.

A testator may execute several wills during his life, and each will may go through several successive drafts. Each time a new will is executed the obvious inference to draw is that the testator intends his estate to be disposed of according to the terms in his most recent will;[83] put negatively, he does not intend earlier wills, or drafts of wills, to have any testamentary effect.[84] The point was forcefully made by Mustill LJ in *Re Berger*,[85] where he said:

> Imagine a document headed with the words, 'This is not a will and is not intended to be admitted to probate.' To hold that it could nevertheless be proved would seem to be not only absurd, and an unjustifiable thwarting of the testator's intentions, but would also contravene the rule that internal evidence can negative animus …[86]

Whilst in most cases a testator will not make his intention – that a draft or memorandum is not to have testamentary effect – express in the same way as happens in Mustill LJ's example, the intention can be inferred from the context: in executing a will, the testator's intention is that his last will supersedes all earlier expressions of testamentary intention.

This basic point, it is suggested, explains why construction cannot be used to correct the error in the above example. In executing the 2015 Will, the clear intention of the testator was that the 2015 Will would replace earlier wills; put negatively, he no longer intended the 2012 Will to have testamentary effect.

[81] It is not entirely clear whether the 2012 Will would be admissible under s 21(1) of the Administration of Justice Act 1982 by reason of the fact that the 2015 Will is not meaningless or ambiguous.

[82] Above, n 53 [34]–[42].

[83] This is normally made express by the inclusion of a revocation clause, whereby the testator revokes all earlier wills and codicils.

[84] *Milnes v Foden* (1890) 15 PD 105.

[85] [1990] Ch 118 (CA).

[86] ibid, 130.

To admit the 2012 Will as evidence of the testator's intended dispositions would frustrate the testator's intention, not give effect to it.[87] For this reason construction cannot give effect to the legacy to Charles.

This error can only be corrected by rectification. As Professor Stevens has explained,[88] rectification operates as a form of partial rescission. In the example given above, the testator's *animus testandi* – that the 2015 Will replace all earlier statements of testamentary intention – is vitiated by his mistaken belief as to its contents and, hence, can be ignored. This conclusion allows the court to give effect to the will that would have existed had the testator *not intended* the 2015 Will to replace earlier testamentary documents, ie it allows the court to consider the 2012 Will, and the legacy to Charles contained therein, as evidence of the testator's intended dispositions.

For these reasons it is suggested that the leading case of *Marley v Rawlings* was correctly decided on the grounds of rectification rather than construction. Consider again the facts: Mr Rawlings had a draft will drawn up for him (Will A), but in the event executed a different draft (Will B). The prima facie inference to draw from his conduct is that he intended Will B to be replace earlier statements of testamentary intention and be the sole source of the terms of his will. It would frustrate his intention to admit Will A as an aid to the construction of Will B. As such, the error cannot be cured by construction. Rectification, on the other hand, works as follows: Mr Rawlings' *animus testandi* – that Will B replace all earlier statements of testamentary intention – is vitiated because he was mistaken as to its contents and, consequently, can be ignored. This allowed the Supreme Court to give effect to the will that would have existed had Mr Rawlings not intended Will B to replace earlier statements of testamentary intention (including those found in Will A).

IV. Conclusion

To conclude, whilst it is possible that certain content errors can be cured by a process of construction, not all can. In particular, where the testator's error lies in a false belief that his will reflects the terms contained in an earlier document, such as a repealed will, draft will or written instructions, it will be necessary to make an application to rectify the will.

[87] See eg *Guardhouse v Blackburn* (1866) LR 1 PD 109; *Thorncroft v Lashmar* (1862) 2 Sw & Tr 479, 164 ER 1083; *White v Pollok* (1882) 7 App Cas 400 (HL(Sc)).

[88] Stevens (n 5) 119. See also *Britoil plc v Hunt Overseas Oil Inc* [1994] CLC 561 (CA) 573.

10

Private Property and Forced Expropriation

Current Challenges in Spanish Law

ENCARNACIÓN MONTOYA MARTÍN

I. Introduction

This chapter explores the constitutional guarantees relating to private property and forced expropriation, as well as those aspects of the regulation of the power of expropriation that are most in need of reform in Spanish law. The modest aim of this work is to give a general overview of expropriation as an institution in the Spanish legal system in order to facilitate and promote comparative law research in relation to private property and, in particular, the power of expropriation – compulsory purchase – from the perspective of the Spanish legal system and English law. For this reason, it is limited to setting out rather briefly the current position of Spanish academic writing and case-law on the right to private property and the forced expropriation of property.

II. Private Property in the Spanish Constitution of 1978

The right to private property is recognised in article 33.1 of the Spanish Constitution of 1978 in the following terms:

> The right to private property and inheritance is recognised.

Article 33.2 states:

> The content of these rights shall be determined by the social function which they fulfil, in accordance with the law.

This constitutional provision reflects the transformations undergone by individual rights in the transition from a liberal abstentionist State to a social State, ie a political organisation that actively intervenes in the private sphere in order to accomplish public interest objectives. In consequence, individual rights are no longer absolute, and property is an example of this. As the Spanish Constitutional Court stated in its very important decision of 26 March 1987:

> The Constitution recognises a right to private property that is certainly configured and protected as a bundle of powers of an individual over things, but also and at the same time as a set of duties and obligations established in accordance with the law taking into consideration the values or interests of the community.[1]

Property is designed not only in the context of power as regards the political organisation, but also in the imposition of a set of obligations on its holder. Indeed, it is this collective aspect of the social function that is the axis on which the concept of property in the Constitution is based, the structural element of its definition. The social function refers to the subordination of individual interests to the superior interests of the community. The social function is linked directly to the very concept of individual rights, in that it is for the legislator, in relation to the various categories of property, to determine the powers that the owner has over them, as well as the way in which, where appropriate, they are to be exercised, preventing those uses or applications that may be contrary to or harmful to the public interest. The Constitutional Court itself has said that there has been a

> diversification of the institution of ownership into a plurality of regulated legal figures or situations with a diverse significance and scope … which is shown by the existence of different types of property with differing legal status depending on the nature of the assets on which, in each case, the right falls.[2]

There has therefore been a clear move away from the unitary concept of property to the assertion in its place of the existence of multiple forms of property (urban, agricultural, cultural, etc). The right of ownership is thus a power designed by reference to function, a right designed by the law. In the Spanish Constitution, property has a legislative character, since it is for the ordinary legislator to determine the content of the property right in its various forms. Such a determination of the content of the property right that is designed to fulfil the social function does not constitute an interference requiring compensation, but will form part of the normal content of each type of ownership. Only those burdens that exceed this normal content will give rise to compensation for forced expropriation under article 33.3 of the Constitution, which states:

> No one may be deprived of his or her property and rights, except on justified grounds of public utility or social interest and with proper compensation in accordance with the provisions of the law.

The question will be to determine to what extent the owner is obliged to bear the limitation of his right without compensation because it is part of the social

[1] STC 37/1987, 26 March (case of the Andalusian Agrarian Reform Law).
[2] ibid.

function or, on the contrary, when there is a total or partial deprivation of the right to property going beyond the social function and giving rise in consequence to expropriation with a right to compensation.

It can be said that when there is property there is no expropriation and, conversely, if there is expropriation it is because there has been a total or partial deprivation of the essential content of the right to property beyond the limitations and burdens imposed by its social function.

The social State not only transforms the concept of the right to private property, but has also given rise to a fundamental review of the principle of forced expropriation which is undergoing 'a process of extension … to all kinds of rights and patrimonial interests and to all categories of public and social aims'.[3]

A. The Nature of the Fundamental Right to Property

The right to private property in the Spanish Constitution is not a fundamental right in the strict sense – it is not one of the 'Fundamental Rights and Public Liberties' listed in Title I, Chapter II, Section 1 of the Constitution – and therefore its regulation is not reserved to 'organic laws'[4] but to ordinary legislation. Moreover, it is not subject to the right of an individual to appeal for protection to the Constitutional Court,[5] an instrument of reinforced protection for those rights that are fundamental rights (in the strict sense) in the Constitution. The Spanish Constitution has not deemed it necessary to include the right to property and its guarantees, including the constitutional limits on expropriation, within this reinforced protection, leaving protection to the ordinary courts, which in turn have the possibility of ruling on the question of unconstitutionality.[6] However, in

[3] STC 166/1986, 19 December, FJ 13; STC 48/2005, 3 March, FJ 4.

[4] See art 81 CE:

1. Organic laws are those relating to the development of fundamental rights and public liberties, those which establish Statutes of Autonomy and the general electoral system, and other laws provided in the Constitution.
2. The passing, amendment or repeal of organic laws shall require an absolute majority of the members of Congress in a final vote on the bill as a whole.

[5] See art 53.2 CE:

> Any citizen may assert his or her claim to the protect the liberties and rights recognised in article 14 and in Section 1 of Chapter II, by means of a preferential and summary procedure in the ordinary courts and, when appropriate, by submitting an individual appeal for protection (*recurso de amparo*) to the Constitutional Court. This latter procedure shall be applicable to conscientious objection as recognised in article 30.

Thus the *recurso de amparo* as an enhanced protection applies only to the rights and freedoms governed by arts 14–29 CE, including conscientious objection governed by art 30. Therefore, the right to property, positioned within the structure of the Constitution in art 33, does not enjoy this enhanced guarantee.

[6] STC 67/1988, 18 April, FJ 4 (*recurso de amparo* by Ruiz Mateos against resolutions of the Council of Ministers authorising or agreeing to the transfer to third parties of some of the shares or holdings

international treaties which have been ratified by Spain,[7] the right to property is considered a fundamental right.

B. Constitutional Guarantees of Property

The right to private property, due to its position in Title I, Chapter II, Section 1 of the Constitution and according to article 53.1 CE,[8] benefits from a double constitutional guarantee: the first is formal, its regulation is reserved to legislation; the second is material, the essential content of the right.[9]

i. Formal Guarantee: Reservation to Legislation[10]

This is a formal guarantee, in accordance with the rule of law, consisting in the fact that the general regime of property rights must be regulated by a rule with the status of legislation, ie by the representatives of the sovereign people. The expression 'in accordance with the law' in article 33.2 of the Constitution makes that reservation more flexible, giving regulation in this area more space than the rule relating to sub-legislative regulation in the context of other fundamental rights.

With the guarantee of reservation to legislation,

> any procedure to remove the subject-matter from the scope of legislation, or any attempt to regulate the content of the right to private property by independent or non-legislative

expropriated from 'Rumasa, Sociedad Anónima' by *Real Decreto-ley 2/1983, de 23 de febrero*, which later became *Ley 7/1983 de 29 de junio, de expropiación por razones de utilidad pública e interés social de los Bancos y otras Sociedades que componen el Grupo «Rumasa, S. A.»*, and against the denial of the right of reversion of property gifted to children or other descendants who have died without issue).

[7] The right to private property was incorporated into the list in the European Convention for the Protection of Human Rights and Fundamental Freedoms ('ECHR') by the first Protocol of 20 March 1952. It is also governed by art 17 of the Charter of Fundamental Rights of the European Union [2000] OJ C364/01.

[8] See art 53.1 CE:

> The rights and liberties recognised in Chapter II of the present Title are binding for all public authorities. The exercise of such rights and liberties, which shall be protected in accordance with the provisions of article 161.1(a), may be regulated only by legislation which shall, in any case, respect their essential content.

[9] For a helpful overview of the doctrine of the Constitutional Court in relation to property and its guarantees in the Spanish legal system, see JM Rodríguez de Santiago, 'Las garantías constitucionales de la propiedad y de la expropiación forzosa a los treinta años de la Constitución Española' RAP no 177, 2008, pp 160–61 ('the core (and, perhaps, something more than that) of the constitutional doctrine on guarantees in art 33 CE was created by the responses of the Constitutional Court, in its first ten years of activity, to the case of the Andalusian Agrarian Reform Law [n 1] and the Rumasa case'. See STC 111/1983, 2 December ('Rumasa 1'); STC 166/1986, 19 December (n 3) ('Rumasa 2') and STC 6/1991, 15 January ('Rumasa 3'); all three are Plenary decisions of the Court; there have been other judgments related to the case issued in proceedings by way of *recurso de amparo*. See, similarly, JM Rodríguez de Santiago 'Artículo 33' in M Rodríguez-Piñero y Bravo Ferrer and ME Casas Baamonde (eds), *Comentarios a la Constitución Española, XL Aniversario*, vol I (Madrid, Fundación Wolters Kluwer, 2018) 1147, 1149 (a seminal work of reference).

[10] See Rodríguez de Santiago 'Las garantías constitucionales de la propiedad y de la expropiación forzosa a los treinta años de la Constitución Española' (n 9) esp 162ff.

regulations, is prohibited, except the referral by the legislator to the collaboration of the rule-making powers of the Administration to supplement the legislative regulation.[11]

A broad collaboration of regulation is enshrined, especially in the regulation of the regime governing immovable property.

Given that Spain is a State that is decentralised through the Autonomous Communities, legislation may be either of the State or of an Autonomous Community depending on the area of jurisdiction in which the particular public interests that impose a specific demarcation of its content are located. As already noted, the regulation of property falls outside the scope of organic laws, as a result of the strict interpretation by the Constitutional Court of the expression 'fundamental rights and public liberties' in article 81.1 CE.[12] It may also be subject to the delegation by the legislator provided for in article 82 CE. In other words, legislative decrees (*Decretos legislativos*) are possible.[13]

Finally, by means of a decree-law (*Decreto-ley*)[14] it is possible to carry out legislative expropriations. Although a decree-law cannot 'affect the rights, duties and liberties of citizens governed by Title I',[15] the Constitutional Court has said that this cannot be given such a broad meaning that it would prevent decree-laws from carrying out particular expropriations, as long as they do not alter 'essential elements' of the regime of forced expropriation.[16]

ii. Material Guarantee: The Essential Content

This is a guarantee imported from German constitutional law.[17] The essential content of any right is given by the set of powers necessary for the right to be

[11] STC 37/1987, 26 March (n 1) FJ 3.

[12] See above, n 4.

[13] The regulation of legislative degrees is found in arts 82–85 CE. They are a form of delegation by Parliament to the Government to draw up a text comprising various articles, or to consolidate existing laws. In short, they are a form of legislative delegation by Parliament that gives rise to a rule drawn up by the Government, ie, the Executive, with the status of legislation provided that it satisfies the requirements of the Constitution. If it does not, the rule drawn up by the Government will not acquire the status and force of legislation, but only that of the rules which the Government itself has power to make, ie, regulations and general provisions which are subordinate to legislation. This is confirmed by art 1.1 *Ley 29/1998, de 13 de julio, Reguladora de la Jurisdicción Contencioso-administrativa*, which allocates to the administrative courts the hearing of claims relating to legislative decrees in so far as they exceed their delegated powers.

[14] See art 86 CE. A decree-law is a rule with the force of legislation approved by the Executive in cases of extraordinary and urgent need. It is provisional, since decree-laws must be ratified or repealed by the Congress of Deputies within 30 days after their promulgation. During this period, they may be passed by *las Cortes* (the legislative bodies) as bills by means of an emergency procedure. For recent examples, see STC 93/2015, 14 May, relating to *Ley 1/2010, de 8 de marzo, reguladora del derecho a la vivienda en Andalucía* and *Decreto-ley 6/2013, de 9 de abril, de medidas para asegurar el cumplimiento de la función social de la vivienda en Andalucía.*

[15] Art 86.1 CE.

[16] STC 111/1983, 2 December (Rumasa 1) (n 9), FJ 8.

[17] Art 19.2 GG (Basic Law for the Federal Republic of Germany): 'In no case may the essence of a basic right be affected' ('In keinem Falle darf ein Grundrecht in seinem Wesensgehalt angetastet werden').

recognisable. In other words, according to the Spanish Constitutional Court, the list of

> powers or possibilities of action necessary to make the right recognisable as belonging to the category described, and without which it ceases to belong to this category and has to be included in another – denaturing it, so to speak. All of this refers to the historical moment in each case and to the conditions inherent in democratic societies when it comes to constitutional rights.[18]

From another methodological angle, neither contradictory nor incompatible with the former, it has also been expressed by the Constitutional Court as 'that part of the content of the right that is absolutely necessary so that the legally protectable interests that give life to the right are really, concretely and effectively protected'.[19]

Thus, 'the essential content is exceeded when the right is subject to limitations that make it impracticable, or unreasonably difficult, or deprive it of the necessary protection'.[20] This means that any specific property law statute must always respect a minimum and non-derogable nucleus of powers in favour of its owner, beyond which the property would cease to exist, giving way to expropriation.

The social function cannot mean the loss or depletion of the economic utility of the property,[21] although limitations can be imposed on the owner as to the use, destination or exploitation of each thing 'aimed at satisfying the public interest as long as the profitability of the owner is safeguarded'.[22]

III. Forced Expropriation

The pre-Revolutionary order in France recognised that public authorities had the possibility of depriving individuals of ownership of their property, subject to compensation as a requirement of natural law. The basis for this was the distinction between the useful domain (*dominium utile*) of private subjects over property and the eminent domain (*dominium eminens*) over all property by the monarch (or by society as a whole, with the advent of enlightened ideas), which meant that if necessary any property had to be put at the service of the public interest, combining eminent and useful domain.

With the French Revolution, the right to property was consecrated as inviolable and sacred, of which no one could be deprived, except where manifestly so demanded by public necessity, lawfully established, and only on condition of fair, prior compensation.[23] In 1810, France promulgated its first forced expropriation

[18] STC 11/1981, 8 April, FJ 8.
[19] ibid.
[20] STC 11/1981, 8 April (n 18) FJ 10; STC 37/1987, 26 March (n 1) FJ 2.
[21] STC 89/1994, 17 March.
[22] STC 37/1987, 26 March (n 1).
[23] National Assembly, *Declaration of the Rights of Man and Citizen* (1789), art 17 ('La propriété étant un droit inviolable et sacré, nul ne peut en être privé, si ce n'est lorsque la nécessité publique, légalement constatée, l'exige évidemment, et sous la condition d'une juste et préalable indemnité').

law, which was designed for the expropriation of immovable property required for the construction of public works and which made the validity of the expropriation conditional upon the legal determination of the ground of public utility; the payment of compensation prior to occupation; and compliance with the procedure established by legislation.

A. The Concept

In Spain, the Forced Transfer Law (*la Ley de Enajenación Forzosa*) was passed in 1836; and then the extensive and detailed Forced Expropriation Law (*la Ley de Expropiación Forzosa*) in 1879, in development of article 10 of the 1876 Constitution; and, finally, the Forced Expropriation Law (*la Ley de Expropiación Forzosa* ['LEF']) of 16 December 1954 and the Decree of 26 April 1957, approving the Regulation of the Forced Expropriation Law (*el Reglamento de la Ley de Expropiación Forzosa* ['REF']). The LEF and the REF are still in force, although with some specific amendments, implementing the provisions of article 32 of the Spanish Charter (*Fuero de los Españoles*) of 1945, which prohibited the penalty of confiscation and provided that 'no one may be expropriated except for reasons of public utility or social interest, subject to proper compensation and in accordance with the provisions of the law'.

The model underlying this legislation was that of the forced expropriation of immovable property for the purpose of carrying out public works. But reality went beyond the initial scheme and movable goods began to be expropriated, as well as expropriations affecting only some part of the property right or other rights or interests of patrimonial content. Therefore, the LEF 1954 extended the concept of forced expropriation.[24] Article 1.1 of the LEF provides:

> The object of this Law is the forced expropriation for reasons of public utility or social interest …, which shall be understood to include any form of singular deprivation of private property or of legitimate patrimonial rights or interests, whatever the persons or entities to which they belong, agreed upon compulsorily, whether it involves sale, exchange, ground rent, lease, temporary occupation or mere cessation of its exercise.

In short, we have moved from the traditional understanding of immovable property required for public works as being practically the only object of the expropriation procedure, to defining as expropriation any alteration of a patrimonial juridical situation, whether the rights are proprietary or merely obligational, and therefore also including movables and incorporeal property.

With regard to the constitutional concept of expropriation, the line that is not always easy to draw is between the regulation of the social function of the property right, which cannot be compensated (article 33.2 CE), and the total or partial expropriation of the right, which is subject to the guarantees of article 33.3 CE and

[24] Note also the REF 1957, which is still in force.

therefore to the duty of compensation.[25] The Constitutional Court has repeatedly stated that for the guarantee of article 33.3 CE to be applied, it is necessary for there to exist the singular deprivation characteristic of all expropriation – in other words, the subtraction or removal of a legitimate right or interest imposed on one or more individuals, a requirement set out in article 1 LEF – but that the legal means of definition of the right, or the general regulation of its content, are not the same thing as this singular deprivation. It is obvious that the legal definition of the content of patrimonial rights or the introduction of new limitations cannot ignore its essential content, since in such a case it would not be possible to speak of a general regulation of the right, but of its deprivation or suppression that, even when predicated as the general norm, would result in a dispossession of individual juridical situations, not tolerated by the constitutional rule unless proper compensation is provided.[26]

In short, the criterion of the singularity of the deprivation to which the ordinary legislator refers in article 1 LEF contrasts with the material criterion of the essential content which is required by the Constitution and which is inferred from articles 53.1 CE and 33.1 CE. This was made clear by Barnés Vázquez.[27] This concept of expropriation has been qualified as a formal concept of expropriation because it uses a formal element of singularity as opposed to generality to characterise the institution, whereas in article 33 CE there is no reference to the mark of singularity of the removal, but only to the total or partial deprivation of the essential content of the right. In its decision 227/1988,[28] the Constitutional Court added to the formal concept (useful in the case of singular expropriations by the Administration or of the legislator) another material concept of expropriation (useful in the face of a legislator regulating patrimonial rights of a general nature), because it connects the border between the social function of the property (article 33.2 CE) and article 33.3 CE (the expropriation) with the material guarantee of the essential content of the right of property (article 33.1 CE).

Furthermore, as Rodríguez de Santiago[29] and others have pointed out, the application of the principle of proportionality must also be taken into account: first, if instead of expropriation another less restrictive measure can be adopted which is equally effective in achieving the public purpose to be served; and secondly, there is a relationship of subsidiarity between expropriation carried out by the Administration and legislative expropriation through the application of the principle of proportionality to the procedural guarantee established in article 33.3 CE.

[25] In its decision 170/1989, 19 October, FJ 8, the Constitutional Court itself states that the line between the deprivation of a patrimonial right and its simple legal incidence or definition based on the social function to which it must be subject (art 33.2 CE) is not always easy to determine.

[26] STC 204/2004, 18 November, FJ 5; STC 227/1988, 29 November, FJ 11; and most recently STC 45/2018, 26 April, FJ 3.

[27] J Barnés Vázquez, *La propiedad constitucional el estatuto jurídico del suelo agrario* (Madrid, Civitas, 1988).

[28] STC 227/1988, 29 November (n 26).

[29] Rodríguez de Santiago, 'Artículo 33' (n 9) 1167–68.

Given that legislative expropriation generally limits the possibilities of defence more intensely, such expropriation is only constitutionally justified in exceptional circumstances, in which the ground for the expropriation cannot be realised with the same effectiveness by the ordinary, less restrictive means offered by the application of the general laws regulating administrative expropriation.

B. Constitutional Guarantees of Forced Expropriation

Article 33.3 of the Constitution states that

> No one may be deprived of his or her property and rights, except on justified grounds of public utility or social interest and with proper compensation in accordance with the provisions of the law.

Expropriation in the Constitution covers all types of property and rights; it requires the concurrence of a ground of public utility or social interest as a legitimate burden; it requires the payment of proper compensation, not necessarily in advance; and it reserves to legislation the regulation of the power of expropriation.

Since forced expropriation is one of the typical exorbitant powers of the public Administration, the constitutional guarantees of forced expropriation are imposed on all public authorities,[30] both on the public Administration, which can be called administrative expropriation, or simply expropriation – which is the ordinary case; and on the legislative authority when in exceptional cases the expropriation is carried out by the legislator.[31] Article 33.3 CE makes no distinction, so it applies to all public authorities. Thus, deprivation of property can occur either through legislation or individual expropriation procedures, or through legislation or general nationalisation procedures.[32] The Constitutional Court has stated in relation to legislative expropriations or expropriations through individual laws that they must respect the guarantees set out in article 33.3 CE: they must respond

[30] According to the ECtHR, it is the Contracting States that commit themselves to recognising the rights and freedoms guaranteed by the Convention system for all persons under their jurisdiction (art 1 ECHR), so that interference with the right to property must be able to relate to the behaviour of any of its organs or authorities, whether they belong to the legislature, the judiciary or the executive. See J Barcelona LLop, 'Privación de la propiedad y expropiación forzada en el sistema del Convenio Europeo de Derechos Humanos' RAP no 185, 2011, p 64.

[31] STC 166/1986, 19 December (n 3) ('Rumasa 2').

[32] In Spain, it is sufficient to recall the well-known case of the expropriation of the Rumasa Group through *Real Decreto-ley 2/1983, de 23 de febrero*, which later became *Ley 7/1983 de 29 de junio* (n 6), which has given rise to case-law at the highest level that has left its mark on the constitutional guarantees of the right to property and on forced expropriation. The justification for this provision was that the Rumasa Group was a conglomerate of companies with unified risk and management, and that some companies – mainly banks – posed a risk to the stability of the financial system, as well as to the protection of the interests of workers and depositors. As a result, the forced expropriation of all the shares representing the capital of the Group's companies was decreed on the grounds of public utility and social interest.

to a purpose of public utility or social interest (*causa expropriandi*);[33] they must guarantee proper compensation; and they must respect the provisions of the law (guarantee of the expropriation procedure), although it admits that it may contain procedural peculiarities with respect to the general procedure that are necessary in light of the exceptional situation by virtue of which the singular expropriation law is approved.[34]

The problem arises with the confrontation between the procedural guarantee and the right to effective judicial protection guaranteed in article 24 CE in the case of legislative expropriations – that is, the possibility for a party subject to such expropriations to raise a defence, a question to which we will return in the section dealing with the procedural guarantee.[35]

i. The Ground of Public Utility or Social Interest is the Legitimate Burden of Forced Expropriation

The first of the guarantees of expropriation established by the Constitution is the public purpose that justifies the expropriation measure. The identification of this falls to the legislator, and indeed its definition is an indispensable requirement, derived from the medial nature of expropriation as an instrument at the service of substantive public ends whose material procurements fall to the Administration.[36]

Directly linked to the ground for the expropriation is the problem of the basis of the right of reversion or redistribution, which raises the relationship between article 33.3 CE and article 54.1 LEF.[37] The right must be linked to the ground. The ground of public utility or social interest is what legitimises the expropriation and must exist not only before but also after the completion, because it is the only reason that legitimises the continuation or maintenance of the deprivation that has been carried out. If, for any reason, the property is not used for its intended purpose, the expropriated person or his successors are entitled to recover the property that was expropriated. In short, the reversion is explained in our

[33] In its most recent decision 45/2018, 26 April (n 26), the Constitutional Court has again declared that the canon of reasonableness inherent in all singular laws is anchored in the first place in their objective justification, which in the case of singular legislative expropriations cannot be other than the concurrence of a ground of public utility or social interest. Therefore, it declared the additional provision 44 *of Ley 39/2010, de 22 de diciembre, de presupuestos generales del Estado para 2011* unconstitutional and null because it considered that it violated art 33.3 CE given that there are no grounds of public utility or social interest to deprive a person of the right to a pension acquired by virtue of the Law.

[34] STC 48/2005, 3 March (n 3).

[35] See below, section III.B(iii).

[36] STC 37/1987, 26 March (n 1), FJ 6.

[37] Art 54.1 LEF provides:

> In the event that the work is not carried out or the service that motivated the expropriation is not established, as well as if there is any surplus part of the expropriated property, or if the basis for the expropriation disappears, the original owner or his successors may recover all or part of what was expropriated, by paying the compensation determined in the following article to whoever is entitled to it.

law by its connection with the ground for the expropriation: if the ground is not fulfilled or is later frustrated, its demise brings with it the right of reversion. The Constitutional Court itself defines the reversion as a patrimonial right inextricably linked to the ground of expropriation.[38]

With regard to reversion, the question of its foundation has been raised – that is, whether the right of reversion is characterised as a right of legal or constitutional configuration. For the Constitutional Court, it does not constitute a constitutional guarantee derived from the ground of public utility or social interest;[39] it is an institution whose existence and regulation is entrusted to the legislator. It is up to the ordinary legislator to regulate it, to moderate it according to the different grounds and circumstances and even to suppress it in a reasoned, proportional and justified manner. In other words, the regulation contained in the LEF does not exhaust the legal regulation of the matter for the Constitutional Court. The LEF constitutes the regime designed for the expropriation of property for the execution of works or services, but this is not the only case, and although it can be applied to other cases by analogy, it does not constitute the general, unique and uniform rule. There may be cases in which the ground is satisfied by the expropriation itself, as was considered in the case of the expropriation of the Rumasa Group shares. This position has been criticised by writers who have correctly taken the view that since it is a right that is inextricably linked to the ground that legitimises the expropriation, it is therefore anchored in the very essence of the expropriation. From this perspective, the consequence can only be the constitutional status of the guarantee of reversion.[40]

ii. Providing Proper Compensation: Compensation as a Patrimonial Guarantee

Article 33.3 of the Constitution requires the payment of proper compensation, or fair payment for the expropriation. It does not require payment prior to taking possession of the expropriated property, since its only requirement is that the deprivation be 'with proper compensation'.

As for the level of this guarantee,[41] the doctrine of the Constitutional Court requires the compensation to correspond to the 'economic value of the property'

See E Montoya Martín, 'Consideraciones sobre el derecho de reversión en la expropiación forzosa' in *Jornadas de Derecho portuario*, Puerto. Memoria 2003–2006 (Puerto de Sevilla, Ministerio de Fomento, 2008) 380–406.

[38] STC 67/1988, 18 April (n 6), FJ 6.

[39] STC 166/1986, 19 December (n 3); STC 67/1988, 18 April (n 6).

[40] See E García de Enterría and TR Fernández Rodríguez, *Curso de Derecho Administrativo I* (Madrid, Civitas, 1998) 323; JM Gimeno Feliu, *El derecho de reversión en la expropiación forzosa*, 2nd edn (Madrid, Civitas, 2003); L Alegre Ávila, 'El derecho de reversión en las expropiaciones legislativas. El caso Rumasa en la jurisprudencia del Tribunal Supremo' RAP no 132, 1993; G De Castro Vitores, *Reversión expropiatoria. Una reflexión en la perspectiva civilista* (Valencia, Tirant lo Blanch, 2001) 120.

[41] Art 1 of the first Protocol to the ECHR does not contain any reference to the obligation to compensate. As the Spanish writer Barcelona LLop shows for the ECtHR (see n 30, 68), the principle of a fair

or to its 'real value'; it then states that between the value of the expropriated property and the compensation there should be a 'proportional balance', a 'reasonable balance between the loss caused by the expropriation and its reparation'; it then goes on to hold that it is sufficient that the compensation is not 'manifestly lacking a reasonable basis', is not 'confiscatory' or simply 'non-existent'.[42]

iii. Procedural Guarantee or the Right to an Effective Defence Against Expropriation

Article 33.3 of the Constitution enshrines the guarantee of the expropriation procedure by providing that the expropriation be carried out 'in accordance with the provisions of the law'. The controversial question has arisen in relation to legislative expropriations when the compatibility of such expropriations with the right to effective judicial protection (under article 24) has been raised.

The problem arises – as Rodríguez de Santiago, among others, has shown – when the Constitutional Court proceeded to interpret the guarantees of article 33.3 CE in accordance with the LEF 1954, instead of carrying out the opposite operation, that is, interpreting the LEF in accordance with the Constitution. In its decision 166/1986[43] (amongst others), the Court has converted the general expropriation procedure of the LEF into a canon of constitutionality of legislative expropriations, giving rise to a sort of supralegalisation of the regulation of expropriation carried out by the LEF, which, however, takes effect at the level of ordinary (sub-constitutional) legislation. The Constitutional Court considers that

balance between the general interest and individual rights calls for compensation in case of deprivation. Compensation is an important element in the analysis of whether there is a fair balance between the interests at stake (those of the community and those of the holder of the right to enjoyment of the property) and whether an excessive burden is not imposed on the person concerned; compensation must be a reasonable sum of money in relation to the value of the property, although the Convention does not in any case guarantee the right to full compensation, as there may be reasonable grounds in the public interest to justify payment of an amount lower than the market value of the property; that is, it appeals to a right of the person concerned which is not formally included in the provision.

[42] STC 166/1988, 19 December (n 3); STC 149/1991, 4 July. STC 149/1991 settles the claims of unconstitutionality against *la Ley 22/1988, de 28 de julio, de Costas*, a case of legislative expropriation by extension by the legislator of the area of public domain of maritime land. According to the Constitutional Court (FJ 8) 'the elimination of existing property rights on land that the Constitution incorporated into the public domain can be considered as deprivation of such property and must therefore give rise to compensation, since this is a matter of respect for the expropriation guarantee, which the Constitution recognises'. It adds that 'there can be no question of the absence of compensation: that is obvious. If the expropriation is carried out precisely by transforming the property into a concession, the economic value of the latter can only be understood as compensation, determined *ope legis*, for the deprivation of the proprietary title. It is not a free choice but an expropriation decision in which the legislation itself sets the quantum of compensation'. Finally, it states that '[f]or the inadequacy of compensation to result in the unconstitutionality of the rule that establishes it for the expropriation of a set of assets, attention must be paid not to the precise circumstances that may arise in each specific case, but to the existence of a "proportional balance" (STC 166/1986) between the value of the expropriated asset or right and the amount of compensation offered'.

[43] STC 166/1988, 19 December (n 3).

the possibilities of defence that the expropriated person possesses in the general administrative expropriation procedure should be the canon of constitutionality also in legislative expropriations. There has therefore been a disturbing constitutionalisation of the general expropriation procedure of the LEF. Rodriguez de Santiago rightly criticises this, giving as an example 'the distinction between the declaration of public utility or social interest and the agreement of need of occupation, as it is carried out in the LEF, underlining that it is not in itself a constitutional distinction derived from article 33.3 CE, despite which the Constitutional Court has used it to examine the constitutionality of a legislative expropriation (STC 166/1986, 19 December, FJ 15A)'.[44] The Court has stated that: 'legislative expropriations … must, in the end, respect the provisions of the legislation' and cannot 'dispense with the guarantee of the expropriation procedure established in the general expropriation legislation, to which they must also be subject (STC 48/2005, 3 March, FJ 5)'.[45]

IV. Weak Points or Aspects Most in Need of Reform in the LEF

In times of the dizzying regulatory changes typical of 'liquid modernity', as expressed by the sociologist Bauman,[46] it is striking that a 1954 law of forced expropriation is still in force in Spain. The question is, how can a LEF from 1954, after more than 60 years in force, be maintained? Spanish writers explain it unanimously by its technical quality, anticipating to a certain extent the constitutional guarantees that would be enshrined in the Constitution of 1978,[47] although this does not mean that there are not critical points that writers unanimously consider to be in need of reform.

It should be pointed out that the most relevant modifications have taken place outside the LEF itself. These are, on the one hand, those that affect the right of reversion by Law 38/1999 on Building Regulations;[48] and on the other hand, the valuation regime in urban planning regulations, currently Royal Legislative Decree 7/2015 approving the revised text of the Land and Urban Renewal Law[49] and Royal Decree 1492/2011 approving the valuation regulations of the Land Law.[50]

[44] Rodríguez de Santiago, 'Las garantías constitucionales de la propiedad y de la expropiación forzosa a los treinta años de la Constitución Española' (n 9) 182.

[45] ibid.

[46] Z Bauman, *Modernidad líquida*, 1st Spanish edn (Mexico DF, Fondo de Cultura Económica, 2003) (originally published in English as *Liquid Modernity*, Cambridge, Polity Press, 2000).

[47] For the genesis of the LEF as well as an analysis of the aspects in need of reform, see E Garcia de Enterría, 'La Ley de Expropiación forzosa de 1954, medio siglo después' RAP no 156, 2001, pp 251–68.

[48] *Ley 38/1999, de 5 de noviembre, de Ordenación de la Edificación.*

[49] *Real Decreto Legislativo 7/2015, de 30 de octubre, por el que se aprueba el texto refundido de la Ley de Suelo y Rehabilitación Urbana.*

[50] *Real Decreto 1492/2011, de 24 de octubre, por el que se aprueba el Reglamento de valoraciones de la Ley de Suelo.*

Given the purpose of the present chapter, we shall just summarise in a general way the main weak points or those that are in need of reform, following the writing of Boix Palop.[51] More detailed development would take us beyond the present context.

A. Forced Expropriation and the Autonomic Model

The LEF 1954 does not, of course, contemplate the Autonomous Communities. The law is not, therefore, adapted to the autonomic model of territorial decentralisation enshrined by the Constitution.

Article 149.1.18 CE attributes to the exclusive competence of the State 'legislation on forced expropriation'. Case-law recognises the State's general competence in expropriation matters, which is full and includes a uniform regulation of the institution of expropriation throughout the State: it includes the procedural guarantee and the patrimonial guarantee, including the criteria for valuations.

The Constitutional Court has upheld the need to reconcile recognition of the Autonomous Communities' capacity to establish, within the scope of their powers, the cases or circumstances in which expropriation is to be applied (the grounds of expropriation) and to regulate jurisdictional and organisational aspects. In this regard, it has stated that

> it is not in doubt that when, under the system of distribution of powers under the Constitution and the Statutes of Autonomy, sectoral legislation falls to the Autonomous Communities, it is those Regions, and not the State, that are responsible for it, they who have the power to define by legislation the cases in which the expropriation instrument may be used by declaring the ground of expropriation necessary in each case, without prejudice to the obligation to abide by the general legislation of the State that guarantees the patrimonial rights of all private subjects equally.[52]

The Constitutional Court has also had to pronounce on the autonomous organs of valuation of forced expropriation created with a composition different from that of the Provincial Juries of Forced Expropriation[53] regulated in article 32 of

[51] A Boix Palop, 'Reformas en materia de expropiación forzosa en un entorno de crisis' in JR Fuentes i Gasó, L Casado Casado and J Gifreu i Font (eds), *Estructuras administrativas y racionalización del gasto público. Problemas actuales de la expropiación forzosa. La Reforma de los entes locales en Italia en el contexto de la crisis económica*, VII Congreso de la Asociación española de Profesores de Derecho administrativo Tarragona, 10 y 11 de febrero de 2012 (Madrid, INAP, 2012) 187–248. In this same collective work, see also M Fuertes López, '¿Una nueva Ley de Expropiación forzosa?' 157–86.

[52] STC 37/1987, 26 March (n 1), FJ 6.

[53] Both the Provincial Juries of Forced Expropriation of the LEF, and the autonomous expropriation bodies that have adopted various different names, are specialised administrative bodies in the field of valuation and determination of the price. Their action is reserved for those cases in which, once the valuation phase has begun, the valuation is not determined by mutual agreement between the owner and the Administration (or the beneficiary of the expropriation). The Jury must also intervene in cases where there is a discrepancy in the fixing of the valuation when the transfer of the expropriated assets is to be reversed.

the LEF. The Autonomous Communities are not obliged to use the Provincial Expropriation Juries regulated by the LEF to implement the expropriations within their jurisdiction, but may set up their own bodies for that purpose. This is tantamount to stating that the creation of these bodies is not covered by the State's competence to establish 'legislation on forced expropriation' regulated in article 149.1.18 CE. The Constitutional Court has also repeatedly declared the constitutionality of these bodies since its decision 251/2006,[54] although this thesis has met with strong criticism from some writers.[55]

B. Administrations with Expropriation Powers

According to article 2.1 LEF only the territorial Administrations are holders of the power of expropriation, given the principle that the superior public powers or functions of authority are reserved to the territorial Administrations. But as Boix Palop has pointed out,[56] a reform of the LEF should reflect on the convenience of making the content of article 2.1 LEF more flexible to provide expressly for the possibility that sectoral laws should permit public bodies that have to occupy land regularly and on a large scale in order to fulfil their functions, to be attributed with expropriation powers in their rules of establishment, which should also, in consequence, provide for the necessary procedural specialities based on their characteristics. In this regard, it should be noted that article 89.2 of Law 40/2015 on the legal regime of the public sector[57] maintains the traditional prohibition on assigning expropriation powers to non-territorial public bodies.

C. The Need to Strengthen Effective Protection of the Expropriated Party in the Expropriation Procedures

We shall just give a general overview of the aspects most in need of reinforcement.

i. The Declaration of the Ground of Public Utility or Social Interest

The presupposition for legitimising the exercise of the expropriation power is that a ground of public utility or social interest is present through the law. Under

[54] STC 251/2006, 25 July, reaffirmed by STC 313/2006, 8 November; STC 314/2006, 8 November; STC 315/2006, 8 November; STC 364/2006, 20 December – despite their different composition.

[55] See eg JA Fernández Torres, '¿Alguien cree de verdad que es conforme a la Constitución la regulación de los Jurados autonómicos de expropiación forzosa? (a propósito de las Sentencias del Tribunal Constitucional 251/2006, de 25 de julio, 313/2006, 314/2006 y 315/2006, de 8 de noviembre)' RUE no 14, 2006, pp 97–108.

[56] Boix Palop (n 51) 206–07.

[57] *Ley 40/2015, de 1 de octubre, de régimen jurídico del sector público.*

article 10 LEF this legislative declaration can be made in a generic way for groups or categories of 'certain works, services or concessions', or in each specific case of a public work or service facility. In practice, generic declarations have become widespread. Article 10 LEF establishes the general rule that the ground of expropriation must be declared by legislation, but allows for implicit declarations as an exception. In practice, the exception has been generalised, so it can be said that the rule in practice is implicit declarations in all types of plans and projects of works and services. The consequence is nothing more than a trivialisation of the declaration of public utility, if not its material disappearance.

Moreover, the fact that such a declaration is made by legislation is not an absolutely essential requirement in the LEF or in article 33.3 CE. On the contrary, it has been considered dysfunctional and disturbing. In this sense, Boix Palop[58] states that it is 'a supposed protective barrier that is in reality a legal ghost without any operation', since the requirement always of a specific administrative procedure would guarantee greater control of the reasonableness and coherence of the decision that declares the public utility, control that in Spain could only be effected by the Constitutional Court in the case of a declaration by legislation.

ii. Reinforce the Procedure for Declaring the Need for Occupation and Reduce the Generalisation of Implicit Declarations

Article 17 LEF provides:

> Once the public utility or social interest has been declared, the Administration will decide on the specific need to occupy the property or acquire the rights that are strictly indispensable for the purpose of expropriation.

But article 17.2 allows the declaration of need for occupation to be made implicitly, by providing that

> when the project of works and services includes the detailed material description referred to in the previous paragraph, the need for occupation shall be understood to be implicit in the approval of the project, but the beneficiary shall be equally obliged to formulate the aforementioned relationship for the sole purpose of determining the interested parties.

In practice, these implicit declarations have also been extended and generalised to works and services projects and plans of all kinds and in sectoral legislation, causing the expropriated party to be defenceless.

In short, it is necessary to develop the specific need for occupation by means of a special procedure in cases of implicit declarations, with a procedure for hearing the interested party.

[58] Boix Palop (n 51) 208–13.

iii. The Generalisation of Emergency Expropriations

We can speak of a real abuse of the emergency expropriation procedure in Spain in the application of article 52 LEF,[59] which allows for the occupation and subsequent payment of the fair valuation. Once again it can be said that the malpractice of the Administrations has turned into a rule what in law is only the exception. When explaining the constitutional guarantees of forced expropriation, it has already been indicated that article 33.3 CE does not require prior payment. The ECtHR admits the perfect constitutionality of regulations that consider payment for the expropriation as an assumption or an essential condition, as well as those, such as that in force in Spain, in which they are given a compensatory value that makes it possible to extend the payment over time. The legal obligation to pay 'within a reasonable time' in the doctrine of the ECtHR refers to the fact that there should not be an excessively long period between the final determination of the price and its payment. This does not exclude the possibility of occupation prior to the determination of the price and therefore also to its payment.[60]

But this practice should be cut back, because it has given rise to irresponsible behaviour by the Administration in the area of public investment, which has been exposed in all its harshness in the economic crisis. Hence, there have been some proposals by writers such as Boix Palop[61] that advocate the appropriateness of introducing the obligation of payment in the budgetary year from the assets destined for those purposes or, at most, budgeted in the year, which would force Spain to behave in fiscal and budgetary matters more in accordance with the European principles in the matter, while improving the position of individuals and the guarantee of their patrimonial indemnity.

On another note, the control of the urgency of the expropriation could be through a clause that would invalidate such expropriations if the works that justified the expropriation were not begun within a short period of time.[62]

iv. The Problem of Valuations[63]

This topic has certainly given rise to a significant litigation. The Spanish valuation model has systematically aimed to depart from market valuation in order to reduce the cost of public works.

The LEF established a duality of criteria that differentiated between valuations in the case of non-urban expropriations (articles 37 to 47 LEF) and urban expropriations, which are regulated in the urban legislation. For the former, it used

[59] Article 52 LEF requires that the declaration be made by agreement of the Government or Council of Ministers and that it refer to a specific work or purpose.

[60] Art 17, Charter of Fundamental Rights of the European Union (n 7). See A Riccio, *La propiedad en el marco del Convenio europeo de derecho humanos* (trans MÁ Fernández Scagliusi, Madrid, REUS, 2018) esp 105–06.

[61] Boix Palop (n 51) 226.

[62] See Fuertes López (n 51) 183.

[63] Fuertes López (n 51) 167 refers to the 'hornet's nest of valuations'.

artificial formulae based on registry values in order to deviate from the market value, giving rise to fierce litigation. The courts ended up applying the residual valuation criteria of article 43 LEF, which allows for valuation using market criteria when the application of the valuation criteria of the LEF results in a significant deviation from the real or market value.

Currently, the LEF valuation criteria are only applicable to movable property and rights and interests with a patrimonial content, after generalisation of the application of the valuation criteria of article 43 LEF by virtue of article 34.1(b) of Royal Legislative Decree 7/2015, approving the revised text of the Law on Land and Urban Renewal:[64] valuations of land, installations, constructions and buildings, and rights constituted over or in relation to them, are governed by the provisions of this Law, whether or not it is a case of urban expropriation, thus unifying the valuation criteria.

The valuation system in our law aims to support as far as possible an objective model, and to limit it by excluding from the value of the property any anticipation of its revaluation, in order to combat speculation.[65] But the courts do not feel comfortable applying values that are significantly different from those of the market when they value the land for the purpose of expropriation, given that significantly deflated valuations have a perverse effect: first, they are systematically appealed against in the courts, and then they end up being systematically revised; if this cannot be contained, it also ends up being very harmful to the interests of the Public Treasury, causing the cost of public works to rise and requiring the rescue of concessions at public expense.[66]

In addition, it is necessary to reduce the deadlines for setting and paying the price, since it can take years for the expropriated party to receive the compensation for the expropriation, with a clear reduction in its value as compensation.

The system of the Provincial Jury of Forced Expropriation established by the LEF (and the equivalent autonomous bodies) are administrative bodies that have proved to be a failure, given the high level of challenges to their decisions in fixing the price. In the end, it is the courts that have the last word.

V. The United Kingdom before the European Court of Human Rights on the Basis of Expropriation

We should refer to two pronouncements of the European Court of Human Rights (ECtHR) on forced expropriation in claims brought against the United Kingdom.

[64] Above, n 49.

[65] It should be noted that according to the ECtHR a valuation well below market value is admissible only in very specific circumstances: the exceptional circumstances must be made explicit and justified. The ECtHR requires that compensation be provided in such a way that it can be seen that it is consequential patrimonial loss that is being repaired. Although this does not necessarily mean that the valuation must be equivalent to the market value, it does at least require a 'reasonable relationship' with it.

[66] For more detail, see Boix Palop (n 51) 227–48.

The first is the judgment of 21 February 1986 in *James v United Kingdom*;[67] and the second, the judgment of 8 July 1986 in *Lithgow v United Kingdom*.[68] Both cases concerned expropriations carried out by Act of Parliament: the first a reform of the legislation on leases imposing compulsory sale in favour of the tenant of the leased property, and the second a law on the nationalisation of certain companies and shares in the aircraft and shipbuilding sector. Therefore, these were not expropriations carried out by the administrative authorities. As is well known, interference with property rights within the scope of the ECHR may concern any State body, power or authority.[69]

In its judgment in *James v United Kingdom*, the ECtHR concluded that compulsory transfer of property from one individual to another may, in certain circumstances, constitute a legitimate means of promoting the public interest under article 1 of the first Protocol to the ECHR.[70] It cannot be inferred from the expression 'public interest' that the property in question must be put into use for the general public or that the community generally, or even a substantial proportion of it, should directly benefit from the taking.[71] A taking of property effected in pursuance of legitimate social, economic or other policies may be 'in the public interest', even if the community at large has no direct use or enjoyment of the property taken.[72] The Leasehold Reform Act 1967 confers on tenants residing in 'houses' in England and Wales held on 'long leases' (over, or renewed for periods totalling over, 21 years) at 'low rents' the right to acquire the freehold of their property, or to obtain an extension of the lease, at specified prices and on specified terms.

The ECtHR considered that

> the notion of 'public interest' is necessarily extensive. In particular … the decision to enact laws expropriating property will commonly involve consideration of political, economic and social issues on which opinions within a democratic society may reasonably differ widely. The Court, finding it natural that the margin of appreciation available to the legislature in implementing social and economic policies should be a wide one, will respect the legislature's judgment as to what is 'in the public interest' unless that judgment be manifestly without reasonable foundation.[73]

The 1967 Act was designed to correct the injustice suffered by tenant-occupiers, by reason of the operation of the system of long-term leases. It was intended to amend the legislation in force at the time, which was considered unfair to such tenants,

[67] (1986) 8 EHRR 123.
[68] (1986) 8 EHRR 329.
[69] For the distinction between the regulation of property (meaning the delimitation of the right) and an interference that constitutes deprivation of property of an expropriatory nature, see the judgments in *JA Pye (Oxford) Ltd v United Kingdom* (2006) 43 EHRR 3 (ECtHR) and (2008) 46 EHRR 45 (ECtHR Grand Chamber).
[70] (1986) 8 EHRR 123 [40].
[71] ibid [41].
[72] ibid [45].
[73] ibid [46].

and to give effect to what was referred to as their 'moral entitlement' to the ownership of their homes:

> Eliminating what are judged to be social injustices is an example of the functions of a democratic legislature. More especially, modern societies consider housing of the population to be a prime social need, the regulation of which cannot entirely be left to the play of market forces. The margin of appreciation is wide enough to cover legislation aimed at securing greater social justice in the sphere of people's homes, even where such legislation interferes with existing contractual relations between private parties and confers no direct benefit on the State or the community at large. In principle, therefore, the aim pursued by the leasehold reform legislation is a legitimate one.[74]

The purpose of the 1967 Act was therefore, in principle, justified, although it was still necessary to show a reasonable relationship of proportionality between the means employed and the aim sought to be realised.[75]

The applicants argued that the right to retain possession – security of tenure – granted to tenants by legislation already in force was an appropriate solution, and that the procedure – the deprivation of property – introduced by the 1967 Act to give effect to the tenant's alleged 'moral entitlement' went too far due to its draconian nature, and found no equivalent in the domestic legislation of any other Contracting State.[76] However, this argument was rejected by the Court:

> The availability of alternative solutions does not in itself render the leasehold reform legislation unjustified; it constitutes one factor, along with others, relevant for determining whether the means chosen could be regarded as reasonable and suited to achieving the legitimate aim being pursued, having regard to the need to strike a 'fair balance'. Provided the legislature remained within these bounds, it is not for the Court to say whether the legislation represented the best solution for dealing with the problem or whether the legislative discretion should have been exercised in another way …
>
> The occupying leaseholder was considered by Parliament to have a 'moral entitlement' to ownership of the house, of which inadequate account was taken under the existing law. The concern of the legislature was not simply to regulate more fairly the relationship of landlord and tenant but to right a perceived injustice that went to the very issue of ownership. Allowing a mechanism for the compulsory transfer of the freehold interest in the house and the land to the tenant, with financial compensation to the landlord, cannot in itself be qualified in the circumstances as an inappropriate or disproportionate method for readjusting the law so as to meet that concern.[77]

There was therefore no violation of article 1 of the first Protocol to the ECHR.

Finally, the applicants argued that the reform of the legislation on leases introduced discrimination in breach of article 14 ECHR on the ground of 'property',[78] on the basis that, first, it was a measure of redistribution of property which applied

[74] ibid [47].
[75] ibid [50].
[76] ibid [51].
[77] ibid [51].
[78] '*fortune*' in the French text of the ECHR.

only to a restricted class of property (long leasehold houses occupied by tenants); and, second, the lower the value of his property the more harshly the landlord is treated.[79] However, the Court considered that such legislation is within the discretionary power of the State and is in accordance with the principle of proportionality, and not discriminatory.[80]

The second case, *Lithgow v United Kingdom*, involved the nationalisation of some of the applicants' assets, namely the aircraft and shipbuilding companies listed in the Aircraft and Shipbuilding Industries Act 1977. The applicants claimed that the compensation that they received was grossly inadequate and discriminatory in violation of article 1 of the first Protocol to the ECHR, together with articles 14, 6 and 13 ECHR, and that, as regards the standard of compensation, no distinction could be drawn between nationalisation and other takings of property by the State, such as the compulsory acquisition of land for public purposes.

However, the Court did not share this view and stated that:

> Both the nature of the property taken and the circumstances of the taking in these two categories of cases give rise to different considerations which may legitimately be taken into account in determining a fair balance between the public interest and the private interests concerned. The valuation of major industrial enterprises for the purpose of nationalising a whole industry is in itself a far more complex operation than, for instance, the valuation of land compulsorily acquired and normally calls for specific legislation which can be applied across the board to all the undertakings involved. Accordingly, provided always that the aforesaid fair balance is preserved, the standard of compensation required in a nationalisation case may be different from that required in regard to other takings of property.[81]

For the Court:

> A decision to enact nationalisation legislation will commonly involve consideration of various issues on which opinions within a democratic society may reasonably differ widely. Because of their direct knowledge of their society and its needs and resources, the national authorities are in principle better placed than the international judge to appreciate what measures are appropriate in this area and consequently the margin of appreciation available to them should be a wide one. It would, in the Court's view, be artificial in this respect to divorce the decision as to the compensation terms from the actual decision to nationalise, since the factors influencing the latter will of necessity also influence the former. Accordingly, the Court's power of review in the present case is limited to ascertaining whether the decisions regarding compensation fell outside the United Kingdom's wide margin of appreciation; it will respect the legislature's judgment in this connection unless that judgment was manifestly without reasonable foundation.[82]

It was held that there was no violation of the ECHR.

[79] (1986) 8 EHRR 123 [73].

[80] ibid [77]. There were also (unsuccessful) grounds of challenge to the Leasehold Reform Act 1967 under arts 6 and 13 ECHR.

[81] (1986) 8 EHRR 329 [121].

[82] ibid [122].

INDEX

***a non domino* acquisitions and transfers, Spanish law (immovable property),** 2, 61
  conflicting interests, 62–63
  defective title, 62–63
  good title/*usucapio* approach, 62, 64
  instantaneous prescription, 28–29
  iustus titulus for usucapio, 62, 64
  nullity, 61–62
  protection of third-party rights, 63–64
  Spanish land registration system, 68–69, 74, 77–78
    title registration, 81–84
    third-party rights, 86–87
    validity of title, 84–86
  title as ownership approach, 64
  warranty against eviction, 62
  wholly *a non domino* transfers, 62
    conclusive title by registration principle, 86
abstraction principle, 93
  Austria, 3, 97–98
  English law, 16, 101, 117
  German law, 95–97, 115, 119, 128, 129–31, 132, 160
acquisition of immovable property, *see* ***a non domino*** **acquisitions and transfers**
Allgemeines Bürgerliches Gesetzbuch **(ABGB) (Austrian Civil Code) (1811),** 97
  casum sentit dominus principle, 104–5
  general entrustment principle, 131
  passing of risk, 104–5
  titulus et modus system, 22, 97
assignment, 167–68
  contract as an asset:
    contract as property, 185–86
    real assignment of contract, 186–87
  contract as object of assignment, 178–79
  contractual rights:
    chose in action, 181–83
    contract and property, distinguishing, 180–81
    property, as, 183–84
  definition:
    English law, 170–71
    French law, 169–70, 171, 172–73
    general definition, 168–69
  English law, 187–88
    chose in action, 181–83
    common law, 171, 177
    contractual rights as property, 183–84
    equity, 170–71, 177
    novation and assignment, 170–71
    subjectivity of contract, 178–79
    transfer, 179–80
  French law, 169–70, 171, 188
    contract and property dilemma, 180–81
    law reform, 173–76
    subjectivity of contract, 178–79
    transfer, 179–80
    valeur patrimoniale/patrimoine, 172–73
  novation, relationship with, 170–71
  obligation v consent, 177–78
  transfer, concept of, 171–73, 179–80
Austrian law:
  Allgemeines Bürgerliches Gesetzbuch, 97
    casum sentit dominus principle, 104–5
    general entrustment principle, 131
    passing of risk, 104–5
  bona fide purchase rules and derivative acquisition, 128
  bona fide purchase rules and protection of third parties, 132
  insolvency, protection against:
    buyers' position, 110
    sellers' position, 112–13
  passing of risk:
    casum sentit dominus principle, 104–5
  property transfer regimes:
    separation without abstraction, 97–98
  titulus et modus system, 22, 97

bona fide purchase rules:
  derivative acquisition:
    delivery, 126, 127–28
    double sale rule, 126
    English law, 124–25

        entrustment principle, 127
        French law, 125–26
        German law, 127–28
        giving of value, 128
        innocent purchaser v original owner, 124–25
        protection of commercial transaction, 125–26
        protection of property, 124–25
    protection of third parties, 129
        Austrian law, 132
        English law, 132–35
        French law, 132
        German law, 129–31
        Spanish law, 69–78
    see also good faith
Bürgerliches Gesetzbuch (BGB) **(German Civil Code) (1896),** 96–97
    bona fide purchase rules, 127–28, 132
    buyers' rights, 106–7
    general entrustment principle, 132
    nemo dat rule, 132
    passing of risk, 104
    sellers' duties, 106
    third-party purchasers, 130
    unjustified enrichment, 119–20
buyers' claims against sellers:
    causal consensual systems, 106
    English law, 106
        conversion, 108–9
    French law, 106
        action en revendication, 107–8
    German law, 106
    performance, 107
    wholly abstract transfer systems, 106

causa, 1–3
    causa civilis obligandi, 21
    cause of the patrimonial attribution, 21
    cause of transfer, 24–26
        cause of obligation distinguished, 24
        power of disposition, 24–25
    fiduciary transfers:
        iusta causa traditionis, 24–26
    iusta causa principle, 20–21
    see also causal consensual systems
causal consensual systems, 93–95, 100–1, 104, 117–18, 133, 148, 154, 174–75
Chancery Division (England), *see* **equity (England)**
Code civil français (Cc) **(French Civil Code) (1804):**
    annulment of contracts, 114–15
    assignment of contract, 175–76, 179, 185, 186
    bona fide purchase rules, 125–26
    obligations, law of, 94–95
    restitution, 120–21
    vindicatio, 108
    see also French law
Código Civil espanol (CC) **(Spanish Civil Code) (1889),** 11–12
    Código de Comercio, relationship with, 28–29
    double sale rule, 26–27
    good faith, 70
    relativity principle, 161
    traditio (immovables), 29–32, 33–34, 38, 44–46, 56–57
    traditio (movables), 27–29, 64
    traditio by means of *escritura pública*, 33–34, 38, 44–46, 56–57
    transfer of ownership, 19–20
    see also Spanish law
Código de Comercio (CCom) **(Spanish Commercial Code) (1885):**
    a non domino acquisitions, 28–29, 64
    Código Civil espanol, relationship with, 28
common law:
    assignment, 6, 170–71, 176–78
    bona fide purchase rules, 124–25, 128, 132–33
    consideration, 21
    contract and conveyance, relationship between, 98–100
        risk, 103–4
    common law rights in land, 140–41
    protection of property, 124–25, 128
    rescission, 114, 116, 117–18
    specific performance, 146
    termination of contract, 114
    unjust enrichment, 121–22
        proprietary restitution, 123–24
    vendor-purchaser constructive trust, 111
    wrongful interference with goods, 108–9
    see also English law
Common Principles of European Contract Law (CoPECL Project), 4–5, 156
conclusive title by registration principle (Spanish law), 2, 15–16, 65–66
    a non domino acquisition, establishment of, 86–87
    acquisition of clean title from transferor, 87
    acquisition of clean title from owner, 87

acquisition for value, 78–79
acquisition of a property right, 68–69
good faith, 65–66
configuration of good faith, 71–75
purchasers' good faith, 69–78
timing of good faith, 75–78
power of disposition, 79–80
protection of third parties, 67–68
purchasers' good faith, 69–71
configuration of good faith, 71–75
timing of good faith, 75–78
title registration, 81–84
validity of title, 84–86
wholly *a non domino* transfers, 86
consensual transfer of ownership, *see* **causal consensual systems**
***Constitución Espanola (CE)* (Spanish Constitution) (1978),** 9
forced expropriation, *see* Forced Expropriation Law
private property, 207–9
fundamental right to property, 209–10
formal guarantees of property, 210–11
material guarantees of property, 211–12
***constitutum possessorium*,** 27, 104, 125, 127–28, 160
contract and conveyance, relationship between, 92–93, 135–36
Austrian law, 97–98
bona fide purchase, *see* bona fide purchase rules
buyers' claims against sellers, *see* buyers' claims against sellers
causal consensual systems, 93–95
contract and conveyance, relationship between, 92–93
English law:
common law and equity, 98–99
deeds, 99–100
inter vivos gifts, 99
real and personal property, 98, 99
sale of goods regime, 100–1
solo consensu principle, 100–1
see also contract and property, interdependence in English law
French law, 93–95
German law, 95–97
insolvency, *see* insolvency, protection against
passing of risk, *see* passing of risk
rescission of contract, *see* rescission
separation without abstraction, 97–98
Spanish law, 13–14, 23, 34–35, 61, 82
unjust enrichment, *see* unjust/unjustified enrichment
wholly abstract transfer systems, 95–97
contract and property, interdependence in English law, 137–38, 151–52
common law rights in land, 140
contracts to transfer rights in land:
contracts of sale of land, 138
transfer of property rights, 139
equitable interests, creation of, 141–42
purchasers' equitable interest under a contract of sale of land, 143–45
specific performance, 145–47
Walsh v Lonsdale, 142–43
equitable rights in land, 140–41
execution of deeds, 139–40
registration of transfers, 139
transfer of movables, 148–49
possession, 149–50
purchasers' right to goods, 150–51
validity:
contracts, 139
transfers, 139
contractual consent, 92
France, 93–95, 113
see also causal consensual systems
construction of wills (English law), 196
admissibility of parol evidence:
law reform, 197–98
construction of contract compared, 199–200
content errors, 198–200
intention, 199–200
literalist approach, 196
law reform, 197–98
parol evidence, 196–98
meaning errors, 200
mirror wills, 198–99
parol evidence:
exclusion of, 196–97
extrinsic evidence, 197–98
law reform, 197–98
limited inclusion, 197–98
rectification compared, 202–3
Spanish law compared, 7–9
constructive trust:
unjust/unjustified enrichment, 123–24
vendor purchaser constructive trust, 111, 143–45

defective title:
a non domino acquisitions and transfers, 62–63, 87

delivery, 2, 12, 34–37
consensual transfer of ownership, 37, 42–45
contractual non-performance, 39–42
delivery as fulfilment of an obligation and delivery as *traditio* compared, 37, 42–45
efficacy of *escritura pública*, 39–42, 44
greater protection of all parties, 160–64
time of execution of the *escritura pública*, 39
see also abstraction principle; *escritura pública, traditio* by means of; *traditio*
double sale, 16–17, 26, 30, 56–57, 86, 126
Draft Common Frame of Reference (2009), 155–57, 165–66
abstract transfer v causal transfer, 164–65
Art.VIII-2:101, 158
delivery/equivalent to delivery, 159
time of transfer, 158–59
transferors' rights, 159
autonomy of will, 159–60
delivery/consensual equivalent to delivery, 159
creditors' rights, 160–64
insolvency, 162–63
par conditio creditorum principle, 163

English law:
assignment, *see* assignment
bona fide purchase rules and derivative acquisition:
double sale rule, 126
innocent purchaser v original owner, 124–25
protection of property, 124–25
bona fide purchase rules and protection of third parties, 124–25, 132–35
buyers' claims against sellers, 106
conversion, 108–9
double sale principle, 16–17
expropriation of private property, *see* European Court of Human Rights
insolvency, protection against:
buyers' position, 109–10
sellers' position, 112, 113–14
property transfer regimes:
common law and equity, 98–99
deeds, 99–100
inter vivos gifts, 99
real and personal property, 98, 99
sale of goods regime, 100–1
solo consensu principle, 100–1
see also contract and property, interdependence in English law
passing of risk, 102, 105
periculum est emptoris, 103
solo consensu principle, 103–4
rescission of contract, 116–17
unjust/unjustified enrichment, 121–24
see also common law; land registry system (England)
equality of treatment:
creditors, for, 162, 164
equitable interests and remedies, *see* **equity (England)**
equity (England), 3–4, 170
contract and conveyance, relationship between, 98–99, 133
proprietary restitution, 123–24
rescission, grounds for, 116–17
contract:
contract of sale of land, 143–45
creation by contract, 140, 141–43
rescission, 117
specific performance, 145–47
Walsh v Lonsdale, 141–43
equitable interests, creation of, 141–42
purchasers' equitable interest under a contract of sale of land, 143–45
specific performance, 145–47
Walsh v Lonsdale, 142–43
equitable rights in land, 140–41
property rights in equity, 138–41
contract of sale of land, 143–45
equitable interests by contract, 141–43
specific performance, 145–47
rescission, 116–17
proprietary restitution, 123–24
vendor-purchaser constructive trust, 110–11
***escritura pública, traditio* by means of (immovable property),** 12, 33–34
action for annulment, 45–46
consensual transfer of ownership, 24, 27
delivery as fulfilment of an obligation and delivery as *traditio* compared, 37, 42–45
defect in the contract, 42
defect in vendors' title, 42
nemo dat quod non habet, 42
delivery, 34–37
consensual transfer of ownership, 37, 42–45
contractual non-performance, 39–42

delivery as fulfilment of an obligation and delivery as *traditio* compared, 37, 42–45
efficacy of *escritura pública*, 39–42
time of execution of the *escritura pública*, 39
performance, relationship with, 24–25
contractual non-performance, 39–42
person not in possession of thing sold, 55–60
prescription, 42
reservation of ownership clauses, 47–51
see also reservation of ownership clauses
sale of a future thing, 51–55
see also sale of a future thing
European Convention on Human Rights:
expropriation of private property:
article 1 of the first Protocol, 225–27
article 13, 227
article 14, 226–27
article 6, 227
European Court of Human Rights:
expropriation of private property:
compensation, 227
discrimination, 226–27
proportionality, 226
public interest, 225–26
security of tenure, 226
United Kingdom, 224–27
eviction:
reverse eviction, 46–47
warranty against eviction, 44, 45–46, 59–60, 62
expropriation of private property, 9
autonomous communities and territorial decentralisation, 220–21
compensation, 217–18
effective defence, right to, 218–19
effective protection of parties, 221–24
French law, 212–13
power of expropriation, holders of, 221
public utility ground, 216–17
effective protection of parties, 221–22
reversion, 216–17
social interest ground, 216–17
effective protection of parties, 221–22
Spanish law, *see* forced expropriation, law of
United Kingdom, ECtHR challenges, 224–27

fiduciary transfers, 24
fiducia cum amico, 24–25
fiducia cum creditore, 24–25
pacto comisorio, 25
iusta causa traditionis, 24–26
trusts
division of ownership, 25–26
Forced Expropriation Law (1954) (Spain):
broad scope, 213–14
compensation, 217–18
emergency expropriation, 223
legal provisions, 213
proportionality, 214–15
public utility ground, 216–17
effective protection of parties, 221–22
public works purpose, 213, 216–17
social interest ground, 216–17
effective protection of parties, 221–22
valuation model, 223–24
weaknesses, 219–20
autonomous communities and territorial decentralisation, 220–21
power of expropriation, holders of, 221
effective protection of parties, 221–24
see also expropriation of private property
French law:
assignment, 167–88
bona fide purchase rules and derivative acquisition:
double sale rule, 126
protection of commercial transaction, 125–26
bona fide purchase rules and protection of third parties, 132
buyers' claims against sellers, 106
action en revendication, 107–8
Code civil français:
annulment of contracts, 114–15
assignment of contract, 175–76, 179, 185, 186
bona fide purchase rules, 125–26
obligations, law of, 94–95
restitution, 120–21
vindicatio, 108
insolvency, protection against:
buyers' position, 109–10
sellers' position, 112, 113–14
passing of risk, 102, 105
periculum est emptoris, 104
private property, right to, 212–13
property transfer regimes:
causal consensual systems, 93–95
rescission of contract, 114–15
transfer of ownership:
French Civil Code, 21–22

transcription system, 30–31
unjust/unjustified enrichment, 119

German law:
bona fide purchase rules and derivative acquisition:
delivery, 127–28
entrustment principle, 127
giving of value, 128
bona fide purchase rules and protection of third parties, 129–31
Bürgerliches Gesetzbuch, 96–97
bona fide purchase rules, 127–28, 132
buyers' rights, 106–7
general entrustment principle, 132
nemo dat rule, 132
passing of risk, 104
sellers' duties, 106
third-party purchasers, 130
unjustified enrichment, 119–20
buyers' claims against sellers, 106
insolvency, protection against, 110
passing of risk, 102
price risk, 102
risk of performance, 102
property transfer regimes:
wholly abstract transfer systems, 95–97
rescission of contract, 115–16
unjust/unjustified enrichment, 119–20
Germanic system of registration, 31, 65
good faith:
conclusive title by registration principle, 69–71
configuration of good faith, 71–75
timing of good faith, 75–78
protection of third parties, 12, 15, 69–78
see also bona fide purchase rules
good title, 20, 62, 64, 124, 134, *see also titulus et modus* system

immovable property:
registration:
Germanic system, 31
Torrens system, 30
traditio, relationship between, 31–32
transcription system, 30–31
traditio, 11–12
conflicts of possession, 29–30
conflicts of ownership, 30–32
registration in public register, 29–32
see also conclusive title by registration principle; *escritura pública, traditio* by means of; land registry system (England); land registry system (Spain)
insolvency, protection against:
buyers' position:
Austrian law, 110
English law, 109–10
French law, 109–10
German law, 110
purchaser protection mechanisms, 110–11
vendor-purchaser constructive trusts, 111
Draft Common Frame of Reference, 162–63
par conditio creditorum principle, 163
sale of goods, 162–63
sellers' position, 111–14
Austrian law, 112–13
English law, 112, 113–14
false appearance of solvency, 112
French law, 112, 113–14
reservation of title clauses, 111–12
sellers' rights *in rem*, 112
title retention clauses, 111–12
intention:
sale of goods, 148–49, 159
wills, 7–8, 189
construction, 196–200
knowledge and approval, 192–95
parol evidence, 197–98, 205–6
rectification, 201–6
see also contractual consent
***inter vivos* declarations of trust,** 195
***inter vivos* gifts:**
English law, 99
French law, 93–94
Italian law:
a non domino acquisitions, 62
Civil Code:
transfer of property, 21
transcription system, 30–31
trusts, 25

knowledge and approval doctrine:
limitations, 195
mistake:
content errors, 193–94
meaning errors, 194–95
probate requirements:
formality requirements, 192
'nature of a will', 191–92

scope of doctrine:
capacity, 193
fraud, 193
mistake, 193–95
validity of wills, 191
challenges, 192–93

land registry system (England), 15
conclusive title by registration principle, 15–16
rectification, 16
reliability of the register, 16–17
see also English law
land registry system (Spain), 14–15
chain of title, 66
conclusive title by registration principle, 65–67
acquisition for value, 78–79
acquisition of a property right, 68–69
acquisition of clean title from owner, 87
acquisition of clean title from transferor, 87
power of disposition, 79–80
protection of third parties, 67–68
purchasers' good faith, 69–78
title registration, 81–84
validity of title, 84–86
wholly *a non domino* transfers, 86
German system compared, 65
inaccuracy:
acquisition of clean title from owner, 87
acquisition of clean title from transferor, 87
wholly *a non domino* transfers, 86
inopposibility, 65
inscription not transcription, 66
presumption of accuracy, 65
property folio system, 66
regulation, 64
verification of title, 65
Latin America, 20, 21
registration system, 31
titulus et modus system, 22–24
legal systems:
comparative law, 89–91
bona fide purchase rules and acquisition from non-owners, 124–35
buyers' claims against sellers, 106–9
passing of risk, 101–6
property transfer regimes, 92–101
protection against insolvency, 109–14
rescission of contract, 114–18
unjust/unjustified enrichment, 118–24
see also Austrian law; English law; French law; German law; Latin America; Spanish law; Swiss law
legitimate title, 24–25

mistakes:
construction of wills, 196
admissibility of parol evidence, 197–98
construction of contract compared, 199–200
content errors, 198–200
intention, 199–200
law reform, 197–98
literalist approach, 196–98
meaning errors, 200
mirror wills, 198–99
parol evidence, 196–98
rectification compared, 202–3
content errors, 190–91, 206
construction of wills, 198–200
knowledge and approval doctrine, 193–94
rectification, 202, 204–5
ignorance distinguished, 190
knowledge and approval doctrine:
challenges to validity, 192–93
content errors, 193–94
formality requirements, 192
limitations, 195
meaning errors, 191
meaning errors, 194–95
'nature of a will', 191–92
probate requirements, 191–92
scope of doctrine, 193–95
testators' mistakes, 190
validity of wills, 191–93
meaning errors:
construction of wills, 200
knowledge and approval doctrine, 194–95
rectification, 203–4
rectification, 201–2
construction compared, 202–3
content errors, 202, 204–5
meaning errors, 203–4
parol terms, 204–6
remedies:
construction, 196–200
knowledge and approval doctrine, 191–95
rectification, 201–6
see also construction of wills; knowledge and approval doctrine; rectification

Mortgage Act (1946) (Spain):
conclusive title by registration principle, *see* conclusive title by registration principle
land registration, 64
property folio system, 66
movable property:
contracts, 148–49
possession, 149–50
purchasers' right to goods, 150–51
possession is equivalent to title rule, 13, 27–29
traditio, 11–12

nemo dat quod non habet, 42, 48, 56, 63, 124–25, 127, 128, 129, 131–33, 150
nullity, 14, 44–45, 67
a non domino acquisitions and transfers, 61–62
validity of title, 84–86
see also rescission

obligation, 92–93
buyers' obligation, 106
causa civilis obligandi, 21
consent and obligation, 20–21, 61–62
delivery as an obligation of the vendor:
delivery as *traditio* compared, 34–39, 43–45, 55
English law, 99, 132, 176–78
contracts to transfer rights in land, 138
French law, 93–94, 119
law reform, 169–70, 171, 174–75
German law, 95–96, 128, 160
sellers' obligation, 107
solus consensus obligat, 20, 101
Swiss law, 105
overriding interests, 17, 144
ownership:
possession distinguished, 11–12
see also transfer of ownership

***pacta nuda* and *pacta vestita* compared,** 21
pacto comisorio:
fiducia cum creditore, 25
***par conditio creditorum* principle,** 162–63
parol evidence:
admissibility, 197–98
exclusion of, 196–97
extrinsic evidence, 197–98
law reform, 197–98
limited inclusion, 197–98
literalist approach compared, 196–98
meaning, 204
passing of risk, 101–2
Austrian law, 104–5
casum sentit dominus, 102, 103, 104–5
English law, 102, 103–4, 105
French law, 104, 105
German law, 102, 104
passing property by consent, 103
periculum est emptoris, 103, 104, 105
price risk, 102, 103
res perit domino, 102
reservation of title clauses, 104, 105
risk of performance, 102
Roman law, 103–4
solo consensu rule, 103–4
Swiss law, 105
person not in possession of thing sold:
escritura pública, 55–60
presumption of *traditio*, 57–58
posesión vale titulo, *see* **possession is equivalent to title**
possession is equivalent to title, 2, 13, 125, 164
acquisition of ownership, 27–28, 125–26
iustus titulus for *usucapio*, 27–28
traditio, 27–29
possession vaut titre, *see* **possession is equivalent to title**
possideo quia possideo, 26
power of disposition, 24–25, 42–43, 61–62
transferors' registered ownership, 79–80, 86
see also a non domino acquisitions and transfers
preferential treatment, 162–63
prescription, 11–12, 19
acquisitive prescription, 12, 57, 72, 74–75, 125–26
movables, 128
instantaneous prescription, 28–29, 126
usucapio contra tabulas, 30
see also usucapio
private property, right to:
French law, 212–13
Spanish law, 207–9
formal constitutional guarantee, 210–11
fundamental nature of the right, 209–10
material guarantee, 211–12
see also forced expropriation
property transfer regimes:
Austrian law, *see* Austrian law
causal consensual systems, 93–95
comparative law, 92–101

contract and conveyance, relationship between, 92–93
English law, *see* English law; contract and property, interdependence in English law
French law, *see* French law
German law, *see* German law
separation without abstraction, 97–98
Spanish law, *see* Spanish law
wholly abstract transfer systems, 95–97
publicising transfers of ownership:
possideo quia possideo, 26
registration in public register, 29–32
traditio, 26–27
see also land registry system (England); land registry system (Spain)

rectification:
land registry system (England), 16
wills, 201–2
construction compared, 202–3
meaning errors, 203–4
parol terms, 204–6
registration (immovables):
Germanic system, 31
Torrens system, 30
traditio, relationship between, 31–32
transcription system, 30–31
see also land registry system (England); land registry system (Spain)
rescission, 114
English law, 116–17
French law, 114–15
German law, 115–16
reservation of ownership/title clauses, 47
in general, 104–5
insolvency, protection against, 111–12
Spanish law:
attachments, 50
full payment of the price, 50–51
purchasers' legal position, 47
scope, 48–50
security, as a, 48
resulting trusts:
unjust/unjustified enrichment, 123–24
reverse eviction, 46–47
Roman law, 6, 11–14
bona fide purchase, 131
retention of title by operation of law, 112
rights *in personam* and rights *in rem*, 137, 170–71
risk allocation, 103, 104
traditio, 103
iusta causa/iustus titulus, 20–21
solus consensus obligat rule, 20–21
warranty against eviction, 62

sale of a future thing:
acquisition of future assets, 54
cause of the contract, 54
delivery as *traditio*, 37, 42–45, 51–52
escritura pública, 51–55
subject matter of contracts, 51–52
delivery by builder of finished construction, 51–53
delivery of land to the builder, 51–53
re-evaluation, 53–54
sale of goods (movables), 153–54
causal consensual model, 101, 116–18, 133
English law, 100
causal consensual model, 101, 117–18, 133
see also Sale of Goods Act (1893); Sale of Goods Act (1979)
fraud, 129–30
functional approach, 154
passing of property and passing of risk, 103
split approach, 154
transfer of full title, 149–50
unitary transfer approach, 154
Vienna Sales Convention, 155
Sale of Goods Act (1893) (UK), 100–1, 135
Sale of Goods Act (1979) (UK), 100–1, 102, 106, 108
bona fide purchase, 134
double sale rule, 126
insolvency of property owners, 110–10, 113
ownership of goods, 160
possession of goods, 150–51
separation principle, 13–14
separation without abstraction, 97–98
see also titulus et modus system
***solus consensus obligat* rule,** 20–21
Spanish Civil Code, *see* ***Código Civil espanol***
Spanish Commercial Code, *see* ***Código de Comercio***
Spanish Constitution, *see* ***Constitución Espanola***
Spanish law:
constitutional law, *see Constitución Espanola*
immovable property, *see a non domino* acquisitions and transfers; conclusive title by registration principle; land registry system (Spain)

property law, institutions and terminology, 11–17
succession law, 7–8
titulus et modus system, 13–14, 23, 34–35, 61, 82
Study Group on a European Civil Code (SGECC), 155–57, 160–61
succession law:
acquisition by succession, 19
French law, 21, 93–94
Spanish law, 7–8
see also construction of wills; knowledge and approval doctrine; rectification; wills
Swiss law:
obligations, 105
passing of risk, 102
periculum est emptoris, 105
registration system, 31–32

testamentary dispositions over property, 7–9
construction, 196–200
knowledge and approval doctrine, 191–95
rectification, 201–6
see also construction of wills; knowledge and approval doctrine; rectification
third-party rights (immovable property):
a non domino acquisitions and transfers, 63–64
protection when acquiring property, 15
registration of title, 16–17
title retention clauses, *see* **reservation of ownership/title clauses**
title-and-delivery system, *see* ***titulus et modus*** **system**
titulus et modus **system,** 1, 13–14
Austrian law, 22, 97
Latin America, 22–24
origins, 22
Spanish law, 13–14, 23, 34–35, 61, 82
traditio, 34–35
Torrens system of registration, 30
traditio, 11–12
contracts not designed to transfer ownership, 26
contracts of sale, 34–35
fiduciary transfers, 25–26
immovables:
conflicts of ownership, 30–32
conflicts of possession, 29–30
registration in public register, 29–32
iusta causa/iustus titulus, 20–21
movables:
possession is equivalent to title rule, 13, 27–29
ownership by third parties, 35
performance, 34–35
publicity, 26–27
registration, relationship between, 31–32
titulus et modus, 34–35
see also delivery; *escritura pública, traditio* by means of
traditio **by means of** ***escritura pública,*** *see* ***escritura pública, traditio*** **by means of**
traditio chartae, 27
traditio ficta, 27, 52, 57–58
transcription system of registration, 30–31, 66
transfer of ownership (generally):
causa, 1–2
cause of transfer and cause of obligation distinguished, 24
cause of the transfer, 24–26
see also causa
causal consensual systems, 93–95, 100–1, 104, 117–18, 133, 148, 154, 174–75
contracts not designed to transfer ownership, 26
fiduciary transfers, 25–26
French Civil Code, 21–22
prescription, 11–12
publicity:
traditio, 26–27
Roman-Canon law, 20–21
separation without abstraction, 97–98
titulus et modus system, *see titulus et modus* system
traditio, 11–12
immovables, 29–32
iustus causa/iustus titulus, 20–21
movables, 27–29
unitary property transfer systems, 2–3, 92–93
wholly abstract transfer systems, 95–97
transfer of ownership (immovables):
English law, 138–47, 151, *see also* land registry system (England)
Spanish law, 29–32, *see also a non domino* acquisitions and transfers; *escritura pública, traditio* by means of; land registry system (Spain)
transfer of ownership (movables), 27–29
Austrian law, 97–98
Common Principles of European Contract Law, 156

Draft Common Frame of Reference, 155–57
autonomy of will, 159–60
delivery/consensual equivalent to delivery, 159, 160–64
creditors' rights, 160–64
insolvency, 162–63
par conditio creditorum principle, 163
see also Draft Common Frame of Reference
English law, 98–101, 148–51
French law, 93–95
German law, 95–97
Spanish law, 13–14, 27–29
Study Group on a European Civil Code, 156
see also sale of goods
trusts:
constructive trusts, 143
vendor-purchaser constructive trust, 111, 143–45
division of ownership, 25–26
fiduciary transfers, 25–26
resulting trusts, 123–24, 133

unitary property transfer systems, 2–3, 92–93
causal consensual systems, 93–95, 100–1, 104, 117–18, 133, 148, 154, 174–75
unjust/unjustified enrichment, 118–19
English law, 121–24
French law, 119
German law, 119–20
interaction with property law:
proprietary theory of restitution, 121–22, 123
rescission, 122–23
resulting trusts, 123–24
remedies, 120–21
proprietary theory of restitution, 121–22
terminology, 119
usucapio, 11–12, 19
a non domino acquisitions and transfers, 62, 64
acquisitive prescription, 12, 57, 72, 74–75, 125–26
movables, 128
instantaneous prescription, 28–29, 126
usucapio contra tabulas, 30

Vienna Convention on Contracts for the International Sale of Goods (CISG), 155

warranty against eviction, 35, 44, 45–46, 59–60, 62
wills, 189
mistakes in, 189–91
construction and rectification compared, 202–3
construction, 196–200
knowledge and approval doctrine, 191–96
rectification, 201–6
see also construction of wills

www.ingramcontent.com/pod-product-compliance
Lightning Source LLC
Chambersburg PA
CBHW071259180926
51613CB00001B/75
* 9 7 8 1 5 0 9 9 2 9 3 3 7 *